Wealth Management and Estate Planning

CCH/Advocis Education Program – Course 4

4th Edition

CCH Canadian Limited
300-90 Sheppard Avenue East
Toronto Ontario
M2N 6X1
1 800 268 4522
www.cch.ca

.CCH
a Wolters Kluwer business

Advocis®
The Financial Advisors Association of Canada

Published by CCH Canadian Limited

Edited by:
Jill Booker, Hon. B.Sc.

The right to use the marks CFP®, CERTIFIED FINANCIAL PLANNER® and CFP is granted under licence by FPSC to those persons who have met its educational standards, passed the FPSC CERTIFIED FINANCIAL PLANNER Examination, satisfied a work experience requirement and abide by FPSC Code of Ethics.

ISBN: 9781554962334

© 2010, CCH Canadian Limited
Fourth Edition

Typeset by CCH Canadian Limited.
Printed in the United States of America.

Preface

Course 4 — Wealth Management and Estate Planning

CCH acknowledges Jamie Aldcorn, CA, CFP, MBA, M.Ed., for the revision of this course. Jamie would like to thank Sandra, his wife, and Jill Booker from CCH Canadian, for their patience and assistance during the preparation of this textbook.

We acknowledge Deborah Kraft, BBA, CFP, CLU, CH.F.C., Kraft Financial Inc., for the original development of this program. Contributors to this course include James Kraft, CA, MTax, CFP, CLU, CH.F.C., TEP, Mary Lawless, B.A., and Dennis Martin, B.A., FMLI, CLU.

We also thank Howard Dixon, CFP, instructor at the University of Victoria, who reviewed the original course material.

About the CFP® Education Program

The CFP® is an internationally recognized designation held by more than 100,000 people in 19 countries around the world. Financial Planners Standards Council (FPSC), a member of the Financial Planning Standards Board (FPSB), has licensed more than 17,000 individuals in Canada.

Qualifying to take FPSC's CERTIFIED FINANCIAL PLANNER (CFP®) Examination is a demanding process. Yet the professional rewards for successful candidates are significant. On average, CFP professionals who have achieved this coveted certification report a substantial increase in gross income and preferred clients in comparison to non-designates.

This CFP® Education Program is an accredited qualifying course of study designed with the CFP certification requirements in mind. By successfully completing this course of study, you'll gain both the knowledge and confidence to help you succeed in obtaining the designation, and in building a thriving financial planning practice. Working with industry experts, we have created five comprehensive courses, containing 28 modules of current and relevant content. Topics covered closely match the CFP® Professional Competency Profile and Examination Blueprint. By focusing on the most important concepts and required skills, this program helps you optimize your study time.

The Competency Profile

FPSC has publicized its "CFP® Professional Competency Profile: FPSC's Standards of Competence for CFP® Professionals". The Competency Profile is based on a comprehensive analysis of the profession and establishes the complete set of financial planning competencies required of a CFP professional. As described by FPSC, the competencies:

- provide a description of what CFP professionals must be able to do in practice;

- offer a description of the abilities that professionals possess; and

- give a representation of the tasks, job-related skills, knowledge, attitudes and judgments required for competent performance by members of the profession.

The Competency Profile reflects current practice, but also considers the expectations of the profession over the next several years.

Impact on CFP Examination Candidates: You can use the Competency Profile to understand the scope of competence required for the CFP Examination. It is the foundation for the blueprint of what is tested on the CFP Examination. All registrants in our CFP® Education Program are strongly advised to visit the FPSC Web site (www.cfp-ca.org) to obtain detailed information pertaining to both The Competency Profile and the CFP® Examination Blueprint.

Impact on CCH Canadian and Advocis as a CFP Education Provider: The Competency Profile will be used to guide the development of our financial planning curriculum to support program registrants in acquiring the knowledge, skills and abilities needed to meet professional requirements. Anticipating the provision of The Competency Profile, our CFP® Education Program has an increased focus on application of knowledge by incorporating:

- study note application pieces that are mini-cases used throughout the program to expand upon or explain concepts;

- additional exercises, problems and/or case studies at the end of each module in each course to help you apply learning and retain knowledge; and

- comprehensive cases that help integrate concepts presented in individual modules.

Our CFP® Education Program will focus on further incorporating changes that meet the requirements of The Competency Profile and related development of Professional Skills and Technical Knowledge. Our commitment to continuous improvement enables us to adapt and evolve the program's study and testing materials to meet the evolving education needs of the CFP professional.

COURSE 4 — WEALTH MANAGEMENT AND ESTATE PLANNING — FOURTH EDITION

This course introduces the student to the fundamentals important to the topics of economics and investing as they relate to key areas of financial planning. It examines a broad array of investment products and explores the subject of personal financial management. The course concludes with estate planning fundamentals, concepts and applications.

Module 15   Economics and Investment Fundamentals

Module 16   Investments — Products

Module 17   Investment Planning

Module 18   Financial Management

Module 19   Estate Planning

Features of this Course

This textbook offers, in both print and online editions, pedagogical features that have been developed to create enhanced learning opportunities.

Detailed Table of Contents — These provide students with a comprehensive summary for each module.

Study Note Application Piece (SNAP) — SNAPs are mini-cases used throughout the program to expand or explain concepts. SNAPs are important for building student confidence in dealing with cases.

Index — There is an index, which provides easy access for locating key terms, for each module, as well as a comprehensive index for the course text.

Software Case Study — Module 14 in this course concludes with a short case study where financial planning software is used as part of the analysis. It is likely that advisors will utilize some type of financial planning software in practice. Financial planning software is commonly used as a valuable tool when working with the retirement planning aspects of a client's financial situation. Students registered in this course are not required to purchase any software, but will have access to the software with the case facts. An educational version of "FP Solutions Advanced" is provided on Disc 1. This allows exploration of the use of software as part of the financial planning process, at your own pace. While this case has been included as study material and provides an example of how software integrates into the retirement planning process, use of the software provided is optional, and will not be tested on the test or exam.

Self-Test Questions & Solutions — There is a section at the end of each module with questions and solutions based on the content of the module for self-testing your comprehension of the material.

End of Module Exercises, Problems and Cases — Additional self-review materials are included in this edition of the study text. You are encouraged to work through these self-test exercises, problems and case studies because they provide further opportunity for you to review and reinforce the concepts learned, as well as prepare for the module tests and the course exam. Please note that the solutions to these additional review materials are not included in the study text.

How do you obtain the withheld solutions?

In-class students can obtain these solutions from your instructor who, in turn, will have received them from CCH. Self-study registrants taking the course online will find the solutions within the course content resident in the "My Courses" section of Training Sphere, the course Web site where you will take your module tests and course exams. Semester-based, self-study students may obtain these solutions from Advocis on request, if not received beforehand.

The additional review materials are located in the study text as follows.

Module 15, Unit 4 contains additional exercises, and a case study.

Module 16, Unit 10 contains additional exercises, and a case study.

Module 17, Unit 3 contains additional exercises, and a case study.

Module 18, Unit 5 contains additional exercises, and a case study.

Module 19, Unit 9 contains additional exercises, and a case study.

The Use of a Financial Calculator — A financial calculator is required for this course. For ease of learning, the Hewlett Packard 10BII is the recommended calculator as helpful hints and calculator instructions within the course material refer to specific features of the HP10BII calculator. The HP10B calculator is an older version of the HP10BII calculator and will work equally as well, although the key locations vary slightly.

Can you use another financial calculator? Definitely yes, provided that your financial calculator has the capability of calculating internal rates of return, the net present value of a stream of future cash flows, as well as time value of money problems. In addition, you should be familiar with the required keystrokes of your own calculator.

The financial calculator utilized for CFP Course One is suitable and meets all of the requirements.

GENDER REFERENCE

To avoid repetition with references to he/she or his/her, the program has been developed utilizing feminine references for even-numbered modules and masculine references for odd numbered modules. The terms he and she are interchangeable throughout the course content unless otherwise noted.

STUDENT EDITION SOFTWARE

Your text includes CDs with educational versions of the following financial planning software products:

- oneSource: CCH Canadian's Financial Planning Research Library; and

- FP Solutions Advanced: CCH Canadian's Financial Planning Software.

Disc 1: CCH Canadian Financial Planning Research Library — This educational version of the extensive electronic research library gives you a wealth of planning information, including the basics of finance, insurance, investment planning, taxation, estate and retirement planning. The CCH library allows you to do key word and phrase searches and will direct you to the information you need. Hypertext links to the references in oneSource will guide you to legislation, commentary, government forms and checklists relevant to your practice or program of study. *Note:* The tests and course exam are based only on the content in the study text.

Disc 2: CCH Canadian Financial Planning Software — The educational version of CCH Canadian's array of financial planning software, which is available in four levels of complexity, includes a demo of *FP Solutions Advanced* software. *FP Solutions Advanced* allows advisors to analyze a client's entire financial situation, including cash flow analysis, and is considered the most appropriate level to accompany the course material. Students can become familiar with the program using the demo and then contact CCH Canadian to receive a free subscription for four months to the commercial version.

THE CFP® EDUCATION PROGRAM: AN OVERVIEW

Course 1 (Advocis 231) — *Financial Planning Fundamentals — Fourth Edition*

This course introduces the fundamentals important to the discipline of financial planning. Students will acquire an understanding of the concepts and applications associated with financial calculations and the analysis of financial statements. The basic concepts of contracting and family law are covered, followed by an analysis of government sponsored benefit programs.

Course 2 (Advocis 232) — *Contemporary Practices in Financial Planning — Seventh Edition*

This course introduces students to basic income tax laws, moving into a more advanced study as these laws relate to areas of financial planning. A review of the professional and ethical responsibilities associated with the role of a financial planner and an understanding of the structures and services within the financial industry are covered in the course. Different forms of business structures are explored in-depth, along with an understanding of trusts.

Course 3 (Advocis 233) — *Comprehensive Practices in Risk and Retirement Planning — Fourth Edition*

Designed to provide students with a comprehensive understanding of the principles and applications related to the concepts of managing risk and retirement planning, this course covers products, issues and practices in the area of insurance and retirement. Included is an understanding of the risk management process along with the retirement planning process moving through the wealth accumulation phase into retirement.

Course 4 (Advocis 234) — *Wealth Management and Estate Planning — Fourth Edition*

This course introduces the student to the fundamentals important to the topics of economics and investing as they relate to key areas of financial planning. It examines a broad array of investment products and explores the subject of personal financial management. The course concludes with estate planning fundamentals, concepts and applications.

Advocis 239 — *CCH/Advocis FPSC-approved Capstone Course — First Edition*

This course begins with a profile of the Canadian financial planning industry, and reviews the professional Code of Ethics, Practice Standards, and the six areas of technical knowledge. The CFP® Professional Competency Profile and CFP® Examination Blueprint are covered along with examination writing techniques. The final section of the course provides the student with case studies and multiple-choice questions to practice and test their knowledge.

PROGRAM COMPLETION REQUIREMENTS

Successful completion of the Capstone Course qualifies students to write the Financial Planners Standards Council's Financial Planning Examination Level 2 (FPE2).

ACADEMIC PARTNERS

For the Instructor

Instructors who have chosen this study guide for their program offering have access to test and exam content for use with the program. Contact us for more information on the implementation of student assessment. PowerPoint slides are available for each module. Instructors also receive complimentary study texts with CCH Canadian student edition software including access to technical support. More information on instructor support material is available from CCH.

For the In-Class Student

Please direct enquiries regarding course content to your instructor; however, you may contact CCH Canadian technical support for queries regarding the educational software in the accompanying CDs contained in the study guide. Identify the course taken and the specific software program when speaking to a CCH Canadian client service representative.

SELF-STUDY LEARNERS

For those who are working through the course on a self-study basis, the following information will be helpful to your success in learning and mastering the content within the program. Self-study learners will have online access to a qualified Study Leader through the Training Sphere Web site. Students will also have access to an online open forum.

Self-study learners may contact CCH Canadian technical support for queries regarding the educational software in the accompanying CDs contained in the study guide. Please identify the course taken and the specific software program when speaking to a CCH Canadian client service representative.

Overview

Upon enrolling, online students will receive a confirmation e-mail from the Training Sphere Web site providing their username and password.

Course Three consists of six modules. Upon completion of each module, students are required to complete a test. After completion of the six module tests, students write a course exam that covers material from all six modules.

Students enrolled in the online version of the course will complete the tests and exam online. If students are enrolled in a paper-based (semestered) version of the program, assignment tests are to be written and submitted at set times. These assignments will be provided at registration, and the course exam will be written at one of the scheduled proctored exam sittings conducted at the end of each of three semesters. Students must select between the semester (paper-based) option and the online option at the time of registration.

The online module tests must be completed in sequential order and are mandatory. Each test is to be completed before the next becomes accessible and all six must be completed to be eligible to write the course exam and pass the course.

THE ONLINE COURSE PROCESS

Step	Action	Module Number	Module Name
One	Study	15	Economics and Investment Fundamentals
Two	Online test	15	Economics and Investment Fundamentals
Three	Study	16	Investments — Products
Four	Online test	16	Investments — Products
Five	Study	17	Investment Planning
Six	Online test	17	Investment Planning
Seven	Study	18	Financial Management
Eight	Online test	18	Financial Management
Nine	Study	19	Estate Planning
Ten	Online test	19	Estate Planning

Step Eleven:

Online students must complete an online exam, which covers Modules 15 to 19 inclusive. The online course must be completed within four months.

If enrolled in the paper-based or semestered version of the course, students must complete a written test assignment and a paper-based course exam that covers Modules 15 to 19 inclusive. This exam will be administered at a designated exam location. There are three semesters per year in which paper-based students may enroll.

Course Marks

Online tests (combined)	40% of total mark
Exam	60% of total mark

To pass this course, the student must obtain a minimum overall grade of at least 60%.

Each test or exam may be written only once.

Students who do not obtain a minimum overall grade of at least 60% may apply to write a paper-based supplemental exam for a fee. This option is available only once.

CCH/ADVOCIS
EDUCATION PROGRAM

COURSE 4
WEALTH MANAGEMENT AND ESTATE PLANNING

MODULE 15
ECONOMICS AND INVESTMENT FUNDAMENTALS

Module 15
ECONOMICS AND INVESTMENT FUNDAMENTALS

Module 15
Economics and Investment Fundamentals

LEARNING OBJECTIVES

✓ Demonstrate and apply a solid comprehension of economic fundamentals relative to inflation, interest rates and interest yield curves.

✓ Understand and explain the concepts and principles associated with monetary policy, fiscal policy, business cycles and economic indicators.

✓ Identify, explain and apply an in-depth knowledge of the different types of investment risk.

✓ Demonstrate a solid comprehension and working knowledge of risk measurement through the concepts of standard deviation and beta.

✓ Understand, explain and apply benchmarks relative to the measurement of portfolio performance and demonstrate a comprehension of time and dollar weighted returns.

✓ Demonstrate a working knowledge of the characteristics, principles and concepts of the efficient market hypothesis as well as the correlation of asset classes; and, explain the Markowitz Theory relative to modern portfolio theory.

OVERVIEW

Economics is the social science that deals with the production, distribution and consumption of goods and services. In simple terms, society has limited or scarce resources and the subject of economics looks at the ways in which individuals and society choose to use these scarce resources.

This module explores the fundamentals of economics, as they relate to knowledge that is valuable to your role as a financial planner. The first unit reviews the topic of gross domestic product, a standard measure of the overall size of the Canadian economy. Everything in the marketplace has a price, but how is that price derived and what factors influence the quantity of goods or services produced? This is followed by a discussion of the factors that influence the concepts of supply and demand.

Canada is like most other modern industrial economies; it goes through significant swings or fluctuations in economic activity. A review of Canadian business cycles provides perspective on fluctuations in economic activity that result in periods of economic expansion or decline. The material then explores various types of economic indicators and discusses how analysis of these indicators and business cycles enables economists to forecast economic trends.

A discussion of the Canadian money supply is followed by an introduction to Canadian monetary and fiscal policy.

The fundamentals of investments are examined in Unit Two, beginning with the concept of yield curves and their integration with economic activity. Next, the phenomenon of inflation is examined, including a review of its causes, controls and effects, which is followed by an overview of deflation.

The concept of systematic and unsystematic risk is introduced, followed by a discussion of the different types of investment risk. Next, a dialogue regarding considerations that should help guide investors when constructing an investment portfolio looks at the topics of opportunity cost, holding periods, measures of investment performance and the calculation of returns.

The unit concludes with a look at Modern Portfolio Theory, an investment approach that attempts to quantify the relationship between risk and return based on the assumption of an efficient market.

Unit 1

Basic Economics

INTRODUCTION

The term *economics* refers to the branch of social science that deals with production, distribution and consumption of goods and services. It considers the efficient use of limited resources to achieve maximum satisfaction. The term *economy* refers to a combination of political structures, rules and arrangements. It relates to how individuals and corporations employ scarce productive resources that have more than one potential use, to create various commodities (products and services) that are distributed for consumption, now, and in the future, among various elements of society.

In a country like Canada, the free-market economy is the "invisible hand" that through the laws of supply and demand determines what goods and services are produced, when, and in what quantities. An economy is considered robust or healthy when it is growing at a good, sustainable pace.

GROSS DOMESTIC PRODUCT

Gross domestic product (GDP) is a formal measure of the total productive output of the final goods and services produced within Canada during a single year. In general terms, GDP is a standard measure of the overall size of the Canadian economy; or, in other words, it measures Canada's economic output. To arrive at the GDP number, the federal government uses thousands of pieces of data from government departments, companies, and private individuals.

GDP takes into account all labour and capital within the geographical boundaries of Canada, ignoring the residency of the labour and ownership of the capital. The GDP account does not, however, include any transfer payments between governments or between the government and individuals (i.e., Old Age Security retirement pensions, employment insurance, welfare payments). To avoid double counting, it also ignores the purchase of all input or intermediate goods such as raw materials, and counts only the final goods and services. For example, GDP would not include the grain used to make a box of cereal, but would include the cereal itself.

The term *real GDP* is used to refer to the GDP after inflation has been taken into account. Real GDP can be extended to measure the total value of all final goods and services produced within Canada, per person, during a specific year, which is then referred to as the *real GDP per capita* (measured in constant dollars).

GDP is the central measure of domestic economic performance. The various tools used by the government to manage the domestic economy are focused on GDP growth. The government closely monitors GDP to identify emerging economic problems. Businesses watch GDP to help forecast revenue and adjust production appropriately. Individuals watch GDP as a gauge of their short-term economic well-being. Productivity and output within a country has a direct impact on that country's standard of living. Real GDP per capita, which measures productivity and output per person, is used as the basis of comparison when assessing Canada's change in standard of living, over time, relative to other countries. While Canada's real GDP decreased 24% in 2009 due to the recession, growth in the last decade averaged 3.5% each year.

It is important to note that GDP measures actual production; it does not measure exchange. In reality, GDP is generated by personal labour combined with business capital, raw materials, energy and technology in a wide array of different industries. GDP can be calculated in two ways: an *expenditure approach* and an *income approach*. The expenditure approach measures the amount spent on all final goods during the target period, whereas the income approach measures the income received by all factors of production integral to producing the final goods. Income, in this instance, includes such items as salaries, rent and profits. These two methodologies lead to the same outcome, except one looks at income received while the other considers expenditures made.

Gross national product (GNP), on the other hand, measures the output generated by residents of Canada, regardless of where the output is produced. The GDP measure places an emphasis on production within the boundaries of Canada; the GNP emphasizes Canadian income that is generated by Canadian residents, regardless of the geographical origin. GNP is calculated from GDP through add-backs and reductions related to investment income. Canadian GNP is lower than Canadian GDP because more investment income flows out of Canada than into Canada. The difference between the two measures is small, amounting to less than 0.05% of the GDP number.

GNP includes such direct items as wages and salaries, company profits and rents. It also includes taxes collected by the federal and provincial governments and investment income, such as dividends, which Canadian residents receive from foreign entities. Similarly, dividends paid by Canadian companies to foreigners are subtracted from GNP, as are imported goods and services not produced by Canadians.

SUPPLY AND DEMAND

Everything in the marketplace has a price. But, why does the used book in the flea market cost $0.50, while the book at a rare bookstore costs $500? Why is one 300-page book worth so much more than another 300-page book? What factors determine the relative price?

PIZZA (1)

Tom is driving home after a late evening at work. His stomach starts to rumble, so he pulls into the local pizza outlet. When he walks in, he discovers that $2.50 will buy him a "ready-to-eat" slice of pizza, prepared just the way he likes it. As he takes the first bite on his drive home, he wonders how the pizza parlor knew he was coming. How did they coordinate it so that an affordable piece of his favourite pizza was ready the second he walked in the store?

Who determines that one young, college-educated man ought to be paid $40,000 to manage a retail store in the local mall, while another young, college-educated man ought to be paid $4 million to bounce a basketball and run up and down a gymnasium floor?

The magic of the system is compounded by the fact that no central strategy group is planning the whole affair. No government figure has told the bookstore, pizza parlor, or basketball team to act they way they do. In capitalist economies, it is the force of supply and demand that coordinates and sets the price in the production and sale of goods and services.

Producers must determine for themselves the appropriate level of supply, driven largely by the existing level of demand. The forces of supply and demand are the ultimate drivers of economic activity coordinated through a free and open market. Buyers communicate with sellers indirectly through their consumption behaviour. The producer will satisfy a buyer's demand for the product, if they can do so at a profitable price. But ultimately, the force of supply and demand coordinates this and almost all market activity.

The analysis of supply and demand can be a very useful analytical tool. There is both a law of supply and a law of demand, and each law works in isolation.

WHAT IS DEMAND?

Demand is often confused with desire. In economic terms, we might say that desire refers to an individual's willingness or strength of motivation to own a good. Demand, on the other hand, has a more narrow definition. *Demand* is the amount of a commodity or service that a consumer desires to own, combined with the capacity to purchase it at a given price.

Utility is another economic term that is linked to demand and desire. *Utility* describes the level of satisfaction that a person gets from consuming or using a specific good or service. It is a subjective term that can and does vary from one individual to the next. The amount of satisfaction derived from owning a good determines its utility to a given person.

LAW OF DEMAND

The relationship between the quantity of a good demanded and price of the good is called the *demand curve*. All other things being equal, the lower the price of a good or service, the higher the quantity demanded of that good or service. This inverse relationship between price and quantity demanded is depicted in Figure 1, which illustrates the shape of the demand curve.

Figure 1
Demand Curve

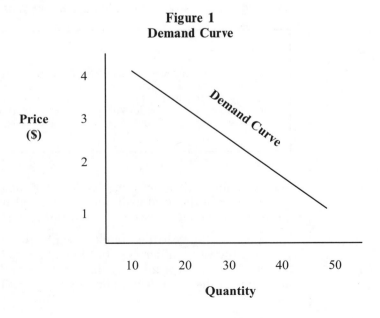

The demand curve slopes downward to the right, reflecting the law of demand:

As price decreases, the quantity demanded increases. Conversely, as price increases, the quantity demanded decreases.

There is utility (satisfaction) from the consumption of a good or service, but as we consume more of the good or service within a given period of time, the additional units consumed offer successively less utility (satisfaction). The decrease in utility accounts for the downward slope of the demand curve, which is referred to as *diminishing marginal utility*. For example, Tom in the Pizza (1) SNAP would get more utility or satisfaction from the first slice of pizza he ate compared to the tenth slice of pizza he consumed.

INFLUENCING DEMAND

From an economics perspective, the basic determinants of demand include:

* price of the good or service;
* changes to the price of related goods (substitute or complementary goods);
* changes to consumers' income or wealth;
* changes to consumers' expectations (i.e., regarding income, price, and/or product availability); and
* changes to consumers' tastes or preferences.

Movements Along and Shifts in the Demand Curve

Economists are typically interested in two different phenomena in respect of the demand curve for a given good or service: movement along the demand curve and a shift in the demand curve.

Movements Along the Demand Curve

Changes in price result in movements along the demand curve. The quantity demanded is sensitive to changes in price; therefore, increases in price result in movement up the demand curve (to the left). Alternatively, decreases in price result in movements down the demand curve (to the right). These two phenomena are sometimes referred to as a *change in quantity demanded*. This type of movement is shown in Figure 2.

Figure 2
Movements Along the Demand Curve

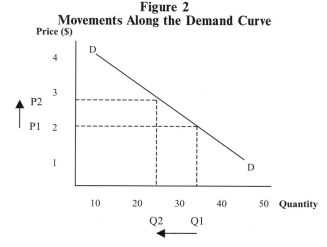

In Figure 2, as the price of the good increases from $2 (P1) to $2.80 (P2), the quantity demanded decreases from 35 units (Q1) to 25 units (Q2).

Of the five factors listed earlier that affect demand, a change to price is the only one that results in movement along the demand curve. Note that we have not yet considered supply influences. The demand curve operates independent of supply influences. It clearly shows that demand for a good or service is sensitive to its price. Holding everything else equal, price increases result in contraction or decrease of demand (movement up the curve), while price decreases result in expansion or increase of demand (movement down the curve).

Returning to the book example, it becomes easier to understand that increases in the price of the used book above $0.50 will cause a contraction of demand, and a decrease in the quantity demanded.

Shifts in the Demand Curve

The impact of a change in price does not mean, of course, that the other four factors listed do not influence the demand curve. They do, but changes in these factors cause a shift in the demand curve rather than movements along the demand curve. Generally, if there is a change in consumer income or taste, or in the demand for substitutes or complements, the demand curve is displaced or shifted either to the right or left of its current position, depending on the nature of the change. This shift in the demand curve is called a *change in demand.*

Consider the Pizza (1) SNAP. When the price of a slice of pizza increases or decreases there will be movements along the demand curve, or changes in quantity demanded that correspond to the change in price. Pizza slices costing $1.00 will cause movement down the curve or expansion of demand. Pizza slices costing $10.00 will cause movements up the curve or contraction of demand.

What might happen if one of the other four factors changes? What if there is a significant income increase for all consumers in the area? The law of demand would predict a shift to the right in the demand curve. By that we mean that there would be a greater demand for pizza slices at the same price.

PIZZA (2)

If the demand for pizza slices averaged 1,000 slices of pizza at $2.50 per slice, the law of demand predicts an increase in consumer income would result in a demand level that is greater than 1,000 pizza slices at the same $2.50 price.

Figure 3
Shift in the Demand Curve

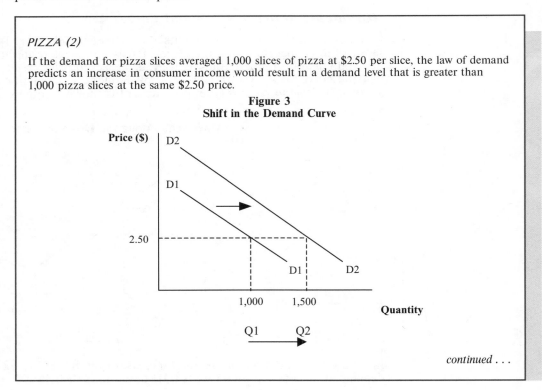

continued . . .

continued . . .

In this example, assuming income levels within the community increased, the demand curve for pizza slices will shift to the right where the price remains constant at $2.50 per slice but the quantity demanded increases from 1,000 slices to 1,500, as shown in Figure 3.

Alternatively, if all income levels within the community decreased, the demand curve should shift to the left causing the quantity of pizza slices demanded to decrease.

In summary, five factors influence the demand curve. Changes in one of these factors — price — will cause movements along the demand curve. A change in any of the other four factors will cause a shift in the demand curve to either the left or the right. A change in price causes movement along the demand curve, and a change in consumer income, tastes, or the demand for substitutes or complements shifts the demand curve for that good.

What is Supply?

Supply is a very simple concept. The quantity supplied is the amount of a good or service a producer is willing and able to sell at a given price during a given period of time.

Law of Supply

The relationship between the quantity of a good produced and the price it can command in the marketplace is called the *supply curve.* All other things being equal, the higher the price of a good or service, the higher the quantity of that good or service that will be produced at that price. This positive relationship between price and quantity of the good or service supplied is depicted in Figure 4, which illustrates the shape of the supply curve. The basic supply curve in Figure 4 shows the amount of a good or service that producers are prepared to produce, and sell at different price levels.

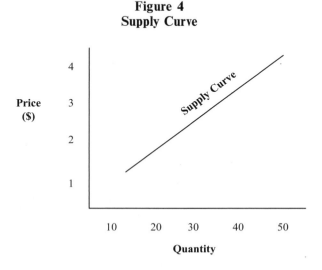

Figure 4
Supply Curve

The supply curve slopes upwards to the right, reflecting the law of supply:

As price increases, the quantity supplied increases. Conversely, as price decreases, the quantity supplied decreases.

Influencing Supply

From an economics perspective, the basic determinants of supply include:

- price of the good or service;
- cost of producing the good or service (i.e., available technologies, price of inputs such as labour or capital);
- price of related goods or services; and
- expectations regarding future price of the good or service.

Movements Along and Shifts in the Supply Curve

Similar to the demand curve, economists are typically interested in two different phenomena in respect of the supply curve for a given good or service: movement along the supply curve and a shift in the supply curve. The analysis of the supply curve is similar to the analysis undertaken with respect to the demand curve.

Movements Along the Supply Curve

Changes in price result in movement along the supply curve. The higher the price, the more producers are willing to supply. The lower the price, the less producers are willing to supply. These changes are also known as *change in quantity supplied*. This type of movement is shown in Figure 5.

Figure 5
Movements Along the Supply Curve

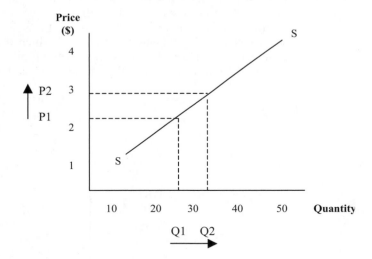

In this example, as the price of the good increases from $2.25 (P1) to $2.90 (P2), the quantity supplied increases from 26 units (Q1) to 34 units (Q2).

PIZZA (3)

Continuing the Pizza SNAP, we can easily see in Figure 6 that if the price of a slice of pizza increases from $2.50 to $10.00, then suppliers would certainly be willing to increase the supply of pizza slices (expansion of supply) at that price.

continued . . .

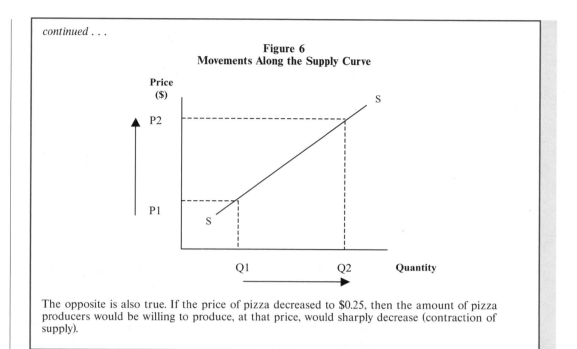

Figure 6
Movements Along the Supply Curve

The opposite is also true. If the price of pizza decreased to $0.25, then the amount of pizza producers would be willing to produce, at that price, would sharply decrease (contraction of supply).

Shifts in the Supply Curve

If changes in price result in movement along the supply curve, then changes in the other factors will cause shifts in the supply curve. A change in one of the factors that causes a supply curve to shift is called a *change in supply*. In the same manner as with the analysis of demand curves, it is important to differentiate between a movement along the supply curve and a shift in the supply curve.

The most common factor that can potentially shift a supply curve is a change to the input costs. Increasing input costs shifts the supply curve to the left. If it costs more to make a slice of pizza that is sold at a given price, then producers will produce fewer pizza slices. Alternatively, decreasing input costs shifts the supply curve to the right, where producers are willing to increase production of pizza slices, as shown in Figure 7.

Figure 7
Shift in the Supply Curve

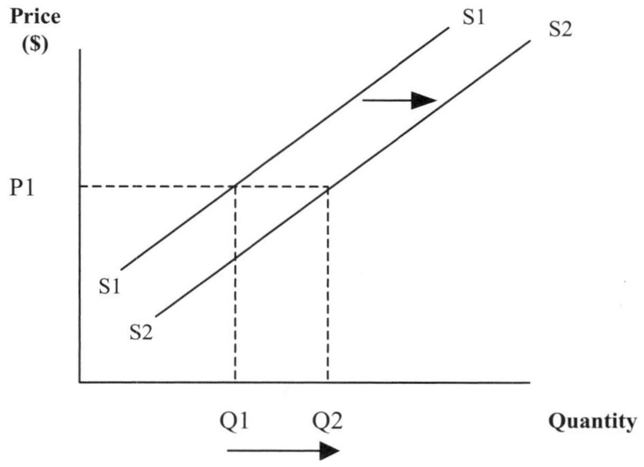

The cost of inputs includes the cost of items such as labour, capital and rent. In addition, an increase in technical proficiency can also shift the supply curve to the right, as shown in Figure 7, because improved technology could result in lower costs. In the pizza SNAP, if the pizza parlour were more proficient in production, it would be willing to produce more pizza at a given price.

The analysis of the supply curve is similar to the analysis undertaken with respect to the demand curve. Different factors influence supply, but only one of them — price — results in movements along the supply curve.

In summary, when the price of the product or service changes, it causes a move along the supply curve for that product where the quantity supplied increases or decreases. When any other factor affecting supply changes, the supply curve shifts.

Market Equilibrium

While the laws of supply and demand are independent phenomena, it is the interaction of the two that coordinates the price and quantity of goods and services that are sold. *Market equilibrium* occurs when the quantity of goods or services supplied equals the quantity demanded. It is the intersection point of the demand and supply curves that influences the quantity and price of the goods or services sold in a market. The price at this point is referred to as the equilibrium price, whereas the quantity at this intersection is referred to as the equilibrium quantity.

Typically, an equilibrium develops in a market situation so that there is no intrinsic tendency to change: the quantity of goods demanded is equal to the quantity supplied. To use the expression favoured by economists: the market clears.

PIZZA (4)

The pizza slice market clears when the price of a slice of pizza is set so that producers produce enough slices to satisfy the demand, which exists at that price, as shown in Figure 8.

Figure 8
Market Equilibrium

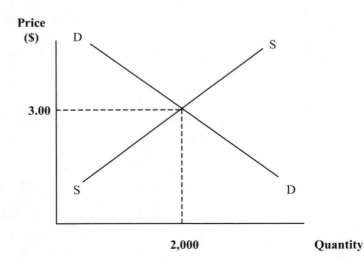

Markets are not always in equilibrium. A market shortage occurs when the quantity demanded at a given price exceeds the quantity that producers are willing and able to supply at that price. Equilibrium would likely be restored in this kind of market by increasing price, which would cause a movement up the demand curve to contract demand. At the same time, it would cause a movement along the supply curve to increase supply. Eventually, a price would be established that restored equilibrium to the market.

At times, market surplus occurs when the quantity of goods supplied exceeds the quantity that is demanded. The implication in this situation is that the market price is too high. Equilibrium would be restored, in this case, by decreasing prices, which would increase demand and decrease supply to the point where the market eventually cleared.

Any free and open market will tend to gravitate towards equilibrium, most of the time. It is this fact that makes free markets stable over the long run.

Price and the Allocation of Resources

The price mechanism of a free market is a powerful means of communication to both producers and consumers. The opposite of a free market is a command economy, where the allocation of resources is decided by central planners who decide how much of any good should be produced. The great downfall of centrally planned economies is the misallocation of resources to products and projects with no productive benefit to society.

A free market, through the price mechanism, is a much more effective means of allocating resources to goods and services with a demonstrable market demand. It is a much better guide for managers who must make investment decisions on what to produce and in what quantities. The free-market pricing mechanism, operating through the interaction of supply and demand, is sophisticated and subtle. It is able to give corporations excellent real-time feedback on the market acceptance of their production decisions.

Aggregate Supply and Demand

Having examined the demand and supply curves for individual markets, we now turn our attention to all markets in our domestic economy. When these individual markets are combined, they are described as an *aggregate market*. In turn, we can review both aggregate demand and aggregate supply curves, and evaluate how factors that influence those curves affect our entire domestic economy.

The aggregate demand curve takes into account the purchases made by consumers, businesses, government, and foreign markets for Canada's entire domestic economy. On the other hand, the aggregate supply curve takes into account the total production of the domestic economy. Understanding aggregate demand and aggregate supply is essential to understanding macroeconomics. The analysis is quite similar to the analysis of demand and supply for a given good or service.

Aggregate Demand

Aggregate demand is the overall quantity of goods and services that is demanded in a given economy at each possible price level (real GDP). Aggregate demand is not simply an individual or market demand curve. Rather, it represents the sum total of all goods and services produced. Conceptually, it shows the total amount that all economic agents (consumers, businesses, and the government) are willing to spend on goods and services at various price levels.

Similar to the individual demand curve introduced earlier, the aggregate demand curve, as shown in Figure 9, is downward sloping to the right, but with an inverse relationship to gross domestic product (real domestic output purchased). Economists generally agree that there are four determinants of aggregate demand:

- consumer spending;

- investment spending;

- government spending; and

- net export spending.

Changes to these determinants could cause a shift in the demand curve.

Figure 9
Aggregate Demand (AD)

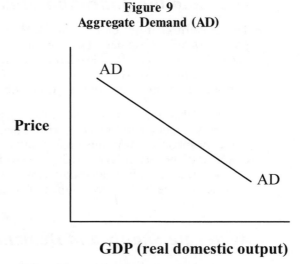

Consumer Spending

The first determinant of aggregate demand is *consumer spending*, which is a function of disposable income and wealth. Real wealth includes financial and physical assets. When real wealth declines, consumers are inclined to buy less at each price level in order to save more, causing aggregate demand to decrease (shift left). Alternatively, when real wealth rises, consumers tend to buy more at each price level, increasing aggregate demand (shift right).

An example of a change in real wealth is the changing value of homes. When the price of homes rises, real wealth increases, which results in increased consumer spending. As the price of homes falls, real wealth contracts and consumers buy less, causing aggregate demand to decline (shift left). In Figure 10, an increase to aggregate demand results in a shift of the aggregate demand curve (AD1) to the right (AD2). Conversely, a decrease in aggregate demand causes a leftward shift in the aggregate demand curve from AD1 to AD3.

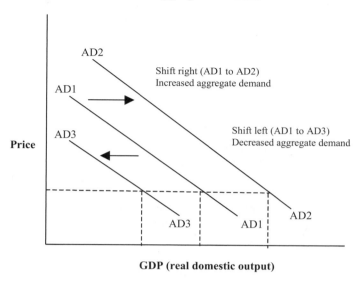

Figure 10
Shifts to Aggregate Demand

Disposable income is defined as the money that consumers have left after they have paid their taxes. As such, personal taxes have an effect on consumer spending. A decrease in taxes provides more disposable income, which leads to increased consumer consumption, causing aggregate demand to increase (shift right). The reverse is also true; as personal taxes increase, consumer spending declines, causing an overall decrease in aggregate demand (shift left).

Changes in consumer expectations relative to the future may affect consumer spending, which flows through to aggregate demand. The expectation of having more income will prompt people to spend more money on consumption, leading to an increase in aggregate demand. A pessimistic outlook about the future will cause consumers to reduce their present consumption, thereby reducing aggregate demand.

Household debt affects consumption because when consumers carry a high debt load from past purchases, it causes a cutback on current consumption, which reduces aggregate demand (shift left). Low levels of household debt have the opposite impact and translate into increased aggregate demand.

Investment Spending

The second determinant of the aggregate demand curve is *investment spending*, which refers to the purchase of capital goods. As investment spending increases, it translates into increased aggregate demand of capital goods at all prices (shift right).

Changes to real interest rates will change investment spending. When real interest rates increase (caused by factors other than price changes), it causes investment spending to fall because the cost of borrowing increases. When investment spending declines, consumers in turn buy less equipment, machinery, and buildings. The result is a decrease in aggregate demand (shift left). The reverse holds true: a decline in real interest rates (caused by factors other than price changes) leads to higher investment spending, causing an increase in aggregate demand (shift right). For example, this type of impact will result because of changes in the money supply that ultimately affect interest rates.

Changes to the expected return on capital investments will shift the aggregate demand curve: the expectation of a higher return increases the demand for capital goods, which increases aggregate demand (shift right). Again, the reverse applies.

Business taxes, technological enhancements and the amount of excess capacity (existing capital not utilized) all affect aggregate demand. Lower business taxes increase corporate after-tax profit, increase investment spending and increase aggregate demand (shift right). Aggregate demand will shift left with an increase in business taxes. Technological enhancements foster higher investment spending and increase aggregate demand. And, when there is excess capacity, it lowers demand for new capital goods and decreases aggregate demand (shift left). A decline in excess capacity promotes investment spending and increases aggregate demand (shift left).

Government Spending

The third element that affects the aggregate demand equation is *government spending*, which includes all expenditures made by the government, but excludes transfer payments to the provinces. Government spending often makes up more than one third of gross domestic product, so it represents a substantial component of aggregate demand. Examples of government spending might include such items as training, salaries and benefits of government employees, advertising of government programs and delivery of programs.

Net Exports Spending

The fourth element of aggregate demand is the level of *net exports*, defined as the difference between total exports and total imports. A change in the amount of purchases made by foreign consumers (caused by factors other than price changes) affects aggregate demand. Higher levels of exports translate into increased foreign demand while lower level of imports suggests increased domestic demand. The level of national income in other countries and exchange rates are the two primary areas that affect this element.

The real GDP in other countries affects Canadian aggregate demand because real GDP in foreign countries determines their consumption, both domestic and foreign. When another country's GDP increases, it increases consumption in that country. This ultimately leads to increased foreign purchases by that country, which benefits Canada when that other country is a trading partner. A decline in another country's real GDP has the reverse affect.

Net exports are sensitive to fluctuations in the real exchange rate. Changes in the exchange rate between Canada and other nations affects Canadian aggregate demand; as the value of the Canadian dollar decreases in relation to a foreign currency, it increases the attractiveness of Canadian products from a foreign perspective. Similarly, Canadians would tend to purchase fewer goods from that foreign country because of the increased cost. The net increase in exports that results shifts aggregate demand to the right. Accordingly, the reverse scenario would shift aggregate demand to the left.

Aggregate Supply

The aggregate supply curve is the sum of all goods and services in an economy. It shows the relationship between price level and quantity of goods and services supplied. The horizontal and vertical axes are the same for aggregate supply as they are for the aggregate demand curve. The vertical axis shows the price level while the horizontal axis shows real economic output (GDP).

However, when analyzing the aggregate supply curve, there is a separation of the short-run region (upward sloping) and the long-run region (slope is vertical). To understand why different regions have a different slope, we need to review the basic relationship between price and output reflected in the aggregate supply curve. In simple terms, the aggregate supply curve shows that output changes from the natural rate of output when the price level changes from the expected price level.

The short-run region of the aggregate supply curve reflects an economy with excess capacity or slack. In this region, price increases will provide the stimulus to increase production, or to put available capital and labour to work. Different economists have put forward different theories to explain how the mechanism might work. When an economy is at full production, as reflected in the long-run region of the curve, and there is no more excess capacity, the only impetus for further increases in output are increases in capital and labour. In this region, price plays no role because regardless of any incremental increase in price level, there is no capacity available to increase supply.

The short-run aggregate supply curve is shown in Figure 11 with an upward line sloping outward to the right.

Figure 11
Short-Run Aggregate Supply (AS)

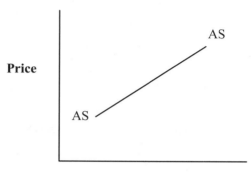

GDP (real domestic output)

Similar to the aggregate demand, there are elements that determine the location of the short-run aggregate supply curve and changes to these elements will shift the curve. A shift to the right reflects an increase in aggregate supply, while a shift to the left depicts a decrease in aggregate supply, as shown in Figure 12. The determinants of aggregate supply include:

- resource prices;

- productivity; and

- taxes and regulations.

Figure 12
Short-Run Aggregate Supply (AS)

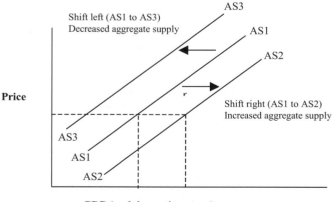

GDP (real domestic output)

Resource Prices

The price of inputs/resources affects production costs (price per unit) and affects aggregate supply. As resource costs increase, production costs increase and aggregate supply decreases (shift left). Conversely, lower resource costs reduce production costs and aggregate supply increases (shift right).

Productivity

Productivity is a measure of average real output per unit of input. A change in productivity affects aggregate supply. Increased productivity means a higher average real output per unit of input and increases aggregate supply (shift right). Lower productivity reduces aggregate supply (shift left).

Taxes and Regulations

Taxes and regulations affect the per unit cost of output. Increasing business taxes or more stringent government regulations (i.e., air pollution) drives up production costs and decreases aggregate supply (shift left). The lowering of business taxes or relaxation of regulations could lower production costs and increase aggregate supply (shift right).

Inflation and Unemployment

Two primary concerns for macro economists are inflation and unemployment. A decline in real GDP causes less economic output, leading to the use of fewer inputs, which causes a decline in employment levels. Declining employment levels translates into higher levels of unemployment, which leads to decreases in the use of available production capacity because plants and equipment are operating at less than full capacity. Ultimately, a decline in real output leads to a decline in real income. This spiralling chain of reactions demonstrates the importance of maintaining a stable level of employment within the country in order to manage economic stability.

The concept of inflation refers to increases in overall price levels, not as simply a one-time increase but a steady increase in price levels over a significant period of time. The effects of sustained inflation can be quite detrimental to an economy, both in the short and longer term. Inflation changes the distribution of income. For example, seniors who rely on a fixed income are affected by inflation because of a reduced ability to purchase goods and services. Alternatively, many government benefits are indexed to inflation, so they are adjusted to recognize inflationary trends. During inflationary times, workers demand salary adjustments to recognize the higher cost of making purchases. In some cases, salary changes may grow faster than price changes; whereas, other times, the opposite may be true. Unanticipated inflation creates uncertainty amongst investors leading to less capital investment which has a negative effect on long-term economic growth.

BUSINESS CYCLE

Canada is like most other modern industrial economies; it goes through significant swings or fluctuations in economic activity. In some years, employment levels are high, most industries are booming and prospects look good. In other years, unemployment levels are high, most businesses are operating with excess capacity and prospects look weak. Economists label the boom years as periods of economic expansion; the periods of economic decline are labelled as recessions or depressions. It is the ebb and flow of economic activity where a country experiences boom years (economic expansion) later combined with bust years (economic contraction) that we call the *business cycle*. A business cycle is the series of ups and downs in the economy.

However, the very words "business cycle" can be misleading. The word cycle tends to be associated with the idea of predictability or regularity, something that can be anticipated and operates according to well-understood patterns. Experience has shown that the timing and duration of economic expansions and contractions are highly irregular and unpredictable. For these reasons, some economists prefer to describe swings in economic activity as economic fluctuations, rather than as part of the business cycle. However, the term business cycle is still frequently used and universally understood.

Most economists also agree that there is nothing inevitable about the occurrence of the business cycle. Nothing in our economic system dictates that we must experience the business cycle. The common view is that certain levels of economic activity ought to be sustainable forever, at least theoretically. In this scenario, once full employment has been reached, the economy could then grow at a rate governed by population increases and technological advances. In this theoretical economic steady state, perpetual sustainable growth would be the norm.

In reality, business cycles do occur. Periods of recovery or expansion culminate in peak economic output, which is later identified as a turning point, and is followed by economic contraction or recession. Recession ends in a trough, which is also, over time, recognized as a turning point, which then subsequently leads to another round of recovery.

Figure 13
Business Cycle

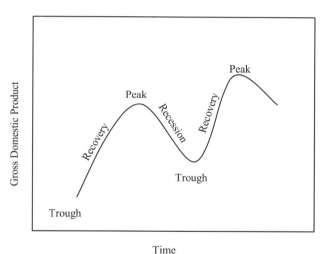

While Figure 13 appears somewhat symmetric, the duration of any period can differ and the cycle tends to be fairly erratic. While erratic, the sequences of stages in the business cycle follow the pattern: recovery/expansion, peak, recession, trough and recovery/expansion. The distinguishing elements between the four phases are the strength of each phase combined with the duration.

Trough

During the *trough* that follows a recession, and less frequently a depression, is the period during which output and employment reach their lowest point. There is no specific duration for a trough, but rather it can last for a relatively short or quite extended period of time.

Overview

Profits:	low
Savings:	high
Spending:	low
Output/production:	lowest point
Employment:	unemployment reaches highest point
Bankruptcies:	reaches highest point
Other notes:	labour costs are high; sales are low; inventories high relative to sales

Recovery/Expansion

The *recovery* stage is also commonly referred to as a period of *expansion* and, as the name suggests, output and employment expand with movement toward full employment and full capacity output.

Overview

Economy:	steadily expanding
Profits:	increasing
Savings:	begins to decrease
Spending:	increasing
Output/production:	increasing
Employment:	increasing
Bankruptcies:	decreasing
Inflation:	stable
Other notes:	sales volume is increasing

Peak

During an economic *peak*, production output is increasing or steady as the economy reaches full production capacity. Similarly, employment is increasing or steady as it moves toward a steady state of full employment. During the peak phase, prices tend to rise.

Overview

Profits:	reaching maximum
Savings:	decreasing
Spending:	increasing
Output/production:	increasing
Employment:	steady or increasing toward full employment
Bankruptcies:	low
Other notes:	output greater than sales; profit margins become thinner; inventories rise

Recession

Having reached a peak in business activity during the prior phase, a *recession* is characterized by a period of at least two consecutive quarters (six months) where there is obvious and continued decline in output, employment and income. During this phase, business activity tends to demonstrate pervasive contraction. Prices tend to fall only after a prolonged recessionary period, which then would likely be classified as a depression.

Overview

Profits:	declining
Savings:	increasing
Spending:	decreasing
Output/production:	decreasing
Employment:	decreasing
Bankruptcies:	increasing
Other:	production capacity is greater than sales potential; reducing output helps reduce the high inventory levels

The effects that these business cycles have on the economy are summarized in Table 1.

Table 1
Business Cycle Economic Impact

	Trough (1)	Recovery/Expansion (2)	Peak (3)	Recession (4)
Savings	High	Begins to decrease	Decreasing	Increasing
Spending	Low	Begins to increase	Increasing	Decreasing
Output/Production	Reaches lowest point	Increasing and moving toward full capacity	Increasing or steady as economy reaches full production capacity	Decreasing
Employment	Unemployment reaches highest point	Increasing and moving toward full employment	Steady or increasing as economy reaches full employment during this phase	Decreasing
Notes		Further into the recovery and before reaching full employment and full capacity production, price levels tend to rise	Price levels tend to increase	*Note:* Statistics Canada normally defines a recession as two consecutive quarters of negative economic growth

While shifts through the business cycle affect everyone, some industries tend to be harder hit than others. For example, industries that are vulnerable to the full impact of the recession phase include:

- producers of consumer durables, such as an automobile or household appliance;

- producers of capital goods, such as machinery used in the production of commodities; and

- the construction industry.

Alternatively, these industries can benefit significantly during the recovery/expansion phase. The rationale for this impact ties to the nature of these items, which are typically non-essential items, so a purchase is easily postponed. In addition, there tends to be just a few producers in these industries, which can result in greater control over pricing of the product. Even during times of recession, some industries are reluctant to adjust prices downward for fear of the long-term repercussions, such as ongoing price wars.

Industries classified as producers of non-durable consumer goods and those classified as service industries tend to be affected by changes in the business cycle, but the impact is typically less dramatic.

Canada, like other nations, works toward the goal of full employment, price stability and continued general economic growth. It is economic or business cycle fluctuations that create challenges as the economy moves off course.

If the business cycle is not inevitable, what causes it to occur? The best answer to this question is that various economic disturbances can collectively move an economy out of a steady state, causing business cycle consequences to occur. A common scenario is that during economic expansion, output increases to the point where price levels increase, which precipitates an interest rate hike to control inflation, which then dampens output to restore price levels.

A great deal of debate exists in the realms of macroeconomics over the most important contributing factors of business cycle effects. Later in this module, the topics of fiscal (government expenditures) and monetary (money supply) policy decisions, made by government in order to manage the business cycle, are explored.

Considering the notion that business cycles are not inevitable, and that the federal government commits many resources to managing the business cycle, many people question why public policy has failed to "cure" business cycles in Canada. The answer to this question is two-fold. The first answer is that neither fiscal nor monetary policy can be implemented with any great precision. The effect of changes in spending, taxes, and monetary position do not precipitate immediate results — long lag times can delay and obscure the results of fiscal and monetary policy.

The second answer is that it is often not clear exactly how much fiscal and monetary stimulus is required to prevent or reverse an economic recession. It is quite easy to overshoot the mark and create other problems when stimulus levels are disproportionate. While government policy may not have eradicated the business cycle, the effects of business cycles on Canadians have been lessened in recent decades through the creation of a social safety net, such as Employment Insurance (EI) and social assistance programs, that buffers the impact of the business cycle for many individuals.

If government policy cannot eliminate the business cycle, the next best thing is to have an early warning system that can predict the onset of changes in the business cycle. This early warning system is made up of a series of economic indicators that economists, policymakers and business managers use to take the "vital signs" of the economy and to predict future changes to the level of economic output.

ECONOMIC INDICATORS

Analysis of business cycles and *economic indicators* enables economists to forecast economic trends by examining the repetitive sequences that occur and to use indicators to provide predictions. Economic indicators either lead, are coincident with, or lag the business cycle. They are measurable economic phenomena that move in concert with changes in the business cycle. Indicators are an inexpensive but useful tool that are used extensively throughout the world.

Leading Indicators

A *leading indicator* is a measurable economic factor that changes before the economic output starts to move in a way that indicates a trend. Some examples of common leading indicators are:

- changes in business and consumer credit;
- average weekly manufacturing hours;
- new orders for plant and equipment;
- new orders for durable goods;

- housing starts;

- initial claims for employment insurance;

- delayed deliveries by vendors;

- new businesses formed;

- new building permits for private housing;

- material prices; and

- stock prices.

Leading indicators are a key gauge of future economic activity. Due to the "noise" that exists in terms of discerning and measuring indicators, a one-month movement in an indicator might be meaningless. Typically, multiple indicators that are evident over more than one month are needed before a trend or pattern is considered confirmed.

Coincident Indicators

A *coincident indicator* is a measurable economic factor that moves in concert, both directly and simultaneously, with economic output, indicating a trend. It indicates the current state of the economy. Some examples include:

- non-agricultural payrolls;

- personal income;

- industrial production; and

- manufacturing and trade sales.

Lagging Indicators

Similarly, a *lagging indicator* is a measurable economic factor that begins to change after the economy has changed to a new pattern or trend. Lagging indicators merely confirm long-term trends but have no power to predict the trend. A lagging indicator confirms that a stage of the business cycle has happened. Examples of lagging indicators include:

- duration of unemployment;

- outstanding loans;

- average prime interest rate charged by banks;

- ratio of consumer instalment credit to personal income;

- change in labour cost per unit of output; and

- ratio of manufacturing and trade inventories to sales.

Figure 14 summarizes the relationship of economic indicators relative to the recovery/expansionary phase of the business cycle.

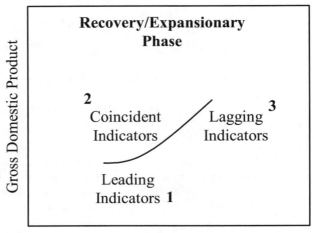

Figure 14
Economic Indicators

CANADIAN MONEY SUPPLY

What Is Money?

In Canada, the value of our money is based strictly on the confidence of the people and organizations that use it. The Canadian dollar would have no value whatsoever without wide acceptance by Canadians who use it as a means of exchange when they buy and sell goods and services. No Canadian can take a Canadian five-dollar bill and present it to the government and demand it be redeemed for something that has an intrinsic value of five dollars.

This has not always been true. Historically, a five-dollar bill had intrinsic value that was vested in gold. A Canadian five-dollar bill was worth five dollars of gold because it was backed by gold. Other nations throughout time have had the value of their money vested in many different objects, in many different forms: cattle, stones, iron, gold, silver, or shells. When money is based on the confidence of the people using it, rather than on an item such as gold with intrinsic value, it is called a fiat or fiduciary money system. The vast majority of the countries in the world currently use a fiat money system. The value of Canadian money is based on confidence and, as such, the Bank of Canada is charged with the obligation to act in ways that maintain the confidence and acceptance of the Canadian dollar.

To ensure that paper money is accepted as the means of payment, the government declares paper money as legal tender, which is the means by which debts are settled. Specific laws are established regarding the printing of money that is used as legal tender. In addition, the government makes the promise not to expand the supply of money in a rapid fashion that will cause the currency to lose its value. When money is expanded rapidly, causing it to lose value, it is referred to as *currency debasement*. This has been a problem for countries with a weak political system that rely on printing additional money as a substitute for raising taxes.

Uses for Money

According to the Bank of Canada, money plays three principal roles:

- a means of exchange;

- a unit of measurement; and
- a means of storing purchasing power for the future.

Means of Exchange

Money is central to the operation of a market. Without money, we would have to use a barter system that requires the exchange of goods and services directly. Money as a means of exchange standardizes and simplifies the operation of a market.

Unit of Measurement

Money allows for easy comparison of the value of goods and services. It is the means by which we price goods and services. It also allows us to compare costs, income, and profit across time. In providing a unit of measurement, money serves as the foundation of the accounting system, allowing us to use information in economic decision-making.

Means of Storing Purchasing Power for Future Use

Money is a means for storing value. It can accumulate as savings and those savings can be lent to others. As a means of storing value, money is simple to use because it allows people to make a contract or perform a service now and be paid for it in the future.

Definition of Money Supply

When economists refer to the money supply or the amount of money in a given domestic economy, they also make reference to four different ways that money can be calculated or defined. The most commonly used measures are M1, also referred to as narrow money, and M2, which is referred to as broad money.

M1 — Narrow Money

The combination of chequing account deposits and other bank deposits that individuals have the right to access (demand) in their entirety are referred to as demand deposits. When reference is made to the M1 money supply, it includes all Canadian currency (bank notes and coins) in circulation, along with all demand deposits held in chartered banks. The M1 money supply can be used for transactions to purchase items, and is measured at a point in time.

> M1 = Currency in circulation + Demand Deposits

M2 — Broad Money

The M2 money supply is a broader measure than the M1 number. It includes everything in M1 plus deposits in chartered banks that are referred to as notice deposits. Notice deposits are those that cannot be used for ongoing transactions but can be easily accessed, often with notice. Personal savings accounts and term deposits are an example of notice deposits.

> M2 = M1 + Notice Deposits

M2+

The M2+ number continues to broaden the measure. It includes everything in M2 plus all deposits at non-bank deposit-taking institutions, money-market mutual funds, individual annuities at life insurance companies and personal deposits held at government-owned savings institutions.

M2++

The M2++ is the broadest measure of money supply. It includes the M2+ number, but also includes all types of non-money-market mutual funds and Canadian Savings Bonds.

CANADIAN FINANCIAL SYSTEM

The Canadian financial system has evolved slowly over the years. Many commentators described the Canadian financial system as having four pillars:

- chartered banks;

- trust and mortgage loan companies;

- insurance companies; and

- securities firms.

Each one of these pillars is a financial intermediary who acts as a link between those who have money to lend or invest and those who want to borrow money or raise equity. One of the key players in the Canadian financial system is the Bank of Canada.

Role of Banking System

A strong and stable financial system is a necessity for a well-functioning economy. The banking pillar in Canada is extremely stable; we have not had a major banking failure in Canada in over 70 years. While the Canadian banking system is fairly complex, it is also highly effective.

The first part of the Canadian banking system is the treasury operation. The treasury, through the Canadian Mint, prints, mints, and stores currency.

The next part of the banking system is the Bank of Canada. The Bank of Canada provides clearing and settlement systems to Canadian chartered banks directly, which allows them to engage safely and efficiently in large financial transactions. The Bank of Canada also serves as a banker to the federal government, buying and selling government bonds. It distributes its profit to the federal government. As well, the Bank of Canada administers international currency reserves and acts as a stabilizer for foreign exchange markets.

One of the most important functions of the Bank of Canada is to manage the Canadian money supply. The Bank of Canada does this through the administration of monetary and interest rate policy.

By regulating the amount of risk that a bank can undertake, the government ensures that depositors will be relatively secure with respect to the deposits they have made, even in situations when economic conditions are poor. Generally, the government regulations imposed on Canadian banks have helped maintain the Canadian banking system as one of the safest and most secure in the world.

Reserve System

At their most basic level of functionality, what do banks do? Generally, we expect banks to accept deposits and make loans. As a financial intermediary, banks preserve the wealth of savers, and act as a predictable source of loans for borrowers. In a simple kind of way, banks are market makers, indirectly matching up savers and borrowers. And, because banks enjoy the trust and confidence of Canadians, depositors are happy to deposit money in a bank, receiving nothing more than a receipt, yet maintaining full confidence that they will be able to demand repayment in the future.

What happens conceptually (but not necessarily in practice) when an individual deposits cash into a local bank? The money is first recorded by the bank and added to the individual's account. The local bank then stores the deposited cash in a vault. The money is eventually removed from the vault of the local bank and taken to a second bank, which is part of the Bank of Canada central bank. The Bank of Canada is not a retail bank; it does not serve individuals or the general public. It is a bank for other banks. The local bank can deposit, withdraw, or take out loans from the central bank.

If an individual walks into the local bank to borrow money, the local bank figuratively removes money from their vault. If it does not have enough on hand, it can approach the central bank and withdraw money from its account there. If the local bank has insufficient funds in its account at the central bank, it can take out a loan from other private banks or from the central bank at an interest rate lower than the rate of interest that the individual will eventually pay to the bank for his loan. This system allows a bank to accept deposits, fund withdrawals and make customer loans without having to maintain all of the deposited cash in their own vault.

And Canadian banks, of course, make money on the spread they earn on the difference between the interest they pay savers on their deposited money and the interest they charge borrowers who borrow the money deposited by the original customer.

Until 1992, banks were required to maintain reserves, a prescribed fraction of their deposits, with the Bank of Canada. This system was gradually eliminated, yet banks continue to maintain reserves with the Bank of Canada either as cash or for settlement of their clearing accounts. Reserves left on deposit with the Bank of Canada are done so at the banks' discretion rather than as a legal requirement.

MINI-WORLD (1)

In this SNAP, assume that we have created a simulated world where the entire money supply is $5,000. Also assume Kerry has deposited $2,000 in her local bank, which pays her no interest. Further, assume that the bank chooses to keep the full $2,000 on reserve with the Bank of Canada (100% reserve ratio), so it is easily accessible when Kerry demands payment.

In this imaginary world, the money supply, after Kerry's deposit has been made, would be reduced to $3,000 since the $2,000 at the local bank would effectively be taken out of the money supply. If, and when, Kerry withdraws the $2,000, the money supply would again be re-established at $5,000.

In Canada, as in other western countries, the banking system does not operate with a 100% reserve requirement. In fact, there are no reserve requirements, yet the banks generally maintain reserves, but at their own discretion. The term *reserve ratio* is used to describe the percentage of the bank's total deposits that are set aside in reserves. The total deposit multiplied by the bank's chosen reserve ratio is equal to the bank's desired amount of reserve.

Continuing the Mini-World SNAP, how would the situation change in terms of money supply if the bank decides to establish its reserve ratio at 20% rather than 100%?

MINI-WORLD (2)

With a reserve level established at 20%, the local bank would keep only $400 of Kerry's $2,000 deposit in reserve. The other $1,600 would be available as money to loan to interested borrowers.

Assume that Anita borrows the $1,600 and subsequently uses the money to purchase furniture from New Look Interiors. Upon receiving the $1,600 as payment, New Look promptly deposits that amount in the bank. Of New Look's $1,600, the bank would keep 20% ($320) in reserve, but the other $1,280 would be available to loan out to a new borrower.

This cycle could potentially repeat itself until such time as all $2,000 of the original deposit is required as subsequent reserve amounts in subsequent loans.

The following are the steps in the cycle of loans.

Loan Number	Amount $
1	1,600
2	1,280
3	1,024
4	819
5	655
6	524
7	419
8	336
9	268
10	215
•	•
•	•
•	•
50	0
Total amount of 50 loans	9,999.89

It is easy to see that the limit or theoretical cap in terms of monies loaned out based on the original $2,000 deposit would be $10,000. However, this does not in itself translate into a $10,000 increase in the money supply. The original $2,000 deposit, which would be held in reserve on the total monies lent out in this series, must first be removed from the original amount of available funds. Therefore, the increase in money supply would be $8,000 ($10,000 - $2,000).

To reconfirm that $2,000 would be the total held in reserve, the following chart looks at the same series of loans, but this time examines the incremental reserve amount associated with each loan.

Loan Number	Reserve Amount $
1	400
2	320
3	256
4	205
5	164
6	131
7	105
8	84
9	67
10	54
•	•
•	•
•	•
50	0.007
Total amount of 50 loans	1,999.97

The term "deposit multiplier" is used to describe the amount by which total bank deposits can increase for every dollar increase in new reserves. This is expanded to the term "money multiplier", which is the amount by which the entire money supply increases.

It is not necessary, of course, to create the series each time to calculate the increase in money supply with respect to a deposit. Rather, the increase can easily be solved utilizing a simple algebraic formula.

$$\text{Deposit Multiplier} = 1 \div \text{Reserve ratio}$$

In the Mini-World SNAP, the deposit multiplier is five, calculated as:

Deposit Multiplier

$= 1 \div 20$

$= 5$

The deposit multiplier is used to calculate the maximum increase in money supply that is associated with a given deposit. The formula for calculating the increase in money supply utilizes the deposit multiplier and the amount of the deposit.

Increase in money supply = (Deposit multiplier × Deposit) - Deposit

The $8,000 increase in money supply, calculated in the Mini-World SNAP can be easily derived through this formula:

Increase in money supply

$= (\text{Deposit multiplier} \times \text{Deposit}) - \text{Deposit}$

$= (5 \times \$2,000) - \$2,000$

$= \$8,000$

The increase in money supply is often smaller than what might be predicted using the formula because households do not always deposit all of their cash holdings. Through this multiplier effect, we can see how the banking system can create money by making loans. As banks become more cautious and increase their desired reserve ratio, the deposit and money multipliers fall and the money supply contracts. Through the effect of creating money, banks can facilitate many transactions with a relatively small deposit amount. In reality, banks are more than just financial intermediaries; they play a role that is integral to the proper functioning of the Canadian economy.

Components of Money Demand

Money demand, at first glance, appears to be a non-issue. If asked, all of us would clearly voice our preference for holding as much money as we can. But, money demand is really a much narrower concept.

Money demand refers to the amount of wealth that society would like to hold in cash and is quite important for understanding the quantity theory of money, which links the demand for money with interest rate levels. In addition, money demand is the basis for the ongoing debate between monetarists and Keynesians on the cause of inflation.

The demand for money can be thought of as a liquidity preference, and it consists of the following motives:

- **Transaction motive:** money intended for expenditure in the near future must be kept on hand.

- **Precautionary motive:** prudent people hold some money to be used in case of emergencies.

Understanding the demand for money is important for economists because they believe the equilibrium rate of interest is found where the supply and demand for money is in equilibrium. In that case, interest rates can be partially explained by changes in the active demand for money due to changes in prices or output.

CANADIAN MONETARY POLICY

When economists refer to *monetary policy*, they are referring to efforts to manage and control the supply of money in the Canadian economy. Monetary policy, in Canada, is the exclusive preserve of the Bank of Canada, which is ultimately accountable to the federal government. The primary objectives of monetary policy are to help the economy achieve full employment, price stability and economic growth. When the Bank of Canada acts to increase the money supply, the policy is called *expansionary*. On the other hand, when the Bank of Canada acts to decrease the money supply, the policy is called *contractionary*.

When the Bank of Canada manages the money supply, it is focused on inflation control. By keeping inflation low, stable and predictable, it achieves an attractive climate that fosters price stability and job creation, leading toward full employment and sustainable economic growth. The target range for inflation established by the Bank of Canada and the federal government is from one to 3%, as measured by the Consumer Price Index.

The total demand for money is comprised of two elements: transaction demands and asset demands. Transaction demands involve the spending of money for goods and services by households and businesses. Asset demand refers to the holding of financial assets in the form of financial investments such as stocks, bonds or simply M1 money supply.

Transaction demand is a function of the nominal GDP because the larger the total value of transactions for goods and services, the greater the demand for money to complete the transactions. As such, transaction demand is directly influenced by changes in the nominal GDP. The relationship of transaction demand to the nominal GDP suggests that transaction demand is independent of interest rate changes.

From an asset demand perspective, there is a trade-off between how much money to hold simply as money or cash and how much to invest. The interest rate is the opportunity cost of holding money as an asset: There is value in holding money because of its liquidity (readily available for use) and there is no risk of loss (low opportunity cost). As the interest rate rises, simply holding money becomes more costly because there is a lost opportunity to earn interest (opportunity cost increases). Conversely, as the interest rate falls, there is less to lose because of the lower level of interest, so people tend to hold more money.

This creates an inverse relationship between the rate of interest and the amount of money people will want to hold (money demanded). Rising interest rates increase the cost of holding money (being liquid). Note that investors are impacted by changes in real interest rates, not the nominal rate. In conclusion, demand for money is inversely related to interest rates and the equilibrium interest rate (price paid for the use of money) is achieved at the point where the demand for money intersects with the supply of money.

As prices or real output increase, businesses and consumers will strive to hold more money in anticipation of undertaking transactions; therefore, an increase in nominal GDP will cause an increase in the demand for money.

When the supply of money is tight, consumers and businesses respond by selling financial assets such as bonds. The quantity of bonds available for sale will outpace the quantity of bonds demanded, which will push the price of bonds downward. The result of lower bond prices leads to higher interest rates. The converse is also true: as the supply of money expands consumers and businesses will tend to lower their money position by increasing their bond holdings, which will push the price of bonds upward.

RELATIONSHIP OF BOND PRICE TO INTEREST RATE

Bond face amount:	$1,000
Bond interest rate:	5%
Current market price of bond:	$ 900

Bond interest is a fixed payment based on the face value of the bond; so in this case, the bond will pay $50 of interest, regardless of the current market price of the bond. Using the time value of money calculations, we know that a single year's return on this bond translates into an interest rate of 16.23%.

We know the following information:
- P/YR = 2
- xP/YR = 1
- PMT = 25
- PV = -900
- FV = 1,000
- MODE = END

SOLVE FOR I/YR which equals 16.2333

Now assume the current market price of the bond was $1,010. A single year's return on this bond translates into an interest rate of 3.97%.

We know the following information:
- P/YR = 2
- xP/YR = 1
- PMT = 25
- PV = -1,010
- FV = 1,000
- MODE = END

SOLVE FOR I/YR which equals 3.9701

Through the supply of money, monetary policy helps determine interest rates. Changes in the supply of money cause changes in the level of consumption and investment. There is no precise formula, although the supply needs to be carefully managed because if the money supply grows too rapidly inflation occurs, whereas too slow can lead to a recession.

There are three basic ways that the Bank of Canada can affect the money supply:

- conducting open market operations;
- transferring government deposits to/from private banks; and
- changing the bank rate, which affects the target for the overnight rate.

Regardless of the method, each one of these actions affects the total amount of currency or deposits available to the public.

Open Market

Open market operations involve the sale and purchase of Canadian government bonds and other government securities. When the Bank of Canada sells a government bond, in effect, the public is exchanging Canadian currency for bonds. The result is a shrinking of the Canadian money supply. The opposite occurs when the Bank of Canada purchases government bonds; the Bank of Canada exchanges currency for bonds. This results in an increase in the money supply. Open market operations are a common tool for any central bank when it comes to controlling the money supply.

Transfers of Government Deposits

A central bank can also influence the money supply by transferring government deposits to the private banks. This provides the private banking system with excess reserves that can be used to increase the money supply through the demand-deposit multiplier or money multiplier. By providing the banks with money, it allows the banks to increase the amount of money they loan. The more that can be loaned, the greater the multiplier effect, which results in a greater increase in the money supply.

Changing the Bank Rate

When private banks have loans with the Bank of Canada, the interest rate charged by the Bank of Canada is referred to as the *bank rate*. The Bank of Canada pays interest on deposits equal to the bank rate less 0.5%.

Private banks borrow from each other at a rate referred to as the *overnight rate*, which is normally lower than the bank rate but is driven by the bank rate. The overnight rate is generally established at an amount between the bank rate and the bank rate less 0.5%. The Bank of Canada manages the money supply through changes to the bank rate, which affects the overnight rate. For the most part, private banks borrow between themselves whenever needed, using the overnight rate. While the Bank of Canada is in a position to lend money to the private banks, the overnight rate is more attractive than the bank rate and, as such, it is more attractive to borrow and lend between each other, rather than involve the Bank of Canada.

When interest rates increase it causes private banks to incur greater costs, if forced to borrow. In turn, banks will adjust their desired reserve ratio, reducing the deposit and money multipliers, thereby tightening the money supply. Alternatively, decreases to the bank rate signal a decrease in costs for the banks.

Expansionary versus Contractionary Monetary Policy

The Bank of Canada can have either an expansionary or contractionary position with respect to monetary policy. Expansionary monetary policy increases the money supply while contractionary monetary policy decreases the money supply.

Utilizing the three ways the Bank of Canada manages monetary policy, *expansionary monetary policy* can be achieved through:

- buying government securities;
- transferring government deposits to private banks; and
- lowering the bank rate.

On the other hand, *contractionary monetary policy* by the Bank of Canada includes:

- selling government securities;

- transferring government deposits from private banks; and

- increasing the bank rate.

Monetary Policy and the Interest Rate

The Bank of Canada's monetary policy can affect interest rates. When the Bank of Canada is pursuing an expansionary monetary policy, and expanding the money supply by purchasing bonds, transferring deposits to private banks, and/or decreasing the bank rate, the interest rate falls. The reason for this change can be explained in two ways. If the demand for money stays constant, the expansion of the money supply caused by expansionary monetary policy causes the interest rate to fall. In this scenario, people are generally eager to make loans but hesitant to take loans. When there is more money in the economy and the demand for money is constant, then the general price of holding money — the interest rate — will be low.

Second, if the Bank of Canada causes an increase in money supply by expansionary policies, the demand and price for loans will decrease. What is important to understand is that the interest rate is the equilibrium factor in the market for funds to be loaned. Therefore, a fall in demand for loans will cause the interest rate to fall as well.

In short, if we hold the demand for money constant, expansionary monetary policy will result in both an increase in supply of funds to be loaned and a decrease in demand, which both act to lower interest rates.

The reverse logic can be applied to contractionary monetary policy. Given a constant demand for money, when money supply is relatively scarce, interest rates tend to increase. *People become hesitant to make loans, but eager to take loans.* And when the Bank of Canada sells bonds, reduces transfers to private banks, or increases the bank rate, the demand for loans tends to increase as money becomes more difficult to source. With the interest rate being the equilibrating factor in the market for funds to be loaned, an increase in the demand for loans causes interest rates to rise. In summary, the Bank of Canada's contractionary monetary policies directly affect the prevailing interest rate.

Figure 15 depicts the economic flow-through of an initiative or action undertaken by the Bank of Canada as a result of a monetary policy decision.

Figure 15
Impact Flow of Monetary Policy

Impact Flow of Monetary Policy

| Bank of Canada undertakes an action following a policy decision | impacts | reserves at chartered banks | impacts | money supply | impacts | interest rates | impacts | investment spending | impacts | aggregate demand | impacts | Prices / GDP |

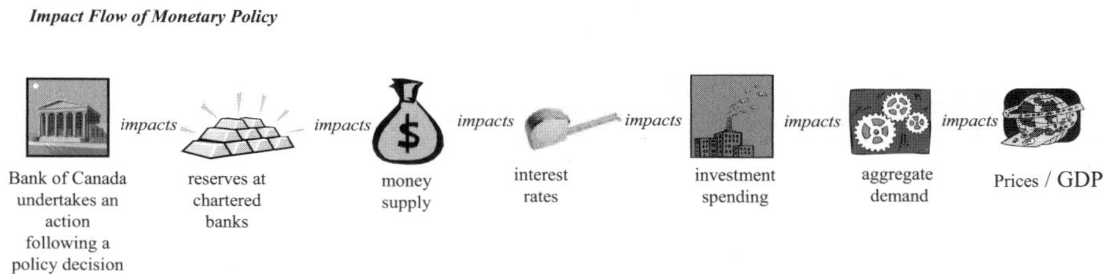

Figure 16 depicts the flow-through of the economic impact that results from a monetary policy decision that is contractionary in nature.

Figure 16
Economic Impact of Monetary Policy — Contractionary

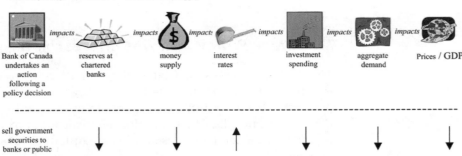

Contractionary monetary policy is concerned with decreasing the money supply. To decrease the money supply, the government wants to reduce the reserves in the chartered bank system, which will cause the banks to reduce lending in an effort to reserve cash, which lowers the bank profit, all leading to less money in the economy.

Selling government securities to the bank or public is one method by which to lower the reserves. Alternatively, the government could retrieve deposits from the banks or increase the bank rate. Either way, the result is to:

lower excess reserves at the bank — reduces the money supply — causes interest rates to rise — causes lower investments — leads to a decrease in aggregate demand and GDP.

Figure 17 depicts the flow-through of the economic impact that results from a monetary policy decision that is expansionary in nature.

Figure 17
Economic Impact of Monetary Policy — Expansionary

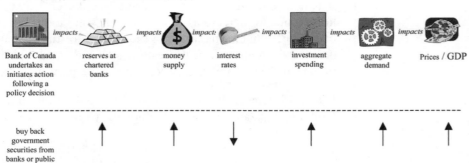

Expansionary monetary policy is concerned with increasing the money supply. To increase the money supply, the government wants to make available more reserves in the chartered bank system which will cause the banks to focus on increased lending which increases the bank profit, all leading to more money in the economy.

Buying government securities back from the bank or public is one method by which to increase the reserves. Alternatively, the government could transfer deposits to the banks or lower the bank rate. Either way, the result it to:

increase excess reserves at the bank — increases the money supply — causes interest rates to fall — causes an increase in investments — leads to an increase in aggregate demand and GDP.

CANADIAN FISCAL POLICY

Fiscal policy, sometimes referred to as government budgetary policy, is the actions taken by the Canadian government to influence the economy through government behaviour regarding spending decisions and tax policy. Fiscal policy can generally be divided into three categories:

- government purchases of goods and services;
- taxes; and
- transfer payments to households (i.e., Old Age Security, Employment Insurance).

Traditionally, certain budgetary actions of the government are considered stimulative. When the government increases government expenditures, reduces taxes, or undertakes a combination of increased government expenditures and reduced taxes, these actions are intended to stimulate growth in the domestic economy over the short term through expansionary policy.

Actions that reduce government expenditures, increase taxes, or undertake a combination of reduced government expenditures and increased taxes, are intended to dampen short-term economic growth through contractionary fiscal policy. The job of government is to enact the right fiscal policy in the right circumstances. This particular challenge is enhanced by the fact that there are long lags, which vary a great deal, between the time government enacts the policy, and when the effects of the policy impact the economy.

The mechanism behind expansionary fiscal policy is straightforward. When the government lowers taxes, consumers have more disposable income. Tax cuts, at the most basic level, shift assets from the government to the populace. Since disposable income is one of the factors that contribute to economic growth (along with government spending, investment, and net exports), tax cuts are associated with increased economic output. In the same fashion, when government spending on goods and services increases, the population receives the money the government spends on those services. Recall that government spending was also one of the factors that contributes to increased economic output, by shifting government assets to the populace. It is through increases in disposable income, and increases in monies spent for goods and services by the government, that expansionary fiscal policy increases economic output.

Contractionary fiscal policy operates in reverse fashion. Increased taxes lowers income, and reduced government spending decreases the shift of government assets to the populace. Since both factors are linked to the level of economic output, contractionary fiscal policy leads to decreases in economic output.

Unit 2
Investment Fundamentals

YIELD CURVES

Types of Curves

The interest rate yield curve is a graphical representation that depicts the relationship between rates of return on fixed-income securities and the maturity dates of those securities. This relationship between yields and time to maturity is often referred to as the *term structure* of interest rates. Normally, the yield curve is positively sloped: longer-term securities have higher yields, while shorter-term securities have lower yields. The yield is simply a measure of the annual return on the security, and the assumption is made that the securities are of similar creditworthiness.

Figure 18
Normal Yield Curve

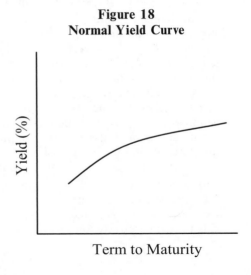

Figure 18 shows a *normal yield curve* where long-term rates are higher than short-term rates, resulting in the upward slope to the right. The general hypothesis of the term structures of interest rates is that the typical yield curve increases at a decreasing rate relative to maturity.

Yield curves are an interpretive and predictive aid to economists and market watchers because they are not always upward sloping. At times, they can be flat, downward sloping or even change directions. When the slope of the yield curve changes, it imparts valuable information about a variety of market and economic phenomena. In fact, there is a strong predictive relationship between the slope of the yield curve and the business cycle. For this reason, the yield curve is often used for forecasting economic activity.

In Figure 19, the yield curve is downward sloping, or inverted, which means yields fall as maturity increases.

Figure 19
Falling Yield Curve

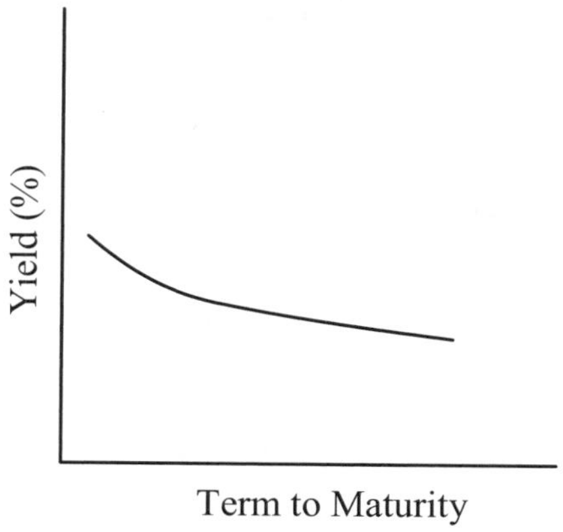

In Figure 20, the yield curve is flat, which means yields are identical across all maturities.

Figure 20
Flat Yield Curve

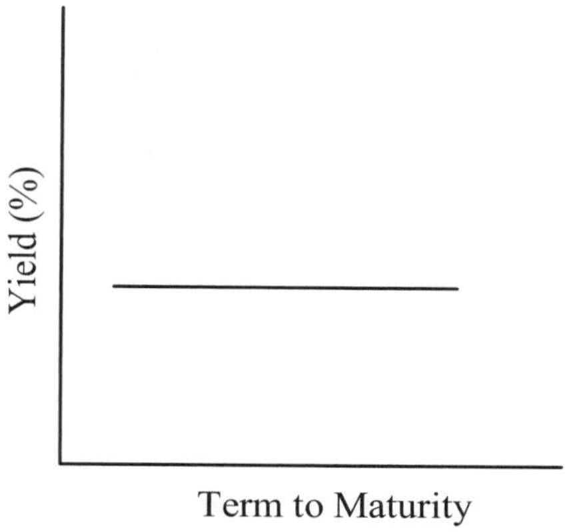

In Figure 21, the yield curve is humped, where yields increase as maturities increase in the shorter term, reach a peak and then through the intermediate and longer-term the yields continue to decline.

Figure 21
Humped Yield Curve

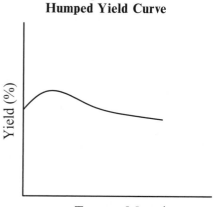

While the yield curve describes the relationship between short- and long-term interest rates, the shape of the curve is often used as a predictor of investor expectations relative to future interest rates. There are three significant theories or schools of thought that are generally used to explain the term structure of interest rates:

- expectation theory;
- liquidity preference theory; and
- market segmentation theory.

Expectation Theory

This theory aligns with the assumption that the yield curve is representative of what people expect rates to be in the future. For example, if a humped yield curve is apparent, perhaps with a peak at about the three-year point, the prediction would suggest that investors expect interest rates to rise for the next three years, after which they will trend downward.

Liquidity Preference Theory

This theory works on the assumption that investors dislike having money tied up and therefore demand a premium return for longer holding periods. The hypothesis is that investors will accept lower yields when it allows them to maintain liquidity. This school of thought provides support for a normal yield curve but provides no support for other types of yield curves.

Market Segmentation Theory

As the name suggests, Market Segmentation Theory works on the premise that investors can be segmented into groups, each with different dominate preferences. For example, in the short-term market, banks play a dominant role, while pension funds and life insurance companies dominate the long-term investment market. In the intermediate market, dominant players include mutual fund companies and casualty insurance carriers. It is believed that the dominant players in each of these markets have little interest in the other markets. The yield curve is thought to be a composite of each of these different segments. This school of thought can be easily aligned with the four different yield curves, shown earlier in this section.

Forecasting Economic Output

The predictive power of yield curves comes from their ability to predict significant interest-rate movements. Investment levels are driven by interest rates, so a tool that can predict significant interest rate increases can also predict significant decreases in economic output. However, when researchers look at the historic efficacy of using yield curves, they find that the predictive power of the yield curve has limitations. Yield curves are better relative predictors of economic output than other macroeconomic and financial variables, but also need to be utilized with caution. For example, yield curve analysis did not successfully predict the 2009 recession, and it did predict other economic downturns that did not materialize.

To give an example of how the yield curve is used to forecast economic activity, we can look at U.S. treasury bills. American economists consider a change in the yield spread between 3-month treasury bills and 10-year treasury notes to be one of the best predictors of a recession, two to four quarters in advance.

Caution is required when interpreting the yield curve as they sometimes can be misinterpreted and give misleading signals, especially during times of financial stress or in the midst of other significant financial dislocations (i.e., stock market panic or major government budget changes). For this reason, the yield curve and other economic conditions must be examined carefully before making predictions based on the movement of the curve's slope.

An anomaly that can subvert the normal yield curve is the "flight to quality" that will drive many investors into short-term guaranteed treasury bills when the world is engulfed in turmoil or uncertainty. The risk-free nature of T-bills tends to attract investors during uncertain times, and the issues with the shortest maturities tend to be the most attractive. During periods of flight-to-quality, the yield curve tends to be volatile. It steepens when money flows into short-term T-bills, and then returns to normal when the uncertainty is over. This pattern is well-enough understood that analysts will use the size and severity of the yield curve as a barometer that mirrors the Bank of Canada's perception about the severity of any given crisis.

The Effect of Government Borrowing

One other large influencer on the yield curve is the change in government budget expenditures. When government increases spending, the government often must also issue debt to fund the increase. The increase in borrowing tends to put upward pressure on interest rates, since higher rates are needed to attract the additional investors. The composition of the maturities of treasury borrowing has the potential to shift the slope of the yield curve. If long-term is the preferred maturity alternative, it will cause long-term rates to rise in relation to short-term rates.

INFLATION

Background

In general, the items we buy cost more now than they did in the past. In the 1920s, a loaf of bread could be purchased for a nickel. Today, that same loaf of bread will cost more than a $2.00. This phenomenon of sustained price increases is what is referred to as inflation. *Inflation* is the percentage change in the purchasing power of a unit of currency over a specific period of time.

Consumer Price Index

Since inflation represents the change in price level from year to year, inflation can be calculated by quantifying the change in a given price index from year to year. The most common and important price index used for calculating inflation is the Consumer Price Index (CPI), which has widespread acceptance. The *Consumer Price Index* is an indicator of changes to the general level of consumer prices, which is referred to as inflation. The purchasing power of money is affected by changes in prices, therefore CPI is useful to all Canadians.

The CPI is used in four unique ways. First, it is commonly used as a benchmark to escalate the given value of a dollar over time in order to preserve the purchasing power of that dollar. As such, it is used as the basis for adjusting general wages and the payments associated with government-sponsored programs including the Canada Pension Plan and Old Age Security.

Secondly, the CPI is useful as a tool to deflate current dollar estimates when there is a need to eliminate the effects of price change. Thirdly, the CPI is integral in the establishment of Canadian economic policy, including monetary policy decisions and impact assessments. The CPI is also widely used in economic research and analysis relative to the causes and effects of inflation along with regional disparities in price changes.

Statistics Canada measures the CPI on a monthly basis by tracking the retail price of a representative basket of approximately 600 goods and services utilized by an average household. Included are expenditures on food, housing, transportation, furniture, clothing and recreation. Items within the basket are given a weight as a percentage of the total based on typical consumer spending patterns. The purpose of the weighting is to reflect actual spending patterns whereby changes to the price of an item with a heavier weighting, such as food, has a bigger impact on the index than an item with a smaller weighting, such as clothing.

Prices within the basket of commodities are measured against a base year, which is currently 2002. This means that the basket of goods was valued at 100 in 2002. The rate of increase for the CPI is typically reported as a percentage increase in the index over the previous 12-month period.

The CPI is incorporated into the formula for calculating inflation as follows:

% Change in Price Level = (((CPI for 2nd time period) - (CPI for 1st time period)) ÷ (CPI for 1st time period)) × 100. See www.bankofcanada.ca/en/inflation_calc.html for an inflation calculation tool.

CPI CALCULATION

In March 2009, the CPI was 114.0 (recall that the base year in 2002 is 100). Twelve months later, in March 2010, the CPI was 115.6. The unadjusted percentage in this twelve-month period between March 2009 and March 2010 is 1.4%.

To calculate the percentage change in price levels, the CPI numbers are input into the formula:

% change in price level

= ((115.6 - 114.0) ÷ 114.0) × 100

= 0.0140 × 100

= 1.4%

CAUSES

In simple terms, inflation results when money is produced at a more rapid pace than the supply of goods and services. This causes a shortage of goods and services relative to the supply of money. The cause and effect relationship drives up the price of goods and services. Rapid economic growth creates consumer confidence, which leads to increased spending. This causes an increase in the demand for loans, putting more money into the economy. This spiralling effect puts upward pressure on the price of goods and services. The basic premise is that inflation occurs when the demand for goods and services outpaces the ability to supply goods and services.

Inflation Control

Although year-to-year changes might be hard to notice, over time Canada has experienced significant increases in what it costs to buy typical consumer goods. Inflation control is an important consideration of Canadian monetary policy because of the impact it has on favourable long-term economic growth. In 2006, the Bank of Canada and Canadian government agreed upon a target inflation rate in the range of one to 3% for the period between 2006 and 2011. The aim is to achieve a rate equal to the 2% mid-point, although a 1% spread either way is within the target range.

The establishment of the target range assists the Bank of Canada when establishing monetary policy actions for maintaining economic growth at a sustainable pace and ensuring a stable price environment.

Effects of Inflation

High Inflation

High inflation erodes purchasing power, thereby impacting the Canadian standard of living. When inflation runs high, uncertainty permeates society because people feel ill equipped to predict future pricing. During high inflationary times, investments tend to be more speculative as individuals attempt to leverage the effects of inflation. This reduces productive investments and creates an environment of temporary success. As inflation spirals upward, people and businesses commonly attempt to insulate themselves by demanding additional wages or prices, which continues to propel the spiralling effect. Individuals on fixed incomes tend to be hardest hit by inflation because there are no additional sources of income to which they can turn.

Low Inflation

During periods of low inflation, the general climate tends to be more predictable; people and businesses feel confident in making longer-range plans. A stable, predictable environment promotes productive investments, leading to increased economic growth. During low inflationary periods, wage and price demands tend to be less onerous with a generally prosperous society that is not experiencing significant price changes. Sustained low inflation becomes reinforcing.

Unexpected Inflation

Actual inflation is comprised of two elements: expected inflation and unexpected inflation. *Expected inflation* is the inflation that economists and investors anticipate. While there is no single method for calculating expected inflation, this number is often the result of consensus surveys or other proxy measures. Unexpected inflation is the missing variable when actual inflation is compared with expected inflation. These three variables create a simple algebraic formula:

Unexpected inflation = (Actual inflation) - (Expected inflation)

If the rate of inflation from year to year differs from what economists and consumers are expecting, then *unexpected inflation* is said to have occurred. Unlike expected inflation, unexpected inflation carries more serious economic consequences. In effect, unexpected increased inflation causes a redistribution of wealth from lenders to borrowers. We know that inflation decreases the purchasing power associated with a given sum of money.

Lenders consider the element of expected inflation when establishing nominal interest rates. If a bank lends money to a borrower at terms that reflect an expected level of inflation, but unexpected inflation strikes, then the money repaid to the bank has less real value than the money that was borrowed.

Of course, if inflation turns out to be lower than expected, then wealth is redistributed from borrower to lender under the exact same premise. In this case, the lender gains since the inflation premium built into the nominal rates is more than adequate.

Interest Rates

The term *real rate of interest* refers to the difference between the interest rate and the expected rate of inflation.

ALLAN

Allan would like to earn a real rate of interest of 4% on his investment portfolio. If the expected rate of inflation is 5%, what nominal rate of interest would Allan need to earn in order to achieve his goal?

To earn a real rate of interest of 4%, when inflation is expected to be 5%, Allan would need to earn a nominal interest rate of 9%.

Note: The above example is simplistic in nature. For financial calculations related to the CFP program and the CFP exam, inflation adjusted return is calculated using the formula (i - infl) ÷ (1 + infl), as taught in previous CFP courses. In this case, Allan would require a nominal return of 9.2% in order to achieve a real rate of return of 4%.

Interest rates incorporate the expected rate of inflation and a return for the lender. The difference between the nominal rate of interest and the real rate of interest is the expected rate of inflation. Included in the "return" aspect of the interest rate is a premium charged by the lender related to the degree of default risk associated with the loan. As the probability of default increases, the premium increases.

Canada's inflation rate has an influence on the supply and demand of Canadian dollars. Investors are attracted to Canadian investments when Canada's interest rate is higher than in other countries, provided Canada's rate of inflation does not exceed that of its trading partners. When Canada's rate of inflation exceeds that of its trading partners, investors typically anticipate that the value of the Canadian dollar will be eroded because of the effects of inflation, so they tend to avoid Canadian investments.

DEFLATION

A sustained decrease in prices, represented by negative changes to the CPI year over year, is referred to as *deflation*. Deflation differs from the concept of *disinflation*, which is simply a decline in the rates of average increases in the rate of CPI. The economic period in the 1930s, known as the Great Depression, when prices declined by about 20% over a four-year period, is Canada's most recent experience with deflation. While many individuals recall the significant drop in CPI, from 12% to 4%, in the early 1980s, this economic period is representative of a period of disinflation, not deflation.

When deflation occurs because of advances in economic productivity, rather than reduced spending, it can have a beneficial influence because the downward pressure on prices causes increases to real income. Some economists cite technological advancements relative to computers as an example of productivity gains.

However, similar to inflation, deflation can also cause harmful effects on a country's economy; it can cause spending habits to contract, resulting in lower prices as economic uncertainty intensifies.

EXCHANGE RATES

Canada has a floating exchange rate where there is no pre-determined value relative to the currency of other countries. Demand and supply for Canadian dollars affects the exchange rate: when demand exceeds supply the value of the Canadian dollar increases and, conversely, the value falls when supply exceeds demand. In addition to the influences of interest rates and inflation, as described earlier, exchange rates are also affected by Canada's balance of trade. When the value of Canada's exports exceeds imports, there is increased demand for Canadian dollars. In addition, investors' expectations relative to Canada's economic outlook will influence the exchange rate. Investors tend to choose investments in Canada, driving up demand for Canadian dollars, when there is a strong, vibrant economic outlook.

INVESTMENT RISK

A general principle of investment works on the premise that risk and return are inter-related: the greater the risk the higher the return. This premise is built on uncertainty about the future.

This section looks at investment risk and how it is quantified and understood by market professionals. The term *investment risk* refers to the variability of investment returns. This variability comes in two forms that can be encompassed into an equation

$$\text{Risk of return} = \text{Company specific risk} + \text{Market related risk}$$

The term *company specific risk* is also known as *unsystematic risk*, and the term *market related risk* is known as systematic risk.

Unsystematic Risk

Looking at risk conceptually, an investment may be subject to risk because of problems associated with the company's operation or profitability. The problem could be anything from labour strife, important patents being refused, or a major product liability suit being brought forward. If an individual's life savings were invested in one company, his risk would be relatively high. He would have, in effect, put all of his eggs in one basket. Are there actions that an individual could undertake to reduce or eliminate this risk? The answer is yes. If the investor broadens his investment base to include a portfolio of companies, he will have diversified away a great deal of the unsystematic risk.

In other words, the effect of problems in one company can be lowered when the individual's stock portfolio is comprised of stock from many different companies. The hallmark feature of unsystematic, company-specific or security-specific risk is that it can be minimized through the diversification of portfolio holdings. In addition, because it can be diversified, the market does not reward investors for assuming this risk. Some estimates suggest that up to 60 or 70% of the risk in a given investment can be attributed to unsystematic risk.

Systematic Risk

Continuing with the conceptual analysis, some of the risk that is inherent in holding an equity investment in a specific company is general market related risk. Certain conditions or events affect not just an individual company, but virtually all companies in the market. For example, a spike in interest rates tends to cause lower levels of investment, and in turn can slow growth or even reverse domestic output. The business-cycle effects will impact virtually all companies in the market. They are, in effect, correlated to the market and, therefore, cannot be diversified away through a portfolio investment strategy.

Other factors that contribute to systematic risk include inflation and currency fluctuations. It is suggested that non-diversifiable, systematic risk can account for up to 30 to 40% of total investment risk. This is the type of risk that the market rewards investors for holding. While systematic risk cannot be reduced by diversification, asset allocation plays an important role in managing this type of risk.

Unsystematic Risk

- company-specific risk

- can be reduced through the diversification of portfolio holdings

- examples include labour strife, patent issue, product liability

Systematic Risk

- market-specific risk

- cannot be minimized through diversification

- examples include interest rates, inflation, currency fluctuations

Influence of Time

In terms of a time horizon, time is on the investor's side. Generally, the longer the time horizon, the more risk an investor can incorporate into a portfolio in exchange for higher returns. If the time horizon is relatively short, investors favour more stable investments with lower risk.

A central issue relative to the length of the holding period is the exposure that investors face with volatile investments early in the holding period. The concept can be illustrated through an example. If an investor buys a highly volatile stock with a mean price of $30 (calculated over the previous 40 trading days), the actual price of the stock might vary between $20 and $40 at any given point in time. Even if the stock performs as the investor expects, and slowly appreciates over time, there will be many days in the short-term where the stock will trade at a price that is lower than the $30 purchase price. If an investor is holding a stock for a short period of time, the risk of needing to liquidate the stock during a low price point is enhanced.

On the other hand, when an investor has a longer time frame, the exposure of having to sell the stock at a low point is greatly diminished because of the appreciation of the stock over the longer time period. It is also assumed that investors with a longer time horizon will have more flexibility in choosing their selling date, thereby avoiding a down day in terms of price.

Types of Investment Risk

The broad term of *risk* associated with an investment is quite general in nature and is not easily quantifiable. However, risk can be divided into a series of categories or types that are more specific in nature. Not every security is subject to every possible type of risk, but rather characteristics of a specific security may make it more susceptible to certain types of risks. The following discussion looks at different categories of risk relative to investments.

Business Risk

Business risk involves the operating risk of the specific company, relative to the volatility of the firm's earnings before interest and taxes (EBIT). Every business is in some respect sensitive to conditions or events that vary the net operating profit or cash flow of the business. Business risk is a broad category and could include items that are as diverse as competitive threat, technological threat or even product cycle threat. The more volatile the firm's operating profit, the greater the firm's business risk.

The cost structure or operating leverage (ratio of fixed to variable costs) of a company contributes an element of business risk to the company. When holding an investment such as an equity security of a company, an investor is exposed to all of the potential operating threats that could negatively affect that business. When a company is said to have a high degree of business risk, it means that it is highly susceptible to factors that could seriously diminish its operating results. Business risk is a form of unsystematic risk.

Financial risk aligns with the probability that the firm will default on its debt. As the firm's debt increases, the risk of default increases. Conversely, decreasing corporate debt lowers the risk of financial default. Holders of bonds are subject to business risk, because there is a risk that the issuing corporation may not have sufficient funds to meet its debt obligation, such as a coupon payment or the funds to redeem a bond upon its maturity.

Market Risk

When an investor purchases a security, in addition to the business risk associated with that security, the risk is compounded by the risks associated with the market in general. In general terms, *market risk* is the sensitivity of an asset relative to changes in the overall market. The best way to describe market risk is to imagine a company (Company A) that has excellent operating results. The company has surpassed expectations with respect to every operating metric of the business. Even when operating results are strong, if the market as a whole has experienced a sharp downturn associated with some external event, the share price of Company A will likely decrease too, notwithstanding its excellent operating results. This effect results from market risk, which is a form of systematic risk. Market risk cannot be avoided through portfolio diversification.

Market risk holds the potential to affect all business or investment opportunities if an economy is hit with periods of very poor economic performance. It is also the risk that the re-purchase value of the security will decline. The longer the period to maturity, the higher the market risk. If an investor needs to liquidate a financial asset prior to its maturity, the investor faces the possibility of market risk.

Reinvestment Risk

Reinvestment risk refers to the investor's ability to take future proceeds and reinvest them in securities that have a similar risk-return profile. If there is a substantial likelihood that future proceeds will have to be reinvested at a lower rate of return, then an investment is said to carry significant reinvestment risk. The term is usually used in reference to fixed income securities.

In a period of falling interest rates, an individual may not be able to reinvest the coupon paid from a given bond at a rate similar to that paid by the existing bond. In this case, there is significant reinvestment risk.

Reinvestment risk must be considered when comparing potential investments of various maturities and various rates of return in a volatile market. For example, if an investor's choice is between investment A, which pays 10% per year for two years, and investment B, which pays 9% per year for five years, the investor would examine the reinvestment risk associated with these investment choices before committing funds. If market interest rates are falling sharply, the case for investment B may be stronger, even though it returns less in the first two years. Reinvestment risk is one of the elements an investor considers as an integral part of selecting appropriate investments.

An investor also faces reinvestment risk when he receives a flow of income during the term of a fixed income security. For example, the income that flows in annually from a bond or preferred share is subject to reinvestment risk when the level of interest at which the income is reinvested is at a rate less than what is being paid on the security itself. In other words, an investor encounters reinvestment risk when the reinvestment rate is below the security's current coupon or interest rate. Reinvestment risk also occurs when an investor receives a coupon or interest payment and simply leaves the income sit idle, even if only in the short-term.

Interest Rate Risk

The *interest rate risk* of an investment describes the effects that interest rates will have on the value of the investment in question. Typically, bond prices are the most sensitive to interest rate risk. If interest rates in the general market are increasing, by default, any bonds held by an investor will be reduced in value to allow a purchaser of the bond to receive the higher market rate should he purchase the bond. Typically, interest rate risk increases as the time to maturity increases. For example, a bond with a long period prior to maturity will experience greater price movement as interest rates change than a bond with a shorter period to maturity. During times of rising interest rates, longer-term bonds will experience a greater price drop than those bonds with shorter periods to maturity. Conversely, as interest rates drop, longer-term bonds will experience a greater price increase.

A similar problem may occur with fixed-rate investments, such as a term deposit that pays a set rate for a given period of time. While the fixed-rate provides protection against falling interest rates, the investor may lose on the up-side because of a commitment to hold the investment until it matures, so the investor is unable to take advantage of increasing interest rates.

Inflation Risk

Inflation or *purchasing power risk* is the probability that price increases will erode the value of an investment. Inflation risk comes into play when making asset allocation decisions. Cash loses its purchasing power over time, when inflation rates are greater than zero. To guard against inflation, investments must obviously be held in an asset other than cash.

Inflation risk is a significant issue for conservative investors who chose to have safety of principal but which ties them to low levels of return. When inflation rates are significant, an important consideration relates to the proportion of investment dollars invested in assets that are highly susceptible to the impact of inflation.

Fixed income securities provide a maximum or capped rate of return, and generally decrease in value because of inflation rate increases. On the other hand, stock prices tend to have an inflation factor built into them, where increases in inflation are generally absorbed by the rising stock price over the long term.

Real estate normally functions with a positive correlation to inflation. As inflation increases, the price of real estate also rises. Conversely, with deflation real estate prices tend to fall.

Marketability Risk

When a financial asset trades in a market with few buyers and few sellers, and no active market making, there may not be a buyer willing to purchase the investment when the seller wants to sell it. In order to induce a buyer in a thin market to buy, the seller often has to discount the selling price. The likelihood of the seller having to use a discount to induce a buyer is referred to as *marketability risk*. In the absence of an active market, many assets need to be discounted in order to be sold.

Liquidity Risk

Liquidity risk is closely linked to marketability risk. If marketability risk represents the probability that an asset will have to be discounted before a buyer will purchase the security, *liquidity risk* is the probability that the investment can ultimately be converted into cash. The more likely it is that the holder of the investment will not be able to convert the investment to cash or will only be able to do so at a substantial loss, the greater the liquidity risk associated with the investment.

Treasury bills are an example of highly liquid assets that can be easily and quickly converted into cash. Real estate is illiquid because of the extended time and complexity required to convert the asset into cash at or near its true value.

As the liquidity of an asset decreases, an investor's demand for a liquidity premium (higher rate of return) increases.

The term *primary market* refers to the initial financial market in which a corporation or government body offers a new issue of securities, such as bonds or stocks. In the primary market, the issuing corporation or government body plays an active role in the initial offering of a new issue of securities. The term *secondary market* is used to describe the role stock exchanges play in capital markets. The majority of trading that occurs on a stock exchange takes place between investors and typically does not involve the company who originally issued the security. This type of trading is commonly referred to as secondary trading, and it is this secondary market that is vitally important to the liquidity of a particular security. The secondary market provides an easily accessible place of exchange.

Political Risk

Every company in existence does business within a given country, which has a unique set of political institutions, government regulations and tax provisions. It may also do business in other countries that have an entirely different political framework. When business decisions are made, they are made with certain expectations about how the political framework of a country operates. Should the political framework change, the business decision might also potentially change.

Therefore, the *political risk* associated with an investment is the risk that the political situation will change within a country to the detriment of the investment. Elements of political risk might be things like the ratification of a tax treaty with another country; the threat of nationalization of assets; or the breakdown of the rule of law. Many countries still have a high degree of political risk, which causes investments in those countries to often trade at a sharp discount.

Exchange Rate Risk

When an investment is denominated in a foreign currency, the investment is subject to the risk of fluctuations in that foreign currency with respect to the purchaser's domestic currency. Consider the scenario where a Canadian purchased an American stock in 2005 and by 2008 that stock appreciated by 20%. If the investor disposed of the stock, after his proceeds of disposition were converted back into Canadian dollars, the investor would likely have ended up with less money than he might otherwise have enjoyed by virtue of the modest appreciation in stock price. The reason, of course, is that the Canadian dollar appreciated in value against the American dollar during that period and investment gains would have, at least partially, been offset by currency losses.

Whenever Canadians invest in foreign securities there are *exchange rate risks* that must be factored into the investment decision. It must be kept in mind that foreign exchange differences can also operate to the advantage of investors. Many Canadian investors who invested in U.S. stocks in the mid 1990s were rewarded not only with superior price appreciation, but also with an exchange rate premium when they converted their U.S. currency back to Canadian dollars if they sold their stock in the late 1990s.

Default Risk

Default risk is the risk that companies will be unable to make the required interest and/or principal payments on their debt obligations, such as bonds. To mitigate the impact of default risk, lenders expect higher rates of return when lending to high-risk companies.

ASSESSING RISK

The risk level associated with an investment during a specific period of time can be measured in two ways:

- the investment's total risk can be measured by its standard deviation; and
- the market risk (systematic) associated with the investment can be measured by its beta.

Standard Deviation

The term *volatility* refers to variances in the return or the price associated with an investment. The more volatile an investment, the wider the swings in price or return. The greater the volatility, the riskier the investment. The volatility of an investment is measured by the standard deviation of the investment's rate of return.

In simple terms, *standard deviation* is the statistical measure of the distance a return is likely to be from the long-term average or mean. Standard deviation is applied to the rate of return of an investment as the method to measure the investment's volatility or risk. The greater the standard deviation, the greater the risk and the more uncertain an investor is of achieving expected returns.

Standard deviation measures the dispersion of the returns around the mean or average return; it does not measure the average return. The more dispersed the returns are, the greater the standard deviation and, therefore, the greater the risk associated with the investment.

SAM (1)

If an imaginary stock had an historical mean return of 12% per year, with no variability, perhaps one could predict that it might have a 12% return in future periods, all other things being equal. But in the real world, a stock with a historical average mean of 12%, likely had years where the stock had a return that was greater or less than 12%. Consider the following numerical summary that depicts the average return of two stocks over a five-year period:

continued . . .

---

continued . . .

	Stock A Return	Stock B Return
Year 1	12%	9%
Year 2	12%	11%
Year 3	12%	16%
Year 4	12%	10%
Year 5	12%	14%
Average Return	12%	12%

If Sam were interested in investing in one of these two stocks in Year 6, both stocks would show an identical average return over the previous five-year period. But, would an investor really be indifferent between the two stocks? The answer, of course, is no. From surface examination, Stock B has historically had much great variability in returns.

Sam wanted to know what kind of variability there might be relative to future expected returns.

Consider the variance equation and its use relative to the historical variance calculation for both Stock A and Stock B. Note that variance is a measure of variability used to characterize the dispersion among the returns.

The variance equation for a probability distribution is:

$\delta^2(r) = \Sigma\ h_i\ (r_i - E(r))^2$

Where,

i = 1 to n

δ^2 is the variance

r is the return

h is the probability

E(r) is the expected return

Since there are five data points, let's assign a 20% probability to each (1 out of 5).

Variance (δ^2)

Stock A

$0.2\ (12 - 12)^2 = 0$

$0.2\ (12 - 12)^2 = 0$

$0.2\ (12 - 12)^2 = 0$

$0.2\ (12 - 12)^2 = 0$

$0.2\ (12 - 12)^2 = 0$

Sum = 0

Stock B

$0.2\ (9 - 12)^2 = 1.8$

$0.2\ (11 - 12)^2 = 0.2$

$0.2\ (16 - 12)^2 = 3.2$

$0.2\ (10 - 12)^2 = 0.8$

$0.2\ (14 - 12)^2 = 0.8$

Sum = 6.8

continued . . .

continued . . .

The standard deviation (SD) is nothing more than the square root of the variance:

Standard deviation $= \sqrt{\delta^2(r)}$

In this case,

Standard deviation

$= \sqrt{6.8}$

$= 2.6$

When the standard deviation is reasonably symmetric and bell shaped, as shown in Figure 22 (normal distribution), the data can generally be interpreted as:

- plus or minus 1 standard deviation covers roughly 68% (68.26%) of the area under the normal distribution curve.

- plus or minus 2 standard deviations covers roughly 95% (95.44%) of the area under the normal distribution curve.

- plus or minus 3 standard deviations covers roughly all (99.74%) of the area under the normal distribution curve.

Figure 22
Standard Deviation

Normal Distribution Curve

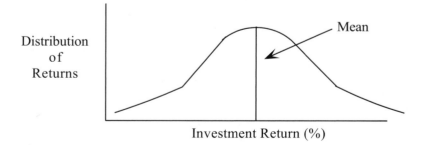

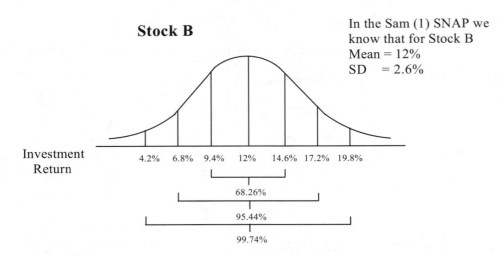

In the Sam (1) SNAP we know that for Stock B
Mean = 12%
SD = 2.6%

Probable return of Stock B is:

— between 9.4% and 14.6% about 68% of the time.

— between 6.8% and 17.2% about 95% of the time.

— between 4.2% and 19.8% almost all of the time.

Interpretation:

— the range 9.4% to 14.6% represents "plus or minus one standard deviation"

— the range 6.8% to 17.2% represents "plus of minus two standard deviations"

— the range 4.2% to 19.8% represents "plus or minus three standard deviations"

SAM (2)

Assuming the underlying distribution is normally distributed, then we know that plus or minus 2 standard deviations covers roughly 95% of the area under the normal distribution curve.

What does this mean in a practical sense?

If Sam is considering this investment choice, and the underlying circumstances have not changed, the probability of Stock A returning 12% was 100% (unrealistic in real-world investing) and the probable return of Stock B is between 6.8% and 17.2%, 95% of the time.

⇨   6.8 is derived using the formula:

expected return less two standard deviations

(12% - (2 × 2.6%))

Note that the numbers inserted into the formula are:

- 12 is the expected return;
- 2 is the number of standard deviations; and
- 2.6 is the standard deviation.

⇨   17.2 is derived using the formula

expected return plus two standard deviations

(12% + (2 × 2.6%),

Note that the numbers inserted into the formula are:

- 12 is the expected return;
- 2 is the number of standard deviations; and
- 2.6 is the standard deviation.

We know that plus or minus 2 standard deviations covers roughly 95% of the area under the normal distribution curve.

BETTY

Betty is considering the purchase of Thru-Way Inc. stock. Based on past returns, the stock has an expected return of 5% with a 3% standard deviation. Given this information, Betty has:

⇨ a 68.26% probability of a return between 2% and 8%;

⇨ a 95.44% probability of a return between -1% and 11%; and

⇨ a 99.74% probability of a return between -4% and 14%.

The calculations for each of these probabilities incorporate the expected rate of return and the standard deviation into the numeric formula. For example, the -4% and 14% are derived as follows:

⇨ 5% - (3 × 3%) = 5% - 9% = -4% and

⇨ 5% + (3 × 3%) = 5% + 9% = 14%

Note that the numbers inserted into the formula are:

● 5 is the expected return;

● 3 is the number of standard deviations; and

● 3 is the standard deviation.

When using standard deviation to determine variances in the return or the price associated with an investment, the analysis uses historic information. Standard deviation does not predict future results, but rather provides historical information only. It is important to analyze the period used in the standard deviation analysis to ensure that it is relevant or to determine if there has been any change that could have a significant influence on the future.

The standard deviation is sometimes expressed as a per cent of the mean, in which case it is known as a *coefficient of variation.*

Standard deviation is a useful measure when comparing single securities or single-asset classes. When using standard deviation as a means of comparison, the period of comparison between two securities should be reasonably consistent. It is also important to have consistency relative to the underlying basis of comparison. For example, are stock dividends included in the return used in the analysis for both securities?

Beta

Beta measures the degree to which a stock's price fluctuates in relation to the overall market, and is calculated using regression analysis. It is a measure of market risk that can be used for measuring the volatility of a security or portfolio of securities in relation to the market. Measuring volatility provides valuable information that can be used in the selection of stocks for an investment portfolio. Beta can be used to compare a stock's market risk to that of other stocks and to the market as a whole. In simple terms, Beta measures the systematic risk of a security. The terms *beta* and *beta coefficient* are used interchangeably.

Beta is a relative number. It does not look at the absolute expected variability of returns, but only at the variability of a stock as compared to the market as a whole. The market, by default, has a beta of one. If a stock within that market also has a beta of one, then it is expected that the stock will mirror the movements of the market. A beta of one indicates that the security's price will move in proportion to the market. If the market increases or decreases by 8%, then it would be expected that the stock would mirror a similar result, increasing or decreasing by 8%, all other things being equal.

A beta greater than one indicates the security's (or portfolio's) price will be more volatile than the market. A beta of less than one indicates the security's (or portfolio's) price will be less volatile than the market.

Beta Value	Volatility
Beta = 0	Cash has a beta of 1, assuming no inflation, because there is no risk.
Beta between 0 and 1	Volatility is less than the market.
Beta = 1	Volatility is equal to the market.
Beta > 1	Volatility is greater than the market.

The beta of a stock reflects the comparative variability of the stock in relation to the variability of the market. A stock with a beta greater than one is more volatile than the market. A stock with a beta less than one is less volatile than the market. It is not unusual for a utilities stock to have a beta that is less than one. Conversely, many high-tech stocks have a beta greater than one.

Investors should understand their personal risk tolerance, as the selection of investments should match their risk preferences. If an investor has a low risk tolerance, he would lean toward investments with a beta of less than one. An investor with a high-risk tolerance would tend to lean toward stocks with a higher level of beta.

TOM

Tom is looking at the stock of two very different companies:
- ⇨ Education Inc. has a beta of 0.5; and
- ⇨ Technoblast Inc. has a beta of 1.7.

Applying the concept of beta, Technoblast Inc. is viewed as 70% more volatile than the market while Education Inc. is considered only half as volatile as the market.

When the beta of a stock is expressed, it is expressed relative to the market, where the market is a benchmark whose beta is said to be one. Many investors in the U.S. use beta to measure the sensitivity of a stock relative to the Standard & Poor's 500 Index. In Canada, the S&P/TSX Composite Index can be used.

To examine how beta helps analysts and investors understand the return of a given investment, consider a basic formula that defines the required investment return.

$R = r_f + \beta (r_m - r_f)$

Where,

R = Required rate of return (or just rate of return)

β = Beta

r_f = risk-free rate

r_m = expected return

TED

Assume that the risk-free rate of return is 4%, and that Ted is contemplating investing in stock of ABC Co. He discovers through research that stock of ABC Co has a beta of 1.8. Assume that the market as a whole is expected, as reflected through the benchmark index, to increase by 10%. Applying this information into the formula introduced above, the required return on ABC Co is calculated as 14.8%.

continued ...

---

continued . . .

$R = r_f + \beta\,(r_m - r_f)$

$R = 4\% + 1.8\,(10\% - 4\%)$

$R = 4\% + 1.8\,(6\%)$

$R = 4\% + 10.8\%$

$R = 14.8\%$

According to this analysis, stock of ABC Co would have a required return of 14.8%. If Ted feels that ABC Co does not have the potential to return 14.8% in the year, he will not be adequately compensated for the risk he assumes in buying the stock.

The beta of the stock is a useful measure for investors to examine when assessing the risk-return profile of a single security, asset class, industry grouping or investment portfolio in comparison to another. Beta typically measures the security's price, disregarding dividend payments.

A security is considered to be completely influenced by the systematic risk associated with the stock market as a whole when the security's beta is one (1.0). With a beta of one, the security will mirror any movements, up or down, in the stock market as a whole. If a security's beta is one and a half (1.5), it is anticipated that the security will mirror movements up or down by an amount equal to 50% more than the market as a whole. And, if a security's beta is only one-half (0.5), it is anticipated that the security will move up or down, in the same direction as the market, by an amount equal to only one-half of any movement in the market as a whole.

When the beta is positive (greater than zero), which is the majority of cases, the direction of any movement is expected to be the same as that of the stock market as a whole. Conversely, when the beta is negative (less than zero), the direction of movement is expected to be the opposite of the market itself. In other words, the price of the security is expected to move up when the market moves down; or, the price of the security is expected to move down when the market moves up. There are a few precious metals and funds that have a negative beta. A fund with a beta of negative one-half (-0.5) is expected to move up in price by half of the amount of the decline in the stock market as a whole.

Beta can be a useful measure in helping investors to achieve specific objectives. For example, if an investor would like to develop a portfolio with a beta of 0.8, he could combine stocks with a beta of 0.2, 1.0 and 1.2. However, similar to the discussion regarding standard deviation, it is important to recognize that beta does not predict future results, but rather is calculated using historical information only.

The majority of stocks have a beta of between 0.75 and 1.25. Many equity-based mutual funds tend to have a beta of less than one (1.0) because of the cash component maintained by most mutual funds. In situations where an investor does not utilize beta as a consideration in the selection of stocks, the beta of the portfolio typically falls in the 1.0 range as a result of averaging.

Systematic risk cannot be diversified no matter how many stocks are selected. On the other hand, security-specific risk (unsystematic risk) can be managed through the number and type of securities selected.

PORTFOLIO DEVELOPMENT

Analysis

Analysis of a company's financial statements provides the opportunity to deepen an analyst's understanding of a company. The statements contain information useful in the evaluation of a company's historical financial performance as well as its future prospects. At the end of the analysis, the financial condition of the company is better understood; areas of risk are identified; asset utilization is evaluated; and comparative financial performance can be identified.

An analyst would typically review three accounting statements for the company: the balance sheet, statement of income and the cash flow statement. In addition, industry comparisons would be performed using information from a third-party information provider such as Standard and Poor's or Moody's, who would have aggregate financial ratios that are useful for comparison purposes. Analysts also use past historical information of the company for the purpose of identifying trends and making comparisons from year to year.

Investing is a complex process that should incorporate numerous considerations. A basic consideration that guides all investors, of course, is rate of return. After all, investors can take their funds and cruise the Caribbean or spruce up the downstairs bathroom. Since they have delayed the gratification that might come with immediate consumption, investors naturally want to be appropriately compensated for experiencing that delay.

Once the decision has been made to invest, an investor has many different markets from which to choose. Traditional, mainstream investment holdings tend to include cash, stocks, bonds and mutual funds. However, there are other alternatives that include options, currencies, futures, commodities and other exotic derivatives, all of which are freely traded through organized markets. In addition, an investor might want to consider something more tangible such as real estate, fine art, hockey cards, stamps, coins or other items that do not tend to trade in highly organized markets.

In developing an investment theory, it is helpful to consider a few fundamentals. Generally, investors are risk averse and prefer to avoid risk whenever possible. When an investor invests in a risk-free asset, such as federal government T-bills, he knows in advance that the return will be guaranteed, but he also knows that the return will be quite modest. Government T-bills are zero risk, low return investments. When an investor selects an investment with risk, the investor will require a premium return, above the risk-free rate of return, to adequately compensate him for assuming the additional risk.

Opportunity Cost

Opportunity cost is a common phrase used by economists. In general terms, it refers to the value of all other goods and services that must be foregone in order to produce one unit of a particular good or service. From an economic perspective, if an economy is operating efficiently, limited or scarce resources leads to the choice, which causes a decision relative to opportunity cost.

Holding Periods

The term *holding period* refers to the length of time over which an investor is assumed to own a particular security. The rule of thumb is that the longer an investment is held, the more immune it becomes to both company-specific unsystematic risk and market-related systematic risk that is inherent in holding an investment. Investor behaviour can be very shortsighted in ignoring this axiom. Unwise investors make long-term decisions based solely on very recent experiences. When long-term investment goals are kept in mind, investors can help maintain the discipline required to avoid short-term myopia.

The antithesis of the long-term investor is the market timer who attempts to exploit the natural variations in the price of an investment. These investors try to buy at the low point of a downward fluctuation and sell at the high point of an upward fluctuation. The problem with market timing is that it is usually only possible to identify high points and low points, retrospectively. It is impossible for investors to know, in advance, when the low point has arrived. In summary, the general rule is that the longer the investment horizon, the more risk or volatility an investor can feel comfortable incorporating into his portfolio.

Measures of Performance

The evaluation of portfolio performance is a critical element for all money managers and investors. Because return is a function of risk, it is impossible to evaluate portfolio performance merely by looking at the reported returns alone. A 14% return, by itself, is a meaningless number. To be meaningful, it has to be compared to returns that were realized on alternative investments bearing the same level of risk.

While it is true that all investors desire superior returns, investors are also risk averse, and there must be a method for determining whether investors have been properly compensated for the risk they have assumed. Therefore, evaluating returns on a risk-adjusted basis is important.

A solution is to compare the returns obtained on a portfolio with the returns that could have been obtained had an investment been made in a comparable alternative. To be useful, the portfolio measurement process must be compared to relevant and obtainable alternatives. Such alternatives are referred to as a *benchmark portfolio*. A benchmark portfolio must be a legitimate alternative that was truly an investment option available for the investor.

The same line of reasoning applies to a bond portfolio. If an investor has assembled a portfolio of non-investment-grade junk bonds, it would be inadequate to compare the returns of that portfolio with the returns on an index made up of bonds rated A or higher.

It is worth noting that even in today's sophisticated investment climate, exact, precise, and universally agreed upon methods of portfolio evaluation are difficult to achieve. The difficulties of identifying a similar-risk benchmark portfolio are non-trivial, representing a significant challenge in the actual assessment of portfolio performance.

There are a number of major sources of indexes used for benchmarking the performance of investment managers. For example, the TSX Group maintains a broad series of indices that track Canadian securities.

Other companies that provide extensive indices include:

* Standard & Poor's

http://www.standardandpoors.com

* Dow Jones

http://www.dowjones.com/

* The NASDAQ Stock Market

http://www.nasdaq.com

Examples of a few of the more popular indices include:

* **S&P/TSX Composite Index**

The precursor to the S&P/TSX Composite Index was the TSE300 Composite Index, which served as a barometer of the Canadian equity market for almost 25 years. After much consultation, the investment community recently decided that the TSE 300 index was no longer a relevant benchmark. The biggest problem with the TSE 300 Index was that the bottom 100 companies represented only 2% of the portfolio, which meant they lacked representation in the index.

When the new index was created, rule changes were made on how the index is to be calculated. These include a reduction to the total number of constituent companies within the index and the movement away from a fixed number (300) of companies that make up the index. The number of companies included in the index will float, contingent on the number of companies that meet all of S&P's criteria for index inclusion. The goal of the index to is to create a portfolio of stocks, weighted by market capitalization size, which almost perfectly reflects the price movement of the entire TSX market.

- **S&P 500 Index**

The S&P 500 is an American index that is designed to represent the leading companies, in leading industries, operating in the United States. They are all large capitalization stocks, and most would be near the top of a list that ranked companies by such measures as sales, profits, assets and net worth. The S&P 500 represents about 80% of the total value of the American stock markets.

- **Dow Jones Industrial Average (DJIA)**

The Dow Jones Industrial Average (DJIA) index is probably the best-known market indicator and is one of the most watched indices in the world. The Dow is made up of 30 American companies, each representing a major industry. Most of them (28) trade on the NYSE, while the rest (Microsoft and Intel) trade on the NASDAQ. The DJIA owes some of its popularity to its longevity. Charles H. Dow and Edward Jones began this famous market-tracking index in the late 1800s. The original index had just 11 stocks, most of which were railroad companies. It was not until 1928 that the DJIA expanded to 30 companies.

- **NASDAQ Composite Index**

The NASDAQ Composite index measures all NASDAQ domestic- and international-based common type stocks listed on The NASDAQ Stock Market. Initiated over 30 years ago, today the NASDAQ tracks over 4,000 companies. The heavy volume of technology related companies that trade through NASDAQ contribute to a volatile index because of the rapidity with which change can occur in the technological industry.

- **Russells 2000 Index**

The Russells 2000 index measures the performance of 2,000 small-cap stocks. The nature of the companies included in this index often reflect newer, small companies with less capital than those that would be included in the S&P 500 and Dow Jones Industrial indices. As such, the index tends to be more volatile.

Calculating Returns

When looking at the performance of a portfolio over a given period of time, it is important to consider how the fund accounts for returns associated with additions or withdrawals from the fund. To do this, the metric should capture both the income component and the capital gains (or losses) associated with any investments. If there are no changes within the portfolio, in its simplest form, rate of return can be calculated as:

$$\text{Return}_{Portfolio} = (\text{Value}_{Ending} - \text{Value}_{Beginning}) \div \text{Value}_{Beginning}$$

If no funds were added to or withdrawn during the measurement period, then this formula would be the only analysis required when evaluating total return of the portfolio. In reality, this calculation does not accurately measure performance of the portfolio if money is withdrawn and contributed to the portfolio at any time during the measurement period. For example, if the portfolio received a large cash infusion right before the measurement period ended, it would distort the ending value of the portfolio. Although it would be simple to merely reverse any withdrawal/contribution to arrive at a close approximation of portfolio performance, timing issues are a problem. Two different methodologies can be used to address this issue: dollar-weighted return and time-weighted return.

Dollar-Weighted Returns

The traditional method of portfolio measurement is to calculate the dollar-weighted rate of return, which is exactly equivalent to the internal rate of return (IRR) metric that is widely used in financial analysis and capital budgeting. Using time value of money principles, the IRR measures the actual return realized on a beginning portfolio value, including any net contributions or withdrawals made during the measurement period.

The advantage of dollar-weighted return is that because it reconciles all cash flows with the period in which they were made, it measures the rate of return to the portfolio owner.

Simply put, it is the appropriate measure to use to determine the change of wealth of the portfolio owner during the measurement period. But the fact that dollar-weighted returns are heavily impacted by the timing of cash flows makes them inappropriate to use when making comparisons to other benchmark indexes, which is a key factor in performance measurement.

Time-Weighted Returns

Because of the limitations of dollar-weighted returns for evaluating portfolio performance relative to benchmarks, the time-weighted rate of return metric was developed. It is used for comparative purposes in situations when contributions and withdrawals occur between the beginning and the end of a period. Time-weighted returns ignore cash flows into the portfolio, and measure the actual rate of return earned by the portfolio manager.

The calculation of time-weighted returns requires information about the value and timing of the portfolio's cash inflows and outflows. Time-weighted returns treat the measurement period as a compilation of many sub-periods, with each sub-period beginning when the fund experiences a cash inflow or cash outflow. The return to the portfolio is then calculated from one cash flow to the next. The last step is to link the rates of return from each sub-period together by computing the compound rate of return over time. If the fund has experienced frequent cash inflows and outflows, substantial calculations are necessary. The advantage of time-weighted returns is that they isolate the performance of the investment manager by eliminating the effects of different cash flows.

The two methods described can often produce very different results. The time-weighted return reflects the rate of return actually realized by the investment manager, while the dollar-weighted return reflects the rate of return realized by the portfolio owner.

Dollar-weighted return is influenced by the timing and size of cash flows, whereas the time-weighted return is not. For this reason, time-weighted return is generally the preferred method when evaluating portfolio performance.

MODERN PORTFOLIO THEORY

Correlation

The term *correlation* is a measure of the relationship between two or more variables. The concept of a correlation coefficient applied to investments is a relatively simple concept that measures the relationship of two or more securities. Will different securities move at the same time, for the same reason and in the same direction? Is the movement of one security dependent on the same reasons, time or conditions as the other security?

The relationship between two securities is considered to have a *positive correlation* when the value of one security increases and so does the value of the other, which is represented by a positive correlation coefficient. Alternatively, the relationship between two securities is considered to have a negative correlation when the value of one security increases while the value of the other decreases, which is represented by a *negative correlation* coefficient.

When two securities move together in perfect tandem, they have *perfect positive correlation*, where a coefficient correlation value of +1 can be assigned. If the securities move in totally opposite directions, they have perfect *negative correlation*, to which the coefficient correlation value of -1 can be assigned. Coefficient correlations range from -1.0 to +1.0. If the movement of one security has no correlation with another, a value of 0 is assigned and the securities are considered to lack correlation.

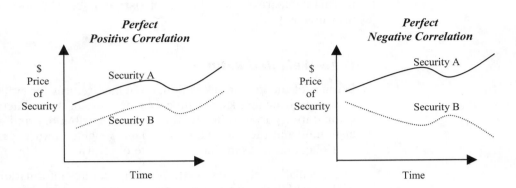

Figure 23
Correlation

As the coefficient of two securities moves closer to +1, the more closely matched are the securities. The left graph in Figure 23 demonstrates two securities that have perfectly positive correlation (+1), and, therefore, are considered perfectly matched securities. On the other hand, the further the coefficient moves away from +1, in the direction of -1, the greater the diversification between the two securities. The right graph in Figure 23 demonstrates two securities that have perfectly negative correlation (-1) and therefore are considered to be completely diversified.

When selecting assets for an investment portfolio, systematic risk can be reduced through the inclusion of securities that are considered to have high negative correlation (moving toward -1, rather than +1).

Markowitz Theory

Harry Markowitz wrote his PhD thesis in 1952, laying the groundwork for Modern Portfolio Theory (MPT), and revolutionizing investment finance in the process. His work on MPT eventually earned him a Nobel Prize in economics in 1990.

The Markowitz Theory starts out by assuming that all individuals are risk averse. In similar fashion to the classical view, he defines risk as the standard deviation of expected returns. However, Markowitz was less interested in measuring risk at the level of the individual security, as he believed that the more important risk determinant was at the portfolio level; each individual investment should be evaluated not on its inherent risk, but on the contribution of risk that it makes to the entire portfolio.

It was this revelation that led Markowitz to add a third element to the standard risk and return elements that were part of classical security analysis of individual stocks. The third element is the correlation of investments to one another (also referred to as co-variation), which has a large impact on risk determination at the portfolio level.

Markowitz realized that the classical view of diversification — to reduce business risk — was ineffective if the second stock purchased was highly correlated to the first stock.

Consider two investments, ABC stock and DEF stock, both of which have the same expected return of 12% and the same risk (standard deviation). Assume that ABC and DEF are perfectly correlated, so that a movement in the price of ABC is mimicked exactly by a movement in DEF. Further, assume that the historical variation of ABC is such that its standard deviation causes the stock to trade between -5% and +5% of its mean.

Markowitz rightly pointed out that if an investor was holding stock ABC and wanted to diversify risk by investing in stock DEF, this diversification would not reduce any risk. The risk of a portfolio containing only ABC, and the risk of a portfolio containing ABC and DEF, would be exactly the same.

Incorporating a slight variation to the assumptions, what if stocks ABC and DEF have the same 12% expected return, and the same standard deviation of -5% to +5% around their mean, but instead of a correlation with each other of +1, they have a perfectly negative correlation of -1. This would mean that when ABC deviated up in price, DEF would be deviating down in price, and when DEF deviated up, ABC would be deviating down. Remember that both stocks have the same general trend upwards as reflected in the fact they both have an expected return of 12%.

When DEF is combined with ABC, and the stocks were perfectly correlated, the risk of the combined portfolio was no lower than if ABC was the only investment. But, what happens to the risk level of the portfolio when the stocks have a perfectly negative correlation? In this case, the risk completely disappears because the deviations cancel each other out.

The expected return of each portfolio in both cases has not changed, as it still remains at 12%. The risk is unchanged with perfectly positively correlated stocks, where the deviations track in tandem. However, risk is eliminated when the stocks are perfectly negatively correlated. The brilliance of the Markowitz Theory suggests that by looking at risk at the portfolio level, it is possible to use the covariance of stocks to reduce the risk of the portfolio without reducing the expected return of the portfolio.

Efficient Frontier Analysis

In a portfolio with a given number of holdings, there is only one possible combination of holdings that will result in the maximum possible return, with respect to a given amount of risk that is assumed. Markowitz labelled the optimum combination of holdings as "efficient", where any other combination of holdings results in a lower return, at that same level of risk.

Portfolios that provide the maximum expected return for a given standard deviation and the minimum standard deviation for a given expected return are termed efficient portfolios. All others are considered inefficient. This would suggest that these inferior combinations of holdings are less efficient. In seeking efficient portfolios, the proportions in which individual securities should be combined needs to be determined, and the sets of efficient portfolios depend on the correlation between the individual securities. The efficient set of portfolios, under the Markowitz Theory, is termed the efficient frontier.

In Figure 24, the efficient frontier is illustrated by the convex curve where the expected return reflects the highest amount of return for a given amount of risk, as measured by the standard deviation.

Figure 24
Efficient Frontier

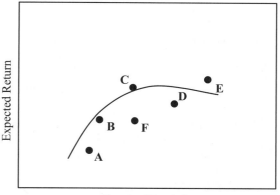

If a line were drawn vertically to connect dots C and F, the amount of risk associated with all portfolios on that vertical line would have the same amount of risk. As such, if dots C and F are different portfolios, the two portfolios are considered to have the same amount of risk but the return on portfolio C is greater than on portfolio F.

The convex curved line is referred to as the efficient frontier, where the portfolios along the line provide the highest return for the various amounts of risk. The area under the efficient frontier has achievable portfolios, but they are less efficient than those on the line.

What must be kept in mind is that every point on the efficient frontier offers the investor the highest return for a particular level of risk. Yet, this still leaves an infinite number of efficient portfolios. The theoretical answer from economists is that the best efficient frontier is the one that is tangent to the indifference curve for the specific investor (the function line that represents all possible combinations of acceptable risk and return combinations).

Practically speaking, modern portfolio theory optimization allows an investor to choose one of two approaches to security selection. One approach is to decide the amount of risk that is bearable to an investor. Perhaps an investor would conclude that he wants to be 95% certain (two standard deviations) to experience no more than a 15% decline in the portfolio during any one year. The investment manager can then construct a portfolio using modern portfolio theory to fall within these constraints. The more common approach would be to have an investor choose an expected return, say 13%, and then the investment manager tries to achieve that result by taking on the least possible amount of risk.

The theory is based on a risk-return approach where an investor must make a trade-off between the expected return on the portfolio and the amount of risk he is willing to assume.

Capital Asset Pricing Model

Concept

The Capital Asset Pricing Model (CAPM) lays out a theory on the relationship between the risk of an asset and the expected return on that asset.

CAPM Assumptions

The CAPM includes several assumptions, as follows:

- investors are risk averse;
- investors favour a high expected rate of return;
- investors have the same investment time horizon (holding period);
- investors can borrow and lend, as much as they want, at the risk-free rate;
- investors pay no taxes or transaction costs;
- investors share the same view on the efficient set for all securities; and
- the securities markets are in equilibrium.

It should be noted that these are simplifying assumptions. No one believes they hold true in the market but, for the model to be verifiable mathematically, these assumptions need to be made. It is the breadth of these assumptions that limits the applicability of the CAPM.

The Role of Beta in Asset Management

The theory suggests that the expected return on an asset is proportional to the extent that its price varies with the market portfolio. This price variability of the market was discussed in a previous section, where it was labelled as systematic risk. In effect, CAPM confirms that investors demand compensation, in terms of expected return, for assuming systematic, non-diversifiable risk.

The CAPM formula was examined previously in the section on beta.

$$R = r_f + \beta \, (r_m - r_f)$$

Where,

R = Required rate of return (or just rate of return)

β = Beta

r_f = risk-free rate

r_m = expected return

The expected return on any asset is equal to the risk-free rate (T-bill rate), plus the risk premium of the market portfolio (against the risk-free rate) times the beta for the asset. If an asset has a beta of one, it has a risk that is identical to the market risk. A beta of less than one equates to an expected return that is less than the market portfolio. A beta that is greater than one equates to an expected return that is greater than the market portfolio.

Market Portfolio

CAPM utilizes reference to a market portfolio that is defined simply as a portfolio of all securities where the proportion of each security held within the portfolio is established as a percentage of the security's market capitalization relative to the market capitalization of all securities. In this theory, the market portfolio is generally not limited to common shares but rather incorporates all types of investments, including common and preferred shares, bonds and real estate. When only common shares are used as the basis of the market portfolio, it may affect the value of this application, depending upon the circumstances.

Security Market Line

The CAPM essentially quantifies systematic risk (non-diversifiable risk) and expresses it relative to the market portfolio. The investor who uses CAPM attempts to find the relationship between risk and return for an efficient portfolio. Efficient portfolios are comprised of alternative combinations of risk and return that can be acquired by combining the market portfolio with risk-free borrowing or lending. This result is referred to as the *security market line* (SML). In other words, the SML is equivalent to the equilibrium relationship between the expected return and standard deviation of the efficient portfolios.

Figure 25
CAPM

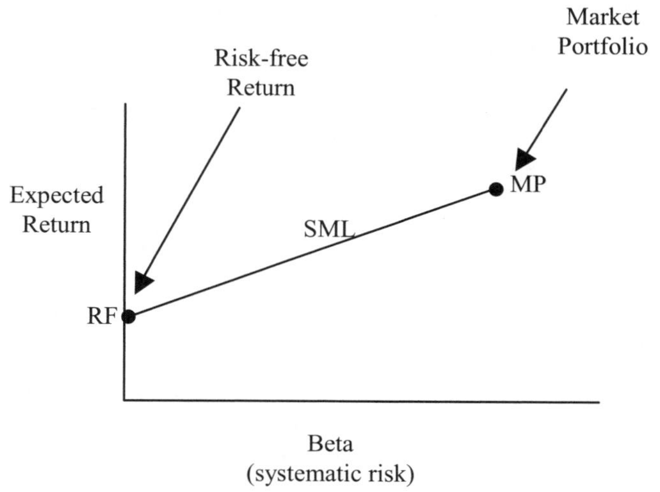

In Figure 25, the risk-free return dot (RF) refers to the hypothetical risk-free rate of return. A security located at this point (RF) on the graph has a beta of zero with an investment return equal to the risk-free rate of return. The MP dot on the graph identifies the market portfolio, while the line between RF and MP is the security market line (SML).

The theory suggests that the RF point is a place that an investor would commonly "park" funds until a more attractive investment opportunity arises. This point may be referred to as the investor's reward for waiting. The slope of the line between RF and MP represents the additional reward an investor receives for accepting an additional unit of risk. It is expected that most securities will fall in and around the SML line and as the SML shifts, so will all market securities resulting in continued close proximity to SML.

Figure 26 depicts the fact that as the price of a security changes, it will move up or down the expected return axis. An increase in the price of a security will cause the security to shift downward, to compensate for a lower expected return. A decrease in the price of a security will cause a shift upward, to acknowledge a higher expected return.

Figure 26
Mispriced Securities

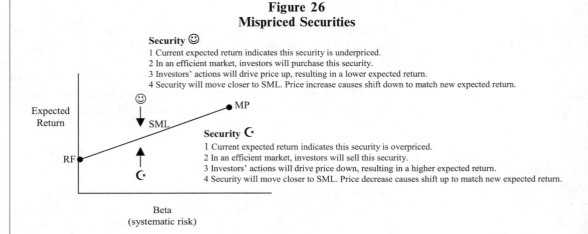

Security ☺
1 Current expected return indicates this security is underpriced.
2 In an efficient market, investors will purchase this security.
3 Investors' actions will drive price up, resulting in a lower expected return.
4 Security will move closer to SML. Price increase causes shift down to match new expected return.

Security ☾
1 Current expected return indicates this security is overpriced.
2 In an efficient market, investors will sell this security.
3 Investors' actions will drive price down, resulting in a higher expected return.
4 Security will move closer to SML. Price decrease causes shift up to match new expected return.

Summary

The CAPM theory suggests that when an investor is evaluating a security, he views the investment's return and systematic risk, commonly referred to as its beta, as two intrinsic elements that directly affect his investment decision. The investor is driven by the motivation that the higher the risk, the greater his potential return relative to the investment. CAPM is an equilibrium-based model that attempts to rationalize the different expected returns for different securities — each security has a different risk associated with it.

Even though the breadth of assumptions casts doubt on the applicability of CAPM in general, it does reinforce the importance of looking at the beta of an asset, or its sensitivity to market risk, when assessing the desirability of holding an asset. In fact, the entire passive investment movement strives to construct investment portfolios that have a beta of one and have returns that reflect the market risk and return.

Arbitrage Pricing Theory

The *Arbitrage Pricing Theory* (APT) was developed on a similar basis as CAPM, except the major difference between APT and CAPM centres on the number of factors that contribute to systematic risk. Recall that in CAPM, the market was used as the sole determinant of systematic risk and beta was constructed to quantify the sensitivity of an asset's return premium relative to market risk. Similar to CAPM, under the Arbitrage Pricing Theory, investment return relates to a security's systematic risk exposure rather than total risk. APT does not make the assumption that all investors behave alike and it does not assume that the market portfolio represents the only risky asset an investor will hold.

APT makes the assumption that there are multiple ways to measure systematic risk, which typically include the risk that arises from unexpected changes in factors. There is a lot of debate on how many factors belong in the APT and what real-world sources of risk they capture. Academics often suggest these factors include such areas as interest rates, inflation, a market index, investor confidence and real business activity. Specifically, the risk premium of an asset is influenced by its sensitivity to these fundamental factors. The theory assumes that all stocks and portfolios are exposed to each of these factors, or systematic risk, which together are referred to as the risk exposure profile of a stock or portfolio. This profile is indicative of how the stock or portfolio is expected to perform under different economic conditions. For example, if investor confidence is lower than anticipated, stocks with high exposure to investor confidence will perform relatively worse than those with low exposures to investor confidence. Likewise, if business activity is better than anticipated, a stock with high exposure to business activity is likely to perform relatively better than a stock with low exposure to business activity.

Supporters of the APT search for opportunities to exploit arbitrage in any earnings expectations for a security. This arbitrage is generally discovered through research. Active followers of APT, arbitrageurs, partake in riskless arbitrage where the same security is simultaneously bought and sold on different markets in order to benefit from small pricing inefficiencies. As well, arbitrageurs undertake risk arbitrage where different securities, each with the same level of risk (beta), are simultaneously bought and sold in order to benefit from perceived pricing inefficiencies.

Using the APT view of systematic risk, each asset has a set of factor loadings rather than just one beta, as was the case with CAPM. Investors continue to invest in arbitrage portfolios as long as they exist, which drives prices up or down, depending upon any current security mispricing. The theory proposes that eventually, all arbitrage possibilities are eliminated and the equilibrium expected return under APT is the linear function of the security or portfolio's sensitivity to the factors.

Efficient Market Hypothesis

Market efficiency is a term that is used to describe the market's ability to disseminate information quickly and comprehensively. Taken to another level, the *Efficient Market Hypothesis* is a theory built on the premise that all known information is instantly reflected in the price of the stock. It is presumed that an efficient market will quickly figure out the meaning of new information, once it is made public. This hypothesis works on the assumption of three different degrees of efficiency: weak form, semi-strong form and strong form.

Weak Form

Weak form market efficiency states that the current price of a stock fully reflects all information contained in past prices of the stock and volumes of trading. In other words, it would be impossible for anyone to study the historical price movements of a stock and learn something (that could be used to their advantage) that was not already known by investors. In this form, all price and volume information known is already incorporated into the price of a security. Weak form efficiency implies that an investor cannot generate excess profits by trading on past trends.

Semi-Strong Form

Semi-strong form market efficiency states that not only is all past price and volume information reflected in the current price, but also all public information of any kind is included in the price. Under this form, it would be futile to research the financial statements of a company because you will never find any information that you can act on to find a stock that is trading for less than its current value. In the semi-strong form of market efficiency, all public information is already fully incorporated in the share price.

Strong Form

The *strong form* of market efficiency states that all information, including public and insider information, is already included in the price of the stock. The strong form is not likely to be true, given the number of people who have profited (and been convicted) for trading on insider information. If it were true, there would be no need for the insider trading laws that currently exist.

The efficient market theory is often used as an example that characterizes how price in a liquid and free market will react to the disclosure of information.

DARRIN

Darrin, president of a large publicly traded company, sent a confidential note to the firm's senior vice president responsible for operations regarding a shift in operations.

An investor who believes that the contents of Darrin's note will immediately impact the price of the company's shares believes in a strong form of efficient market. In reality, it is unlikely that all private information of this nature is immediately known and reflected in the price of the company's shares.

Post-Modern Portfolio Theory

The greatest contribution of modern portfolio theory was the establishment of a formal risk-return framework for investment decision-making. However, modern portfolio theory is limited by measures of risk and return that do not always represent the realities of the investment markets. With modern portfolio theory, risk is defined in terms of variability of returns around the mean return, and is measured by the standard deviation of the return. In other words, modern portfolio theory treats all uncertainty in the same way — the upside variance is identical to the downside variance. Post-Modern Portfolio Theory was formulated to overcome these types of issues.

In the post-modern portfolio theory approach, downside risk is clearly distinguished from upside volatility. In post-modern portfolio theory, only volatility below the investor's expected return translates into risk; all returns above the expected rate are merely a risk-free opportunity for premiums above the expected return.

In post-modern portfolio theory, the target rate of return is called the minimum acceptable return. Post-modern portfolio theory uses downside risk and asymmetrical return distributions, to provide investors with flexibility and accuracy in creating efficient portfolios that would not be possible using the traditional symmetrical Markowitz mean-variance methodology.

Sharpe Ratio

The *Sharpe ratio* was created by William Sharpe, a professor of finance at Stanford University, and one of the pioneers in portfolio theory. The Sharpe ratio is a measure of risk-adjusted return, showing the excess return per unit of total risk.

The ratio is a measure of the combined results of returns and risks of various assets within a portfolio. The ratio can be calculated by subtracting the risk-free rate of return from the rate of return for the portfolio and dividing the result by the standard deviation of the portfolio's return. The higher the Sharpe ratio, the more reward that can be expected per unit of risk assumed. The result of subtracting the risk-free rate of return from the portfolio return is referred to as the excess return.

$$\text{Sharpe Ratio of} \times = (r_x - r_f) \div SD_x$$

where,

x = portfolio

r_x = portfolio return

r_f = risk free rate of return (i.e., return on T-bill)

SD_x = portfolio standard deviation

This ratio provides a tool to assess the return generated by the portfolio compared with the amount of risk undertaken to achieve the excess return. In simple terms, it identifies the unit of return per unit of risk.

Unit 3
Self-Test Questions

QUESTIONS

Question 1

With regard to the concepts of supply and demand, which of the following statements are true?

1. The laws of supply and demand are interrelated phenomena where a change to the supply curve will affect the corresponding demand curve.

2. The laws of supply and demand are independent phenomena where a change to the supply curve will not affect the corresponding demand curve.

3. Market equilibrium is the point where the quantity of goods supplied is equal to the quantity demanded.

4. Market equilibrium is the gap between the supply and demand curves that arises when the price of a product is adjusted.

     a. 1 and 3 only

     b. 1 and 4 only

     c. 2 and 3 only

     d. 2 and 4 only

Question 2

Which of the following factors will cause the aggregate demand curve to shift to the left?

     a. Increases in consumer real wealth.

     b. High levels of consumer debt from past purchases.

     c. Increases in consumers' disposable income.

     d. Consumer expectations of rising income.

Question 3

Place the following business cycles in linear order.

1. Recovery/Expansion

2. Peak

3. Trough

4. Recession

     a.   1, 2, 3, 4

     b.   1, 3, 2, 4

     c.   2, 4, 3, 1

     d.   4, 2, 1, 3

Question 4

Which one of the following statements regarding economic indicators is true?

     a. Leading indicators include stock prices, housing starts and new orders for durable goods.

     b. Leading indicators include housing starts and the duration of unemployment.

     c. Coincident indicators include personal income, stock prices, and industrial production.

     d. Coincident indicators include outstanding loans and personal income.

Question 5

Which of the following items are included in the composition of Canada's M1 money supply?

1. Currency held outside of banks

2. Demand deposits

3. Notice deposits

4. Money market mutual funds

5. Canada Savings Bonds

    a. 1 and 2 only

    b. 1 and 3 only

    c. 3 and 4 only

    d. 2, 4 and 5 only

Question 6

With regard to interest rates, which of the following statements is/are true?

1. Holding money becomes more costly as interest rates fall.

2. Interest rate is the opportunity cost of holding money.

3. There is an inverse relationship between the rate of interest and the amount of money demanded.

    a. 1 only

    b. 2 only

    c. 1 and 3 only

    d. 2 and 3 only

Question 7

To increase the money supply, the Bank of Canada could:

1. Transfer government deposits to the banks.

2. Sell government securities to the bank or public.

3. Lower the bank rate.

    a. 2 only

    b. 3 only

    c. 1 and 3 only

    d. 1, 2 and 3

Question 8

A normal yield curve is:

    a. vertical.

    b. horizontal.

    c. negatively sloped.

    d. positively sloped.

Question 9

According to the liquidity preference theory of the term structure of interest rates, which one of the following statements is true?

    a. Investors will accept lower yields if it allows them to maintain liquidity.

    b. There is no unique link between liquidity and an investor's yield preferences.

    c. The shorter the term to maturity, the higher the expected yield.

    d. Investors with a preference for liquidity are insignificant when compared to the total market.

Question 10

With regard to systematic risk, which of the following statements is/are true?

1. Inflation and currency fluctuations contribute to systematic risk.

2. Systematic risk is diversifiable.

3. Labour strife in a single company is classified as a systematic risk.

    a. 1 only

    b. 2 only

    c. 1 and 3 only

    d. 2 only 3 only

Question 11

Which one of the following types of risk is defined as "the sensitivity of an investment asset relative to changes in the overall market"?

    a. Interest rate risk

    b. Market risk

    c. Business risk

    d. Liquidity risk

Question 12

The volatility of the expected return on a single security is typically measured using:

    a. standard deviation.

    b. beta.

    c. systematic risk.

    d. unsystematic risk.

Question 13

Which one of the following options would typically be used to measure how a stock's price will mirror fluctuations in the market as a whole?

    a. Standard deviation

    b. Beta

    c. Systematic risk

    d. Unsystematic risk

Question 14

Stanley has narrowed his investment decision down to two possible stocks: ABC stock, which has a beta of 0.75, and XYZ stock, which has a beta of 1.25. With regard to these two stocks, which of the following statements is true?

    a. It is expected that movements in ABC stock will occur in the same direction as movements in the market while XYZ stock will move in the opposite direction to the market.

    b. It is expected that movements of XYZ stock will mirror the market by an amount equal to 125% more than the market as a whole.

    c. It is expected that movements of ABC stock will mirror the market by an amount equal to three-quarters of any movement in the market as a whole.

    d. The volatility of ABC stock is greater than the market while XYZ's volatility is less than the market.

Question 15

Which one of the following theories is based on the premise that "all known information is instantly reflected in the price of the stock"?

    a. Markowitz Theory

    b. Capital Asset Pricing Model

    c. Sharpe Ratio Theory

    d. Efficient Market Hypothesis

QUESTIONS & SOLUTIONS

Question 1

With regard to the concepts of supply and demand, which of the following statements are true?

1. The laws of supply and demand are interrelated phenomena where a change to the supply curve will affect the corresponding demand curve.

2. The laws of supply and demand are independent phenomena where a change to the supply curve will not affect the corresponding demand curve.

3. Market equilibrium is the point where the quantity of goods supplied is equal to the quantity demanded.

4. Market equilibrium is the gap between the supply and demand curves that arises when the price of a product is adjusted.

    a. 1 and 3 only

    b. 1 and 4 only

    c. 2 and 3 only

    d. 2 and 4 only

Answer: c

    ⇨   2. The laws of supply and demand are independent phenomena where a change to the supply curve will not affect the corresponding demand curve.

    ⇨   3. Market equilibrium is the point where the quantity of goods supplied is equal to the quantity demanded.

Reference: Pages 15-14 to 15-15

Question 2

Which of the following factors will cause the aggregate demand curve to shift to the left?

    a. Increases in consumer real wealth.

    b. High levels of consumer debt from past purchases.

    c. Increases in consumers' disposable income.

    d. Consumer expectations of rising income.

Answer: b

    ⇨   b. High levels of consumer debt from past purchases.

Reference: Pages 15-15 to 15-18

Question 3

Place the following business cycles in linear order.

1. Recovery/Expansion

2. Peak

3. Trough

4. Recession

    a. 1, 2, 3, 4

    b. 1, 3, 2, 4

    c. 2, 4, 3, 1

    d. 4, 2, 1, 3

Answer: c

    ⇨ c. 2, 4, 3, 1

  Reference: Pages 15-20 to 15-24

Question 4

Which one of the following statements regarding economic indicators is true?

    a. Leading indicators include stock prices, housing starts and new orders for durable goods.

    b. Leading indicators include housing starts and the duration of unemployment.

    c. Coincident indicators include personal income, stock prices, and industrial production.

    d. Coincident indicators include outstanding loans and personal income.

Answer: a

    ⇨ a. Leading indicators include stock prices, housing starts and new orders for durable goods.

  Reference: Pages 15-24 to 15-26

Question 5

Which of the following items are included in the composition of Canada's M1 money supply?

1. Currency held outside of banks.

2. Demand deposits.

3. Notice deposits.

4. Money market mutual funds.

5. Canada Savings Bonds.

    a. 1 and 2 only

    b. 1 and 3 only

    c. 3 and 4 only

    d. 2, 4 and 5 only

Answer: a

    ⇨ 1. Currency held outside of banks.

    ⇨ 2. Demand deposits.

  Reference: Pages 15-27

Question 6

With regard to interest rates, which of the following statements is/are true?

1. Holding money becomes more costly as interest rates fall.

2. Interest rate is the opportunity cost of holding money.

3. There is an inverse relationship between the rate of interest and the amount of money demanded.

    a. 1 only

    b. 2 only

    c. 1 and 3 only

    d. 2 and 3 only

Answer: d

    ⇨ 2. Interest rate is the opportunity cost of holding money.

    ⇨ 3. There is an inverse relationship between the rate of interest and the amount of money demanded.

Reference: Pages 15-32 to 15-34

Question 7

To increase the money supply, the Bank of Canada could:

1. Transfer government deposits to the banks.

2. Sell government securities to the bank or public.

3. Lower the bank rate.

    a. 2 only

    b. 3 only

    c. 1 and 3 only

    d. 1, 2 and 3

Answer: c

    ⇨ 1. Transfer government deposits to the banks.

    ⇨ 3. Lower the bank rate.

Reference: Pages 15-32 to 15-36

Question 8

A normal yield curve is:

    a. vertical.

    b. horizontal.

    c. negatively sloped.

    d. positively sloped.

Answer: d.

    ⇨ d. Positively sloped.

Reference: Pages 15-38 to 15-39

Question 9

According to the liquidity preference theory of the term structure of interest rates, which one of the following statements is true?

    a. Investors will accept lower yields if it allows them to maintain liquidity.

    b. There is no unique link between liquidity and an investor's yield preferences.

    c. The shorter the term to maturity, the higher the expected yield.

    d. Investors with a preference for liquidity are insignificant when compared to the total market.

Answer: a

    ⇨   a. Investors will accept lower yields if it allows them to maintain liquidity.

    Reference: Page 15-40

Question 10

With regard to systematic risk, which of the following statements is/are true?

1. Inflation and currency fluctuations contribute to systematic risk.

2. Systematic risk is diversifiable.

3. Labour strife in a single company is classified as a systematic risk.

    a. 1 only

    b. 2 only

    c. 1 and 3 only

    d. 2 only 3 only

Answer: a

    ⇨   a. Inflation and currency fluctuations contribute to systematic risk.

    Reference: Pages 15-45

Question 11

Which one of the following types of risk is defined as "the sensitivity of an investment asset relative to changes in the overall market"?

    a. Interest rate risk

    b. Market risk

    c. Business risk

    d. Liquidity risk

Answer: b

    ⇨   b. Market risk

    Reference: Pages 15-46 to 15-47

Question 12

The volatility of the expected return on a single security is typically measured using:

    a. standard deviation.

    b. beta.

    c. systematic risk.

    d. unsystematic risk.

Answer: a

    ⇨   a. standard deviation.

    Reference: Pages 15-49 to 15-53

Question 13

Which one of the following options would typically be used to measure how a stock's price will mirror fluctuations in the market as a whole?

    a. Standard deviation.

    b. Beta.

    c. Systematic risk.

    d. Unsystematic risk.

Answer: b

    ⇨ b. Beta.

Reference: Pages 15-53 to 15-55

Question 14

Stanley has narrowed his investment decision down to two possible stocks: ABC stock, which has a beta of 0.75, and XYZ stock, which has a beta of 1.25. With regard to these two stocks, which of the following statements is true?

    a. It is expected that movements in ABC stock will occur in the same direction as movements in the market while XYZ stock will move in the opposite direction to the market.

    b. It is expected that movements of XYZ stock will mirror the market by an amount equal to 125% more than the market as a whole.

    c. It is expected that movements of ABC stock will mirror the market by an amount equal to three-quarters of any movement in the market as a whole.

    d. The volatility of ABC stock is greater than the market while XYZ's volatility is less than the market.

Answer: c

    ⇨ c. It is expected that movements of ABC stock will mirror the market by an amount equal to three-quarters of any movement in the market as a whole.

Reference: Pages 15-53 to 15-55

Question 15

Which one of the following theories is based on the premise that "all known information is instantly reflected in the price of the stock"?

    a. Markowitz Theory.

    b. Capital Asset Pricing Model.

    c. Sharpe Ratio Theory.

    d. Efficient Market Hypothesis.

Answer: d

    ⇨ d. Efficient Market Hypothesis.

Reference: Pages 15-65 to 15-66

Unit 4

Module 15 Exercises and Case Study

MODULE 15 EXERCISES

1. Determine if the following statements are True or False. If the statement is False, explain why.

   a. Economics is a social science that deals with the production, distribution and consumption of goods and services.

   b. The GDP measures the output generated by residents of Canada, regardless of where the output is produced.

   c. GNP is larger than GDP because more investment income flows out of Canada than into Canada.

   d. The demand curve illustrates that the lower the price of a good, the higher the quantity demanded of that good.

   e. Changes in price of an input from $1 to $2 would result in a shift of the supply curve to the right.

   f. A recession is characterized by a period of at least two consecutive quarters of declining output, employment and income.

   g. A leading economic indicator is a measurable economic factor that changes with economic output, indicating a trend.

   h. M1 money supply includes all Canadian currency in circulation, all demand deposits and notice deposits held in chartered banks.

   i. Canadian chartered banks are required to maintain a reserve ratio with the Bank of Canada.

   j. When the Bank of Canada acts to increase the money supply, the policy is called contractionary.

   k. Inflation is the percentage change in the purchasing power of a unit of currency over a specific period of time.

   l. Actual inflation = expected inflation - unexpected inflation.

   m. The exchange rate of Canadian dollars compared to American dollars is affected by differences between the two countries' interest rates, inflation and balance of trade.

2. Explain the two methods for calculating GDP.

3. What are the five basic determinates of demand? Explain how each determinant affects a movement along or shift in the demand curve.

4. Identify the common determinants of supply and demand.

5. Explain the term market equilibrium. Why do free and open markets tend to move towards market equilibrium normally?

6. List the four determinants of aggregate demand and the three determinates of aggregate supply?

7. If business cycles are not inevitable, why has government fiscal and monetary policies failed to "cure" business cycles in Canada?

8. Explain the three principal roles money plays in our economy.

9. What functions does the Bank of Canada perform within the Canadian banking system?

10. Define monetary policy and explain the primary objectives of monetary policy.

11. List the three ways that the Bank of Canada can affect the total amount of currency or deposits available to the public.

12. Utilizing the three ways the Bank of Canada manages monetary policy, explain what actions the Bank would use to achieve an/a:

   a. Expansionary policy

   b. Contractionary policy

13. Define fiscal policy and list the three categories of government fiscal policy.

14. Discuss how the expectations theory, liquidity preference theory and market segmentation theory explain the term structure of interest rates.

15. Explain the four ways the CPI is used in Canada.

16. Explain how the CPI is calculated by Statistics Canada.

17. Explain the differences between unsystematic and systematic risk and how each risk can be effectively managed.

18. Briefly explain the different types or categories of risks related to investments.

19. The risk level of an investment can be measured by its standard deviation, the investment's total risk, its beta and the systematic market risk associated with the investment. Explain the terms standard deviation and beta in regards to the risk level of investments.

20. The Efficient Market Hypothesis is based on the premise that all known information is instantly reflected in the price of the stock. Explain the three different degrees of efficiency: weak form, semi-strong form and strong form.

CASE STUDY — AN ECONOMIC UTOPIA

The economy of Utopia, a country in the Euro-Americas, has not been performing very well lately. Housing starts are down 7%, and new orders for durable goods are down 5% from last year. Claims for employment insurance are starting to increase as the companies in Utopia lay off workers due to low sales levels and high inventory levels. The manufacturing sector has seen several months of declining production, employment, and profitability. With all of the recent layoffs, the citizens of Utopia have started to fear that they may lose their jobs, so they have reduced their spending on non-essential goods to save as much cash as possible.

You have been recently elected as the mayor of Utopia based on your promise to improve the economy and bring prosperity to the country. Prepare a written economic plan for Utopia. In your plan, address the following questions:

a. Identify, with supporting reasons, the business cycle that Utopia is currently experiencing. What types of economic indicators support your assessment?

b. What monetary policies do you recommend the Central Bank of Utopia implement? Address the impact of your recommendations on the money supply, interest rates, investment levels, aggregate demand, and GDP.

c. What government fiscal policies should be implemented?

d. Why is it difficult to exactly predict the impact that changes in monetary or fiscal policies would have on the economy of Utopia?

Topical Index

CCH/ADVOCIS
EDUCATION PROGRAM

COURSE 4
WEALTH MANAGEMENT AND ESTATE PLANNING

MODULE 16
INVESTMENTS — PRODUCTS

Module 16
INVESTMENTS — PRODUCTS

Module 16
Investments — Products

LEARNING OBJECTIVES

✓ Understand, explain and apply a working knowledge of corporate and government bonds, common and preferred shares, mortgage-backed securities and the concepts associated with derivatives.

✓ Demonstrate proficiency in the application of concepts and technical knowledge relative to treasury bills, guaranteed investment certificates and term deposits, mutual funds and segregated funds.

✓ Discuss and demonstrate a solid comprehension of the characteristics and concepts associated with tax-sheltered investments, including limited partnerships, flow-through shares and income trusts.

✓ Explain and demonstrate competence and a working knowledge of the tax consequences associated with investments in stocks, bonds, mutual funds and segregated funds.

OVERVIEW

This module explores the characteristics, concepts and technical aspects of a wide breadth of financial instruments that are important to the comprehension and application of knowledge in a financial planning role. It builds on concepts and issues discussed in Module 15 that will assist in the analysis, synthesis and evaluation of investment products relative to the investor's specific circumstances.

Unit 1
Select Fixed-Income Securities

INTRODUCTION

A fixed-income security is an investment vehicle that provides certain cash flows at future points in time. The cash flow could be a single amount, which is referred to as a *pure-discount security*. Alternatively, if the security involves a series of cash flows, it may be referred to as a coupon paying security. A fixed-income security often involves a date after which there are no additional cash flows, in which case the date is referred to as the maturity date. On the maturity date, the investor's principal is normally returned along with any unpaid cash flow owing to the investor.

While there are many types of fixed-income securities, this unit explores only a selection of these securities, including:

- treasury bills;
- commercial papers;
- bankers' acceptances;
- guaranteed investment certificates (GICs) and term deposits;
- index-linked GICs; and
- mortgage-backed securities.

Other types of fixed-income securities include bonds, debentures and preferred shares, which are examined in later units.

TREASURY BILLS

Nature

Treasury bills, commonly referred to as T-bills, are short-term debt instruments issued by the federal government which are sold through the Bank of Canada to large financial institutions during a bi-weekly auction. These institutions repackage T-bills and make them available to the public in amounts as small as $1,000. Treasury bills are considered money market instruments, which means that they are generally a safe, short-term investment that provides a reasonably low level of return. Money-market instruments are often used as a short-term holding place for funds.

Government of Canada T-bills are issued with maturities of approximately three, six and twelve months, and less frequently, for even shorter periods.

From an investor's perspective, T-bills are highly liquid and carry a very low level of risk. A T-bill does not pay interest, but rather sells at a discount relative to its maturity value. The phrase maturity value of a T-bill is used interchangeably with the phrase *face value*.

Taxation

Despite the fact that T-bills are bought at a discount and mature at face value, if the T-bill is held to maturity, investment returns are treated as interest income.

FRANK

Frank purchased a T-bill for $965 on May 1. The T-bill matured at $1,000, 182 days after purchase. The $35 difference between the purchase price of $965 and the T-bill's face value of $1,000 is treated as interest income, for income tax purposes.

If a T-bill is sold prior to maturity, the difference between the original price and the proceeds of disposition usually results in both interest income and a possible capital gain or loss. To calculate the capital gain or loss, the investor has to subtract the interest accumulated to the date of disposition.

JESSE

Jesse bought a T-bill on June 1 for $19,750. The T-bill's term is 92 days and its maturity value on September 1 is $20,000. However, he sold it on August 1 for $19,975. The quoted yield rate was 5.022%.

Jesse calculates interest on the T-bill as follows.

Interest to be included in income (can be calculated using the yield rate or by using the number of days)

= Purchase price × Effective yield rate × Number of days T-bill held ÷ Number of days in the year

= $19,750 × 5.022% × (61 ÷ 365)

= $165.76

Or, using the number of days method:

($20,000 - $19,750) × 61 days ÷ 92 days = $165.76

continued . . .

---

continued . . .

Jesse calculates his capital gain as follows:

Proceeds of disposition	$ 19,975.00
Minus: Interest	- 165.76
Net proceeds of disposition	$ 19,809.24
Minus: Adjusted cost base	- 19,750.00
Capital gain	= $ 59.24

Strategies

Considered a very safe investment, treasury bills provide investors with a highly liquid security. While the investment return is reflective of the T-bill's very low level of risk, it is commonly favoured as a place to park money for short-term periods when an investor wants to avoid any risk relative to the loss of capital.

T-bills can provide a source of income for investors, although the rates are relatively low and therefore expose the investment to inflation risk.

U.S. T-bills are commonly used as a hedge against U.S. exchange rate risk, if the investor anticipates a drop in the value of the Canadian dollar. In the course material, you can assume any reference to a T-bill is a Canadian T-bill unless otherwise noted.

COMMERCIAL PAPER

Nature

Commercial paper is a short-term debt security issued by corporations, typically for the purpose of financing accounts receivable and inventories. It is a negotiable corporate promissory note that is not generally secured by corporate assets, although it could be backed by a line of credit or by a parent company. Many large Canadian companies finance their short-term debt by issuing bankers' acceptances or commercial paper, and purchasers tend to be large institutional investors.

Commercial paper may be freely traded without reference to the issuer and normally pays a higher return than a T-bill. Commercial paper carries a higher risk than T-bills and the overall quality is highly dependent upon the financial strength of the issuing company.

Short-term usually means up to one year in maturity for commercial paper and commonly not longer than 270 days.

Taxation

The income earned on commercial paper is interest income. If the instrument is held to maturity, the investor will report the income as interest. If the instrument is sold prior to maturity, the investor will have interest income and may realize a capital gain or loss equal to the difference between her adjusted cost base (ACB) and net proceeds of disposition.

Note that an investor must report accrued interest annually, if the investment is for longer than one year.

Strategies

The use of commercial papers addresses the three investment objectives: security of principal, liquidity and income flow. The security is a direct obligation of the issuing company that can be sold by the investor prior to maturity. While the investment is only as good as the issuing corporation, careful assessment of the issuing company will help manage the investor's risk.

BANKERS' ACCEPTANCE

Nature

A *bankers' acceptance* is a short-term promissory note issued by a corporation bearing the unconditional guarantee (acceptance) of a major chartered bank. It is a debt instrument, where repayment of the principal and payment of the interest is the responsibility of the issuer but guaranteed by a bank. Comparatively, it is lower in risk than a commercial paper, and generally more liquid.

Taxation

The income earned on a banker acceptance is interest income. If the instrument is held to maturity, the investor will report the income as interest.

Note that an investor must report accrued interest annually, if the investment is for longer than one year.

Strategies

Investment in bankers' acceptances addresses the objectives of security of principal, liquidity and income flow. The security is a direct obligation of the issuing bank and can be sold prior to maturity. While the investment is only as good as the issuing bank, careful assessment of the issuing bank will help manage the investor's risk.

GICS AND TERM DEPOSITS

Nature

A *guaranteed investment certificate* (GIC) and a *term deposit* are debt instruments issued by banks, trust companies or other financial institutions that guarantee investors a fixed rate of interest for a set term. The investment period for a term deposit/guaranteed investment certificate can be measured in days, months or years. Depending upon the financial institution, these debt instruments can be purchased for short durations such as 30, 60 or 90 days. They may also be available for investment periods of one, two, three, four and five years, and some institutions offer terms that extend well beyond five years.

At the end of the investment term, the instrument matures and the financial institution returns the principal and any interest payments owing to the investor. The minimum amount of principal required for investment will differ by financial institution.

An important consideration in the selection of a term deposit/guaranteed investment certificate is the redemption privilege. The instrument may be *redeemable* or *non-redeemable*. A redeemable guaranteed investment certificate is one where the investor has the right to redeem the instrument during the term of the investment, but where the financial institution likely reserves the right to apply a market value adjustment to the rate of interest paid on the instrument.

A *market value adjustment* involves an adjustment to the interest rate to compensate the issuing institution because of an early redemption. If, for example, the rate of interest on a deposit was set as 3% annually, and now market conditions warrant that the financial institution will need to pay a higher rate of interest to a new investor, the financial institution will reflect this by paying a lower interest rate than what was originally promised.

While a market value adjustment may be applicable, the fact that the investment is redeemable makes it a liquid asset.

EMILY (1)

Two years ago, Emily purchased a $25,000, five-year redeemable guaranteed investment certificate from a local financial institution. The rate of interest for the investment was set at 2.4% annually. Emily has encountered an unexpected financial need to access the principal of this investment, so she will redeem the certificate early.

Interest rates in the market place have increased so the financial institution will now have to pay a higher rate of interest of 3.1% to a new investor to replace Emily's investment in its portfolio. The financial institution will apply a market-value adjustment to Emily's investment, to reflect their increased cost. The rate of interest paid on Emily's investment, for the time it was held, will be reduced from 2.4% to 1.7%.

Funds held within a non-redeemable investment certificate are non-liquid because they are inaccessible to the investor throughout the full duration of the investment.

EMILY (2)

Three and a half years ago, Emily purchased a five-year, non-redeemable guaranteed investment certificate with a local financial institution. Because the investment is non-redeemable, Emily cannot access the funds until maturity, at the end of the five-year term.

GICs and term deposits generally pay a higher rate of interest than a bank savings account, and non-redeemable certificates normally command a marginally higher interest rate than redeemable instruments with otherwise similar characteristics.

Taxation

The income earned on a GIC is treated as interest income. Note that an investor must report accrued interest annually, if the investment is for longer than one year.

EMILY (3)

Three and a half years ago, Emily purchased a five-year, non-redeemable guaranteed investment certificate with a local financial institution. If she invested $10,000 on October 1, 2008 in a GIC that pays 5% interest, compounded annually, what is the income tax consequence?

We know that the maturity value of the GIC will be $12,762.82. However, what is the annual tax consequence?

Taxation Year	Interest Reported
2008 — 3 months	nothing
2009 — 12 months	$ 500.00
2010 — 12 months	525.00
2011 — 12 months	551.25
2012 — 12 months	578.81
2013 — 10 months	607.73
total interest report	$ 2,762.79
initial investment	10,000.00
maturity value	$12,762.79

Strategies

A GIC can address investment objectives that include security of principal and income flow.

> *ELLEN*
>
> After the unexpected death of her spouse, Ellen found that she was consistently short of income needed to meet her ongoing living expenses. This shortfall was causing Ellen to sporadically dip into her non-registered savings, yet capital preservation had been identified by Ellen as an important investment objective.
>
> To address this ongoing income need, Ellen invested $100,000 in a non-registered GIC that paid her a monthly income equal to the investment earnings. The investment earnings allowed Ellen to subsidize her monthly income, and also allowed her to preserve her $100,000 of non-registered capital.

Guaranteed investment certificates and term deposits are subject to inflation risk as well as reinvestment risk.

INDEX-LINK GIC

Nature

Similar to a regular GIC, an *index-linked guaranteed investment certificate* (index-linked GIC) normally provides the investor with a guarantee that her principal will not be eroded. The difference between a regular GIC and an index-linked GIC arises from the handling of the interest component. An index-linked GIC generally pays no interest throughout the term of the GIC, but instead the return is linked to a stock market index, typically a well-known index from Canadian or international markets.

If the stock market index, to which the investor's GIC is linked, rises during the term of her investment, the investor gains. However, most index-linked GICs do not provide the investor with the full gain, but rather the interest payment is based on a percentage (such as 80%) of the rise in the index, with a cap applied to the total return, perhaps 20% or 25%. In addition, the institution normally limits the downside so, in this respect, the investment return cannot be negative.

Because product innovation is important for attracting investors' dollars, the features of index-linked GICs can be quite varied. Some institutions may allow early cash-out, at set times throughout the investment term, while others may not provide for any early redemption prior to the selected term. The breadth of features is quite varied across the institutions.

Taxation

Gains on an index-linked GIC are taxed as interest income, which means that there is no tax advantage to the investor. However, the interest income on an indexed-linked GIC is reported upon maturity. This offers an advantage over non-indexed GICs, where the interest income is reported on an accrual basis. Tax on the income earned on an indexed-linked GIC is deferred, because interest earned in one year could be lost in a subsequent year if the index experiences negative movement.

Strategies

The fact that the index-linked GIC offers a guarantee associated with the return of principal addresses the objective of security. The link to the stock-related index ties the investment return to the volatility of the stock market, increasing the risk relative to the amount of investment return. Yet, under the risk-return principle, it provides the opportunity for greater return than would otherwise be available through a regular GIC. An investor who selects an index-linked GIC needs to be aware that indices go up and down over time.

An index-linked GIC that does not provide a minimum guaranteed return leaves the investor open to a greater loss of purchasing power through inflation than a regular GIC. If the index to which the GIC is linked falls, or does not rise, the investor receives a return of her initial investment, which could equate to no investment earnings over the period during which the GIC is held.

An index-linked GIC should not normally be considered for short-term investments. Rather, the market-related elements of an index-linked GIC suggest that a longer investment horizon is more appropriate, generally not less than three to five years.

MORTGAGE-BACKED SECURITIES

Nature

A mortgage-backed security is created when a pool of mortgages are packaged to create what is referred to as a *mortgage-backed security* (MBS) that can be bought and sold by investors.

The majority of mortgage-backed securities, in Canada, are created through the NHA Mortgage-Backed Securities Program (NHA-MBS). Under the NHA program, the Canada Mortgage and Housing Corporation (CMHC), a government agency, has an established program where approved financial institutions are permitted to package mortgages into an NHA-MBS, provided the mortgages meet specific qualifications. The common qualification is that all NHA-MBSs are comprised of residential mortgages insured by CMHC, under the *National Housing Act* (NHA).

To qualify to issue an NHA mortgage-backed security, the issuing institution must be a chartered bank, trust company, insurance company, credit union, caisse populaire or a loan company. In addition, the qualifying institution must meet specific criteria set out by the NHA program.

The terms of the security can range from as short as six months up to 25 years, although five years is the most common term. There are four categories of mortgage pools that can be packaged into a NHA mortgage-backed security:

1. exclusive homeowner;

2. multi-family;

3. social housing; and

4. any combination of the first three.

As mortgages, these investments are backed by the security of the real estate. In the case of mortgages that fall under the NHA-MBS program, mortgage loan insurance is a requirement when the mortgage is issued, so the *National Housing Act* unconditionally guarantees NHA mortgage-backed securities.

MBSs may be issued either directly in the name of the individual owner or in the name of the securities firm. Where registration is in the name of the securities firm, this is commonly referred to as being registered in the *street name*. By registering the security in the street name, it facilitates negotiability where it can be readily bought and sold. Any time a security is maintained in street name, the financial institution maintains individual ownership records.

With mortgage-backed securities, investors receive a regular monthly pass-through payment. This monthly income consists of a blend of principal and interest payments from the pool of mortgages, which is paid directly to the investor by the central payor and transfer agent. Only NHA-MBS issues have a guarantee issued by CMHC on behalf of the Government of Canada.

NHA mortgage-backed securities are sold in multiples of $5,000. Market conditions have a direct impact on the yield of mortgage-backed securities because the vehicles are interest-rate sensitive. The yield on a mortgage-backed security is normally higher than for government bonds with similar maturities. New issues of NHA mortgage-backed securities are packaged and offered at interest rates that reflect current market conditions. Subsequent trading of the security occurs in the secondary market where the price of the security fluctuates with movements in the interest rate: price declines as interest rates increase and price rises as interest rates fall.

The yield is calculated as the present value of all payments compared with the cost of the security. The after-tax yield is calculated taking into account the cash flows received in various years, as well as the tax liability in each applicable year.

The features and characteristics of the mortgages packaged into a pool may differ. For example, if the mortgages within the pool allow the mortgagor to pay more than the scheduled principal repayment, or to pre-pay a portion or all of the outstanding debt, these types of adjustments may affect the monthly payment to the investor and the subsequent yield on the investment.

Similar to government bonds, the issuer of an NHA-MBS is not required to prepare a detailed prospectus. Instead, a prescribed information circular is created for each new issue, providing investors with details specific to that particular security.

NHA-MBS securities are quite popular in Canada, with an active secondary market. While NHA mortgage-backed securities can be purchased as a non-registered investment, they are also eligible investments for inclusion in RRSP and RRIF portfolios. Valuable features of the NHA-MBS include the guarantee and the regular monthly cash flow.

Taxation

Interest income on a mortgage-backed security is fully taxable but the capital receipts are not. This means that as each payment is received, the investor must record the interest and the principal portion separately. The capital portion of each receipt will lower the investor's ACB in the instrument.

Strategies

Any mortgage-backed security has the backing of the real estate on which the mortgage is held. When mortgage insurance (NHA or private) backs the mortgages held within the pool, there is an increased level of security beyond simply the real estate value associated with the mortgage. MBSs are subject to reinvestment risk because of the reinvestment need associated with the interest income and return of principal over the term of the security.

Mortgage-backed securities are considered high-quality investments and are fairly liquid, having an active secondary market where the security can be sold prior to maturity. The regular income flow is an attractive characteristic and often appeals to investors who are in the retirement phase of life. Comparable investments tend to be Government of Canada bonds, although the yield of MBSs is more attractive when considering securities of comparable maturities.

CONCLUSION

The purchase of fixed-income securities does not guarantee an investor's return of capital, nor does it guarantee a specific flow of cash, but, for the most part, they tend to be lower-risk investments that are associated with safety of principal. Fixed-income investments are typically included in an investment portfolio as part of a well-balanced portfolio or where a regular income flow is an important objective.

Unit 2
Bonds and Debentures

INTRODUCTION

Bonds and debentures are debt instruments representing a loan from the investor to the issuer. In return, the issuer of the bond or debenture promises to pay the investor a specified rate of interest during the term of the security, and to repay the face value at maturity. Bonds and debentures fall under the investment umbrella of *fixed-income securities* and are often referred to as *debt securities*.

With the exception of Government of Canada bonds, bonds are generally secured by physical assets owned by the issuing company. If the issuer defaults on scheduled payments, the assets that back the bond issue are subject to legal claim by the bondholders. A debenture is secured only by the general credit of the issuing corporation and is considered to present a greater risk for the investor than a bond.

A bondholder ranks higher than a holder of a debenture in terms of claims against the issuer's assets. For these reasons, a debenture generally commands a higher rate of interest payable to the investor and is therefore a more costly means of borrowing for the issuing company. Throughout the remainder of this section, the term *bond* will be used interchangeably to refer to a bond or debenture, unless otherwise noted.

Government of Canada bonds are not secured by physical assets, but rather are backed only by the government's promise to pay. This unsecured element of Government of Canada bonds means that they more appropriately align with the definition of debentures, but traditionally the term bond is used rather than debenture.

NATURE OF A BOND

Face or Par Value

The terms *face value, par value* and *denomination* are commonly interchangeable and refer to the monetary value of the bond at maturity, excluding any interest owing to the bondholder. In other words, the face value is the principal amount of the debt obligation owed by the issuing institution when the bond matures.

Issuer and Bondholder

The purpose of issuing bonds is to raise capital for the issuing institution. *Issuers* of a bond include the federal government, a provincial or municipal government, government agencies and public corporations. The investor who owns the bond is commonly known as the *bondholder* or the *bondowner*.

Bond Price

A bond is normally issued at par, and is referred to as trading at par or face value when it is bought or sold at its par or face value. Once a bond is issued, future trading of that bond normally occurs in the secondary market, and while newly issued bonds tend to sell at or about face value, bonds traded in the secondary market will fluctuate in price in response to changing interest rates. When a bond trades at a price in excess of its face value, it is said to trade at a *premium*. When a bond trades at a price below its face value, it is said to be selling at a *discount*. The phrase *market price* refers to the prevailing price at which the bond is bought or sold.

Bonds have unique terminology where the bond's par or face value is commonly referred to as a base of 100 and the bond trades in units relative to the base. For example, when a $10,000 bond is trading at par, it is said to be priced at 100. If the bond sells at 98, it has sold for $9,800 ((98 ÷ 100) × $10,000). On the other hand, if the bond sells at 102, it has sold for $10,200 ((102 ÷ 100) × $10,000).

AYDEN

Ayden owns a $25,000 bond issued by Tele Corporation and has the opportunity to sell it at 105. If Ayden completes the trade, he will receive $26,250, derived as ((105 ÷ 100) × $25,000).

After selling the Tele Corporation bond, Ayden plans to purchase a bond issued by TV Ltd. The TV bond has a face value of $50,000 and a market value of $55,000. If Ayden completes this purchase, he will pay $55,000 for a bond with a face value of $50,000, which is a $5,000 premium.

Maturity Date

The *term* of a bond refers to the length of time between when the bond is issued and the point in the future when the bond must be redeemed. The *maturity date* is the date on which the bond issuer must pay back the money borrowed through the issuance of the bond. On the maturity date, the face value is repaid to the investor along with remaining interest payments. The maturity date determines the term of the bond such as one, five, or perhaps thirty years.

The expression *term-to-maturity* describes the period of time between the current date and the date on which the bond matures. When the bond is first issued, the term to maturity aligns with the term of the bond. As time passes, the term to maturity decreases. A bond's term provides a sense of how volatile a bond may be if interest rates change.

Bonds are generally classified by the length of time remaining until maturity, where:

- *short-term bonds* mature in the next few years;

- *intermediate-term* bonds come due within three to ten years; and

- *long-term bonds* mature in more than ten years, and up to thirty years.

Coupon Rate

The term *coupon* is used in reference to the annual interest payable on the bond and is a percentage of the face amount. Interest payments on a bond are normally paid every six months, although the coupon rate is quoted as an annual rate.

ALEX

Alex owns a $10,000 bond that has a 5.5% coupon rate. Each year, Alex will receive two equal payments of $275 on this bond, which are calculated as: ((Face Amount) × (Coupon Rate)) ÷ 2

= ($10,000 × 5.5%) ÷ 2

= $550 ÷ 2

= $275

continued . . .

---

continued . . .

While the coupon rate on this bond is 5.5% annually (also referred to as the nominal interest rate), the effective rate of interest Alex earns on this bond is 5.58%.

We know the following information:

- P/YR = 2
- NOM% = 5.5

SOLVE FOR EFF%, which equals 5.5756

Similar to any debt obligation, the issuance of a bond carries with it specific terms and conditions to which the issuer is financially bound. The higher the credit rating of the issuing institution (borrower), the more favourable the terms upon which desired funds can be borrowed. The coupon rate associated with a bond will be influenced by general interest rates, the level of risk associated with the issuer and any security associated with the bond.

The issuer of a bond will need to attract investors and to do so will be competing with a wide range of other investments. To attract investors, the level of interest rate will need to be competitive relative to interest rates associated with investments of a similar nature. In addition, bonds follow the normal risk-reward pattern where the level of risk associated with the issuing institution will influence the coupon rate on the bond. The more financially secure a borrower is, the lower the coupon rate. Alternatively, the higher the level of risk associated with the borrowing institution, the higher the coupon rate.

The third element associated with the coupon rate is the type of security, if any, associated with the bond. An unsecured bond will necessitate a higher interest rate than one secured by assets. Where assets secure the bond, the quality of the assets will influence the coupon rate needed to attract investors.

With the exception of income bonds, the interest obligation associated with a bond is a debt of the company and payment is not contingent upon the company's success or profitability.

Settlement Date

The *settlement date* is the date on which a trade must be finalized or settled. This is the date when the buyer must pay for and the seller must deliver the security. For a bond or stock, the settlement date is usually three business days after the date the trade was executed.

ABLE CORPORATION (1)

Anita paid $25,000 to purchase a bond issued by Able Corporation, when it was first offered. This five-year bond was issued on September 1, 2007 and is scheduled to mature August 31, 2012. The Able Corporation bond has a $25,000 face value and a 6% coupon rate.

continued . . .

continued . . .

Bond issuer:	Able Corporation
Bondholder:	Anita
Par Value:	$25,000
Bond issue date:	September 1, 2007
Bond maturity date:	August 31, 2012
Term:	Five years
Coupon rate:	6%
Coupon payment:	$1,500 annually, but because bond interest is normally paid semi-annually, Able Corporation will pay Anita $750 on the last day of February and August 31 during the term of the bond.
Annual Effective Interest:	6.09%

We know the following information:
- P/YR = 2
- NOM% = 6.0

SOLVE FOR EFF%, which equals 6.0900

Principal Debt Obligation:	On August 31, 2012, Able Corporation owes a principal repayment of $25,000 to Anita.

The Able Corporation bond, purchased by Anita, had a five-year term, which was considered an intermediate-term bond when she purchased it.

On August 31, 2010, Anita has the opportunity to sell the bond for $22,000, which is the bond's current market price. If Anita decides to accept the $22,000, she will be selling the bond at a discount because she will receive less for the bond than its face value.

Basic Taxation

In general terms, the taxation of bonds occurs in three specific ways:

- tax on the coupon payment (interest);
- tax that may arise if a bond is sold prior to maturity; and
- tax that may arise when the bond matures, if the bond was purchased at a discount or premium.

The coupon payment is taxed as ordinary interest income, as discussed in Module 5.

When a bond is disposed of prior to maturity, for an amount other than what the investor paid for it, the investor will incur either a capital gain or a capital loss. Where the proceeds of disposition are greater than the original cost, the investor will incur a capital gain. Where the proceeds of disposition are less than the original cost, the investor will incur a capital loss.

This same theory applies if a bond is held to maturity, but was originally purchased at a price other than its face value. When a bond is redeemed for its face value and this face value is greater than the original cost, the investor incurs a capital gain. Alternatively, if the face value is lower than the original cost, the investor incurs a capital loss.

BARBARA

On January 1, 2009, Barbara paid $15,000 for a bond issued by Keyboard Corporation. The bond had a face value of $15,000, and a coupon rate of 5.15%. On December 31, 2010, Barbara sold the bond for $17,500.

The annual coupon payments that total $772.50 are taxed as ordinary income and are fully taxable to Barbara on an annual basis.

In 2010, when Barbara sold the bond, she incurred a capital gain of $2,500 on the sale of the bond. The $2,500 is taxed as a capital gain. The sale of the bond will increase Barbara's 2010 taxable income by $1,250 (50% × ($17,500 - $15,000)).

Marketability

With the exception of non-marketable government bonds, most bonds can be bought and sold in the open market, but, as discussed earlier, the current market price of the bond will fluctuate with market interest rate changes.

Strategy

As market interest rates rise and fall, there is a direct effect to the market value of the bond. A rise in market interest rates, above a bond's coupon rate, means that investors will be willing to pay less for the bond because they need to purchase the bond at a rate that provides them with a return equal to the current market rate. On the other hand, if market interest rates fall below the coupon rate on the bond, investors will be willing to pay more for the bond because the premium is warranted by the higher coupon rate.

As discussed in Module 15, interest rate risk increases as the time to maturity increases. A bond with a long period prior to maturity will experience greater price volatility as interest rates change than a bond with a shorter period to maturity. This interest rate effect suggests that if an investor's objectives include minimizing the loss of principal, and if he selects bonds that are likely not to be held until maturity, it is generally more advantageous to select bonds with shorter periods to maturity. Interest rate changes have a lower impact on price changes for shorter-term bonds than on longer-term bonds.

Interest rates are affected by changes in the inflation rate. When the inflation rate rises, it normally pushes interest rates up, which in turn causes bond prices to fall.

Another risk faced by bondholders is reinvestment risk. As coupon payments are received and bonds mature, in a period of falling interest rates, an individual may not be able to reinvest the funds in a subsequent security that pays a rate of return similar to the existing bond. The staggering of investment maturities is a technique that lowers the investor's overall reinvestment risk. For example, by incorporating bonds with one-, five- and ten-year maturities into her portfolio, an investor is able to lower the reinvestment risk because the money comes due at various times, not all at once. As bonds mature, funds can be reinvested at prevailing rates.

Bonds are subject to credit risk; if the corporation's credit rating changes, it will have a direct impact on the price of the bond. Deterioration of a corporation's credit rating increases the risk of default on the bond, which in turn causes investors to demand a greater return for taking on that additional risk. If an investor currently holds a bond of a corporation whose credit rating is reduced, the risk of default on the bond has increased, and in turn the price of the bond will fall.

The market price of a bond is influenced by the bond's coupon rate and the features of the bond. If two bonds are identical except one pays a higher coupon rate than another, the bond with the higher coupon rate will be less volatile relative to changes in market interest rates.

The term to maturity of a bond will also affect the market value of a bond. The longer the term to maturity, the more volatile the price of the bond because of the uncertainty of what may happen during the period leading up to maturity. Investors seek a higher return for bonds with longer terms to maturity. And conversely, the shorter the period to maturity, the lower the expected return. Longer terms to maturity present increased risk and uncertainty and investors look to be compensated for their willingness to accept the longer-term risk.

When an investor feels interest rates are likely to fall, she may decide to purchase bonds on the premise that falling interest rates will increase the price of the bonds and therefore generate a profit to the investor.

GOVERNMENT BONDS

Marketable Bonds

The federal, provincial and municipal governments all issue marketable bonds, which represent debt obligations of the issuing government. Typically, the Canadian government's marketable bonds, also known as *Canadas*, are backed by the credit of the Canadian government and not by specific assets. The terms of government-issued bonds range from one to thirty years, and normally pay a fixed semi-annual interest amount throughout the term of the security.

These bonds cannot normally be redeemed prior to maturity, but can be bought and sold in the open market. A bond bought at par and held until maturity will receive the investment return established in the bond's interest rate. The price of the bond, in the open market, will vary with market interest rates.

Some government issues include a call feature that provides the issuer with the right to call the bond issue, prior to maturity, at a predetermined price that is slightly above par. As well, some issues may include a purchase fund where the government retires a portion of the debt in advance of the issue's maturity date. The government retires the debt by repurchasing existing bonds in the open market at a price which is generally at par or slightly less than par.

BOB

Bob recently paid $48,250 to buy a $50,000 Government of Canada bond with a 6.25% coupon. The market price of this government bond was $48,250, which represents a discount relative to the $50,000 face value. The annual interest paid on the bond is $3,125, which Bob will receive as two equal instalments of $1,562.50.

Government of Canada Real Return Bonds

A *Government of Canada real return bond* is a marketable bond that pays semi-annual interest based on a real interest rate. Interest payments are adjusted in relation to the cost of living as measured by the Consumer Price Index (CPI). Real return bonds are sold by the Bank of Canada to large financial institutions, through a quarterly auction, and the financial institutions re-sell the bonds to retail investors.

Each real return bond has a nominal principal value of $1,000 and is an unsecured debt obligation of the Canadian government. The real yield on a real return bond is dependent upon inflation activity during the term of the bond. The interest element of the bond is comprised of a coupon interest payment that is paid through semi-annual instalments throughout the term of the bond; and an inflation compensation entitlement payable at maturity.

These types of bonds provide the investor with protection against inflation over the long-term, helping to preserve the investor's purchasing power. As government of Canada debt, the risk of default is low so the bond carries a reasonably strong level of security. A real return bond cannot be redeemed prior to maturity, but can be bought and sold in the open market. The market value of the bond will fluctuate in relationship to changing interest rates and, like any other bond, the sale of the bond prior to maturity could result in a capital gain or loss.

Canada Savings Bonds

Canada Savings Bonds (CSBs) are non-marketable debt instruments issued by the Government of Canada. They are redeemable on demand by the registered owner, at anytime. If cashed during the first three months following the issue date, the bondholder receives only the face value of the bond. After the first three months, the bondholder receives the face value of the bond plus any interest owing up to the end of the month prior to the date of redemption. Ownership of CSBs cannot be transferred from one investor to another, but rather an investor may dispose of the CSB through redemption.

There are two types of bonds available:

- regular interest bonds (R-series); and
- compound interest bonds (C-series).

Interest on R-series bonds is paid annually, on the bond anniversary, until maturity. Payments are either through a cheque to the bondholder or as a direct deposit into the bondholder's bank account. Interest on the C-series is automatically reinvested and compounds throughout the term of the bond.

Canada Savings Bonds may be purchased by Canadian residents, up to specified limits, and may be registered in a single name, as joint ownership with the right of survivorship or as tenants in common. CSBs may be owned by individuals, estates, charitable organizations and personal trusts.

CSBs are eligible investments for an RRSP or RRIF. An individual may hold CSBs as a direct RRSP or RRIF investment known as The Canada RSP and The Canada RIF, or they may be held within a self-directed RRSP or self-directed RRIF.

The bonds may be purchased directly over the Internet or by telephone, through payroll deduction, and through most financial institutions such as banks, credit unions and investment dealers. Only the C-series is available through payroll deduction.

The sale of the bonds begins in October of each year and generally lasts until April 1, although the Minister of Finance may end the sale at any time. The time frame for purchase through payroll deduction is much shorter.

Backed by the Government of Canada and highly liquid, CSBs guarantee a minimum interest rate, although the interest rate could be increased, at the government's discretion, if warranted by market conditions.

While Canada Savings Bonds provide the investor with a secure investment, the modest rate of return leaves the investor subject to significant inflation risk. The highly liquid nature of the CSBs makes them a reasonable choice for the liquid portion of an investment portfolio, although the income and maturity value is subject to reinvestment risk.

Taxation

Income from Canada Savings Bonds is reported on an annual basis. Interest on the regular interest bonds is reported in the year it is received, whereas interest on the compound interest is reported on an accrual basis. Tables published by the Bank of Canada provide holders of compound interest bonds with details of the accrued interest that must be reported annually for income tax purposes.

Canada Premium Bonds

A *Canada Premium Bond* (CPB) is similar to a Canada Savings Bond in that it is issued and guaranteed by the Government of Canada. Similar to a CSB, the Canada Premium Bond is available in two types: the regular interest series (R-series) and the compound interest series (C-series).

At the time of issue, the interest rate on Canada Premium bonds is higher than the rate of interest on Canada Savings Bonds because, unlike CSBs, Canada Premium Bonds can only be redeemed once each year, on the anniversary date and for the 30 days that follow. An exception to this restriction is permitted when CPBs are held within The Canada RIF and redemption is necessary to facilitate a periodic payment.

CPBs are eligible investments for an RRSP or RRIF. Similar to Canada Savings Bonds, CPBs can be held by an individual as a direct RRSP or RRIF investment known as The

Canada RSP and The Canada RIF, or may be held within a self-directed RRSP or self-directed RRIF.

Taxation

The taxation for Canada Premium Bonds is the same as for Canada Savings Bonds.

Provincial and Municipal Bonds

Similar to the federal government, the provinces, territories and municipal governments also utilize bonds and similar debt securities to finance major initiatives. For example, a provincial or territorial government might borrow funds through a bond issue to finance a public works project. Provincial bonds are commonly referred to as *provincials*, whereas municipal bonds may be referred to as *municipals*.

Provincial and municipal bonds are considered to have a lower liquidity than a Government of Canada bond, which means the issuing institution would incur a higher cost to issue debt security. This higher cost means that the issuing institution would need to pay a higher interest component, than would be the case for Government of Canada bonds, in order to attract investors.

CORPORATE BONDS

Nature

Bonds issued by a corporation differ from equity because the principal and interest on the bond issue is a debt obligation of the issuing corporation. The corporation has a commitment that requires it to meet the debt obligation as it falls due, and failure to do so will put the corporation into default relative to the bond issue. In the event of default, bondholders can seek legal recourse.

The corporation's payment of interest to the bondholder is a deductible business expense for the corporation. As a business expense, bond interest payments are deducted from the corporation's earnings prior to the calculation of corporate income tax, thereby reducing the firm's earnings before taxes.

The risk associated with a corporate bond is higher than the risk associated with a government bond and, subsequently, the interest paid on a corporate bond would be higher than on a government bond to reflect this increased risk. The stability associated with a corporate bond is dependent upon the financial strength of the issuer. A corporate bond is generally considered to have greater security (less risk) than stocks.

Corporate bonds are considered a senior debt obligation of the issuing company. While creditors have priority over bondholders to claims against the assets of the company in the event of company dissolution, bondholders take priority over preferred and common shareholders.

The long-term nature of bonds often makes them attractive for inclusion in investment portfolios designed to fund long-term retirement and education costs.

Types of Bonds

There are numerous types of bonds that are described by a variety of different names. The following is a discussion of the more common types of bonds.

Extendible Bond

An *extendible bond* is one where the bondholder is permitted to extend the maturity of the bond for a longer period of time than the original maturity date indicates. An extendible bond is attractive because it provides the investor with the ability to respond to changes in interest rates. For example, if current interest rates have dropped compared to the bond's coupon rate, opting to extend the bond's maturity allows the investor to benefit from the higher interest rate for an extended period of time. On the other hand, if current interest rates have increased compared to the bond's coupon rate, the bondholder would likely opt to redeem the bond and use the resulting capital to reinvest at the higher interest rate.

ALBERT

Albert is the bondholder of a five-year extendible bond with a April 15, 2010 maturity date. The coupon rate on the bond is 6.9%, compared with a current market interest rate of 4.5%. Albert opted to extend the bond for an additional two years rather than redeem it on April 15, 2010. The bond's coupon rate of 6.9% was more attractive to Albert than the 4.5% that he felt he could obtain on a comparable investment, if he opted to redeem the bond.

Retractable

As the name suggests, a *retractable bond* is the opposite of an extendible bond. The holder of a retractable bond is permitted to redeem the bond at face value prior to the scheduled maturity date. For example, a 10-year retractable bond may allow for early redemption, perhaps at the five or seven year mark. If current interest rates are higher than the coupon rate, a bondholder may choose to exercise the early redemption feature. She could use the proceeds of the redemption to reinvest at a rate higher than she was receiving on the bond. If, however, the coupon rate remains higher than the current interest rates, the bondholder would likely not redeem the bond early.

BETTY

Betty is the owner of a ten-year retractable bond with a March 15, 2015, maturity date. Betty had the option to redeem the bond at par on March 15, 2010, when current market interest rates were 4.25%. The coupon rate on the bond is 7.25%. In this case, Betty would likely not have exercised the retractable feature, but rather would have continued to hold the bond, given the attractive coupon rate.

Convertible Bond

A *convertible bond* permits the bondholder to exchange the bond for a predetermined number of common shares of the bond issuer's corporation, at certain times during the life of the bond. Quite often, the conversion does not involve any cash, but simply a straight trade of the bond for a specified number of common shares.

The ratio of the bond's par value over the number of common shares per bond is used to calculate the conversion ratio. The conversion price is simply the bond's par value divided by the number of common shares offered per bond. In other words, the conversion price refers to the amount of the bond's par value that the investor must forego in order to acquire one common share. The bond's current market price does not affect the calculation of the conversion ratio or the conversion price.

Conversion ratio = # of common shares per bond

Conversion price = (Bond's par value) ÷ (# of common shares per bond)

> *BILLY (1)*
>
> Billy owns 100 X-Corp bonds, each with a par value of $500. Each X-Corp bond is convertible to 15 common shares of the company.
>
> The conversion ratio for an X-Corp bond is 15.
>
> The conversion price is $33.33 ($500 ÷ 15).
>
> Billy must give up $33.33 of X-Corp bond value in exchange for each common share.

Convertible bonds tend to offer a lower rate of return than non-convertible bonds because of the hybrid nature of the investment. The convertible bond carries with it the risk level of a bond but also provides the investor with the potential for appreciation in relation to the company's common share value. A bondholder might opt to exchange a convertible bond for corporate shares if the corporation's common share value is on the rise.

> *BILLY (2)*
>
> Continuing the Billy (1) SNAP, if the current market price of the X-Corp shares is $39.50 per share, the conversion value of the bond is $592.50 ($39.50 per share × 15 shares per bond). If the current market price of the bond is $650, then the bond has a conversion premium of $57.50 ($650 - $592.50), when the market value of the common shares is $39.50.

Details relative to the conversion feature of any single bond issue are quite specific and can often be fairly complex. While additional cash payments are not typically required, it is possible that the conversion feature could incorporate a cash component that requires a payment from the investor in addition to surrendering the bond. There is no typical time frame for conversion but rather the debt issuing institution will create its own criteria. For example, a bond could have an initial period during which no conversion is permitted (i.e., one year). Alternatively, there could be a time schedule with a conversion scale where the ratio increases or decreases at various points. Characteristically, convertible bonds include a level of protection for the investor relative to stock dividends and stock splits.

Callable Bond

A *callable bond*, also known as a *redeemable bond*, is one where the issuer has the right to redeem the bond at a specified price and at a specified date, prior to the bond's maturity date. The issuer's right to redeem the bond is also known as its right to call the bond, which aligns with the name assigned to this type of bond.

It is most likely that the bond will be issued with an initial period during which the bond cannot be called, but will include a time frame during which the issuer has the right to call the bond. If the issuer opts to call the bond, the bondholder is usually paid a premium over the face value of the bond. The premium is identified at the time the bond is issued, but is only paid if the bond is called. The intention behind the premium is to reward the investor for the loss of future interest associated with the investment.

If interest rates have declined since the bond was issued, the issuer will likely refinance their bonds at a lower rate of interest; therefore, the issuer will call the bond and reissue at a lower interest rate. The call date is the date on which the bond may be redeemed by the issuer before maturity. Investors should be aware of the call date when buying a bond, as the interest payments are only guaranteed up to that date.

Floating Rate Bond

A *floating rate bond* is a bond where the interest rate paid on the bond fluctuates with changes in the market conditions, and is often pegged to the yield on a benchmark security such as the interest rate on T-bills.

Income Bond

The interest payment on an *income bond* is tied to the issuing corporation's profitability. Interest is paid to the bondholder based on the company's profit performance, and the non-payment of interest, due to poor financial results, is not viewed as a default on a debt obligation.

Mortgage Bond

As the name suggests, a *mortgage bonds* is backed by real property. These types of bonds can be issued as a first or second mortgage bond with first mortgage bonds having a higher claim priority over second mortgage bonds, in the event of default. The variation in risk associated with first and second mortgage bonds is reflected in a higher interest rate for the second mortgage bonds relative to first mortgage bonds.

Strip Bond

Strip bonds, also referred to as *strips* or *zero coupon bonds*, are bonds that have had the interest payments separated from the principal repayments. As the name suggests, the coupons have been removed or stripped from the bond, usually by the investment dealer, so there is no regular coupon payment associated with the security. The stripped coupons are sold off to investors with specific objectives, whereas the remaining strip bond is sold to a separate investor, one who generally does not require a regular flow of interest payments that would normally come with the purchase of a regular bond. Strip bonds are sold at a discount to the face value of the bond and are redeemed at face value.

CARL (1)

On March 1, 2010, Carl purchased a strip bond with a face value of $10,000 and which matures in exactly five years after his purchase date. Carl purchased the $10,000 bond for $7,700.

If Carl holds the bond to maturity, he will earn an investment return of 5.4% based on a purchase price of $7,700 and a maturity value of $10,000.

We know the following information:

- P/YR = 1
- xP/YR = 5
- PMT = 0
- PV = -7,700
- FV = 10,000

SOLVE FOR I/YR, which equals 5.3663

Note: When completing time value calculations relative to strip bonds, there is inconsistency in the industry on the use of 1 or 2 compounding periods (the xP/YR value in time value calculations). For purposes of this course, we will use the value of 1 for strip bonds only, unless otherwise noted.

Strip bonds do not pay any money until maturity, so an investor does not have the ongoing worry of reinvestment risk that might otherwise be prevalent with bonds that pay a regular cash flow. There is, however, an annual tax component associated with strip bonds, which tends to make them a popular choice for tax-sheltered investments such as RRSPs and RRIFs.

If a strip bond is held to maturity, it is redeemed for its face value. However, the price of strip bonds in the secondary market tends to be quite volatile, increasing the risk exposure for investors who do not hold the bond until its maturity.

Taxation

For income tax purposes, strip bonds are treated as a prescribed debt obligation. While strip bonds do not provide the bondholder with interest from coupon payments, the bondholder is required to include in income, each year, a notional amount of interest. The calculation of a notional interest amount that is deemed to accrue each year takes into account the difference between the bond purchase price and its face value at maturity. The calculation must incorporate compounding at least once each year.

CARL (2)

Continuing Carl's SNAP, assuming the bond is held as a non-registered investment, what amounts are reported annually for income tax, if he holds it until maturity?

Investment	$7,700	
Maturity Value	$10,000	

Taxation Year	Income Tax	
2010	zero	
2011	$ 413.21	($7,700 × 5.3663%)
2012	$ 435.38	(($7,700 + $413.21) × 5.3663%)
2013	$ 458.74	
2014	$ 483.36	
2015	$ 509.31	
TOTAL	$2,300.00	

Upon disposition, the bondholder will have a notional interest component that must be included in income. Where there is a disposition of a strip bond prior to maturity, capital treatment is available when the sum of the proceeds of disposition and all notional interest accrued and included in income is greater or less than the total purchase price. If the amount received on such a disposition exceeds (is less than) the total of the purchase price and the amount of all notional interest accrued and included in income, the excess will be treated as a capital gain (loss).

BOND RATING AGENCIES

Independent bond rating agencies provide information to investors that assist with decisions relative to the quality of a security. The three main credit rating agencies that cover the Canadian bond market are:

- Dominion Bond Rating Service (DBRS) (http://www.dbrs.com);

- Standard and Poor's (http://www.standardandpoors.com); and

- Moody's (http://www.moodys.com/cust/default.asp).

These agencies undertake analysis and assign a rating (using the letters of the alphabet) that, in their opinion, reflects the degree of risk associated with the company and subsequently the investment. Investors use these ratings as an indication of the probability of default by the issuer. An example of the ratings assigned through DBRS is shown in Table 1.

Table 1

DBRS Ratings

AAA — highest credit quality
AA — superior credit quality
A — satisfactory credit quality
BBB — adequate credit quality
BB — speculative credit quality
B — highly speculative credit quality
CCC, CC and C — very speculative credit quality and in danger of default on interest and principal
D — in default on either interest or principal

Typically, bonds are classified as *investment grade* or *speculative*. The top four ratings for each of the agencies are normally considered investment grade (i.e., AAA through to BBB as ranked by DBRS), whereas classification from the fifth level (i.e., BB) and lower is considered speculative.

DILBERT

A neighbour mentioned to Dilbert that he was purchasing bonds issued by Woo Nelly Corporation. Based on the information provided by his neighbour, the bonds sounded attractive to Dilbert, who was quite excited about the possibility of capturing a good deal.

Before proceeding with any purchase, Dilbert learned that the Dominion Bond Rating Service had given the bond a BB rating. Based on this assessment, the Woo Nelly Corporation bond is classified as speculative. This caught Dilbert by surprise and caused him to reconsider any purchase.

The term *high-yield bond*, also commonly referred to as a *junk bond*, is generally applied to corporate bond issues where the credit rating is classified in the speculative category. These types of bonds are typically issued by emerging mid-cap corporations who require cash to finance growth. The high yield associated with these types of bond issues appears attractive, but with the attractive yield comes the increased risk of default on the interest and principal as noted by the rating agencies' ranking. Aggressive investors may look to high-yield bonds as an alternative to stocks.

Unit 3
Common Shares

INTRODUCTION

As discussed in Module 7, every corporation must have share capital. The term *share* is used to refer to a shareholder's proportionate interest in the capital of the corporation. Shareholders are owners of the company. The term *common share* refers to basic shares of a company that represent the equity or ownership in the corporation.

Another type of share is a preferred share that has some of the characteristics of a common share but also carries preferential rights with regard to the receipt of dividends or redemption upon the dissolution of the corporation. Depending upon the rights set forth for preferred shares in the corporation's charter, a preferred share generally does not have entitlement to share in the growth of the company, but in most cases, is eligible for dividend payment prior to dividend payments to common shareholders.

NATURE

Structure

A common share is also referred to as a *common stock. Authorized share capital* refers to the maximum number or value of shares that a corporation may issue as prescribed in the corporation's charter. While the authorized share capital is set out in the charter, a corporation is not obliged to issue all of its share capital but may retain it for future use or may never issue it. The portion of the authorized share capital that has been issued by the corporation is referred to as *issued capital*, while the shares that have been issued and fully paid for are termed *paid-up capital*. For the most part, shares must be fully paid for when issued, so the terms *paid-up capital* and *issued capital* are commonly used as interchangeable.

Dissolution

While a corporation is liable to the full extent of its debts, a shareholder cannot be held liable for the debts or obligations of the corporation. In the event of business failure, a creditor may attempt to seize the assets of the company, but has no claim against personal assets of the shareholder. A shareholder's financial risk is limited to the loss of her investment used for the purchase of shares, nothing more.

As owners of the company, common shareholders share in the corporation's performance — good and bad. An obvious benefit associated with the ownership of common shares is the right to participate in the profits of the company, through dividend payments. As a common shareholder, there is the possibility of losing all or part of the original investment in the event of company dissolution. Common shareholders have the lowest ranking relative to claims against the firm's assets upon dissolution of the company. While a common shareholder has the greatest growth opportunity, she also has the greater risk relative to bonds and preferred shares.

Ownership Transfer

Common shares can be transferred from one shareholder to a new shareholder, simply by transferring the shares to another person or company (subject to discretionary transfer restrictions established in private or closely held corporations). Upon the registration of a share transfer, the new shareholder becomes entitled to the rights offered through share ownership.

The death or personal events, such as bankruptcy, of a shareholder do not affect the legal existence of the corporation.

Common shares normally carry voting rights, often one vote per share, although the rights are outlined as part of the stock issue. In addition, common shares normally have the right to share proportionately in any declared dividend, along with the pre-emptive right whereby the shareholder has the right to maintain proportional ownership through the purchase of additional stock, if a new stock issue takes place.

When a company issues more shares it dilutes the value of existing shares.

Classes of Shares

While common and preferred shares represent two different forms of stock, a corporation may create distinctions within each of these forms of shares with the creation of different classes of shares. The purpose of creating classes of shares is to separate the rights associated with the shares. For example, a company may allocate voting power to a certain group of shares and not other groups. Or, the company could allocate ten votes per share for a specific class of shares and perhaps only one vote per share for another class.

General Terminology

Par Value

The term *par value* is simply an arbitrary number assigned to each share of stock. Typically, the par value is established as a low amount and shares are commonly issued for an amount higher than the stated par value, in which case there are two entries on the company's books:

- common stock (based on par value times the number of shares outstanding); and
- paid-up capital or capital contributed in excess of par value (based on the number of shares outstanding times the capital received in excess of the par value).

While not all companies assign a par value to their share capital, a stated value must be recorded in its place when the company accounts for the issued shares on its books.

Book Value

The book value of a share is a ratio of the company's shareholders' equity divided by the number of common shares outstanding.

Market Value

The market price of a share of stock, for a publicly traded company, is the last reported price at which the security was exchanged.

INVESTMENT EARNINGS

An investor who holds common stock will generate investment returns in two ways:

- the receipt of dividends; and
- capital appreciation through the market value of the common shares increasing more than your investment.

Dividends

Payments

The board of directors of a corporation possesses the sole authority to authorize a payment, referred to as a dividend, out of the company's current profits or retained earnings. Dividends may be in the form of:

- cash (cash dividend);
- stock (stock dividend); or
- other property.

Dividends are a fundamental component of the investment return on a common share, although there is no requirement that a company must pay dividends. Companies that do not pay regular dividends are typically in a progressive growth period and investors would normally look toward the capital appreciation as the significant element of return on the common share. Those companies that are beyond the high growth stage, and no longer have a high need to consistently reinvest profits into the company, quite often pay dividends to the shareholder.

Dividends are not considered a business expense and are not tax deductible. The board of directors has no obligation to declare a dividend, and they do not become a liability of the firm until they have been declared. The amount of dividend may differ by class of share.

Once a company begins making dividend payments, investors often come to expect a regular pattern of payments, so companies frequently try to maintain consistency as an important means for maintaining investor confidence. However, the company is under no obligation to meet this expectation.

When a company makes a one-off extra dividend payment, it is often referred to as a *special* or *extra dividend*, which helps to manage investor expectations that the payment is not intended to form part of the regular dividend pattern.

The expected volatility of earnings will have a direct influence when a firm's board of directors is considering the payment of dividends. As well, the board of directors will consider the effect the dividend will have on the company's cash flows.

Cash Dividend

A cash dividend, the most common type of dividend, is accomplished through a cheque issued by the company payable to the shareholder. The term *regular dividend* is often used interchangeably with the phrase *cash dividend*.

Stock Dividend

When a company issues additional shares of stock as payment of a dividend, instead of cash, the shares issued are referred to as a *stock dividend*. A stock dividend may be used when the company wants to preserve cash while still providing a benefit to the shareholders.

Important Dates

Declaration Date

The date on which the board of directors authorize and announce the date and amount of the next dividend payment is referred to as the *declaration date*.

Record Date

The *record date*, set by the corporation, is the date on which an individual must own shares in order to be eligible to receive a declared dividend.

Ex-Dividend Date

The *ex-dividend date*, also referred to as the *ex-date*, is the first date of the ex-dividend period. Any stock trades that occur from the ex-dividend date onward are ineligible to receive the declared dividend. Stocks traded during the ex-dividend period will normally trade for an amount less than in the period just prior to the ex-dividend date, because the declared dividend will not be paid to the new owner, but rather to the old. The price of the stock will normally fall in proportion to the amount of the declared dividend.

Cum Dividend

As the antithesis of ex-dividend, the phrase *cum dividend* means *with dividend*. Where a new owner purchases a stock after a dividend is declared but prior to the ex-dividend date, the new owner is eligible to receive the declared dividend.

Liquidating Dividend

A *liquidating dividend* is normally paid to shareholders when a company is going out of business. The amount of the liquidating dividend is calculated based on the funds that remain after the company has satisfied all higher-standing claims.

A *liquidating dividend* has unique tax issues in that it is comprised of a regular taxable dividend and a return of capital. The amount of the liquidating dividend that exceeds the paid-up capital is a taxable dividend and the paid-up capital amount is paid to the shareholder tax-free. Paid-up capital is generally the original subscription price of the share as first issued.

Dividend Reinvestment and Share Purchase Plans

A *dividend reinvestment plan* (DRIP) provides shareholders with the opportunity to automatically purchase additional shares of the company with their dividend payment. Purchases are made shortly after the dividend payment and the purchase price is calculated as the average of the share price over the prior few days. There is generally no commission associated with the purchase and the purchase of partial shares is permitted. It is quite common for companies to offer shareholders a small reduction in the share price (i.e., 5%) of shares purchased with dividends in order to encourage participation in a DRIP. In order to sell the shares purchased through a DRIP, the shareholder simply requests a share certificate from the company.

A *share purchase plan* (SPP) is quite similar to a DRIP, in that the shareholder can send the company additional money that is used to purchase more shares on a set date. This set date quite often coincides with a dividend payment date. It is quite common for companies to establish an upper and lower limit relative to the amount that can be purchased through this method.

Capital Appreciation

Capital appreciation on a stock is simply an increase in the market value of the stock. When the value of a share grows, the owner of that share benefits from the increased market value.

TOM (1)

Three years ago, Tom purchased shares of ABC Company when the market price was $6.50 per share. Today, the market value of a share of ABC Company is $7.55. The difference between Tom's purchase price of $6.50 and the current market price of $7.55 is referred to as capital appreciation.

Tom will only realize the benefit of the share's capital appreciation if he sells a share.

The converse is also true in that the value of a share is volatile and is not limited to growth but could also decline in value. When the value of a share declines relative to the original purchase price, the owner will experience negative investment earnings, which can translate into an investment loss.

TOM (2)

At the same time that Tom purchased shares of ABC company, he also purchased shares of TUV Inc. The original cost of TUV shares was $8.90 per share. Today, the TUV shares have a market value of $7.90. The difference between Tom's original purchase price of $8.90 and the current market price of $7.90 is an investment loss. However, Tom will only realize the loss if he opts to dispose of the shares.

STOCK PURCHASE

Initial Public Offering

The phrase *initial public offering* (IPO) is used to describe the process where a private company first sells its stock to the public. Quite often, IPOs are initiated for smaller companies seeking capital to expand their operation. This process is also referred to as *going public*. The purchase of shares through an IPO is considered risky because there is no frame of reference as to how the market will react to the share offering on the first day of trading.

The market in which an investor has the opportunity to purchase a newly issued security, such as through an IPO, is referred to as a *primary market*. In a primary market, securities are purchased directly from the issuing company. Subsequent trading of the security takes place in the *secondary market*. In simple terms, the secondary market is one where previously issued securities trade without the involvement of the issuing company.

In general terms, the IPO process is as follows:

- The private company, who wants to go public, contacts an underwriting firm. The underwriting firm is an investment banker who works with the private company to price the securities and complete the extensive filing requirements.

- The private company prepares a *preliminary prospectus* or *red herring* that provides extensive details regarding the company and the securities issue. The term *red herring* is used because this document can be updated several times during the IPO process and includes a statement written in red to state that the company is not attempting to sell the shares until final approval is received by the securities commission.

- Upon receiving final approval from the securities commission, a final prospectus is prepared by the company, which includes the price of the issue, benefits and restrictions.

Secondary Market

The secondary market refers to the stock market. In the stock market, or secondary market, investors trade previously issued securities between themselves and the issuing company is not involved. The secondary market is categorized as either an auction market or a dealer market. The Toronto Stock Exchange is an example of an *auction market* where parties congregate and announce the price they are willing to pay (bid) and the price they are willing to sell (ask) for a particular security. The convergence of buyers and sellers theoretically results in an efficient market.

A *dealer market* is one where parties do not congregate but rather the dealers specialize and buy or sell a particular security according to demand. The dealer derives a profit from the difference between the posted bid and ask price associated with its particular security. In this market, dealers buy and sell out of personal inventory. NASDAQ is an example of a dealer market. Most bonds trade in this type of market.

There are different types of market exchanges, such as the New York Stock Exchange, where the trading of securities takes place on the trading floor in a face-to-face situation. This arrangement is commonly referred to as a *listed exchange*. A second type of exchange is the *over-the-counter* (OTC) exchange, of which NASDAQ and the Toronto Stock Exchange are examples. With an OTC exchange, there is no central location or face-to-face encounter, but rather trading occurs through computers and telecommunication networks that connect dealers.

Share Purchase

Cash

When an investor purchases stocks through a stockbroker, the investor maintains an account with the dealer that in many instances is referred to as a cash account. The stock purchase is paid for with funds maintained in the cash account.

Margin

In addition to the purchase of shares for cash, an investor may use the concept of margin as a means to increase her purchasing power. Buying shares on margin is simply a means to buy shares for a combination of cash and a loan, where the loan is money borrowed from the investor's security firm. The use of borrowed funds allows the investor to leverage her investment in stocks.

A margin account is much like that of a secured line of credit where the owner of the account can borrow funds up to a maximum limit, with the cash balance and securities acting as collateral. The portion of the purchase price an investor must deposit into the account is referred to as the *margin*. The margin is also the investor's initial equity in the security purchased.

As owner of the account, the investor agrees to maintain a minimum margin in the account. If the balance in the account drops below the minimum required level (a margin deficiency), the investor is required to place additional funds into the account. A shortfall can be covered through the deposit of additional cash or margin-eligible securities into the account or through the sale of sufficient securities to cover the shortfall. Margin accounts are available through registered investment dealers who charge interest on any loaned funds. In many senses, the account is set up like a demand loan and interest is charged on any outstanding loan balance.

Option trading can only occur if an investor has a margin account and not all stocks can be bought on margin. Security regulators establish the *maximum loan value*, a set percentage of the value of the investment, that the investment dealer is permitted to loan to the investor, although firms are free to establish even more vigorous standards. The maximum loan value differs by type of security. An example of the maximum loan value established, by the Investment Industry Regulatory Organization of Canada (IIROC), for securities other than bonds or debentures, is shown in Table 2.

Table 2
Securities
(excluding bonds and debentures)

Price Per Share of Security	Maximum Loan Value
$2.00 or above	50% of market value
$1.75 to $1.99	40% of market value
$1.50 to $1.74	20% of market value
less than $1.50	No opportunity for margin

Source: IIROC, Dealer Member Rule 110.2(f).

FRIEDA (1)

Frieda plans to buy 300 shares of Media Inc. at $10 per share through the use of her margin account. Determine the total value of Frieda's purchase of Media Inc., the maximum loan value and the minimum margin requirement. Where necessary, use the information in Table 2 and disregard commissions.

Total market value of Frieda's purchase:

300 shares × $10/share

= $3,000

Maximum loan value:

Market value × 50%

= $3,000 × 50%

= $1,500

continued . . .

---

continued . . .

Initial margin loan:

(Total market value) - (Maximum loan value)

= $3,000 - $1,500

= $1,500

Using a combination of cash and her margin account, Frieda can purchase 300 shares of Media Inc., a total market value of $3,000, with only $1,500 of cash. Frieda's investment dealer will loan her the remaining $1,500 required to complete this purchase and Frieda will in turn pay interest on the outstanding loan balance.

While the investor has an outstanding loan, she is required to maintain a minimum amount in her margin account. Changes to the market value of the security will impact the total value of the security held, which in turn will affect the loan balance. When the actual value of the loan exceeds the maximum loan value, the investment dealer will request the investor to place additional cash in the margin account. A request from the dealer for additional funds to cover a *margin deficiency* is referred to as a *margin call.*

While many dealers provide the investor with prior notice if an account is running a margin deficiency and a margin call is necessary, the dealer typically has the right to undertake an immediate sale of the collateral securities without prior notice. The securities held in the account are collateral for a margin loan, and if a sale is undertaken to cover a margin deficiency, the investor will pay full commissions on the sale.

FRIEDA (2)

Assume the market value of Media Inc. falls to $8 per share. What impact does this have for Frieda?

    ⇨   We know that the maximum loan value permitted is:

50% × 300 shares × $8

= $1,200

      ⇨   We know the initial margin loan was $1,500.

Therefore, Frieda has a margin shortfall of $300, which is calculated as the difference between the initial loan margin ($1,500) and the current maximum loan value ($1,200).

If Frieda does not have the funds available to meet the margin call for $300, her investment dealer will sell a portion of her shares of Media Inc., even though it may cause Frieda to incur a loss on the investment.

FRIEDA (3)

Assume the market value of Media Inc. increases to $12 per share. What impact does this have for Frieda?

    ⇨   We know that maximum loan value permitted is:

50% × 300 shares × $12

= $1,800

      ⇨   We know the initial margin loan was $1,500.

Therefore, Frieda has a balance of $300 in her margin account, greater than what is required. This overage is calculated as the difference between the current maximum loan value ($1,800) and the initial loan margin ($1,500). Frieda is free to withdraw the $300 or to use it toward the purchase of another security on margin.

Assume Frieda decides to sell her shares. What is the outcome?

continued . . .

continued . . .

In this case, Frieda could sell the shares at $12 per share, repay her loan of $1,500 and exit with a profit of $600 (commissions have been excluded).

⇨ Current value of investment (300 × $12/shares) $3,600

⇨ Frieda's initial investment $1,500

⇨ Repayment of margin account $1,500

⇨ Profit $600

An investor who uses a margin account must be prepared to meet any margin call and, as such, needs to have funds immediately available to make up any shortfall or be prepared for the possibility of shares being sold by the investment dealer. A margin account represents leverage; it is a loan that allows the investor to purchase a larger amount of a security. However, borrowed funds must always be repaid and if the value of the stock decreases, an investor is still liable for the original debt, which can be a very risky position.

FRIEDA (4)

In the Frieda (1) SNAP, we know that Frieda purchased 300 shares of Media Inc. at $10 per share, although she initially borrowed $1,500 to make this purchase.

If the price of Media Inc falls to $4 per share, the total value of Frieda's purchase declines to $1,200. While the value of the stock is now only $1,200, Frieda still has an obligation to pay the initial $1,500 that she borrowed in order to make the original purchase.

Note that margin accounts may also be used for the purchase of qualified bonds and debentures. The process is similar and incorporates minimum loan value requirements.

Short Selling

Another form of leverage commonly used by investors is the short selling of a security, which an investor typically considers when she feels the price of a security is likely to fall.

Using the strategy of short selling, an investor who believes that the price of a security is likely to fall will borrow shares of the security from her investment dealer and sell the borrowed shares at what the investor believes to be a high price. The investor retains the obligation to return the borrowed shares at a point in the future, when requested by the owner. The sale of borrowed shares, in these circumstances, is referred to as *selling short.*

In the future, if the price of the shares falls, the investor buys the shares at a more favourable price (more favourable than the price at which the shares were sold short) and returns the shares to the investment dealer. The investor's profit is the difference between the price at which she sold the short shares and the price at which the shares were purchased for return to the investment dealer.

If the price of the shares does not fall, as the investor anticipates, she must still purchase shares for return to the investment dealer, in which case the investor could incur a loss.

This type of leveraging strategy is also subject to minimum margin requirements established through the provincial security commissions. Table 3 outlines the minimum loan value for short selling as dictated by IIROC. Note that the minimum balance that the investor must hold in her margin account fluctuates with the value of the security.

Table 3
Short Selling Securities
(excluding bonds and debentures)

Price Per Share of Security	Credit Required
$2.00 or above	150% of market value
$1.50 to $1.99	$3.00 per share
$0.25 to $1.49	200% of market value
less than $0.25	Market value + $0.25 per share

Source: IIROC, Dealer Member Rule 100.2(f).

The underlying premise associated with a short selling strategy is that the price of the security will fall, allowing the investor to replace the borrowed security through a purchase of shares at a lower price. If this premise does not hold true, the investor could incur a loss. To protect the potential loss if the price of the security rises, an investor may place a purchase order that instructs the investment dealer to purchase a predetermined number of shares of the security if the price reaches a specific level.

GEORGE (1)

George feels strongly that the share price of Search Inc. will fall substantially over the next six months, so he has sold short 1,000 shares of Search Inc. George sold the shares at $5 per share. Use information in table 3, where needed. (Disregard commissions.)

The $5,000 of proceeds from the sale was deposited in George's margin account. Because this was undertaken as a short sale, George is required to maintain a minimum balance in his margin account of $7,500, so he must deposit an additional $2,500 ($7,500 - $5,000).

Initial minimum margin required in account

150% × market value

= 150% × (1,000 shares × $5/share)

= 150% × $5,000

= $7,500

Note that the minimum balance that George must hold in his margin account fluctuates with the value of the Search Inc. shares.

GEORGE (2)

When the price of Search Inc. shares falls to $3, George decides to close out his position by purchasing 1,000 shares and transferring ownership back to the dealer. This cancels his current obligation that requires the replacement of 1,000 shares.

What is George's investment return on this transaction?

⇨ George originally sold 1,000 shares for $5 per share, which generated total revenue of $5,000.

⇨ George completed the transaction when he purchased 1,000 shares at $3 per share, which cost him a total of $3,000.

⇨ The difference between George's revenue and cost on this transaction was $2,000 ($5,000 - $3,000).

⇨ George was required to deposit $2,500 in the margin account.

Therefore, George's return on the investment is 80% ($2,000 ÷ $2,500).

STOCK SPLIT

From time to time, a company may decide to declare a stock split, which is merely an increase to the number of shares outstanding, with a corresponding adjustment to the share price. Companies characteristically opt to declare a split in an effort to increase the attractiveness of the company's shares to an investor. When the price of a share has risen to a certain level, some companies feel that a stock split helps to bring the share into a more desirable price range. A stock split does not change the company's revenue or reduce expenses and does not change the stockholder's equity or ownership proportion of the company.

EDNA

Edna owns 500 shares of Tel Optical Inc. at a current share price of $75 and a total value of $37,500 (500 × $75). If Tel Optical Inc. declares a 2-for-1 stock split, the total value of Edna's shares of Tel Optical Inc. remains at $37,500, but the number of shares Edna owns will increase to 1,000 while the price of a share will drop to $37.50.

The 1,000 shares is based on a 2-for-1 stock split, which means each of Edna's 500 shares is now worth 2 shares (500 × 2), for a total of 1,000 shares. The new price of $37.50 is derived as half of $75.00, based on a 2-for-1 split.

The total value of Edna's portfolio of Tel Optical Inc. remains unchanged at $37,500.

MARKET VIEW

The terms *bull* and *bear market* are used to describe markets where there is consensus with regard to long-term movements of significant proportion.

Bull Market

A *bull market* is characterized by a prolonged period of rising stock prices, when GDP is growing and the economy is very strong. Investors who are optimistic about the market, and believe stock prices will continue to increase, are viewed as having a bullish outlook.

Bear Market

A *bear market* is characterized by a prolonged period of declining stock prices in a weak economic environment. When investors are pessimistic about the market, believing stock prices will continue to fall, they are viewed as having a bearish outlook.

CORPORATE STRATEGY

The benefits of issuing common stock over debt, for a corporation, include the fact that the funds generated through a stock issue do not have to be paid back and dividends are paid only if the company earns sufficient income. A decision regarding the payment of dividends lies with the board of directors.

Unit 4
Preferred Shares

INTRODUCTION

Preferred shares of a company are considered a form of equity investment; however, they are also considered a fixed-income security because a level of income is often fixed through the promise of specific dividend payments.

NATURE

While corporations issue preferred shares as a form of equity, they differ from common shares in a number of ways.

Voting Rights

Preferred shares typically do not provide the holder with voting rights.

Dividends

A preferred share will normally have a stated dividend amount, which represents a fixed payment to the shareholder. The annual dividend associated with the share is commonly paid in quarterly instalments. The dividend feature on preferred shares makes preferred shares of taxable Canadian corporations a tax-preferred type of investment. To review the dividend tax treatment refer to Module 5.

DONALD

Donald owns 100 preferred shares of Hi Corp. The shares have a dividend rate of 6% and a par value of $100. The annual dividend payment associated with each preferred share is $6. If dividends were paid, Donald would normally receive $1.50 for each share on a quarterly basis.

As discussed under the common share section, a corporation is not legally required to pay dividends. This statement is also true of dividends associated with preferred shares. The company is under no obligation to pay a dividend and can defer a dividend indefinitely. The omission of a dividend payment does not create any legal liability for the issuer of the security. However, the corporation must pay dividends on preferred shares before a dividend payment can be made to a common shareholder.

Many preferred shares are *cumulative*, which means that all missed dividend payments must be paid before the company can pay dividends to common shareholders. This cumulative feature does not create a legal liability for the corporation but simply provides the preferred shareholder with an assurance that any dividend arrears will be forthcoming before any dividend payments are made to the holders of common shares. If the preferred share is not cumulative, the company is under no obligation to catch up on missed dividends to preferred shareholders before making dividend payments to common shareholders.

Some preferred shares incorporate an additional feature known as *participating*. With participating preferred shares, under specific conditions, the shareholder is entitled to additional dividend payments above the stated dividend rate.

Dissolution

If a company is dissolved, preferred shareholders have the right to receive the par value or a stated liquidation value for each share, which takes precedence over the rights of common shareholders. The priority of preferred shares in the dissolution process is behind bond-holders but ahead of common shareholders.

OTHER FEATURES

Similar to common shares, preferred shares can have a number of additional features that can enhance their attractiveness to an investor. The term *straight preferred* share is a phrase commonly used to describe a simple preferred share without additional enhancements.

Convertible

Some preferred shares offer a *convertible* feature where the preferred shares can be exchanged for a specified number of common shares. The ratio of exchange is stated in the details of the preferred share.

The addition of the convertible feature to a preferred share tends to increase the volatility of its price because of the link to the corporation's common shares.

Retractable

Some preferred shares offer a *retractable* feature where the preferred shareholder can force the issuing corporation to buy back the shares at a specified price on a specific date.

Callable

Preferred shares can be issued with a *callable feature*, where the issuing corporation has the right, with specified notice, to call the shares in for redemption. A share that does not include a call feature is referred to as non-callable, and the company has no right to call the share.

Purchase or Sinking Fund

Some preferred shares may be issued with a *purchase fund*, where a corporation has the right/obligation to retire a certain number of preferred shares, under prescribed conditions (i.e., the share price is at or below a specified amount on a given date).

Less common is the use of a *sinking fund*, where an issue of preferred shares is gradually retired over a period of years.

Other

The design of preferred shares can be very diverse and can include such features as the addition of a warrant, a variable or floating interest rate associated with the dividend payment and even a foreign payment component.

WHY PREFERRED SHARES?

Preferred shares can be an attractive form of capitalization for a corporation because they do not commit the issuing company to the repayment of debt on a specific date, whereas a bond issue does. There is no specific maturity date to which a company is committed and a missed dividend payment does not put the company into default.

The design of a preferred share issue can be developed around the specific financial needs and status of the corporation. The benefits derived by the company translate into a higher cost for an issue of preferred shares than for a debt issue. In turn, investors are attracted to preferred shares because of the preferential tax treatment of dividends from Canadian corporations.

Dividends on preferred shares are paid with after-tax corporate dollars, which is more costly to the corporation than a debt issue where interest payments are tax deductible to the corporation.

When an investor is considering the purchase of preferred shares, evaluation of the company's net income will help assess the adequacy of funds to cover the preferred dividend commitment. Independent credit assessment of the issuing organization is also helpful in analyzing the business risk associated with the security.

STRATEGY

Similar to bonds, preferred shares are attractive to investors who have an interest in a regular income flow. In contrast to bonds, Canadian preferred shares are considered tax-advantaged investments because the dividend income is eligible for the gross-up and dividend tax credit.

Preferred shares are subject to the risk associated with interest rate changes. As interest rates rise, an investor selling the preferred share will need to reduce the price in order to attract a prospective buyer. Therefore, similar to bonds, the price of preferred shares moves in the opposite direction to interest rates.

Unit 5
Derivative Securities

INTRODUCTION

A derivative is a financial instrument whose value is dependent on the value and characteristics of an underlying security. The underlying security could be a currency, bond, stock or commodity. Examples of common financial derivatives include: put options, call options, futures and swaps.

OPTIONS

An *option* is the right, but not the obligation, to sell or buy an underlying security during a given period for a specified price, which is commonly referred to as the *strike price*. An option is considered a security just like a stock or bond and includes very specific terms and conditions. The underlying security associated with an option is typically in standardized units of 100. For example, an equity option is comprised of 100 stocks.

It is important to note that the purchase of an option provides the owner with the right, but not the obligation, to do something. An option carries with it a specific expiration date, after which the right expires if it has not been previously exercised. If the owner chooses not to evoke the rights within the option by the expiration date, the option simply expires. During the period that the option can be exercised, the option has value. If the option expires, it becomes worthless. An option is a contract associated with an underlying asset where the option derives its value from the performance of the underlying security.

Call Option

When an investor owns an option to buy a specific security, it is referred to as a *call option*. Ownership of a call option gives an investor the right, but not the obligation, to buy a specific security, bond, commodity or other financial instrument at a specified price within a specified time frame. The purchase of a call option is similar to taking on a *long* position in a stock. Those who own a long position in a security want the price of the security to increase.

An investor who buys a call option hopes that the price of the underlying security will increase before the option expires. As the price of the underlying security increases, a call option becomes more valuable. A call option with an exercise price of $50 that expires in May is described as a May 50 call.

Put Option

When an investor owns an option to sell a specific security, it is referred to as a *put option*. Ownership of a put option gives the investor the right, but not the obligation, to sell a specific amount of an underlying security, bond, commodity or other financial instrument at a specified price within a specified time frame. The investor purchases this right, a put option, by paying a premium to the seller of the option. The only financial commitment is the premium that the buyer of an option pays for the right, and any associated commissions. The seller of the option receives the premium, but in return has assumed an obligation to buy the security, if the option is exercised.

An investor who buys a put option hopes that the price of the underlying security will decrease before the option expires. As the price of the underlying security decreases, a put becomes more valuable. Put options can be used to manage price risk; they protect against lower prices.

A put option with an exercise price of $50 that expires in May is described as a May 50 put.

Nature of Options Market

The Players

Owners of a put or call option are known as *buyers*, because they buy a specific right. Once the buyer owns the option, she becomes a *holder*. Two other participants, a call seller and put seller, are integral to the completion of the option market. Those who sell a call or put option are referred to as *writers* of the option. A seller of an option receives a premium payment from the buyer of the option.

If the holder of an option exercises the option, the writer is contractually bound to buy/sell the underlying security from/to the option holder as the agreement states.

Seller (has a short position) Obligated to buy or sell, if option buyer exercises option Receives $ for obligation	Call Writer	Put Writer

Buyer (has a long position) Exercising the option is the holder's choice. Pays $ for right	Call Holder	Put Holder

The Process

The buyer of an option pays a premium to the writer of the option, where the term *premium* refers to the cost of the option. The phrase *strike price* refers to the price of the underlying security at which the option may be exercised — security bought (call) or security sold (put). Depending upon the position that the investor holds, the movement of the security in relationship to the strike price prior to the expiration date determines if the holder can make a profit by exercising the option.

An investor will purchase a call option when she expects the price of the underlying security to increase. For the holder of a call option, the price of the security must rise above the strike price in order to make a profit. A call option is *in-the-money* when the market price of the underlying security is above the strike price.

An investor will purchase a put option when she expects the price of the underlying security to decrease. For the holder of a put option, the market price of the security must fall below the strike price in order to make a profit. A put option is *in-the-money* when the market price of the underlying security is below the strike price.

The term *in-the-money* is used to describe the position at which the option is worth money and the holder can exercise the option in order to generate a profit. The amount by which an option is *in-the-money* (could generate a profit) is commonly referred to as the *intrinsic value* of the option. Table 4 describes the terminology used to describe the market price of the security in relationship to the strike price.

Table 4
Market Price Relative to Strike Price

If the market price is:	Call Option	Put Option
a. Above the strike price	in-the-money	out-of-the-money
b. At the strike price	at-the-money	at-the-money
c. Below the strike price	out-of-the-money	in-the-money

An option's premium is its intrinsic value plus time value. Intrinsic value is the amount by which the security is in-the-money. The time value element is the price associated with the possibility of the option increasing in value. In reality, options always trade above intrinsic value.

Writer of a Call

The writer of a call option is paid a premium, from the buyer, in exchange for the writer's agreement to sell shares at a strike price. If the price of the stock increases above the strike price, the call buyer will likely exercise the option, thereby requiring the writer to sell the stock to the call holder at the strike price. The writer of a call option expects the market price of the security to remain relatively stable, below the strike price, at least until the expiration of the call option.

Investors write call options as a means to generate additional income on their portfolio. The profit to the writer of a call option is the premium she receives for writing the call option. If the option is exercised, the writer is obligated to sell the stock at the strike price and therefore gives up any appreciation beyond the strike price. If the price of the underlying security does not appreciate beyond the strike price, which is the writer's hope, then the option simply expires. The writer of a call option is viewed as having a short position, which is said to be short in a call.

Writer of a Put

The writer of a put option is paid a premium, from the buyer, in exchange for the writer's agreement to buy shares at a strike price. If the price of the stock falls below the strike price, the put holder will likely exercise the option, thereby requiring the writer to buy the stock from the put holder at the strike price. The writer of a put expects that the market price of the security is reasonably stable and will not fall below the strike price.

An investor writes put options as a means to generate additional income on her portfolio. The profit to the writer of a put option is the premium she receives for writing the put option. If the option is exercised, the writer is obligated to buy the stock at the strike price. If the price of the underlying security does not fall below the strike price, which is the writer's hope, then the option simply expires. The writer of a put option is viewed as having a short position, which is said to be short in a put.

EDWARD — COVERED PUT

Edward owns 1,000 shares of News Link Corporation. Although Edward feels some uncertainty about the current market conditions, he does not yet want to sell his shares of News Link Corporation. To offset his uncertainty, Edward buys put options on shares of News Link Corporation for $2.25 per share. Through ownership of the put options, Edward now has the right to sell his shares of News Link Corporation, any time in the next three months, at the option's strike price.

If the market price of News Link Corporation's shares falls below the strike price, Edward would exercise his put option whereby he would sell the News Link Corporation shares at the strike price (which is above the market price).

If the market price of News Link Corporation shares does not fall, Edward takes no action but simply lets the put option expire.

By purchasing the put option, Edward invests an amount equal to the price of the put option in order to reduce his risk of loss. If the anticipated drop in the market value of the shares does not occur, Edward's cost is simply that of the price of the put options. If the anticipated drop in the market value of the shares does occur, Edward has reduced his price risk associated with the shares of News Link Corporation.

EDWINA — CALL OPTION

Edwina is a reasonably sophisticated investor who feels very bullish about the market. Based on Edwina's research, all factors suggest that the price of Turn Point Inc. shares will increase over the next several months. Yet, Edwina still feels some uncertainty about the prediction.

Rather than simply buying shares of Turn Point Inc., Edwina opts to purchase call options. The call option provides Edwina with the right to buy shares of Turn Point Inc., at the option's strike price. For example, if the current market price is $20, Edwina might purchase a call option that allows her to purchase the shares at $25 per share — the strike price.

If the market price rises, as Edwina expects, and the market price exceeds the strike price on the call option, Edwina would exercise her right to purchase shares of Turn Point Inc., and then immediately re-sell the shares for a profit.

If the market price does not rise as Edwina expects, Edwina simply lets the call option expire without taking any action.

For a modest investment, Edwina's purchase of the call option provides her with the opportunity to participate in potential market growth.

Tables 5 and 6 summarize two different scenarios: one where the market price exceeds the strike price and the other where the market price is less than the strike price.

Table 5
Transaction One

Strike price: $12

Market price: $15

Call Option

HOLDER has the right to buy the stock at $12.
If the market price is $15, the option is ***in-the-money,*** where the market price exceeds the strike price.

WRITER is obliged to sell the stock at $12, if the holder chooses to exercise the option.

Given this current position, the holder would likely exercise the option, resulting in a profit to the holder.

Put Option

HOLDER has the right to sell the stock at $12.
If the market price is $15, the option is ***out-of-the-money*** because the market price exceeds the strike price.

WRITER is obliged to buy the stock at $12, if the holder chooses to exercise the option.

Given this current position, the holder would not exercise the option.

Table 6
Transaction Two

Strike price: $20

Market price: $15

Call Option

HOLDER has the right to buy the stock at $20.
If the market price is $15, the option is ***out-of-the-money,*** because the market price is less than the strike price.

WRITER is obliged to sell the stock at $20, if the holder chooses to exercise the option.

Given this current position, the holder would not exercise the option.

Put Option

HOLDER has the right to sell the stock at $20.
If the market price is $15, the option is ***in-the-money*** because the strike price exceeds the market price.

WRITER is obliged to buy the stock at $20, if the holder chooses to exercise the option.

Given this current position, the holder would likely exercise the option, resulting in a profit to the holder.

COLLIN and DANIEL

When ABC Inc. had a market price of $20, Collin purchased a call option (ABC Inc. November 30) contract that allows him to purchase 100 shares of ABC Inc. at a strike price of $30. He paid $2 per option for a total cost of $200 (100 options per contract). Collin is considered the call option holder who has the right to purchase 100 shares of ABC Inc. at a price of $30 per share prior to the expiration of the option contract in November.

Daniel, who owns 100 shares of ABC Inc., is the writer of the call option. In return for Daniel's agreement to sell 100 shares of ABC Inc. at $30 per share prior to the end of November, if called, he receives a total premium of $200 ($2 per call).

What is the likely consequence if the market price of ABC Inc. increases to $50?

As the call holder, Collin has the right to purchase 100 shares of ABC at $30 per share. If he exercises his call, he will purchase 100 shares at a total cost of $3,000. In turn, he could sell the shares in the market for $50 per share, which would generate revenue of $5,000. The difference

continued . . .

continued . . .

between Collin's $5,000 revenue and $3,000 cost leaves a gain of $2,000. After allowing for the original cost of the call option, $200, Collin is left with an $1,800 gain.

This $1,800 gain represents a 900% return on investment where an investment of $200 (original cost of option) resulted in a net gain of $1,800.

Collin did not have to use a call option to achieve this profit, as he could have merely purchased the shares at $30, and later sold them at $50. However, the purchase of a call option allowed Collin to limit his risk while leveraging his investment.

Daniel, the writer of the call option, receives the premium of $200. When Collin decides to exercise the call option, Daniel is obliged to sell 100 shares of ABC at $30 per share. This means that Daniel loses the opportunity to benefit from the appreciation in the price of the stock beyond the $30 strike price. It is likely that Daniel did not expect the price of ABC to increase in the way that it did.

What is the likely consequence if the market price of the ABC Inc. increases to $25?

As the call holder, Collin has the right to purchase 100 shares of ABC at $30 per share. If he exercises his call, he will purchase 100 shares at a total cost of $3,000. In turn, he could sell the shares in the market for only $25 per share, which would not generate a profit when compared with his cost.

Given that the market price of the shares is below of the break-even point for Collin, it would not be advantageous for Collin to make the purchase so he would not likely exercise the option. The only cost that Collin would incur is the $200 required to purchase the call option.

Daniel, the writer of the call option, receives the premium of $200, regardless of whether or not Collin exercises the option. If Collin has not exercised the call option by the time it expires, Daniel continues to own his ABC shares and is free to deal with the shares in any way he pleases.

Why Use Options?

Call Options

Call options are used by investors primarily for speculation, hedging, leverage and as coverage against a short position.

Speculation

The term *speculation* involves the anticipation of large movements, up or down, in the price of a particular security. Through the purchase of a call option, speculators use the premium as an investment that they are willing to risk in return for a superior return should they be able to accurately predict an increase in the price of the particular security.

Leverage

The only cost to the purchaser of an option is the price of the premium that is paid to the writer. For a small amount, the price of the premium, the investor is able to leverage her investment, which allows her to take advantage of the capital appreciation of a share beyond the strike price.

Coverage Against a Short Position

When the investor expects, but is not certain, that the price of a stock will fall, a call option can be used to hedge against an upward movement in the price of a security. The investor can short the stock and then purchase a call option to cover the position.

Put Options

Hedge

An investor will use a put option as a means of insurance where the option is purchased by the investor as insurance against a downturn in a particular stock. Using put options, investors can cost effectively limit the downside associated with a particular investment while enjoying the full benefit of the upside.

DONALD

Donald owns 10,000 shares of STU Company where the current market price is $25 per share. Donald could purchase a 100 put option contract on STU Company shares for a premium of $1.50 per share, which totals $15,000. The strike price of the put option is $20. Through the purchase of the put option contract, Donald is able to ensure that he can sell his 10,000 shares for $20 per share up until the put option contract expires.

If the price of the STU Company shares falls below the $20 strike price, Donald would likely exercise his put options. If the price of the stock falls to $15 per share, the put option acts as insurance that protects Donald so he will receive at least $20 per share. Donald also has another option. Rather than exercising the option, Donald could sell the put options on the open market, which should garner at least $5 per share (the difference between the strike price of $20 and the current market price of $15). This $5 per share represents a total of $50,000, which represents the intrinsic value of the option. There is also a time value associated with the intrinsic value. The $50,000 generated through the sale of the options compensates Donald for the loss he will incur in the value of the stock.

If the price of the STU Company shares increases above the current market price of $25, then Donald would not exercise the put options. If, for example, Donald decides to sell the shares when the market price is $40, he will incur a profit (excluding commissions) which equals the difference between his original purchase price and the price at which he sells the shares, in this case $40. His profit would be reduced by the $1.50 per share premium paid for the options.

The use of put options reduces Donald's risk of a price decline. Once purchased, the put options contract will either be exercised by Donald, expire, or can be traded on the options market.

Straddle

A *straddle* is an investment strategy whereby an investor holds a position in both a call and put option, on the same security, each with the same strike price. An investor would utilize this type of strategy if she is expecting significant changes in the price of the underlying security, but it is not clear as to the direction of the potential change. Typically, straddles are used in a volatile market.

The double protection of a call and put purchase means that the investor has the opportunity to gain if the price of the security either increases or decreases by the end of the expiry period. If the market price increases, the investor would exercise the call option, whereas if the price decreases, she would exercise the put option.

DONNA

Donna has followed the activities of Redo Inc., which is in the process of restructuring its finances. Donna anticipates that the market will respond either very positively to the restructuring efforts or very negatively. Although Donna is uncertain as to which way the market will react, she feels that there will be a strong response that will impact the value of the Redo Inc. shares.

Given Donna's strong feelings, she has decided to undertake a straddle position where she will purchase a put and call option on Redo Inc. shares, both for a six-month period, expiring in January. The details are as follows:

— January 25 call @ $1.50 premium
— January 25 put @ $2.00 premium

In the following discussion, disregard any commissions paid on any transactions.

Donna has purchased 1 call and 1 put option on the shares of Redo Inc. that expires in January (6 months from now) and each has a strike price of $25. This transaction gives Donna the right to:

● buy 100 shares of Redo Inc. at $25 per share. The call option becomes attractive when the market price of Redo Inc. rises above the $25 strike price.

● sell 100 shares of Redo Inc. at $25 per share. The put option becomes attractive if the market price of Redo Inc. falls below the $25 strike price.

continued . . .

continued . . .

The cost of this straddle is $350, calculated as:

$(100 \times \$1.50) + (100 \times \$2.00)$

As discussed previously, the underlying asset associated with an option is typically in standardized units of 100 and the premium applies to each unit of the underlying asset.

To determine the break-even price at which Donna will make a profit if the call or put is exercised:

Exercise Price of Call

(a) $25 + ($350 ÷ 100)

= $28.50

Exercise Price of Put

(b) $25 - ($350 ÷ 100)

= $21.50

If the price of Redo Inc. stock increases beyond $28.50, or decreases to a level below $21.50, Donna will make a profit on this transaction.

If the price of the security falls to $20, then she would exercise her put and sell 100 shares at $25. She will buy 100 shares at $20 and sell 100 shares for $25, making a $500 gain. Her cost to earn the $500 gain was $350.

If the price of the security rises to $30, then she would exercise her call option to buy 100 shares at $25. She will buy 100 shares for $25 and then immediately sell them for $30, making a $500 gain. Her cost to earn $500 was $350.

Options Summary

- An option is a derivative because its value is derived from an underlying asset.
- A call option gives the call holder (buyer) the right to buy the underlying asset at the specified price during a specified period. The call holder hopes that the price of the asset will increase.
- A put option gives the put holder (buyer) the right to sell the underlying asset at the specified price during a specified period. The put holder hopes that the price of the asset will decrease.
- The term strike price is used to describe the price for which the underlying asset can be bought or sold.
- The term premium is used to describe the cost of the option.
- The term holder is used to refer to the buyer of a put or call option.
- The term writer is used to refer to the seller of a put or call option.
- Options are used primarily for hedging and speculation.
- The underlying asset associated with an option is typically in standardized units of 100 and the premium applies to each unit of the underlying asset.

WARRANT

A certificate issued by a corporation that entitles the holder to purchase a specified number of the corporation's common stock at a predetermined price, for an extended period of time, is referred to as a *warrant*. The purchase price of the security associated with the warrant is normally higher than the current market price of the underlying security. The features of a warrant are very much like that of a call option, where the holder of the warrant has the opportunity, but not the obligation, to exercise the warrant prior to its expiration. There is no common period for which a warrant is valid; the corporation who issues the original security establishes the lifespan of a warrant.

A warrant may be issued as an independent certificate, which is common when it is used as an alternative to a cash or stock dividend. A warrant may also be issued as a complement to another security, quite commonly preferred shares and bonds. When issued as an enhanced feature to another security, the warrant entitles the shareholder or bondholder to purchase a specified number of the firm's common stock at a predetermined price, for an extended period of time.

A firm may attach warrants to another security as a means to increase the attractiveness of the bond or share because the warrant increases the investor's opportunity for profit. If the market price of the stock associated with the warrant increases to a level above the pre-established price in the warrant, an investor could turn a profit by exercising the warrant. She could purchase the shares at the predetermined price established in the warrant and could immediately resell them for a profit. If the market price of the stock does not increase to a level beyond the pre-established price in the warrant, the warrant simply expires.

A warrant holds value and can be bought and sold on the secondary market. If a warrant is attached to another security, the terms associated with that specific warrant will dictate whether it can be detached and traded independent of the security with which it was originally issued.

While a warrant has similarities to a call option, there are differences. A true call option involves two independent investors, while a warrant involves an investor and the company who issues the stock. When an investor exercises a call option, the transaction is independent of the corporation; when a warrant is exercised, it involves the corporation who receives the cash and distributes the shares to the shareholder.

EMMA

Three years ago, Emma purchased 1,000 preferred shares of Caps Lock Inc. Emma was attracted to the shares because they included warrants that provide the opportunity to purchase Caps Lock Inc. common shares. Each preferred share has one warrant attached that expires June 30, 2011, and which allows for the purchase of one common share at $30 per share.

When Emma purchased the preferred shares, the common stock of Caps Lock Inc. was trading at $18 per share. Three months ago, the common shares were trading in the $28 range.

Emma just confirmed that the common shares are now trading at $34 per share. If Emma exercises her 1,000 warrants, she will purchase 1,000 common shares of Caps Lock Inc. at $30 per share and can immediately resell the shares at $34 per share. Emma will earn a profit of $4 per share (excluding commissions) for a total profit of $4,000.

If Emma believes the price of a Caps Lock Inc. common share will go above the current value of $34, she could wait longer in an attempt to capture an even greater profit from the warrants.

RIGHTS

When a corporation undertakes the issuance of additional corporate shares, existing shareholders may be given the right to purchase new shares in proportion to the number of existing shares that they already own. A *right*, sometimes referred to as a *subscription warrant*, provides the shareholder with the opportunity to purchase a prescribed number of newly authorized shares in order to maintain her proportional ownership of the existing corporation.

This purchase opportunity takes place prior to the sale of the new shares to the general public and is quite often limited to a very specific, short period of time. It is this short, limited period that is a distinguishing feature between a right and a warrant. During a limited period of time, existing shares trade *cum rights*, which means *with rights*. Subsequently, the shares trade *ex-rights*. The market price of the existing shares will adjust according to the cum rights and ex-rights provisions attached to the shares. Rights have value and commonly trade in the secondary market.

FORWARD CONTRACT

In its simplest form, a *forward contract* is a private contract where two parties agree to exchange an item in the future at a predetermined price.

ELMER

Elmer wants to attend all figure skating competitions at the next Olympics. He is told that he could book a ticket now that will allow him entry to all skating events at the winter Olympics and that he can pay $2,500 at the time he picks up his ticket on the day of the first event. Or, Elmer could wait and purchase his ticket at the entry gate on the day of the first event, and pay whatever the going rate is at that time.

If Elmer proceeds and opts to book his ticket now, he guarantees himself entry to all figure skating events during the next Olympics for the price of $2,500. By taking this action, Elmer enters a forward contract, which removes the risk that he would have to pay more than $2,500 for the ticket. Elmer is obliged to meet the terms of the contract, even if the price of the ticket falls to an amount far less than $2,500.

FUTURES

A *futures contract* is a standardized forward contract, which is traded on an organized exchange. The exchange acts as an intermediary between the buyer and seller, with both the buyer and seller entering separate contracts with the exchange.

A future is a derivative investment that derives value from the underlying asset. Futures are amongst the oldest financial instruments and date back to the 18th century when they were used in the trading of rice and silk in Japan. Today, futures are a financial contract where the sale or purchase of a commodity or security occurs, at a specified price, with delivery in the future. The trading of futures takes place on a commodity exchange. Future contracts can be terminated through a compensatory transaction (equal and opposite transaction) executed any time prior to the expiration of the original contract.

An investor can have one of two positions in a futures contract: a short or long position. Where an investor buys a futures contract and agrees to receive delivery, she is viewed as having a *long position*. Where an investor sells a futures contract and agrees to make delivery, she is viewed as having a *short position*.

Other terminology includes:

- **Face value:** The value is the forward price multiplied by the quantity of items agreed to in the contract.
- **Forward price:** Is the price determined by the seller and buyer on a future date.
- **Spot price:** The current actual cash price for immediate sale/exchange in the market.

Each futures contract is developed based on a standardized set of specifications that outline the conditions related to the agreement. For example, the contract will describe the nature of the futures contract such as details about the commodity, currency, financial instrument or index. The quantity and the settlement date are important to the specifications. The price of the underlying security is not a standardized item included in the contract. Futures contracts are quite liquid as they are actively traded on an exchange.

Uses of Futures

To lock in a predetermined price, the producer of a good will sell futures contracts. By selling the futures contract, the producer eliminates the risk of price fluctuations and creates price protection. As well, if the market price of a good is quite high and the producer of a good wants to lock in the price, she will sell futures contracts. If the price of the good decreases prior to the delivery date, the futures contract has value.

Futures are commonly used to reduce risk. For example, if a farmer who produces corn anticipates that the price of corn will fall by the time his crop is ready for market, he could insulate himself through the use of a futures contract. Using a futures contract, the farmer could agree now to sell his corn in the future at a specific price. This type of risk management is commonly referred to as hedging.

Speculators are risk takers who buy or sell futures contracts with the primary objective of making a profit. They have no interest in the actual good, so have no interest in price protection.

Future contracts are a form of leverage because, for a small investment, the investor acquires the opportunity to create a significant return. On the other hand, leverage also includes significant risk because it can lead to substantial losses.

Investments in metal such as copper and platinum are actively traded as futures. The global nature of metal products makes the price quite volatile, so this risk is actively managed through hedging against adverse price movements. The futures market in New York handles more gold futures than any other market in the world. While the price of gold is dependent on supply and demand, there is a tremendous amount of speculation in gold futures, which has an impact on price.

Clone Fund

The term *clone fund* is commonly used to describe a mutual fund that uses derivatives to replicate the strategy and performance of another fund or index. In simple terms, the clone fund invests a portion of its assets directly in the fund it strives to mirror, and then the remaining assets of the clone fund are invested in derivative contracts and other offsetting securities to provide coverage for the derivates.

As discussed in Course 3, prior to January 2005, registered plans were subject to rules that limited direct holdings of foreign content to 30%. Clone funds were commonly used as a means for investors to increase their percentage of holdings in foreign assets, beyond the 30% limit. This was achieved through the use of derivatives.

To work around the rule, a clone fund invested a portion of its assets in foreign holdings, commonly up to 30%. Additional assets were invested in Canadian derivative contracts that were intended to track the performance of the foreign fund, with the remainder in other securities to cover the derivates. This process allowed the clone fund to retain its classification as a Canadian security, but when the foreign content of the clone fund was combined with the investor's direct foreign content, the result was an amount greater than the basic 30%.

Through the use of derivatives, an investor was able to expand her foreign holdings in an RRSP or RRIF. Since the 2005 Budget eliminated the 30% foreign content rule, clone mutual funds are being phased out.

SWAP

A *SWAP*, as the name suggests, is an exchange of one security for another where qualities of the respective securities differ and the trading parties are looking for alternative securities to meet revised investment objectives. For example, a simple interest rate SWAP may occur between two investors where the cash flows of a bond with fixed interest payments are exchanged for the cash flows of a bond with a floating interest rate, where both bonds have the same principal amount. These types of arrangements can be beneficial when two investors each have a comparative advantage (lower opportunity cost) in opposite markets, so by swapping they can both benefit.

A currency swap involves a similar theory where two investors exchange principal and interest in one currency for the same amount in another.

Unit 6
Mutual Funds

INTRODUCTION

The term *investment fund* is used to describe a large portfolio of securities purchased with a pool of funds contributed by many investors, and which investment professionals manage. The large sums of money, which are invested in accordance with the objectives of the fund's prospectus, allow the fund manager to buy many securities so that returns are not heavily dependent on the ups and downs of a few investments. There are two major types of investment companies:

- a closed-end investment company; and
- an open-end investment company, which is commonly referred to as a mutual fund company.

CLOSED-END INVESTMENT FUNDS

A *closed-end investment fund* is one that is established as a corporation where a limited number of shares are issued by the corporation, and where the number of shares remains fixed. Similar to common stock, where after the initial offering the shares trade in the secondary market, shares of a closed-end trust normally trade on a stock exchange or in the over-the-counter market between investors without involving the corporation.

The capital raised through the initial public offering (IPO) is used by the corporation to make investments in accordance with the fund's stated objectives. The number of shares associated with a closed-end investment fund remains fixed and only changes if the corporation decides to raise additional capital by issuing additional shares. The market price of shares of a closed-end fund fluctuates based on supply and demand; it seldom matches the fund's net asset value.

Closed-end investment funds often focus on a specialized type of investment such as bonds or precious metals. A closed-end investment fund is generally considered to have low liquidity because an investor cannot simply request redemption but rather is subject to the forces of supply and demand in the open market. There must be a willing buyer for the closed-end investment fund before the fund owner can dispose of her shares. In some situations, the size of the closed-end fund is small, which could further affect liquidity because of the very low trading volume.

Shares of a closed-end investment fund that trade at a level below the net asset value per share are considered to trade at a discount, whereas the shares are considered to trade at a premium if they trade at a higher price than the net asset value.

The volatility of closed-end funds tends to be higher than open-end funds because, while both funds have a net-asset value, the closed-end funds normally trade at a discount or premium, not net-asset value. As the variance between net-asset value and the actual trading price shifts, the larger the variance between the fund's discount and premium, the greater the fund's price volatility.

Because shares of a closed-end fund trade on an organized exchange, investors pay brokerage fees to purchase and sell shares, but normally there are no other fees. Expenses incurred by closed-end funds tend to be lower than those incurred by open-end funds since there are few costs associated with ongoing distribution of the funds.

UNIT INVESTMENT TRUSTS

A *unit investment trust* (UIT) is a holding of mutual fund assets, quite often invested in debt-securities such as bonds and debentures. When selecting a UIT, the investor purchases units of a fixed portfolio of investments that has a pre-determined life span, after which the holdings are liquidated (most often mature).

A trust manages the flow of funds, paying investors in the UIT interest or dividends along the way and a return of capital upon the portfolio's maturity. While UITs are not common today, they were popular in the past for investors interested in a steady income flow and a long investment horizon. The life span of a UIT often runs in the 10, 20 and 30-year range. There tends to be very little performance information, which makes it difficult to make valid comparisons with alternate investments.

OPEN-END INVESTMENT FUNDS

Initially developed to provide greater flexibility than what is available through closed-end investment funds, an *open-end investment fund* continuously issues and redeems units directly from the fund itself. Today, the majority of mutual funds are open-end funds and the term *mutual fund* is used synonymously with the term open-ended investment fund. There are two types of open-end mutual funds: mutual fund corporations and mutual fund trusts. Both types of open-end mutual funds operate under similar objectives, but the structure and subsequent taxation of the two types of operations differs. With a trust, the operation is subject to trust laws with trustees responsible for the governance of the operation, whereas a board of directors oversees the operation of an incorporated fund.

Open-end funds continuously issue and redeem units so the number of units outstanding varies from day-to-day. The term *net sales* is used to describe the situation where the number of units sold was greater than the number redeemed. Conversely, the term *net redemptions* describes the situation where more units were redeemed than sold.

REASONS FOR INVESTING IN MUTUAL FUNDS

Professional Management

Each mutual fund has an individual or team of professional money managers responsible for selecting and managing the portfolio of securities held within the fund. The investment professionals are experts in their field and have the knowledge, information, time and resources necessary to make informed investment decisions. Continuous research and monitoring provides the fund managers with important information used to actively manage the fund. Portfolio managers must meet high standards of education and experience and be registered by provincial securities commissions.

Diversification

Mutual funds provide smaller-size investors with the opportunity for diversification of assets across many securities. This allows the investor to reduce her exposure to the risk associated with any single or small group of securities. In addition to the general diversification that occurs because of the fund's objectives and management style, investors in mutual funds also benefit from securities regulations that limit the holdings of any single security to 10% of the fund's total assets.

Liquidity

For the most part, a mutual fund investment is quite liquid because the investor can sell all or a portion of her units on any business day. Owners of mutual funds have a right to redemption. The mutual fund must redeem the shares when requested and securities regulations define how the processing must occur. In most cases, an investor will have access to her funds within a matter of a few days after having submitted a written request for redemption. While most mutual funds are valued daily, real estate funds are an exception.

Disclosure

The mutual fund industry is heavily regulated and subject to extensive disclosure requirements, placing significant accountability on the fund companies.

Scheduled Purchases

Many mutual fund companies provide investors with access to scheduled purchase plans where an investor purchases mutual funds on a regular basis (i.e., monthly) using automatic debits from her bank account.

As well, the automatic reinvestment of disbursements from a mutual fund is commonly offered by many fund companies, which allows the investor to continually acquire additional shares of the fund.

Transfers

Mutual fund companies commonly allow investors to transfer assets between funds available within the same fund organization, at little or no charge. These types of transfers provide an investor with the opportunity to reorganize her holdings without incurring significant costs.

OTHER CONSIDERATIONS

No Capital Guarantee

When investing in a mutual fund, an investor does not receive any guarantees relative to the capital that she invests. Her capital investment is subject to the volatilities of the marketplace, similar to common shares. There is risk associated with all mutual funds. The loss of capital is possible and should be an important consideration in the risk assessment when selecting appropriate investments that align with the investor's personal objectives.

No Performance Guarantee

It is important for investors to understand that there are no guarantees associated with a mutual fund's performance. While a fund may have performed well in the past, past performance is no indication of future performance. Similar to other types of investments, mutual funds carry risk and are subject to market volatility. In addition, an investor cannot select the price at which she wants to purchase or dispose of units; units are acquired or disposed of at the net asset value established on the day of the transaction. This value cannot be predicted in advance.

NET ASSET VALUE

The term *net asset value per share* (NAVPS) refers to the price at which units of a mutual fund are purchased and sold. The formula for calculating NAVPS is:

NAVPS = ((Market value of the fund assets) - (Total liabilities)) ÷ (# of units outstanding)

This formula can be further reduced to:

NAVPS = (Net asset value of fund) ÷ (# of units outstanding)

With the exception of real estate funds, the NAVPS for most funds is calculated on a daily basis.

> *XYZ MUTUAL FUND*
>
> XYZ mutual fund was comprised of securities that, on July 10, had an aggregate market value of $5,300,000. This same day, the fund had liabilities of $600,000 and there were 800,055 units of the fund outstanding.
>
> On July 10, the fund's:
> ⇨ net asset value was $4,700,000 ($5,300,000 - $600,000); and
> ⇨ net asset value per share (NAVPS) was $5.8746 ($4,700,000 ÷ 800,055).

OPERATIONAL ISSUES

Disclosure

Disclosure is an important means for investors to acquire valuable information that assists in the selection of appropriate investments. A fund's prospectus or simplified prospectus is the company's primary communication medium that provides investors with disclosure that covers a broad range of topics including:

- mutual fund issuer;
- management of the fund;
- investment objectives of the fund;
- risk factors involved in the purchase of fund units;
- the initial offering price of mutual fund units;
- details about how to purchase and redeem fund units;
- the commission structure and any other fees payable;
- management expense ratio (MER); and
- the fund's audited financial statements.

The regulation of mutual funds is provincially driven, so rules and regulations may differ by jurisdiction. In many jurisdictions, legislation requires that the prospectus be delivered to the purchaser within a specific time frame. Several provinces set this time as "within two days of placing an order". While the delivery of a prospectus is not required in all situations, it does play an important role in many jurisdictions and is an excellent source of information.

For example, in many jurisdictions, the purchaser of a mutual fund has the right of withdrawal after having placed a purchase order. The purchaser can exercise this right through written notice to the dealer no later than midnight on the second business day after the purchaser receives a copy of the simplified prospectus.

In some jurisdictions, the purchaser also has the right to rescind a purchase within 48 hours after having received the trade confirmation.

Management Expense Ratio

Like any other business, mutual funds incur expenses to operate. Management expenses such as the cost of marketing, administration and investment management are typical of the types of expenses that are covered through the fund's management fee. The *management expense ratio* (MER), expressed as a percentage of the total assets held in the fund, refers to the management fees charged directly to the fund. While the MER is deducted before the reporting of a fund's return, management expenses do lower the overall performance of a fund because the expenses are deducted from the fund's assets and ultimately reduce the investor's overall return. In essence, the MER represents foregone earnings. MERs, which are listed in the fund's prospectus, will differ by type of fund and by company.

The MER provides a way to compare management and other costs from one fund to another, as it is expressed as a percentage of the fund's average NAV during the year. A MER represents the percentage of each dollar in the mutual fund's portfolio that is being used to operate the fund and includes all fees payable by a fund except interest, taxes and brokerage fees.

MER =
(All fees and expenses payable during the year) ÷ (Average net asset value for the year)

All mutual funds charge a MER. The higher the MER, the greater the return the fund must achieve before making money for the investor.

Sales Charges

The sale of mutual funds to investors can result in the payment of commissions to the dealer and advisor associated with the sale. Commissions are also commonly referred to as *loads* or *sales charges* and are commonly applied when mutual fund units are purchased or sold. These loads or sales charges may or may not directly affect the client, financially. Funds are commonly grouped according to their commission structure, which is defined as:

- Front-end loads;
- Deferred sales charges; and
- No-loads.

Front-End Load

A mutual fund may charge a fee, referred to as a *front-end load*, where the investor is charged a fee based on a percentage of total assets purchased. After allowing for fees, the balance of the investor's capital is invested in the applicable fund. Front-end charges are negotiable between the investor and her advisor/dealer (i.e., commonly 1 to 5% of the amount invested). The advisor/investor has the discretion to establish any fees, including a zero fee. This fee represents a charge to the client, at the time of purchase, for the sales commissions paid to the advisor/dealer.

The fee associated with a front-end load is incorporated into the calculation that arrives at a purchase price per unit. When purchasing funds that have a front-end load, the purchase price per unit is derived from the formula:

Purchase price per unit = (NAVPS) ÷ (1.0 - Sales charge)

ANDREW

Andrew has $15,000 that he plans to use for the purchase of RT mutual funds. If Andrew purchases the funds when the NAVPS is $5 and he is charged a 2% front-end sales charge, how many units will Andrew purchase?

Because the purchase is subject to a front-end sales charge, Andrew's $15,000 will purchase only 2,940 units, because the 2% sales commission is calculated on the purchase price.

Purchase price per unit

= (NAVPS) ÷ (1.0 - Sales charge)

= ($5) ÷ (1.0 - 0.02)

= $5 ÷ 0.98

= $5.1020408

continued . . .

---

continued . . .

Number of units purchased

= Total amount ÷ Purchase price per share

= $15,000 ÷ $5.1020408

= 2,940 shares

Commission

The commission for this transaction is $300, derived as: 2% × $5.1020408 × 2,940 shares

There is no charge to the investor when units initially purchased with a front-end load are eventually sold.

Deferred Sales Charges

With funds that are sold on a *deferred sales charge* (DSC) basis, the mutual fund company pays a commission to the advisor/dealer and there is no direct charge to the investor. This leaves the full amount of the investor's funds available to purchase units of the applicable fund. However, the funds that the investor purchases are then subject to a redemption fee, based on a declining schedule that eventually dissipates after a number of years. The redemption fee schedule is typically high in the early years after an initial purchase but declines as time passes. The asset base against which the schedule applies can differ between companies, where some apply the schedule against the original amount and others apply it against the asset base at the time of redemption.

Typically, the fund company allows the investor to move funds between the family of funds without facing any redemption fees (back-end loads). In addition, the investor is frequently permitted to redeem up to a specified percentage of the funds annually (i.e., commonly 10%), without incurring redemption charges. The asset base against which the 10% amount applies may differ by company.

BARBARA

In January 2007, Barbara purchased $12,000 of PQR mutual funds on a DSC basis, when the NAVPS was $8. The fund's deferred sales charge schedule is shown below.

Redemption Period	Charge (based on original assets)
During first year	6%
During second year	4%
During third year	2%
During fourth year	1%
After fourth year	0%

In February 2010, when the NAVPS was $12, Barbara decided to redeem the PQR mutual funds. Barbara's redemption occurs in the fourth year when a 1% deferred sales charge applies. The result is a $120 fee with net proceeds of $17,880.

continued . . .

continued . . .

  Original Purchase

      $12,000

      1,500 units ($12,000 ÷ $8)

  Current Market Value

      $18,000 (1,500 units × $12)

  Applicable DSC

      $120 ((1,500 units × $8) × 0.01)

  Net Proceeds from Redemption

      $17,880 ($18,000 - $120)

What is the impact if the deferred sales charge is based on the assets at redemption rather than at the time of purchase? (Assume the rest of the schedule remains unchanged.)

If the asset base against which the sales charge applies is changed to reflect the value at the time of redemption, Barbara's total charge increases to $180, a 50% increase.

  Original Purchase

      $12,000

      1,500 units ($12,000 ÷ $8)

  Current Market Value

      $18,000 (1,500 units × $12)

  Applicable DSC

      $180 ((1,500 units × $12) × 0.01)

  Net Proceeds from Redemption

      $17,820 ($18,000 - $180)

No-Load

A *no-load fund* is just that; a fund where the investor is not subject to direct charges such as front-end loads or deferred sales charges when a fund purchase is made. As well, there is no charge at the time when units are sold.

Service Fees

In addition to any sales commission, the fund company typically pays an annual fee to the advisor/dealer that is based on a percentage of the fund's value. This commission, frequently referred to as a *service fee* or *trailer*, is intended to compensate the advisor/dealer for her ongoing service and advice to the client. Service fees are generally paid regardless of whether the fund was purchased as a front-end load or a DSC. In the case of no-load funds, the fund company may or may not pay a service fee and, if it does, it may be based on a minimum volume of assets. The service fee is paid by the fund company and is not a direct charge to the client.

FUND CLASSIFICATIONS

There are literally hundreds of different mutual funds offered for sale throughout Canada. An important distinguishing factor is the grouping of mutual funds by their investment objectives and the types of securities held within the fund's portfolio. The three broad asset classifications are:

- income;
- growth; and
- growth and income.

Within each of these broad asset classifications, mutual funds are further categorized relative to the risk and volatility. The risk element of a mutual fund can be judged by the volatility associated with the rate of return earned by a fund. Those funds whose rate of return is fairly even over time are generally considered low-risk funds, whereas those funds that experience wide variations in the return are viewed as high-volatility funds. The risk-reward assessment relative to the investor's risk tolerance is an important consideration when selecting appropriate investments, and mutual funds are no exception.

Asset Classification

Income	**Growth**	**Growth & Income**
Money Market Fund	Equity Fund	Balanced Fund
Mortgage Fund	Global/International Fund	Asset Allocation Fund
Bond Fund	Speculative Fund	
Dividend Fund	Real Estate Fund	

Money Market Funds

Money market funds are comprised of low-risk short-term investments such as government T-bills, corporate papers, bankers' acceptances and other short-term securities. The objective of money market funds tends to focus on the generation of income without risk to the investor's capital. In most cases, money market funds are valued differently than other mutual funds in that they have a fixed value of $1 or $10. The return associated with money market funds is purely income.

The return on money market funds fluctuates with general interest-rate levels. They are attractive to investors whose main motivation is to earn a greater rate of return than typical bank savings accounts, but with little risk. The money market fund is also commonly used as a holding place while an investor ponders longer-term investment decisions or as a place to hold a liquid portion of an investor's investment portfolio.

While money market funds are typically considered quite low risk, there is the need for a word of caution. In an excessively low interest rate environment, such as what Canada experienced in 2009, an unusual situation could arise. If the investment return on a money market fund falls below the amount of the MER, there is the possibility that an investor could lose capital. For example, this could occur if the money market fund is returning only 1%, but the MER on a fund is 1.25%. This is a relatively new issue at the time of writing, because of the noticeably low interest rate environment. A way around the problem is for a fund to lower its MER; however, the fund is under no obligation to do so, so there is some potential risk for the investor.

Mortgage Funds

A mortgage fund is one that is comprised of mortgages, generally on residential properties, and mortgage-based securities. The volatility of a mortgage fund tends to be quite low, although it is more risky than a money market fund but less risky than a bond fund. The return on a mortgage fund is income oriented.

Bond Funds

As the name suggests, bond funds invest in bonds. The types of bonds, such as government issued bonds or corporate bonds, will vary according to the objectives of the fund. Some funds may include all types of bonds while other funds may focus on a specific type of bond. For the most part, bond funds are focused on the creation of income, although a small degree of capital appreciation may be prevalent due to bond trades. The risk associated with a bond fund is pegged in the low to medium range and is generally considered more volatile than a mortgage fund.

Dividend Funds

A dividend fund is comprised of preferred and common shares that demonstrate a regular pattern of dividend payments. The fund generates a combination of income and capital appreciation. Generally more volatile than bond funds, dividend funds are viewed as investments that carry a medium level of risk.

Real Estate Funds

As the name suggests, the composition of investments within a real estate fund tend to be just that, real estate. Typically, the real estate is commercial and industrial in nature and includes properties such as shopping malls and office buildings. These types of mutual funds, unlike others, are permitted to borrow money for the acquisition of assets.

The asset value on a real estate fund is established through valuation of the properties held within the portfolio, which results in the establishment of unit prices on a less frequent basis than other mutual funds. Prices are commonly set on a monthly or quarterly basis. Return from the fund occurs in several ways, including income from the property rentals and capital gains. Depending upon how a fund handles the capital cost allowance, some unit holders may receive an allocation of a capital cost allowance deduction, which can be deducted against distributed rental income. The fund's prospectus outlines how these types of issues are handled.

Real estate funds are not readily redeemable, as investors may be required to provide advance notice and there may be specific dates on which redemptions can occur. The timing for delivery of the proceeds from redemption can be affected by the availability of cash within the fund. The risk level of a real estate fund is medium in nature, where the risk is commonly viewed as higher than a dividend fund but less than a balanced fund.

Balanced Funds

A balanced fund is one that targets a range of securities, including bonds, preferred shares and common shares. The fund's objective is to provide a combination of income, through bonds and preferred shares, and growth, through common shares held within the portfolio. The fund's investment strategy sets out the parameters relative to the percentage of holdings of different types of securities. The risk level of the balanced fund is described as medium in nature. A balanced fund is considered riskier than a bond or dividend fund, but has a lower risk than an equity fund.

Asset Allocation

The asset allocation fund can include a combination of bonds, preferred shares and common stocks, depending upon the fund manager's assessment of market conditions. The investment objective of asset allocation funds is similar to balanced funds: a combination of income and growth. The risk level is viewed as medium to high, depending upon the nature of the assets within the portfolio.

Equity Funds

An equity fund is comprised of stocks, which are mainly common shares. The types of common shares held within a fund can be very specific or can be quite broad depending upon the fund's objectives and investment direction. For example, a narrowly focused fund may specialize in one sector of the market such as financial services or health care. Returns on equity funds will vary. Some funds may target capital gains, while other funds may generate a more balanced combination of capital gains and dividends.

In general terms, equity funds are considered high risk because of the general volatility associated with stocks. Similar to the risk assessment associated with common stocks, the risk factor associated with different types of equity funds will vary. For example, an equity fund that targets high growth is considered to be at the highest risk level, similar to a specialty fund that might focus on a particular country or sector. As an offset to the high degree of risk, equity funds have the potential for higher returns than other less-risky types of funds.

International and Global Funds

International and global funds are generally comprised of securities from a variety of countries, where the securities may include stocks and bonds. The funds may be single focused and include only one type of security, such as stocks, or may include a combination of stocks and bonds. These types of funds are considered high risk and, because of the risk factor, they have the potential for higher returns. The composition of countries represented in the portfolio will also influence the risk assessment as will the currency exchange rate.

Speculative and Venture Funds

Speculative funds, also commonly referred to as venture funds, are comprised of shares of high-risk companies with high growth potential. These types of companies tend to be reasonably small where the risk of bankruptcy can be relatively high. This risk element trades off against the potential for substantial returns, particularly through capital gains. These types of funds tend to be viewed as those with the highest level of risk.

Risk/Return Summary

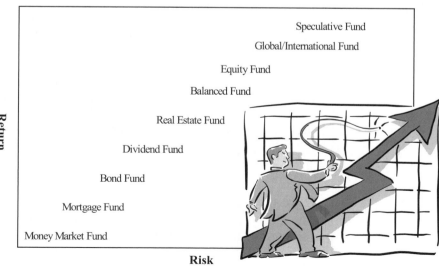

PERFORMANCE EVALUATION

Comparison

When assessing mutual fund performance, return on the fund is one result, but to truly measure performance it is important to understand how the fund's performance compares with similar funds or relevant indexes. The comparison should consider funds with similar objectives or an index with similar holdings. There are two main types of benchmark comparisons:

- *Peer group average:* assesses the returns of a select group of funds that have similar investment goals and policies.
- *Market index:* measures return of the market or a key segment of market.

Different segments of the financial markets can perform quite differently. Simply comparing one bond fund to another, or one stock fund to another, does not provide the investor with relevant benchmarks. Consider a bond fund — how many different types of bonds are available? The quality of the bonds, the maturities and the type of bond (government versus corporate) can deliver quite different performance results. To make a valid comparison when comparing a .fund to an index, the market sector plays a key role. The concept of risk and return is important in this discussion because there will be wide gaps if an investor considers only the numerical rate of return in isolation of the qualitative factors that influence risk relative to the investor's risk tolerance.

To enable these types of comparisons, an investor should look at peer group comparisons. To assess the performance of one mutual fund holding, a performance comparison should reference the results of competitive funds in the same peer group. Peer group reports should be looked at from a medium and longer-term time frame, as it minimizes the blips and extraordinary issues (both positive and negative) that could distort short-term results. To be valid, it is essential that comparisons be done on a similar time frame.

Independent companies that measure the performance of mutual fund companies commonly use a format termed *quartile rankings*. This type of report sorts the array of mutual funds according to their asset class, where all funds of a similar class are grouped into a common segment. The performance of all companies within that segment is compared, relative to others in the segment. The report works on quartiles, whereby the top 25% of the companies are ranked as performing in the first or top quartile. This same structure applies to the remaining three quartiles: those companies whose performance is between 50 and 75% are in the second quartile; those between 25 to 50% are in the third quartile, and the fourth quartile picks up the companies that performed in the bottom 25%. The reports compare historic performance and make comparisons based on short, medium and longer-term time periods. These types of reports are valuable when assessing a fund's overall performance, but it is important to reinforce that past performance of a fund is no indication of future performance.

The investor's goal is seldom so simple as to achieve the highest possible return, but is more likely aligned with an overall investment strategy that is targeted at the achievement of specific financial goals while undertaking an acceptable level of risk. The selection of mutual funds that form part of an investor's portfolio should not be done in isolation but needs to be considered in a manner similar to the acquisition of other securities that integrate into the investor's overall investment strategy. Investment mix, diversification, personal objectives, time horizons and risk tolerance must all be considered and incorporated.

Investment Risk

The incorporation of a variety of stocks and bonds into the asset composition of a mutual fund means that the mutual fund is subject to market volatility similar to the securities held within the fund. When investing in mutual funds, the general practice of investing for the long term should be a key consideration.

Mutual funds whose objective is to provide income will incorporate interest sensitive investments such as bonds and treasury bills. This type of fund is subject to interest rate and reinvestment risk. Market and business risk could be significant issues for equity-based funds, and could involve exchange rate and political risk, depending upon the nature of the fund.

Single-sector funds subject the investor to sector risk because of the high concentration of securities in a single industry. Sector funds lack the benefit of diversification and may expose the investor to industry related issues that could depress the fund's return.

Risk assessment cannot be done in isolation but instead should be incorporated into the investor's overall investment strategy.

DOUG

Thirty-year-old Doug has worked hard to accumulate $10,000 in savings. This is the most he has ever saved, and it represents his total savings, other than the $50,000 of equity in his home. Doug is determined to invest in non-registered mutual funds as he sees the value of starting a regular investment account.

The $10,000 is not required for ongoing living expenses and Doug feels strongly that it can be invested for the long term. He is concerned about capital preservation and is interested in a fund that provides a medium level of risk and a corresponding return.

An extensive understanding and knowledge of Doug's personal circumstances, including his current financial situation, risk tolerance and investment objectives, is important in the selection of appropriate mutual funds.

AVERAGE RETURN

The fund's annual return is reported after expenses, and incorporates the assumption that distributions have been reinvested in the fund.

PURCHASE/WITHDRAWAL MECHANISMS

Systematic Withdrawal Plan

A *systematic withdrawal plan* (SWP) is one where the investor sets up, with the fund company, a pre-arranged schedule of withdrawals from the investor's mutual fund account. The withdrawal is based on a pre-established time schedule, quite often monthly, where the company is authorized to make a withdrawal of a specific dollar amount or number of units. The funds withdrawn from the investor's mutual fund account are placed directly in her bank account or she receives a cheque from the fund company.

A systematic withdrawal plan can serve a variety of needs where a regular income flow is required, such as:

- minimum payment requirements out of a registered plan, such as a RRIF;
- a flow of funds needed to meet a debt obligation that entails a regular payment schedule (i.e., monthly car payment or monthly property tax payment); or
- the provision of funds to provide an ongoing income or income supplement.

A systematic withdrawal is established by the owner of the investment asset and can be increased, decreased or terminated at the investor's discretion. As such, it is highly flexible in meeting the investor's income needs.

> *DARLENE*
>
> Darlene retired this past year, when she turned age 58. While her gross monthly income of $1,800 from her company pension plan is valued, it does not provide Darlene with sufficient income on which to live. For this reason, Darlene plans to draw on her savings as needs arise.
>
> To help manage her cash flow, Darlene has decided to use a systematic withdrawal plan from her non-registered mutual funds as a means to cover her property taxes and supplement her income flow, for the upcoming year.
>
> Darlene has set up a pre-authorized payment for the property taxes, where the town in which she lives draws $230 from her bank account on the 15th of each month. To cover this $230 monthly payment and to provide an additional $500 monthly income supplement, Darlene has put an SWP in place that provides her with a net monthly withdrawal of $730 on the first of each month, from her non-registered mutual funds. The fund company automatically deposits this $730 in Darlene's bank account.

Note that each withdrawal of mutual funds, whether as a single lump sum amount or through an SWP, is considered a redemption of the underlying fund.

Cheque Writing

A number of fund companies now offer investors the opportunity to have cheque writing privileges on a money-market type of account. This type of service allows the fund companies to compete with other financial institutions because investors can have immediate access to funds while the funds are still earning a basic level of interest, an amount that exceeds many basic chequing accounts.

Dollar Cost Averaging

A common investment strategy is *dollar cost averaging*, where an investor invests a fixed amount of money on a regular basis, quite often monthly or quarterly, that is used to purchase mutual funds. As the price of the fund shifts, the investor will buy fewer shares in the months that the unit value increases and more shares in the months when the unit value declines. This strategy is commonly used when the price of a fund fluctuates, as the objective is to level out the average unit cost.

> *BONITA*
>
> Bonita uses dollar cost averaging to purchase units in XYZ fund, on a DSC basis. Her monthly bank withdrawals and unit purchases, for the first six months of this year, are summarized below (disregard sales commissions):
>
> | Month | Bank Withdrawal | XYZ Unit Price | # of Units Purchased |
> |-------|-----------------|----------------|----------------------|
> | Jan | $ 300 | $5.00 | 60.0000 |
> | Feb | $ 300 | $5.25 | 57.1429 |
> | Mar | $ 300 | $5.19 | 57.8035 |
> | Apr | $ 300 | $5.30 | 56.6038 |
> | May | $ 300 | $4.90 | 61.2245 |
> | June | $ 300 | $5.01 | 59.8802 |
> | Total | $1,800 | | 352.6549 |
>
> *continued . . .*

> *continued . . .*
>
> During the first six months, Bonita purchased 352.6549 units of XYZ fund. Her purchase price ranged from a low of $4.90 per unit to a high of $5.30. The average price of the units purchased during this time frame was $5.1041.
>
> Using dollar cost average, Bonita was able to smooth out the purchase price of the units. If Bonita had used the $1,800 to make a single purchase, her unit cost may have been higher or lower than the average cost of $5.1041. Note that on three purchase dates, Jan, May and June, Bonita's unit cost was equal to or lower than the average, while in February, March and April the purchase price exceeded the average.

STRUCTURE

A *fund management company* manages the day-to-day operations of the fund, and, in most cases, its investment portfolio. Management services include administrative services, research, portfolio management, legal services in connection with the prospectus and audit services.

The *portfolio manager* is responsible for the investment decisions of the fund, including the purchase and sale of securities and determining asset mix. Portfolio managers may be hired externally, may be internal managers, or may be a combination of both, and are guided by the fund's investment objectives as stated in the prospectus. The goal of all portfolio managers is to generate the best return for the fund's investors while operating within the fund's investment objectives.

The distribution of mutual funds occurs through *distributors*. Examples of distributors include:

- financial institutions such as banks, trust companies or credit unions who sell their own family or group of mutual funds;
- brokerage firms who sell a variety of mutual fund offerings, as well as other securities;
- mutual fund dealers who sell a variety of mutual fund offerings;
- mutual fund management companies, if registered as a dealer, may sell their own family or group of mutual funds; and
- independent financial advisors and consultants, who are appropriately licensed and also contracted with a mutual fund dealer as a mutual fund salesperson, may sell a variety of mutual fund offerings; and depending upon other licenses, may also offer other securities or insurance products.

A *registrar* is responsible for maintaining records relative to the tracking of securities that are issued and redeemed. Duties of the registrar include:

- maintaining a record of issued securities;
- verifying cancelled security certificates; and
- examining and recording the issue and replacement of certificates.

The *transfer agent* is responsible for maintaining investor information. Duties include:

- maintaining a register of unit holders;
- maintaining records of purchases and redemptions;
- disbursing distributions; and
- preparing and mailing income tax receipts.

In practice, most mutual fund companies combine the duties of the registrar and transfer agent.

A *mutual fund salesperson*, who must be appropriately licensed to sell mutual funds, may also be referred to as a *registered salesperson*. This role is permitted and/or required to:

- solicit sales;

- discuss mutual fund investment alternatives;
- distribute fund prospectuses and other sales materials;
- complete new client account applications; and
- accept client purchase and redemption requests.

A rule referred to as *know your client* (KYC) is intended to protect investors and must be followed by the mutual fund sales representatives. Mutual fund salespeople must complete/update a KYC questionnaire with the investor, quite often at the time of purchase of any mutual funds, as a means to ensure that the specific products are appropriate given the investor's personal circumstances. The salesperson must be fully aware of an investor's current financial situation, risk tolerance and investment objectives in order to act in the investor's best interest. KYC information normally includes information relative to the investor, such as:

- investment objectives and needs;
- investment knowledge level;
- risk tolerance;
- annual income;
- net worth;
- age;
- occupation; and
- information relative to the investor's spouse.

A role, referred to as a *custodian*, is responsible for the safekeeping of the cash and securities belonging to the mutual fund. Mutual fund assets must be held separate and apart from other assets of the mutual fund management company. The custodian receives all income earned by the fund and its portfolio and makes all payments on behalf of the fund. A custodial agreement between the fund and the custodian outlines how the custodian will hold the fund's assets and how the two parties will interact with each other. If securities are to be held outside of Canada, a sub-custodian agreement may be signed between the domestic custodian and a foreign custodian.

INCOME TAX IMPLICATIONS

Mutual Fund Trusts

A mutual fund can hold a variety of securities that includes such instruments as bonds, debentures, preferred shares or common stock. The mutual fund will buy and sell securities that may result in capital gains to the mutual fund itself. Each type of security owned by the mutual fund has its own income tax implications where the security may provide straight income that is fully taxable or where the security is considered to be a tax-preferred investment.

Investment income within a mutual fund retains its character when it is allocated to the investor. This can be an attractive feature, as investors can benefit from tax-advantaged investments such as capital gains and dividends. A capital loss realized within a fund (due to the sale of a capital asset) does not pass through to the investor but rather is used to reduce capital gains within the fund.

A mutual fund unit represents capital property owned by the investor. When an investor buys a unit of a mutual fund, the unit has an adjusted cost base (ACB) that is used in the calculation of any applicable capital gains or losses realized upon disposition of the unit and directly attributable to the investor. This type of transaction is completely separate from transactions within the mutual fund itself.

The mutual fund's net asset value per share is directly affected by any distributions made by the fund. A distribution from the fund to its unit holders creates an offsetting decrease in the value of the NAVPS. To avoid taxation within the mutual fund trust itself, distributions of allocated income must be made to the unit holders by mid-December.

CARLEY

Carley owned units of PQR mutual fund. When the NAVPS of the fund was $12, the fund made a distribution of $3. Immediately following the $3 distribution, the NAVPS for PQR was $9, which represents a $3 reduction due to the distribution.

Taxation of Allocations

Allocations that a mutual fund makes to investors who hold non-registered funds must be reported as income to the investor in the year of the allocation. The holder of the mutual fund units on the date of the allocation is the person or entity responsible for the tax.

This impact can be particularly disturbing to investors who make a fund purchase in the period just prior to year-end, and where the fund makes an allocation just prior to its year-end. The investor will be subject to tax on any allocations. It is often wise to time a purchase so that the investor avoids this type of scenario.

Participation in programs that provide for the automatic reinvestment of distributions does not change the tax consequence triggered by the allocation. Investors are still subject to any applicable tax consequences.

Mutual Fund Corporation

When a mutual fund operates under the structure of a corporation, investment income is not a direct flow through to the investor as with a mutual fund trust; instead, investment income is paid to the investor as ordinary dividends and capital dividends from the mutual fund corporation. As discussed in Module 6, the income tax consequences for the investor would be the same as for dividends or capital gains.

Unit 7
Segregated Funds

INTRODUCTION

The term *segregated fund* is used to describe a pool of investments that are held and managed separate from other assets of a life insurance company. These segregated funds, which have many similarities to mutual funds, are the investment side of any investment fund insurance product sold by life insurance companies. Only life insurance companies offer segregated funds. According to the *Income Tax Act* (the "Act"), a segregated fund is deemed to be owned by a trust where the policy owner, also referred to as the unit holder, is deemed to be the beneficiary of the trust. For simplicity throughout this unit, the terms *unit holder* and *policy owner* will be used interchangeably.

COMPARISON TO MUTUAL FUNDS

The following discussion highlights a number of similarities and differences between segregated funds and mutual funds. It is not intended to be a comprehensive summary, but simply highlight a few key areas important to the general positioning of these two similar but different products.

Similarities

Similar to mutual funds, segregated funds are a pool of investment assets where the securities held within the pool can be as diverse as with mutual funds. Segregated funds can include securities such as stocks, bonds or treasury bills.

Investors purchase and sell segregated funds as a unit of the fund, with each unit having a defined price, similar to that of a mutual fund.

As with mutual funds, professional money managers who have strong investment knowledge and expertise are charged with the responsibility for managing the fund's investment performance.

BCD SEGREGATED FUND

BCD segregated fund holds a variety of securities that have an aggregated market value of $50,000,000 on March 31. On this same day, the fund's liabilities totaled $500,000 and the total number of units outstanding was 1,500,000. The fund's net asset value was $49,500,000, which was calculated as:

Net asset value = (Market value of assets) - (Liabilities)

Net asset value

= $50,000,000 - $500,000

= $49,500,000

The net asset value per share (NAVPS) of the fund is $33, calculated as:

NAVPS = (Net asset value) ÷ (# of units outstanding)

NAVPS

= $49,500,000 ÷ 1,500,000

= $33

The net asset value per share (NAVPS) of BCD segregated fund on March 31 was $33.

Differences

Life Insurance

Segregated funds, which are less commonly referred to as *individual variable insurance contracts* (IVIC), are considered insurance products and are regulated by the *Uniform Insurance Companies Act* and not by any provincial securities act. Segregated fund products are sold only through individuals who are licensed to sell insurance products.

As a life insurance product, a segregated fund policy has an owner, annuitant and a beneficiary. The annuitant can be described as the measuring life against which contractual issues such as guarantees are measured. As such, a segregated fund policy has an owner and annuitant, where these two roles can be the same individual or different individuals, for non-registered policies. The owner retains the right to name the beneficiary. The owner and the annuitant must always be the same for a registered policy.

Guarantees

Segregated fund contracts include a guarantee of the principal. Unlike mutual funds where there is no guarantee of principal, segregated fund contracts are required by law to guarantee that at least 75% of the invested principal, less any withdrawals, will be returned to the policy owner upon maturity of the contact or upon death.

Many insurance carriers provide guarantees greater than 75% and it is not uncommon to see a 100% guarantee. A segregated fund contract matures on the date set by the insurance carrier. The maturity date cannot be less than 10 years after the contract was issued, and many carriers establish the date at 10 years, although a number higher than 10 years is quite possible.

For contracts where there is a flow of funds into the contract, beyond simply the initial deposit, the principal guarantee (deposit less withdrawals) cannot be less than 10 years after the date of each principal deposit. In other words, the maturity guarantee period normally tracks with each principal deposit.

For policies that have not yet matured and where the annuitant has not died, there are no guarantees. If a segregated fund policy is surrendered prior to the expiry of the guarantee period, the policy owner is entitled to receive the cash surrender value of the contract, with no guarantees triggered.

DOREEN

Doreen purchased a segregated fund policy on March 1, 2008, with a $25,000 deposit. She made two subsequent deposits of $25,000 each, into the policy on March 1, 2009 and March 1, 2010. Assume the policy provides the standard 75% guarantee upon maturity or death, and that the plan follows the minimum 10-year period for the guarantee. Doreen named herself as the policy owner and annuitant.

Death Benefit Guarantee

If Doreen dies on September 10, 2010, when the market value of her policy is $67,000 compared with the $75,000 of original principal deposited into the policy ($25,000 on each of March 1 of 2008 to 2010, inclusive), how much would Doreen's designated beneficiary receive?

The market value of Doreen's policy is $67,000, which is greater than the guarantee of $56,250 (75% × 75,000). Therefore, Doreen's designated beneficiary will receive $67,000.

If Doreen dies on November 3, 2010, when the market value of her policy is $52,000, how much would Doreen's designated beneficiary receive?

continued . . .

> *continued . . .*
>
> At a market value of $52,000, this amount is less than the death benefit guarantee of $56,250. In this case, Doreen's designated beneficiary would receive the $52,000 plus an additional $4,250 because the death benefit guarantee (75% of $75,000) is greater than the policy's current market value.
>
> **Redemption**
>
> Assume Doreen does not die, but rather remains healthy and decides to redeem the policy on September 10, 2010, when the market value of the policy is $67,000. In this case, Doreen will receive the $67,000 less any surrender charges. The early redemption of the policy prior to maturity means there is no guarantee of principal.

It is not uncommon for some insurance carriers to provide policy owners with the option to reset the principal guarantee at different points in time. While the specific terms may differ by carrier, generally this option provides the policy owner with the opportunity to re-establish the principal guarantee for death, or maturity, or both, at the current fair market value of the policy's assets. The re-setting of the principal amount generally accompanies an update to the guarantee period where it too re-starts.

Beneficiary Designation

The insurance aspect of segregated funds provides the policy owner with the opportunity to protect the funds from creditors of the policy owner, under specific conditions, by naming a beneficiary within a prescribed class, as discussed in Module 10; or by naming an irrevocable beneficiary.

From an estate planning perspective, the naming of a beneficiary provides the opportunity for the assets to pass to the named beneficiary without passing through the policy owner's estate, where the policy owner and annuitant is the same individual.

Assuris Coverage

Assuris provides insurance protection to policy owners of segregated funds with guarantees, should the insurance carrier become insolvent, as discussed in Module 8.

Process

When an investor purchases segregated funds, they do not acquire ownership rights in the funds themselves, which is the case with mutual funds. Rather, the normal process involves the insurance carrier's purchase and registration of the funds in the carrier's name, which then holds the funds for the sole benefit of the policy owner. The policy owner's rights are derived from the contract she holds with the insurance carrier. In simple terms, units of segregated funds are owned by segregated fund life insurance contracts, which are owned by individual policy owners.

The family of segregated funds offered by insurance companies typically is quite broad, with each fund having a specific investment objective. Segregated funds issue a *summary information folder*, which is the equivalent of a prospectus issued by a mutual fund company.

INCOME TAX IMPLICATIONS

Income Flow

The nature of segregated funds is that of an *inter vivos* trust, but where the Act requires that any taxable income earned by the trust must flow through to the beneficiaries of the trust. Investment income earned by a segregated fund retains its nature and flows through to the policy owners. This allows the policy owner to benefit from tax-advantaged investment income within the fund, such as Canadian dividend income and capital gains. Any income allocations are taxed to the policy owner in the year the allocation is made.

Capital losses also flow through to policy owners, which differs from the discussion in the mutual fund section where losses are used to offset capital gains and are not a direct flow through.

A unique issue with segregated funds is that income allocations from a segregated fund are made on December 31 to all those policy owners who owned units anytime during that year. This means that policy owners who owned funds but had redeemed those funds sometime during the year will be included in any allocation made to policy owners.

Disposition

When a policy owner purchases a segregated fund contract, the units of the contract have an adjusted cost base (ACB) attached to the contract. Acquisition fees for segregated funds are not deductible when the contract is first acquired and are not added to the contract's ACB. Rather, the acquisition fee is maintained separately and is reported by the insurance carrier to the policy owner as a capital loss at the time of disposition.

A disposition is deemed to have occurred should the policy owner redeem her units or a portion of her units. In addition, transfers during the owner's lifetime can also trigger a deemed disposition. A disposition of a segregated fund contract will trigger the realization of an accrued capital gain or loss.

Unique attributes of a segregated fund policy require closer examination relative to the tax consequences upon death.

ANN (1)

Ann and Robert, a married couple, have a non-registered investment portfolio with combined assets that total $275,000. To diversify their investment holdings, they decided to move $50,000 of savings from a maturing term deposit held by Ann to a segregated fund policy.

The couple did not want to transfer assets between themselves, so Ann will continue to be the owner of the segregated fund policy, but she does have the opportunity to name herself or someone else, such as Robert, as the annuitant of the plan. The annuitant is the life against which the insurance company will base the guarantees and, as such, ensure that the individual is younger than the maximum age for issue (most companies impose a maximum age for issue). In this case, Ann has chosen to name herself as owner and annuitant, and Robert as beneficiary.

A segregated fund policy matures upon the death of the annuitant and the policy owner is required to report any accrued capital gains. There are no options available for the owner to defer any gain.

ANN (2)

As owner and annuitant, if Ann should die, the policy matures and any accrued capital gain must be reported. Under this structure, there is no opportunity for the investment to roll to Robert on a tax-free basis.

As beneficiary, Robert will receive the proceeds of the death benefit under the policy directly without the assets passing through Ann's estate. However, Ann's death will trigger tax consequences that cannot be deferred through a spousal rollover.

If the owner and annuitant are different individuals, then there are two separate events that could occur: death of the owner and death of the annuitant.

- Upon the death of the owner where the owner is not the annuitant, the policy continues in effect and is treated like any other disposition of capital. In this case, ownership of the policy could transfer to the surviving spouse on a tax-free rollover basis.

- Upon the death of the annuitant where the annuitant is not the owner, the policy matures and the proceeds are paid out under the terms of the contract to the beneficiary. Any tax consequences arising from the accrued capital gain or loss accrue to the policy owner.

ANN (3)

Assume Ann names herself as owner and beneficiary, and Robert as annuitant of the policy.

If Ann should die, the policy will be treated like any other capital property and is eligible to be transferred to Robert on a tax-free rollover basis.

Alternatively, if Robert as the annuitant should die, the policy matures, and Ann, as policy owner, is responsible for any accrued capital gain or loss on the policy.

The appointment of a successor owner on a segregated fund policy can provide an estate planning opportunity. When the policy owner and annuitant are two different individuals, naming a successor owner provides a structure that allows the policy to pass directly from a deceased policy owner to the successor owner, without passing through the deceased owner's estate. This does not eliminate the tax consequence arising from death, but is a planning opportunity in other ways. Keep in mind that the annuitant is still living, so the death of the policy owner does not cause the contract to mature or terminate; ownership simply transfers to the successor owner, and the deceased owner incurs any relevant tax consequences. Spousal rollover would be possible under these circumstances.

For non-registered policies, the annuitant may be the same or different from the policy owner. Where permitted by the terms of the contract, consideration of a joint annuitant and the appointment of a successor owner are planning techniques that may provide value, depending upon the total circumstances. When undertaking any decisions, it is important to ensure that a strategy that achieves one objective does not cause the loss of another, perhaps equal or more important, benefit.

Guarantee

In situations where the guarantee under a segregated fund policy is greater than the market value at the annuitant's death or maturity, the insurance company will make up the difference, sometimes referred to as a *top-up*. The top-up amount is taxed as a capital gain. The investor will also incur a capital loss as the market value of the policy is less than the original capital invested. The capital gain on the top-up and the capital loss on the policy offset each other.

ELLEN

Ellen owned a policy where the original capital was $10,000. At maturity, the policy is surrendered when the market value is $8,000. The life insurance carrier pays Ellen a $2,000 top-up as a guarantee under the segregated fund policy. Ellen claims a $2,000 capital gain resulting from the receipt of the top-up and she claims a corresponding $2,000 capital loss relative to the policy's lost capital ($10,000 original investment less the $8,000 market value at surrender).

BENEFITS OF SEGREGATED FUNDS

As discussed earlier, segregated fund contracts offer a guarantee of principal upon maturity or death. This guarantee provides a level of comfort for investors who want to undertake market-sensitive investments, but with the knowledge that there is a provision for the return of original capital, less any withdrawals, up to a specified percentage in the event of premature death.

In many cases, the guarantee is more than the minimum 75% and may be as high as 100%, depending upon the company. In addition, the knowledge that the investor has this guarantee upon the plan's maturity provides reassurance to the investor that, should the value of the market-related investments fall, she is eligible for the guaranteed value upon the plan's maturity.

The benefit of a beneficiary designation, successor owner and creditor protection were discussed earlier.

Investment income earned by a segregated fund policy retains its nature and flows through to the policy owner. This allows the policy owner to benefit from tax-advantaged investment income within the fund, such as Canadian dividend income and capital gains/losses.

OTHER CONSIDERATIONS

Similar to mutual funds, segregated funds may have different commission structures, including a front-end load, deferred sales charge and no-load.

Like mutual funds, segregated funds also have management expenses that are referred to as MERs. From a consumer perspective, the MERs tend to be higher on segregated funds than on regular mutual funds, generally because of the guarantees incorporated into segregated fund policies. The higher the guarantee (i.e., 75% versus 100%), the greater the cost to the insurance carrier and therefore the greater the impact on the MER.

Most insurance companies restrict the sale of segregated fund policies to annuitant's under age 80, and sometimes even younger, because of the death benefit guarantee.

SELECTING APPROPRIATE FUNDS

The types and breadth of segregated funds are similar to mutual funds with similar risk and reward issues. Each segregated fund has a specific investment philosophy and investment style that should form part of any investor's selection process. Segregated funds should not be looked at in isolation, but should be considered relative to the investor's investment strategy as a whole. Issues such as the investor's objectives, risk profile, tax situation, time horizon, and unique needs satisfied by segregated funds all form part of the considerations when selecting appropriate investments.

Segregated funds may be suitable in a variety of situations, but each must be looked at relative to the investor's total circumstances. The following list provides a few examples of where segregated funds may be a suitable option.

- In situations where creditor protection is important, such as business owners, professionals, company officers or directors and self-employed individuals.
- Segregated funds may work well as part of an investor's estate plan, where the death benefit guarantee could be valuable.
- For individuals reaching retirement, the maturity and death benefit guarantee could be attractive.
- Conservative investors may find the maturity guarantees and re-set options attractive features.
- Aggressive investors may rely on the maturity guarantee as an offset against the risk associated with higher risk funds.

Unit 8

Other Investment Structures

EXCHANGE TRADED FUNDS

An *exchange traded fund* (ETF) is an investment fund which invests in a pool of securities which mirror a stock index such as the S&P500. ETFs trade on stock exchanges like regular common shares and can be purchased or sold at any time of the day in contrast to mutual funds, which can only be sold based on the net asset value of the mutual fund at the end of each day. There are no sales loads or investment minimums required to purchase an ETF. ETFs are usually not actively managed funds, which decreases the operating costs and reduces the amount of capital gains for tax purposes. ETFs may be attractive as investments because of their low operating and transaction costs, tax efficiency, and stock-like features, such as limit orders, short selling and options compared to mutual funds.

HEDGE FUNDS

Hedge funds are speculative funds which are allowed to use aggressive strategies that are unavailable to mutual funds, including selling short, leverage, program trading, swaps, arbitrage, and derivatives in an attempt to achieve above average returns. They utilize borrowed money to leverage their returns (and losses) and are not a very liquid investment. Investors in hedge funds pay a management fee as well as a percentage of the profits. Such funds are considered extremely risky and suitable for high-wealth investors only.

LABOUR-SPONSORED INVESTMENT FUNDS

Nature

Labour-sponsored venture capital corporations (LSVCCs), also referred to as *labour-sponsored investment funds* (LSIFs), were initially brought forth by the provincial governments in Quebec and Saskatchewan, and the federal government eventually embraced the concept. These types of investment corporations are designed as a means to elicit investment funds from the general public that are used as venture capital to support Canadian businesses. The term *labour* is used in the title because unions must be involved in the sponsorship of the funds.

Shares in an LSVCC or LSIF are eligible for a non-refundable federal tax credit and may also qualify for a provincial tax credit. The federal credit is very straightforward: 15% of the investment amount, based on the cost of acquiring the shares, is available as a credit up to a maximum investment of $5,000 (or credit of $750) in the taxation year that the investment is made, or in the previous taxation year if the investment is made in January or February. Many provinces provide additional tax credits on provincial taxes payable, but as discussed in Modules 5 and 6, each province sets its own tax schedule so the availability and amount of the tax credit may differ by province.

In a province where the provincial tax credit matches the federal tax credit, an investor may be eligible for combined annual maximum federal and provincial tax credits of $1,500 ($750 federal + $750 provincial), on an investment of $5,000. The federal tax credit requires that the investor maintain ownership of the funds for a minimum of eight years. The sale or disposition of funds prior to the end of the required holding period will result in the loss of previously claimed tax credits. Similar requirements are established in provinces that provide tax credits.

While there is no limit as to the number of shares an individual may purchase, there are annual limits relative to the maximum tax credit available to the investor. The tax credit must be used in the year in which it is earned; otherwise, any unused portion of the credit is lost.

Applications

Labour-sponsored investment funds may be purchased as non-registered funds, but are also qualified investments for a Registered Retirement Savings Plan (RRSP) and a Registered Retirement Income Fund (RRIF). The purchase of shares directly by the RRSP generates a non-refundable tax credit for the RRSP contributor on her personal income tax return. While it is possible to purchase the shares personally (as non-registered investments) and then transfer the shares as a contribution in kind into an RRSP, this route is less efficient from a total income tax perspective.

GARY

(a) Non-Registered Purchase

Gary has recently purchased $5,000 in shares of a labour-sponsored investment corporation. Assuming that Gary lives in a province that matches the federal government's non-refundable tax credit, and Gary is in a 45% marginal tax bracket, what is Gary's after-tax cost of the share purchase? (Disregard commissions.)

After-tax cost = Cost[1] × (100% - (Federal tax credit% + Provincial tax credit%))

After-tax cost

= $5,000 × (100% - (15% + 15%))

= $5,000 × 70%

= $5,000 × 0.70

= $3,500

The after-tax cost of Gary's investment is $3,500. This means that if his $5,000 investment grows in value, he will incur a substantial profit. Conversely, if his $5,000 investment falls in value, it would have to fall below $3,500 before he suffers a loss.

(b) Direct RRSP Purchase

Gary has decided to make a $5,000 contribution to a spousal RRSP on which his wife, Jennifer, is the annuitant. Gary's $5,000 contribution is used by the RRSP to purchase shares of an LSIF. Gary will be entitled to both the federal and provincial non-refundable tax credits associated with this contribution. In addition, he will benefit from the tax deferral associated with the $5,000 RRSP contribution.

After-tax cost = Cost[2] × (100% - (Federal tax credit% + Provincial tax credit%) - MTR)

After-tax cost

= $5,000 × (100% - (15% + 15%) - 45%)

= $5,000 × 25%

= $1,250

Gary's after-tax cost is $1,250.

(c) Non-Registered Purchase, Then Into an RRSP

If Gary purchases the shares personally, and then transfers the funds into his RRSP as a contribution in kind, he will lose the value of the tax credits when calculating his RRSP contribution amount.

TAX-SHELTERED INVESTMENTS

Limited Partnership

As discussed in Module 7, a limited partnership is a partnership that includes at least one general partner and one limited partner. Under provincial legislation, the majority of provinces have what is referred to as a *Limited Partnership Act*, or a similarly named act. This act allows for the creation of a limited partnership where one partner (a limited partner) contributes capital but is not involved in the ongoing business operations. The limited partner has limited liability for the debts and liabilities of the partnership.

---

[1] To a maximum of $5,000.

[2] To maximum of $5,000.

In a limited partnership, the general partner is responsible for managing the business operation and is personally liable for the debts and obligations of the partnership. The limited partner is generally a passive investor.

Characteristics

Liability

The characteristics and attributes of a *general partner* in a limited partnership are the same as those discussed relative to partners of a general partnership. A general partner of a limited partnership is personally liable for the debts and obligations of the partnership. Each general partner is jointly and severally liable. A judgment against the partnership can be satisfied with the assets of any one or all of the general partners, creating a significant exposure to financial risk for the general partner.

Limited partners are not liable for the debts and obligations of the partnership, provided they do not participate in the management of the partnership. The financial exposure for a limited partner is capped to the amount of his investment. To retain the status of a limited partner, the limited partner must remain passive and not participate in the active management of the business operation in any way.

Limited partnerships are commonly used as a structure for tax-advantaged investments where a corporation acts as the general partner (sometimes referred to as the promoter) and there are numerous limited partners whose only involvement is in the contribution of capital as a limited partner. While the general partner has unlimited liability, because the partner is a corporation which generally holds few assets, the liability in this structure is minimal. The limited partners are exposed to a loss of no greater than their contribution.

Taxation

The Act views the taxation of a limited partnership in the same manner as a general partnership with a few exceptions that are discussed in the following sections, entitled *At-Risk Rules* and *Income Attribution*.

At-Risk Rules

A limited partner is limited in the deduction of his allocation of partnership losses incurred by the partnership. The amount of allocated partnership losses that can be deducted by a limited partner is limited to the amount at-risk less certain deductions as defined in section 96 (2.1 to 2.7) of the Act.

The at-risk amount has a special calculation that looks at elements such as:

- limited partner's adjusted cost base of his partnership interest; and
- the amount of the partner's share of the current year's income and proceeds of disposition for resource property.

Losses that become non-deductible to a limited partner, because of the tax rules, can be carried forward indefinitely as deductions against future income from the same partnership.

Income Attribution

Income attribution rules come into play when a taxpayer loans, gifts or transfers funds to a spouse, common-law partner or a related minor who then uses the funds to invest in a limited partnership. In this situation, the Act specifies that income from the limited partnership is treated as property income, rather than business income, and is attributed to the transferor as described in subsection 96(1.8) of the Act.

> *BELINDA AND BOBBY*
>
> Belinda transferred $50,000 to her spouse Bobby, who used the money to purchase an interest in a limited partnership called Blades Marketing. Bobby's share of business income from his limited partnership in Blades Marketing was $8,000 during the first year of the investment.
>
> Because the funds for investment in Blades Marketing originated through Belinda, the $8,000 of business income will be deemed to be property income, attributable to Belinda.

Income Trusts

An *income trust*, also commonly referred to as an *income fund*, is a publicly traded trust that typically offers a long-term stream of income. There are generally three types of income trusts:

- resource royalty trusts, which typically focus on natural resources such as gas and oil;
- real estate investment trusts (REITs), which are discussed later under the real estate section; and
- infrastructure and business trusts, which are often industry-based and include such areas as power, pipelines, horticulture and telecommunications.

Income trusts have increased in popularity because they have become an easier method through which companies can access funds compared with the establishment of an IPO. Most Canadian income funds are typically structured as a mutual fund trust for tax purposes, and are considered Canadian property for investments in registered savings programs such as an RRSP or RRIF. Because an income fund is established as a trust, income flows through and is taxed in the hands of the investor, who is referred to as the unit holder.

The establishment of an income trust includes the preparation of a prospectus with specific disclosure requirements. Income funds tend to provide investors with a high yield, stable income. They are considered very liquid and are attractive because they offer the benefits of flow through income.

Income trusts do present one area of concern relative to the liability of the unit holder. If a trust were to go bankrupt or experience a catastrophic lawsuit, there is the possibility that the unit holder could be held responsible. While a shareholder of a corporation is insulated from the debts and liabilities of a corporation, the nature of an income trust is not that of a corporation but rather the relationship is structured as a trust. There is a significant question as to whether a unit holder can be held responsible for the debt obligations of the trust, if the trust is unable to fulfill its obligations.

The increased popularity of income trusts in the past few years suggests that many retail investors do not consider this liability to be a significant concern, yet it does not remove the risk. While there is debate as to whether a unit holder could be held ultimately responsible, the current laws suggest this is indeed possible. However, at the time of writing, limited liability legislation was enacted in Ontario, Alberta, Quebec and Saskatchewan.

Income trusts, also referred to as publicly-traded flow-through entities (FTEs), are an increasingly significant presence in Canadian business. These entities have grown dramatically over the past few years and now represent over $200 billion in market capitalization.

A major reason for the proliferation of these entities — and a major reason for the concern they have generated — is the unbalanced income tax treatment that applies to them and their investors. FTEs and their investors have enjoyed substantially lower combined income tax rates than large corporations and their shareholders. The combination of corporate income tax and the shareholder's tax on the dividend was significantly greater than the tax an otherwise identical investor would pay on income distributed by a FTE. In its 2006 Budget, the Government resolved this difference for those investors, by reducing the rate of federal tax on dividends from large Canadian corporations

In October 2006, the Government announced a measured response to the tax imbalance created by FTEs. Measures in the Tax Fairness Plan include:

- A Distribution Tax on distributions from publicly traded income trusts and limited partnerships. Under the new rules FTE's tax treatment will be more like that of corporations, and their investors will be treated more like shareholders. These changes took effect beginning with the 2007 taxation year for trusts that begin to be publicly-traded after October 2006, but will only apply beginning with the 2011 taxation year for those FTEs that were already publicly-traded.

Flow-Through Shares

The term *flow-through shares* describes a type of tax-advantaged investment related to shares of Canadian companies operating in resource exploration. When investors provide money to Canadian corporations, who meet specific criteria, for exploration or development work or for the acquisition of a resource property, certain tax deductions normally afforded to the corporation can alternatively flow through to the investor and can be used as a deduction in calculating the investor's income.

The intention is to help corporations finance riskier types of exploration and development with restrictions on the types and amounts of expenses eligible for this tax-advantaged treatment. This reference to "riskier types of exploration and development" is an important consideration. The price of stock in the resource industry is highly volatile, which tends to be compounded by the high-risk nature of the flow-through company's activities. There is a high risk that an investor could lose capital. Using the risk-reward theory, with high risk comes the opportunity for a corresponding high return, but this is not without substantial volatility and risk.

In some provinces, flow-through shares may have a minimum holding period, such as one year, and quite often the price of the shares is pushed higher than regular shares of the company because of the tax benefits. The price of flow-through shares is affected by price changes in the commodities market. If the price of the commodity has recently reached a low point, the volatility and risk will tend to be somewhat lower, whereas if the commodity price has recently peaked, there tends to be greater volatility and risk.

Flow-through shares provide immediate and long-term tax advantages to an investor, which tends to attract investors in the higher marginal tax bracket.

INTERNATIONAL INVESTMENTS

Foreign Holdings

While ownership in Canadian equities is common either directly, or indirectly through the ownership of mutual or segregated funds, the Canadian equity markets represent only a very small percentage of the total world markets. To be truly diversified, many investors extend their portfolios into international investments. This could be as simple as investments in American markets or could extend to other non-Canadian investments.

Investments outside of Canada carry the normal risk associated with a selected security, but also involve additional risk relative to social, political, and currency risk, as well as market volatility, access to public information and liquidity risk depending upon the country to which the investment is attached.

Investments in emerging markets often involve debt or equity securities. Typically, emerging markets are considered less mature, and are subject to higher inflation and volatile growth. Potential growth in this market can be attractive to some investors, but the application of the standard risk-reward philosophy suggests this market represents very high risk because of the high degree of volatility. Many emerging markets do not allow short selling, which can eliminate an effective hedging strategy. The volatility associated with investments in emerging markets is considered very high.

Taxation

From a Canadian perspective:

- interest income and dividends received from foreign investments are fully taxable; and
- capital gains or losses on foreign investments are eligible for capital gains treatment.

The tax withholding rates by foreign countries will differ, depending upon the country. To recognize foreign taxes that may have been paid on foreign income, Canadians are eligible to claim a foreign tax credit.

REAL ESTATE

Direct Holdings

Direct holdings in real estate can be segmented into broad categories, such as:

- residential;
- offices;
- retail; and
- industrial.

Quite often an individual owns the personal residence in which she lives, such as a house, condominium, co-operative or townhouse. The purchase and ownership of one's personal residence is typically the most substantial investment many individuals make in their lifetime. Home ownership tends to have a long-term horizon associated with the purchase decision. In addition to a home, some individuals may own a recreational property such as a cottage or hobby farm.

In addition to a direct investment in one's personal residence or recreational property, an investor may choose to make direct investments in any of the four broad categories of real estate. An individual investor may make a direct purchase of real estate or may be a partner in the direct purchase of real estate, which is then leased or rented to another individual.

FANNY

Fanny and two friends decided to pool their available resources to collectively purchase two town-house units as investment properties. Each of the three investors contributed $75,000 for a total of $225,000, which was used as the capital to purchase the two town-house units. The units were rented out to families.

Fanny's primary objective with this investment was the potential for capital appreciation.

The number of real estate transactions is very limited in comparison to stocks or bonds. The liquidity of a real estate investment is subject to the availability of an interested buyer at the time that the investor decides to dispose of the property and, for this reason, real estate is considered to have very low liquidity.

Mortgages

An investor may also make an indirect investment in real estate by holding a mortgage on another individual's property.

FRANK

This past May, Frank inherited $200,000, which he wanted to place in a broad array of investments. He chose to use $50,000 of the capital to lend as a mortgage on a private residential property. Frank's lawyer connected him with an individual who was looking for a private first mortgage.

Frank lent the $50,000 to Andrew Cummings as a mortgage on Andrew's personal residence. A schedule of monthly payments, based on a 25-year amortization period, was established at an interest rate of 5% for each of the first five years of the mortgage.

This schedule provided Frank with the opportunity to earn what he felt was a competitive rate of interest on the $50,000 and his exposure for losing the capital was negligible because the $50,000 was backed by a property valued at $210,000.

Real Estate Investment Trusts

Holdings in real estate can be established through the purchase of units in a *real estate investment trust* (REIT), which is a trust that owns real estate properties and/or mortgages. When a REIT includes aspects of both real estate property ownership and mortgages, it may be referred to as a hybrid REIT, whereas an equity REIT involves only the ownership of real estate (no mortgages) and a mortgage REIT involves only real estate debt (mortgages).

While REITs have operated in the United States for some time, they have only gained momentum in Canada during recent years. A number of REITs now trade on the Toronto Stock Exchange, where investors may purchase and dispose of units of the REIT in the same manner as a stock. Equity REITs that trade on large stock exchanges are often highly liquid and frequently pay quarterly distributions.

In simple terms, REITs are pools of funds, structured as an investment trust, that provide investors with a flow of income, although the flows will vary depending upon the assets held within the trust. For income tax purposes, REITS in Canada are considered mutual funds and are eligible investments for inclusion in registered portfolios such as an RRSP and RRIF. As discussed under the *Income Trust* section, REITS are established as a trust and, as such, investment earnings retain their character as they flow through to investors.

Distributions from a REIT are a combination of taxable income and a return of capital. A REIT is able to generate cash to payout as a return of capital because of its ability to shelter income with capital cost allowance. Any return of capital reduces an investor's adjusted cost base.

PRECIOUS METALS

Precious metals have played an economic role throughout recorded history. For example, gold reserves have, in the past, been used as the backing to a country's currency, although this is no longer the case.

Precious metals are used as a hedge against inflation during periods of economic uncertainty. Typically, the tangible nature of precious metals and wide international acceptance helps in the retention of value, despite inflation. During periods of severe political or international unrest, some investors may opt for precious metals because of their universal acceptance. Precious metals are generally considered liquid assets.

COLLECTIBLE ASSETS

In this case, the term *collectible asset* is used to refer to assets that investors tend to collect and hold such as coins, stamps, jewellery, antiques and artwork. With the exception of the antique category, these types of collectibles all fall within the definition of listed personal property, a special subset of personal-use property, as defined in section 54 of the Act. These types of assets tend to command high transaction costs where intermediaries often charge a substantial fee, such as a percentage of the transaction price, in order to bring together buyers and sellers.

Collectibles are considered to have very low liquidity as it can take some time to bring together a buyer and seller. A collectible does not provide the investor with any income earnings during the holding period, but rather any profit is attained through appreciation of the asset. It is common for investors to incur expenses for insurance and storage of collectible items, which will reduce any overall appreciation gain.

INSURANCE

The selection of appropriate investments for the cash value of a universal life (UL) insurance policy should take into consideration all of the issues discussed relative to the risk-reward philosophy. For example, an individual who has a very high risk tolerance may lean toward equity-based investments that have high volatility and high return opportunities. On the other hand, an investor who has a very low risk tolerance, and could not afford any erosion of capital, may lean toward guaranteed investments where the rate of return is known in advance. Others may look for a balance of investments that provide some opportunity for growth, but with a manageable level of volatility. UL policies are considered permanent insurance products and, as such, the selection of investments for the cash value will often include consideration of the longer-term nature of the product.

Unit 9
Self-Test Questions

QUESTIONS

Question 1

Albert has saved $25,000 in anticipation of his daughter's wedding that is scheduled for next fall, 18 months from now. He has made a commitment to provide $25,000 toward the cost of the wedding, and wants to ensure that any investment he undertakes with the savings between now and next fall does not impact negatively on his capital. Which of the following types of investments would be suitable for Albert?

1. Mutual fund — balanced fund

2. Segregated fund — bond fund

3. Mortgage-backed security

4. Term deposit

5. Preferred shares

6. GIC

    a. 4 only

    b. 4 and 6 only

    c. 1, 3 and 5 only

    d. 2, 5 and 6 only

Question 2

An investment in Canada Premium Bonds would be subject to which of the following types of risk?

1. Political

2. Liquidity

3. Marketability

4. Inflation

5. Business

    a. 4 only

    b. 2 and 4 only

    c. 1, 3 and 5 only

    d. 2, 4 and 5 only

Question 3

With regard to strip bonds, which one of the following statements is true?

    a. Strip bonds are sold at a premium and are redeemed at face value.

    b. The price of strip bonds tends to be fairly stable.

    c. There is no annual tax consequence associated with a strip bond when held as a non-registered investment.

    d. Strip bonds are typically not a suitable option if the investor requires a regular flow of income.

Question 4

With regard to corporate bonds, which of the following statements are true?

1. They represent an equity investment in the corporation.

2. Failure to make an interest payment to bondholders, when due, will put the corporation into default relative to the bond issue.

3. There is a higher risk associated with a corporate bond than a government bond.

4. Preferred shareholders have higher priority than bondholders over claims to corporate assets, in the event of company dissolution.

5. The stability associated with a corporate bond is dependent upon the financial strength of the issuer.

6. Bond interest payments lower the corporation's earnings before taxes.

    a. 1 and 4 only

    b. 2 and 6 only

    c. 1, 3, 4 and 5 only

    d. 2, 3, 5 and 6 only

Question 5

Martin is considering short selling shares of XYZ Company. With regard to this strategy, which of the following statements are true?

1. Short selling is a form of leverage.

2. It is likely that Martin expects the price of XYZ shares to increase.

3. Martin will be required to fulfill any margin call.

4. Martin will be required to replace the borrowed security.

5. If the price of shares does not move as Martin expects, his only cost is a small premium he paid for the right to sell short.

    a. 1 and 3 only

    b. 2 and 5 only

    c. 1, 3 and 4 only

    d. 2, 4 and 5 only

Question 6

When comparing common and preferred shares, which one of the following statements is **false**?

    a. Preferred shares typically do not include voting right, whereas many common shares do.

    b. Preferred and common shares rank equal in priority relative to claims to corporate assets, in the event of company dissolution.

    c. The company is under no legal obligation to pay dividends to preferred or common shareholders.

    d. The corporation must pay dividends to preferred shareholders before a dividend can be paid to common shareholders.

Question 7

Laura's broker called to advise her that the call option she owns on XYZ stock was "in-the-money". This means that:

    a. the market price is below the strike price.

    b. the market price is at the strike price.

    c. the market price is above the strike price.

    d. the market price exceeds the strike price by 15%.

Question 8

Leah used $25,000 to purchase HIJ mutual funds when the NAVP was $8.80. She and her broker agreed to a 1.5% front-end sales charge on this purchase. What is the total number of units Leah will purchase with this transaction?

    a. 2,784.0884

    b. 2,798.2986

    c. 2,840.9091

    d. 2,883.5063

Question 9

Rachel is considering the purchase of either mutual funds or segregated funds to add to her portfolio of non-registered investments. From the following list of considerations that she has compiled, which of the statements is/are true?

1. Segregated funds allow Rachel to eliminate exposure of the investment to probate fees.

2. The MER on segregated funds tends to be higher than on mutual funds.

3. Mutual funds offer different fee options, such as front-end load and deferred sales charges, whereas segregated funds are always sold on a no-load basis.

4. Segregated funds provide Rachel with a guarantee of principal, which is not available for mutual funds.

    a. 4 only

    b. 1 and 2 only

    c. 2 and 3 only

    d. 1, 2 and 4 only

Question 10

A labour-sponsored investment fund:

1. may be purchased as a non-registered fund.

2. is a qualified investment for an RRSP or RRIF.

3. qualifies for a federal tax credit and can be carried forward up to three years.

4. qualifies for a federal tax credit equal to 15% of the investment up to a maximum investment of $10,000.

    a. 1 and 2 only

    b. 3 and 4 only

    c. 1 and 3 only

    d. 2 and 4 only

QUESTIONS & SOLUTIONS

Question 1

Albert has saved $25,000 in anticipation of his daughter's wedding that is scheduled for next fall, 18 months from now. He has made a commitment to provide $25,000 toward the cost of the wedding, and wants to ensure that any investment he undertakes with the savings between now and next fall does not impact negatively on his capital. Which of the following types of investments would be suitable for Albert?

1. Mutual fund — balanced fund

2. Segregated fund — bond fund

3. Mortgage-backed security

4. Term deposit

5. Preferred shares

6. GIC

      a. 4 only

      b. 4 and 6 only

      c. 1, 3 and 5 only

      d. 2, 5 and 6 only

Answer: b

      ⇨   4. Term deposit

      ⇨   6. GIC

Reference: Integrated throughout the module

Question 2

An investment in Canada Premium Bonds would be subject to which of the following types of risk?

1. Political

2. Liquidity

3. Marketability

4. Inflation

5. Business

      a. 4 only

      b. 2 and 4 only

      c. 1, 3 and 5 only

      d. 2, 4 and 5 only

Answer: b

      ⇨   2. Liquidity

      ⇨   4. Inflation

Reference: Pages 16-21

Question 3

With regard to strip bonds, which one of the following statements is true?

　　a. Strip bonds are sold at a premium and are redeemed at face value.

　　b. The price of strip bonds tends to be fairly stable.

　　c. There is no annual tax consequence associated with a strip bond when held as a non-registered investment.

　　d. Strip bonds are typically not a suitable option if the investor requires a regular flow of income.

Answer: d

　　⇨　d. Strip bonds are typically not a suitable option if the investor requires a regular flow of income.

Reference: Pages 16-25 to 16-26

Question 4

With regard to corporate bonds, which of the following statements are true?

1. They represent an equity investment in the corporation.

2. Failure to make an interest payment to bondholders, when due, will put the corporation into default relative to the bond issue.

3. There is a higher risk associated with a corporate bond than a government bond.

4. Preferred shareholders have higher priority than bondholders over claims to corporate assets, in the event of company dissolution.

5. The stability associated with a corporate bond is dependent upon the financial strength of the issuer.

6. Bond interest payments lower the corporation's earnings before taxes.

　　a. 1 and 4 only

　　b. 2 and 6 only

　　c. 1, 3, 4 and 5 only

　　d. 2, 3, 5 and 6 only

Answer: d

　　⇨　2. Failure to make an interest payment to bondholders, when due, will put the corporation into default relative to the bond issue.

　　⇨　3. There is a higher risk associated with a corporate bond than a government bond.

　　⇨　5. The stability associated with a corporate bond is dependent upon the financial strength of the issuer.

　　⇨　6. Bond interest payments lower the corporation's earnings before taxes.

Reference: Page 16-22

Question 5

Martin is considering short selling shares of XYZ Company. With regard to this strategy, which of the following statements are true?

1. Short selling is a form of leverage.

2. It is likely that Martin expects the price of XYZ shares to increase.

3. Martin will be required to fulfill any margin call.

4. Martin will be required to replace the borrowed security.

5. If the price of shares does not move as Martin expects, his only cost is a small premium he paid for the right to sell short.

       a. 1 and 3 only

       b. 2 and 5 only

       c. 1, 3 and 4 only

       d. 2, 4 and 5 only

Answer: c

     ⇨   1. Short selling is a form of leverage.

     ⇨   3. Martin will be required to fulfill any margin call.

     ⇨   4. Martin will be required to replace the borrowed security.

Reference: Pages 16-35 to 16-36

Question 6

When comparing common and preferred shares, which one of the following statements is **false**?

       a. Preferred shares typically do not include voting right, whereas many common shares do.

       b. Preferred and common shares rank equal in priority relative to claims to corporate assets, in the event of company dissolution.

       c. The company is under no legal obligation to pay dividends to preferred or common shareholders.

       d. The corporation must pay dividends to preferred shareholders before a dividend can be paid to common shareholders.

Answer: b

     ⇨   b. Preferred and common shares rank equal in priority relative to claims to corporate assets, in the event of company dissolution. In fact, preferred shares rank higher than common shares.

Reference: Pages 16-38 to 16-39

Question 7

Laura's broker called to advise her that the call option she owns on XYZ stock was "in-the-money". This means that:

       a. the market price is below the strike price.

       b. the market price is at the strike price.

       c. the market price is above the strike price.

       d. the market price exceeds the strike price by 15%.

Answer: c

     ⇨   c. the market price is above the strike price.

Reference: Pages 16-41 to 16-46

Question 8

Leah used $25,000 to purchase HIJ mutual funds when the NAVP was $8.80. She and her broker agreed to a 1.5% front-end sales charge on this purchase. What is the total number of units Leah will purchase with this transaction?

    a. 2,784.0884

    b. 2,798.2986

    c. 2,840.9091

    d. 2,883.5063

Answer: b

    ⇨ b. 2,798.2986

Solution:

    ⇨ $(8.80) \div (1.0 - 0.015) = 8.9340$

    ⇨ $25,000 \div 8.9340 = 2,798.2986$

Reference: Pages 16-56 to 16-57

Question 9

Rachel is considering the purchase of either mutual funds or segregated funds to add to her portfolio of non-registered investments. From the following list of considerations that she has compiled, which of the statements is/are true?

1. Segregated funds allow Rachel to eliminate exposure of the investment to probate fees.

2. The MER on segregated funds tends to be higher than on mutual funds.

3. Mutual funds offer different fee options, such as front-end load and deferred sales charges, whereas segregated funds are always sold on a no-load basis.

4. Segregated funds provide Rachel with a guarantee of principal, which is not available for mutual funds.

    a. 4 only

    b. 1 and 2 only

    c. 2 and 3 only

    d. 1, 2 and 4 only

Answer: d

    ⇨ 1. Segregated funds allow Rachel to eliminate exposure of the investment to probate fees.

    ⇨ 2. The MER on segregated funds tends to be higher than on mutual funds.

    ⇨ 4. Segregated funds provide Rachel with a guarantee of principal, which is not available for mutual funds.

Reference: Pages 16-68 to 16-73

Question 10

A labour-sponsored investment fund:

1. may be purchased as a non-registered fund.

2. is a qualified investment for an RRSP or RRIF.

3. qualifies for a federal tax credit and can be carried forward up to three years.

4. qualifies for a federal tax credit equal to 15% of the investment up to a maximum investment of $10,000.

      a. 1 and 2 only

      b. 3 and 4 only

      c. 1 and 3 only

      d. 2 and 4 only

Answer: a

      ⇨   1. may be purchased as a non-registered fund.

      ⇨   2. is a qualified investment for an RRSP or RRIF.

Reference: Pages 16-74 to 16-75

Unit 10
Module 16 Exercises and Case Study

MODULE 16 EXERCISES

1. Determine if the following statements are True or False. If the statement is False, explain why.

    a. A bond is secured by the general credit of the issuing company and is considered to be riskier for an investor than debentures.

    b. A bond that trades at a price above its face value trades at a discount.

    c. Investment grade bonds are ranked as BBB and above by DBRS.

    d. A margin call is a request from a dealer for additional funds to cover a margin deficiency.

    e. A stock split increases a shareholder's proportion of the company.

    f. Strip bonds are sold at a discount to the face value of the bond and are redeemed at face value.

    g. A cash dividend is normally paid to shareholders when a company is going out of business.

    h. When an investor owns an option to sell a specific security, it is called a call option.

    i. Mutual fund investment losses are covered by government insurance.

    j. Labour-sponsored investment funds are considered more risky than investing in a well-balanced mutual fund.

2. Match the following terms with their definition.

    _____ Treasury bill

    _____ Commercial paper

    _____ Bankers' Acceptance

    _____ GIC

    _____ Mortgage-backed securities

    a. Debt issued by banks, trust companies that are guaranteed by the government.

    b. A negotiable, short-term corporate promissory note.

    c. Highly liquid, safe, short-term debt instruments issued by the federal government.

    d. A short-term promissory note issued by a corporation bearing the unconditional guarantee of a major chartered bank.

    e. Debt issued by banks, trust companies or other financial institutions that guarantee investors a fixed rate of interest for a set term.

3. Explain the different taxation effects for treasury bills, commercial paper, and GICs if they are held to maturity compared to sold prior to maturity.

4. What is the difference between a bond's coupon interest rate and the market interest rate?

5. What factors affect the coupon rate offered on a bond?

6. George purchased two bonds. Bond A, with a coupon rate of 6%, was bought at a discount of $200 three years ago and was held to maturity this year. Bond B, dated January 1, 20X5 with a coupon rate of 7%, was purchased January 1 at face value, but sold prior to maturity on May 30 for $900. Calculate the amount George will be taxed on each bond.

7. Explain the differences between extendible, retractable, convertible and callable bonds. Which of the bond types benefit the bondholder more than the bond issuer?

8. Explain the two ways in which an investor who holds common stock generates investment returns.

9. Why would a company issue a stock dividend *versus* a cash dividend?

10. What is the importance of the ex-dividend date to the value of a stock?

11. When would an investor use a short-selling strategy?

12. Why would a company choose to issue common or preferred shares instead of corporate bonds?

13. Explain when an investor would use a call option, a put option or a straddle investment strategy.

14. Compare and contrast the characteristics of warrants and call options.

15. Discuss the reasons why an investor would invest in mutual funds instead of individual stocks?

16. Mutual funds are typically classified as income, growth, and growth and income funds. What factors are used to classify the different types of mutual funds?

17.   1. Classify the following mutual funds as
   a. (1) low risk/low return;
   b. (2) medium risk/medium return; or
   c. (3) high risk/high return,
   2. Identify each as an income, growth, or growth and income type of mutual fund.

Example: mortgage fund = (1), income
   - money market fund _____
   - equity fund _____
   - speculative fund _____
   - bond fund _____
   - balanced fund _____
   - dividend fund _____

18. Discuss the main similarities and differences between segregated funds and mutual funds.

19. What are the income tax implications of segregated funds?

20. Discuss four characteristics of LSIFs.

CASE STUDY — KIMMI AND MARC'S INVESTMENTS

Marc and Kimmi were referred to you by one of your current clients. The couple tell you that although they have purchased investments from several different mutual fund salespeople, they have never had a comprehensive financial plan prepared. Marc and Kimmi are both 33 years old, and were married eight years ago.

Marc's Investments, Registered

Marc has one self-directed RRSP account. He purchased $20,000 of units in the Wondergrowth International Small Cap Fund two years ago, and bought $10,000 of units in the Wondergrowth Venture Labour Sponsored Fund last year. Marc's pension plan assets are managed by the Moon Insurance Company and are distributed as follows:

- $8,000 Moon Canadian Mortgage Fund

- $4,000 Moon Canadian Dividend Fund

Marc's Investments, Non-Registered

Exactly one year ago, Marc maxed out his $10,000 line of credit at BigBank and then invested the proceeds in a direct trading account at the InternetTrade online brokerage firm. He invested the proceeds as follows:

- $6,000 in common shares of XYZ Communications (purchased for $5,000)

- $10,000 in the Soaring Investments Precious Metals Fund (book value of $4,000)

- $5,000 in the Soaring Investments Global Equity Fund (book value of $1,000)

Kimmi's Investments, Non-Registered

Kimmi has a self-directed RRSP at BigBank, and her holdings are as follows:

- $5,000 Government of Canada Bond (4.5% interest, matures in 2013)

- $4,906 Province of Ontario Bond (strip bond, matures in September 2010, yield to maturity of 2.5%

- $5,000 XYZ Communications Corporate Bond (5% interest, matures January 1, 2020)

Risk Profile

Both Kimmi and Marc describe themselves as conservative investors, and they are uncomfortable seeing the value of their portfolios change dramatically over the short term.

Required

a. What types of questions would you ask Kimmi and Marc to comply with the "Know Your Client" rule?

b. Comment and make recommendations, if appropriate, on Kimmi's investments and Marc's current portfolio in regard to their stated risk profile.

c. Explain how Marc would be taxed if he sold his Soaring Investments Global Equity Fund.

d. Explain how Kimmi is taxed on the interest she earns on the Government of Canada Bond.

e. Calculate the market price of Kimmi's XYZ Communications Corporate Bond investment if current market interest rates are 6%. Assume it is January 1, 2010 today. Explain why the current market price is different than the face value of $5,000.

Topical Index

CCH/ADVOCIS
EDUCATION PROGRAM

COURSE 4
WEALTH MANAGEMENT AND ESTATE PLANNING

MODULE 17

INVESTMENT PLANNING

Module 17
INVESTMENT PLANNING

Module 17
Investment Planning

LEARNING OBJECTIVES

✓ Understand, explain and apply a working knowledge of the different types of active and passive investment strategies.

✓ Explain and demonstrate an in-depth knowledge of the concept of investment diversification, including its importance and various methodologies through which diversification can be achieved.

✓ Understand, explain and apply an in-depth working knowledge of the concept of leverage including its advantages and disadvantages.

✓ Discuss and demonstrate a solid comprehension of the attributes and concepts associated with fundamental and technical analysis.

✓ Demonstrate a comprehensive working knowledge of various investment returns, including current yield for stocks and bonds, yield-to-maturity and market value of bonds.

OVERVIEW

The general investment principle that risk and return are interrelated is evident across the returns of various investment products. Fixed-income products, such as treasury bills and GIC products, provide lower average returns to the investor than products such as common shares. The low level of risk, close to risk-free, of treasury bills provides the investor with known information, such as the investment return, which takes place in a relatively short time frame. There is little uncertainty with a treasury bill. On the other hand, common shares represent a much greater unknown for the investor, so in return for taking on this additional risk, the investor demands a higher level of return. There is a clear trade-off between risk and return.

Given the variance in risk and return, is there a better or more preferred security? At a broad level, the answer to this question is no. Each product offers unique features, elements, risks and returns that will be a good fit in some situations and not a good fit in others. On its own, a product cannot be judged as good or bad, but rather needs to be considered relative to a specific investment situation.

To help clients manage their investments, advisors need to have a solid comprehension of the client's objectives and personal circumstances. They must have a good grasp of the different assets that are available for investment purposes and be skilled at evaluating investments to determine the attractiveness of an asset relative to the given set of circumstances.

This module continues to build on the knowledge gained in Modules 15 and 16. As well, you will have acquired important knowledge in earlier modules, such as many tax-related issues in Modules 5 and 6, that will not be repeated in the investment modules but are assumed to be a prerequisite foundation.

BEHAVIOURAL FINANCE

Another investment planning area a financial planner should be aware of is behavioural finance. Behavioural finance studies the relationship between psychology and money, examining how one's perceptions, desires, and fears affect the financial decision making process. If advisors can learn to recognize and understand what drives people to make irrational investment decisions, they may be able to prevent both themselves and their clients from making these mistakes. Those interested in reading more on the subject should consider "Beyond Greed and Fear", written by Hersh Shefrin, and published by the Oxford University Press in 2002.

Heuristics

Heuristics are rules of thumb, mental shortcuts, guidelines, or strategies which people use to solve problems and make decisions. Behavioural finance is interested in how relying on heuristics may lead to biases and/or errors in judgment. The three key elements are: availability, representativeness, and anchoring.

Availability

When asked to assess the probable frequency of an event, people tend to base their answer on recently acquired information. This heuristic helps to explain why new information can have a short-term, disproportionate effect on the price of a company's shares. If a company announces particularly good first quarter results, for example, it will be widely reported and the share price may surge temporarily, but unless these results are indicative of a fundamental change in the company, the share price is likely to revert to its previous level.

Representativeness

If someone is asked to predict the likelihood that A belongs to category B, they will often think something similar — a comparable known thing or experience — and base their response on that. For example, one may be inclined to think that simply because a firm shares some of the traits of, and is in the same industry as, under performing companies that it is also a poor investment.

Anchoring and Adjustment

This describes a person's tendency to focus heavily on, or anchor to, one specific piece of information or reference point, and adjust expectations from there. An investor may not react appropriately to a positive earnings announcement from a company that, in the past, did not perform very well. If she ignores fundamentals and dismisses the improvement as temporary, she may miss out on an opportunity to buy because she has mentally anchored the stock price at a low level.

Prospect Theory

The "Prospect Theory" attempts to explain how people make choices when they are confronted with risk, or when an outcome is unknown. Basically, people prefer sure things, but they also found that the pain people experience as a result of a loss is stronger than the pleasure they derive from an equal gain. It may feel good to find a $100 bill, but it hurts more to lose one. This phenomenon is called *loss aversion*. Another example occurs when an investor holds on to investments that have lost a significant amount of value in hopes that the stock will increase in the future and she will break even.

Endowment Effect or Divestiture Aversion

If people already own something, they attribute a higher value to it. As a result, they will demand more to give up an object they already possess than they would be prepared to pay to acquire it. For example, a home owner may expect to sell her home for a higher price than comparable homes because she thinks it is worth more.

Status Quo Bias

Given the choice people prefer to stick with the *status quo* even though it is no more attractive than the other options available to them. For instance, if the employer's contributions to a defined contribution pension plan are automatically deposited into one fund, members may be more likely to remain in that fund even though it is unsuitable given their financial circumstances. *Status quo* bias is also tied to the concept of loss aversion, since people may fear the loss of the *status quo* more than they value the potential gain that could result from making change.

Overconfidence

When people are overly confident in their ability to make a rational decision, or an accurate prediction about the direction the stock market is heading, they may be prepared to accept more risk than the situation really warrants. Overconfidence can also cause investors to under-react to new information, fixed in a belief that their initial investment choice was a good one. One way to deal with overconfidence is to eliminate part of decision making process. Rather than try to select individual securities, the investor can purchase the entire market through an index fund, for example.

Demographics

A person's age, culture, social and educational background may also affect the ability to make decisions. A study found that highly-educated males who are nearing retirement, who have received investment advice, and who have experience investing for themselves, tend to have a higher certainty level and are therefore more prone to overconfidence.

Escalation Bias

Once someone has made a decision they may remain emotionally attached to it, becoming more even committed despite being presented with new information that proves their initial choice was a poor one. It explains why, instead of selling, investors will ride losing investments into oblivion, pouring new money into a losing and doomed investment while telling themselves that they are "averaging down" and buying the stock a bargain price. Investors can counteract escalation bias by consistently re-evaluating their portfolio using pre-determined, fixed criteria, e.g., the investor decides she will only hold shares that have P/E Ratio less than X, or by asking an independent person for an opinion.

Mental Accounting

Many people do not see their finances as a whole, but instead divide their funds into several separate accounts, assigning a specific purpose to each one. The rules of mental accounting are not neutral — the source of the funds affects how they are spent. For example, if someone were to receive a $1,000 tax refund, she may have no qualms spending it on an expensive holiday. She would be reluctant, however, to withdraw the very same $1,000 from her retirement savings.

Herd Mentality

The human tendency to follow the actions of the larger group is sometimes called the herd mentality, herding, or crowding. The most recent Canadian example of herding is the widespread enthusiasm for Bre-X, a mining company which in the early and mid-1990s claimed to have found a massive gold deposit in Busang, Indonesia, which increased the stock price widely. Eventually, the gold find was discovered to be untrue and the company went bankrupt.

Like mental accounting, herding contradicts traditional economic theory, which suggests that fundamentals and the law of supply and demand regulate prices, and that agents act independently of others.

Unit 1
Measuring Return

INTRODUCTION

There is no single methodology used for calculating investment returns achieved through different investment alternatives. This section looks at methods for measuring investment return for a variety of investment options including treasury bills and bonds. The concept of duration is explored followed by a discussion regarding the valuation of stocks.

TREASURY BILLS

Quoted Yield

Treasury bills are purchased at a discount and mature at face value. The difference between the purchase price and maturity value is used to calculate the discount rate and quoted yield. For example, a one-year $1,000 treasury bill that is purchased for $950 has a discount rate of 5.3% ($50 ÷ $950). It is important to note that the $50 of earnings is based on the original investment of $950, not the maturity value of $1,000.

The *quoted yield* on a treasury bill is based on the discount rate and is derived from the formula:

Quoted Yield

= (((Value at end of period) - (Value at beginning of period)) ÷ (Value at beginning of period)) × (365 ÷ Days to maturity) × 100

= (((Face value) - (Purchase price)) ÷ (Purchase price)) × (365 ÷ Days to maturity) × 100

The quoted yield is a simple interest rate that does not take into account the reinvestment of the interest earned on the investment instrument. When working with Canadian T-bill yield calculations, the formula uses a year based on 365 days.

This same yield concept applies to a commercial paper.

HERMAN (1)

Herman purchased a 180-day Canadian treasury bill for $98,900 with a maturity value of $100,000. What is the quoted yield on Herman's T-bill?

The quoted yield is 2.2554%.

Quoted Yield = (((Face Value) - (Purchase price)) ÷ (Purchase price)) × (365 ÷ Days to maturity) × 100

= (($100,000 - $98,900) ÷ $98,900) × (365 ÷ 180) × 100

= 2.2554%

Purchase Price

If we know a particular quoted yield, then we can determine the purchase price.

Purchase price = Face Value ÷ (1.0 + ((Quoted yield) × (Days to maturity) ÷ 365))

HERMAN (2)

Herman wanted to purchase a 180-day Canadian treasury bill with a quoted yield of 2.2554% and a maturity value of $100,000. What is the purchase price on Herman's T-bill?

The purchase price of Herman's T-bill is $98,899.98.

Market Price

= Face Value ÷ (1.0 + ((Quoted yield) × (Days to maturity) ÷ 365)

= $100,000 ÷ (1.0 + (2.2554% × 180 ÷ 365))

= $100,000 ÷ (1.0 + (0.022554 × 0.49315))

= $100,000 ÷ (1.0 + 0.0111225)

= $98,899.98

HERMAN (3)

Herman purchased a 120-day Canadian treasury bill for $99,250 with a maturity value of $100,000. If there are 30 days remaining on Herman's T-bill, and the quoted yield for 30-day T-bills is 1.2144%, what is the market price of Herman's T-bill?

The market price of Herman's T-bill is $99,900.30.

Market Price

= Face Value ÷ (1.0 + ((Quoted yield) × (Days to maturity) ÷ 365)

= $100,000 ÷ (1.0 + (1.2144% × 30 ÷ 365))

= $100,000 ÷ (1.0 + (0.012144 × 0.082192))

= $100,000 ÷ (1.0 + 0.000998)

= $100,000 ÷ 1.000998

= $99,900.30

U.S. Treasury Bills

When working with yield calculations for U.S. T-bills, a year is based on 360 days, not 365. This slight variance from the calculation for Canadian T-bills results in a slightly higher yield for comparable U.S. T-bills. As with any investment held in a foreign currency, a U.S. T-bill is subject to foreign exchange risk.

HERMAN (4)

If the bond Herman purchased in the Herman (2) SNAP were a U.S. bond, the market price would be $98,884.88.

Market Price

= Face Value ÷ (1.0 + ((Quoted yield) × (Days to maturity) ÷ 360)

= $100,000 ÷ (1.0 + (2.2554% × 180 ÷ 360))

= $100,000 ÷ (1.0 + (0.022554 × 0.50))

= $100,000 ÷ (1.0 + 0.011277)

= $98,884.88

Effective Annualized Yield

The calculation of effective yield takes into account the benefit of compounding. For T-bills shorter than one-year, effective yield will be higher than the quoted yield because the calculation assumes a reinvestment of the earnings.

HANNAH (1)

Hannah bought a 91-day T-bill, issued by the federal government, for $99,350. Calculate the effective annualized yield on Hannah's T-bill.

The quoted yield on Hannah's T-bill is 2.6242%.

Hannah's effective annualized return on this T-bill is 2.6502%, which is marginally higher than the quoted yield of 2.6242%.

We know the following information:

- P/YR = 1
- xP/YR = 0.249315068 [91 ÷ 365]
- PMT = 0
- FV = 100,000
- PV = -99,350

SOLVE FOR I/YR, which equals 2.6502

HANNAH (2)

Hannah also bought a 181-day T-bill, issued by the federal government, for $9,800.25. Calculate the annualized effective yield on Hannah's T-bill.

The quoted yield on Hannah's T-bill is 4.1102%, while the effective annual yield is 4.1528%.

Quoted Yield

= (($10,000 - $9,800.25) ÷ $9,800.25) × (365 ÷ 181) × 100

= 4.1102%

Effective Yield

We know the following information:

- P/YR = 1
- xP/YR = 0.495890411 [181 ÷ 365]
- PMT = 0
- FV = 10,000
- PV = -9,800.25

SOLVE FOR I/YR, which equals 4.152795616

BONDS

Market Price

Determining a bond's market value, also commonly referred to as *current market price*, is nothing more than determining the present value of the future expected cash flows associated with owning the bond. The cash flows, of course, come in two forms: the semi-annual coupon payment and the redemption of the bond at its face value when it reaches maturity. In other words, the value of the bond is nothing more than the present value of the stream of income payments and the lump sum payment upon maturity. With this information, the current market price of a bond is easily calculated using time value of money calculations.

HARRIETT

Harriett is considering the purchase of a Nomega Corp bond with a face value of $20,000 and 20 years remaining to maturity. The coupon on the Nomega bond is 5%, while the current market interest rate is 7%. What price should Harriett pay for the Nomega bond? (Disregard taxes.)

Based on these details, Harriett should be willing to pay $15,728.99 for the Nomega Corp bond.

We know the following information:

• P/YR = 2	{interest is paid 2 times each year}
• xP/YR = 20	{20 years to maturity}
• I/YR = 7	{use the current market rate}
• PMT = 500	{($20,000 × 0.05) ÷ 2}
• FV = 20,000	{at maturity Harriett will receive $20,000}
• MODE = END	

SOLVE FOR PV, which equals -15,728.9855

The payment is derived by multiplying the face value of $20,000 by the coupon rate of 5%, and dividing the result by two to reflect the semi-annual nature of bond coupon payments. The I/YR is arrived at by using the prevailing market interest rate of 7%. The bond has 20 years left until maturity.

If Harriett pays $15,728.99 for this bond and the bond pays her $500 twice each year for 20 years, along with a return of the par value of $20,000 at the end of 20 years, the bond will have generated a 7% annual nominal return, which is the prevailing market rate.

The annual effective rate of return on this bond is 7.12%.

We know the following information:

- P/YR = 2
- I/YR = 7.0
- EFF% = 7.1225% [[SHIFT] EFF%]

The market price of a bond moves in the opposite direction to interest rates. As prevailing interest rates rise, the price of the bond will decrease. As prevailing interest rates decrease, the market price of the bond will increase.

JOAN

Joan owns a 15-year bond issued with a face value of $100,000 and a coupon rate of 5%. A buyer is interested in Joan's bond at a time when the prevailing market interest rate is 3.5%, and there are five years left until the bond reaches maturity. What is the current market price of Joan's bond? (Disregard taxes.)

The prevailing interest rate is less than the current coupon rate, so Joan can expect to realize a premium when she sells the bond. Given the information described above, the current market price of the bond is $106,825.92.

We know the following information:

- P/YR = 2
- xP/YR = 5
- I/YR = 3.5
- PMT = 2,500
- FV = 100,000
- MODE = END

SOLVE FOR PV, which equals -106,825.9172

If Joan sells the bond at its current market price, she will realize $106,825.92 on the sale of this bond. The buyer can afford to pay a $6,825.92 premium over face value ($106,825.92 - $100,000) because the semi-annual interest payments are based on an amount higher than the prevailing market rate.

We can see that this bond sells at a premium to its face value, which is what we would expect from a bond that has a 5% coupon rate, which is substantially higher than the market rate of interest of 3.5%.

Note that the market value of a strip bond is calculated in a similar manner, using time value of money calculations. When entering the data into the time value formula, the payment amount is entered (into PMT location) as zero, because there are no coupon payments associated with the strip bond. The other item that may differ between a regular bond and a strip bond is the compounding periods. With most normal bonds, two compounding periods are incorporated into the formula because coupon payments typically occur semi-annually. With strip bonds, there is no flow of coupon payments. For purposes of this course, assume one annual compounding period is used when calculating the market value of a strip bond, unless otherwise noted in the SNAP or question details.

Current Yield

The phrase *current yield* refers to the rate of return on a bond, which is calculated using the bond's current market price. Current yield does not consider the reinvestment of coupon payments received by the bondholder and does not incorporate any capital appreciation or loss that may occur (i.e., bond purchased at 92 but it matures at 100 or bond purchased at 105 but is disposed of at 98).

This calculation is helpful to an investor who is assessing his current annual income from a specific investment.

Current Yield = ((Annual interest payment) ÷ (Current market price)) × 100

HAROLD (1)

Harold owns a 20-year bond, with a $25,000 par value, issued by T-Corp. The bond has a coupon rate of 7.3% and a current market value of $26,500. What is the bond's current yield?

Annual Interest Payment

= $25,000 × 0.073

= $1,825.

Note: The annual interest payment is based on the bond's par value and is not affected by the current market price.

Current Yield

= ((Annual interest payment) ÷ (Current market price)) × 100

= ($1,825 ÷ $26,500) × 100

= 0.0689 × 100

= 6.89%

The current yield on Harold's T-Corp bond is 6.89%. The current yield should not be confused with the coupon rate. In this case, the coupon rate is higher than the actual current yield on the bond.

HAROLD (2)

Harold also owns a 15-year bond, with a $25,000 par value, issued by Alpha Corp. The bond has a coupon rate of 8.6% and a current market value of $20,000. What is the bond's current yield?

continued . . .

---

continued . . .

Annual Interest Payment

= $25,000 × 0.086

= $2,150

Current Yield

= ((Annual interest payment) ÷ (Current market price)) × 100

= ($2,150 ÷ $20,000) × 100

= 0.1075 × 100

= 10.75%

The current yield on Harold's Alpha Corp bond is 10.75%, whereas the coupon rate is 8.6%.

Yield-To-Maturity

The most widely used measure of yield in the bond market is *yield-to-maturity*, which measures the total rate of return on a bond over its lifetime. Conceptually, the yield-to-maturity is merely a calculation of the bond's internal rate of return (IRR). Specifically, the calculation factors are the price paid for the bond, the accrued interest income including the semi-annual nature of the coupon payments, payment of the face value of the bond at the maturity date, the prevailing interest rate on comparable investments and the period remaining until the bond matures.

The yield-to-maturity of a bond purchased at face value and held to maturity is equal to the coupon rate.

GAIL (1)

Gail is considering the purchase of a Nalpha Corp bond with a $15,000 face value. The bond was originally issued 20 years ago, but has only 10 years remaining. The coupon on the bond is 12%, while the current market price is $17,000. If Gail purchases the bond today, what is her yield-to-maturity on the Nalpha Corp bond?

If Gail pays the current market price of $17,000, which is more than the bond's par value, we can deduce that her yield-to-maturity will be an amount less than 12%. Why? Because Gail will pay a premium for the bond, and the 12% coupon rate is calculated only on the par value.

Using a time value of money calculation, and solving for the nominal interest rate, derives a yield-to-maturity of 9.87%.

We know the following information:

- P/YR = 2
- xP/YR = 10
- PMT = 900
- FV = 15,000
- PV = -17,000
- MODE = END

SOLVE FOR I/YR, which equals 9.8718

The calculation of the yield-to-maturity utilizes the nominal interest rate. If the resulting interest rate is converted to an effective rate, the end product is the *effective yield-to-maturity*.

GAIL (2)

The yield-to-maturity on Gail's Nalpha Corp bond is 9.87%. This rate is equivalent to an effective yield-to-maturity of 10.11%.

We know the following information:

- P/YR = 2
- xP/YR = 10
- PMT = 900
- FV = 15,000
- PV = -17,000
- MODE = END

SOLVE FOR I/YR, which equals 9.8718

Convert nominal I/YR of 9.8718% to effective rate, which equals 10.1154% (by pressing [[SHIFT] EFF%]).

Yield-To-Call

When calculating the yield to maturity of a callable bond, the calculation is referred to as a *yield-to-call*, because the formula assumes that the bond is called at the earliest date. In addition, the formula assumes that the future value of the bond, normally the face value, will be the full amount paid to the bondholder at redemption, including the face value, plus any financial enhancement attributed to the company's decision to retire the debt obligation prior to maturity. The yield-to-call is calculated based on a nominal rate of interest. When the nominal rate of interest is converted to the effective rate, the phrase *effective yield-to-call* is utilized.

IVAN

Ivan is buying a Pomega Corp bond with a $10,000 par value that was originally issued 20 years ago, but has 15 years remaining. The bond is callable at the 10-year point, five years from now. The bond includes a financial enhancement of $250 if it is called prior to maturity. The coupon rate is 10%, while the current market price is $11,000.

What is the yield-to-call on this Pomega Corp bond?

The yield-to-call on Ivan's bond is 7.95%.

We know the following information:

- P/YR = 2
- xP/YR = 5
- PMT = 500
- FV = 10,250
- PV = -11,000
- MODE = END

SOLVE FOR I/YR, which equals 7.9539

What is the effective yield-to-call on this Pomega Corp bond?

To derive the effective yield-to-call, the nominal rate of 7.95% is converted to an effective rate, which equals 8.11%

continued . . .

continued . . .

We know the following information:

- P/YR = 2
- xP/YR = 5
- PMT = 500
- FV = 10,250
- PV = -11,000
- MODE = END

SOLVE FOR I/YR, which equals 7.9539

Convert nominal I/YR of 7.9539% to effective rate, which equals 8.1121%.

PREFERRED SHARES

Preferred shares are typically considered fixed-income investments with an annual cash flow. Many features of preferred shares mirror those of bonds, with the exception of the maturity date.

Current Yield

The current yield of a preferred share can be calculated utilizing annual dividend information and the security's current market price, similar to a bond.

Current Yield = ((Annual dividend payment) ÷ (Current market price)) × 100

JOHN (1)

John plans to purchase preferred shares of T-Corp, which have a $100 par value and a dividend rate of 6.95%. The current market price per share is $90. What is the current yield of the T-Corp preferred share?

Annual Dividend Payment

= $100 × 0.0695

= $6.95

Note: The annual dividend payment is based on the preferred share's par value and is not affected by the current market price.

Current Yield

= ((Annual dividend payment) ÷ (Current market price)) × 100

= ($6.95 ÷ $90) × 100

= 0.0772 × 100

= 7.72%

The current yield on John's T-Corp preferred share is 7.72%. The current yield should not be confused with the dividend rate. In this case, the dividend rate is lower than the actual current yield on the share.

JOHN (2)

John plans to purchase preferred shares of X-Corp, which have a $100 par value and a dividend rate of 4.95%. The current market price per share is $110. What is the current yield of the X-Corp preferred share?

continued . . .

continued . . .

Annual Dividend Payment

= $100 × 0.0495

= $4.95

Current Yield

= ((Annual dividend payment) ÷ (Current market price)) × 100

= ($4.95 ÷ $110) × 100

= 0.0450 × 100

= 4.50%

The current yield on John's T-Corp preferred share is 4.50%. The current yield should not be confused with the dividend rate. In this case, the dividend rate (4.95%) is higher than the actual current yield (4.50%) on the share.

Market Price

Determining the *market price* of a preferred share incorporates the cash flow derived from the dividend and the prevailing market rate.

Market Price = (Dividend payment) ÷ (Prevailing market rate)

JOHN (3)

John is considering the purchase of preferred shares of Y-International Corp, which have a par value of $75 and a dividend rate of 5.8%. If the prevailing market rate for similar types of investments is 6.5%, what is the current market price of John's Y-International Corp preferred share?

Market Price

= (Dividend payment) ÷ (Prevailing market rate)

= ($75 × 0.058) ÷ 6.5%

= $4.35 ÷ 0.065

= $66.92

Given the current prevailing market rate of 6.5%, the market price of the Y-International preferred share is $66.92.

HOLDING PERIOD RETURN

While the yield-to-maturity is an indicator of a bond's overall return, it is not a useful measure for other securities, such as stocks, that do not mature. As well, the yield-to-maturity calculation assumes that the investor will hold a bond until maturity, which is not always the case. In addition, this measure has gaps relative to the assumptions made with regard to the handling of income flows. For example, the yield-to-maturity does not take into account that an investor might use income flows to purchase additional securities.

The phrase *holding period return* refers to the total return on an investment, income plus capital appreciation, during a specific holding or time period. The total return is compared with the total cost of the investment. It is a measure that is useful regardless of the type of security, so it works well for stocks as well as bonds.

The formula for calculating the holding period return makes several assumptions, including:

- the selection of a specific time period during which the security will be held; and
- all income flows are used to purchase additional units of the security (even if it is partial units).

Using this information, the total value of the security at the end of the holding period is divided by the total value of the security at the beginning of the holding period, to derive a period value.

Holding period return = (((Closing value) - (Opening value)) ÷ (Opening value)) × 100

This formula could also be rewritten as:

Holding period return = [((Total value of security at end of holding period) - (Total value of security at start of holding period)) ÷ (Total value of security at start of holding period)] × 100

MAXINE (1)

On January 1, Maxine bought 500 preferred shares of Old Corp Ltd. for $68 per share. The par value of these shares was set at $50 per share with a dividend rate of 5.6%. On each of March 31, June 30, September 30 and December 31, that same year, Maxine received a $0.70 dividend per share.

Throughout that year, the market price of Old Corp shares was:

$70.25 per share — March 31

$71.00 per share — June 30

$69.50 per share — September 30

$71.50 per share — December 31

Calculate Maxine's holding period return for this single year.

The holding period return assumes all income flows are used to purchase additional units of the security, so each dividend received by Maxine is used to purchase additional shares of Old Corp Ltd.

Dividends received and additional shares purchased

March 31

(500 × $0.70) ÷ $70.25)

= 4.98 additional shares

Cumulative shares 504.98 (500 + 4.98)

June 30

(504.98 × $0.70) ÷ $71.00

= 4.98 additional shares

Cumulative shares 509.96 (504.98 + 4.98)

September 30

(509.96 × $0.70) ÷ $69.50

= 5.14 additional shares

Cumulative shares 515.10 (509.96 + 5.14)

December 31

(515.10 × $0.70) ÷ $71.50

= 5.04 additional shares

Cumulative shares 520.14 (515.10 + 5.04)

continued . . .

---

continued . . .

One-year holding period return (January to December inclusive)

= (((Total value of security at end of holding period) - (Total value at start of holding period)) ÷ (Total value of security at start of holding period)) × 100

= ((520.14 × $71.50) - (500 × $68)) ÷ (500 × $68) × 100

= ($37,190 - $34,000) ÷ $34,000 × 100

= $3,190 ÷ $34,000 × 100

= 9.38235%

= 9.4%

Maxine's return during this single year holding period was 9.4%.

In simple terms, a security's holding period return looks at the total rate of return on an investment over a specified period of time and can be used with any type of security.

DURATION

Overview

A tool referred to as *duration* is used to measure the price sensitivity and risk related to fixed-income securities. In other words, it is used to predict expected changes in the price of a fixed-income security relative to an interest rate change. Portfolio managers commonly use duration to measure the expected market value gain or loss relative to an interest rate change; it allows them to manage volatility.

Duration is a useful tool to track a bond portfolio's price volatility, perhaps within a target range. If the portfolio's duration creeps above or below the target range, appropriate sale or purchase actions can be used to rebalance the portfolio to the target range.

Duration is simply the weighted-average time to maturity for the cash flow on a fixed-income security, such as a bond. Using the time value of money concept, we know that a dollar today is worth more than a dollar in the future. This same concept applies to the cash flows associated with a fixed-income security. Under the duration calculation, all cash flows are time-weighted, including any interest and principal payments. The duration is calculated as the point when the time-weighted cash flows equal the current market price of the security.

Duration = (PV of all time-weighted cash flows discounted at the security's YTM) ÷ (Current market price)

Note: YTM refers to yield-to-maturity.

Application

Using the example of a five-year bond, we know that the bondholder will receive coupon payments twice each year for five years and, at the end of the five years, he will receive the lump sum par value of the bond. Figure 1 depicts the cash flow expectations associated with a five-year bond. In this example, the duration is 4.37 years.

Figure 1
Cash Flow Summary

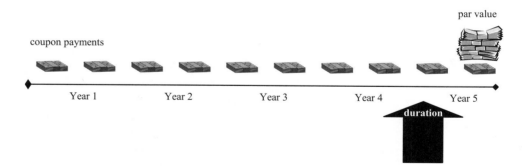

coupon payments

par value

Year 1   Year 2   Year 3   Year 4   Year 5

duration

MAXINE (2)

Maxine owns a bond as follows:

Par Value: $10,000

Coupon Rate: 6.7%

Market Value: $11,000

Years to Maturity: 5

We know the following information that will be used in the calculation of the bond's duration:

⇨   Coupon payment of $335 calculated as (($10,000 × 0.067) ÷ 2)

⇨   Yield-to-maturity 4.4473%

- P/YR = 2
- xP/YR = 5
- PMT = $335   [calculated as (($10,000 × 0.067) ÷ 2)]
- FV = 10,000
- PV = -11,000
- MODE = END

SOLVE FOR I/YR, which equals 4.4473

With this data, we are ready to begin the duration calculation.

Duration

= (PV of time-weighted cash flows discounted at the security's YTM) ÷ (Current market price)

Table 1
Maxine's Bond
Duration Calculation

Period Months	Cash Flow	Weighted CF	PV of Weighted CF
6	335.00	167.50	163.86
12	335.00	335.00	320.58
18	335.00	502.50	470.42
24	335.00	670.00	613.58
30	335.00	837.50	750.29
36	335.00	1,005.00	880.76
42	335.00	1,172.50	1,005.20
48	335.00	1,340.00	1,123.81
54	335.00	1,507.50	1,236.79
60	10,335.00	51,675.00	41,473.11

discount rate	4.44730%
PV of weighed CF	48,038.40
current market value	11,000.00

DURATION | **4.37** |

Table 1 demonstrates the methodology for determining duration. The cash flows from each year are multiplied by the "n" when they are received. For example, in the 6-month row, the cash flow of $335 is multiplied by 0.5 to reflect the time-weighting associated with the fact that the money will be received six months from now (half of one year) resulting in a weighted cash flow of $167.50. In the 36-month row, again there is a cash flow of $335, but this time it is multiplied by three to represent the number of years until the cash flow is received and results in a weighted cash flow of $1,005. The 60-month row recognizes the cash flow associated with the interest payment for the final six months of the bond's maturity and the receipt of the principal.

The next step in Table 1 is to determine the present value of each time-weighted cash flow. The fourth column is the present value of each time-weighted cash flow. For example, the number in the fourth column for the 36-month period is $880.76, which is derived as the PV of $1,005. The calculation of duration is beyond the scope of this course.

We know the following information:

(*Note:* Because we're working with periods of 6 months rather than one year, adjustments are made in the entry of the data into the formula.)

- P/YR=1
- xP/YR = 6   {six six-month periods}
- I/YR = 2.2236   {4.4473 ÷ 2, the interest rate for a six-month period}
- PMT = 0
- FV = 1,005
- MODE = END
SOLVE FOR PV, which equals -880.7629

The sum of the PV of the time-weighted cash flows is divided by the market price of the bond to determine the bond's duration, which, in this case, is 4.37 years.

If a fixed-income security has only one payment, such as a strip bond where there are no payments until the par value of the bond becomes due at maturity, the duration of that bond is its term to maturity.

A common rule of thumb associated with duration is:

The price of a security will change x% given a 1% change in interest, where x is the security's duration.

Applying this rule of thumb, a security with a duration of six years would generally be expected to move up or down in price by about 6% for each 1% change in the interest rate. With a single number, duration summarizes a bond or portfolio's sensitivity to interest rate changes.

Suppose a portfolio has a duration of eight years. That portfolio will appreciate about 8% for each 1% decline in interest rates. If that portfolio has a duration of three years, a one percent interest rate increase is expected to cause a decline of about 3% in the portfolio's value. Duration acts as a multiplier used to predict the percentage change in price resulting from an interest rate change.

Duration can also be referred to as the point at which the price risk and coupon reinvestment risk are offsetting. Small coupon payments cause the duration to extend outward in time to balance off against the high principal repayment at the end of the term.

MELANIE

Melanie owns two identical bonds, except the coupon payment of bond A is based on a rate of 3.1%, whereas the coupon payment for bond B is 5.4%. Bonds A and B each have the same five-year term and same face value. The only differentiating element between these two bonds is the coupon payment, which means the duration of the two bonds will differ.

If the market interest rate is 6%, then Bond A is worth $876.31 and Bond B is worth $974.41. However, their durations are 4.64 years and 4.44 years, respectively, as shown in Table 2.

BOND A

- P/YR = 2
- xP/YR = 5
- I/YR = 6
- PMT = 15.5
- FV = 1,000
- MODE = END

SOLVE FOR PV, which equals -876.31206

BOND B

- P/YR = 2
- xP/YR = 5
- I/YR = 6
- PMT = 27
- FV = 1,000
- MODE = END

SOLVE FOR PV, which equals -974.4094

continued . . .

---

continued . . .

Table 2
Melanie's Bond Comparison
Duration Calculation

Period Months	Bond A			Bond B		
	Cash Flow	Weighted CF	PV of Weighted CF	Cash Flow	Weighted CF	PV of Weighted CF
6	15.50	7.75	7.52	27.00	13.50	13.11
12	15.50	15.50	14.61	27.00	27.00	25.45
18	15.50	23.25	21.28	27.00	40.50	37.06
24	15.50	31.00	27.54	27.00	54.00	47.98
30	15.50	38.75	33.43	27.00	67.50	58.23
36	15.50	46.50	38.94	27.00	81.00	67.84
42	15.50	54.25	44.11	27.00	94.50	76.84
48	15.50	62.00	48.94	27.00	108.00	85.26
54	15.50	69.75	53.46	27.00	121.50	93.12
60	1,015.50	5,077.50	3,778.14	1,027.00	5,135.00	3,820.92

	Bond A		Bond B
discount rate	6.00000%	discount rate	6.00000%
PV of weighed CF	4,067.97	PV of weighed CF	4,325.80
current market value	876.31	current market value	974.41
DURATION	**4.64**	**DURATION**	**4.44**

In Melanie's case, Bond A will appreciate about 4.64% for each 1% decline in interest rates, whereas Bond B would typically be expected to appreciate about 4.44%. Conversely, an increase of 1% in interest rates would typically cause a slightly larger decline in Bond A's value when compared to Bond B.

When all factors are equal except the coupon payment, the bond with the higher coupon payment will have the shorter duration. As duration shortens, the volatility of the price declines. Conversely, the longer the duration of the bond, the higher the price volatility.

It is common for portfolio managers to alter the duration of a fixed-income investment portfolio in relationship to changes in economic cycles. For example, during a period of recovery or expansion there is a tendency to reduce duration, whereas the opposite strategy, increase duration, is applied during a period of recession.

IMMUNIZATION

Bondholders are subject to interest rate and reinvestment risk. The calculation of yield-to-maturity assumes all coupon payments are reinvested at the security's yield-to-maturity. In reality, if market interest rates change during the term of the bond, the bondholder loses or wins depending upon the actual change.

Changes to market interest rates during the term of the bond drives the price of a bond up or down, which will affect the bondholder if the bond is sold prior to maturity. It is interesting to note that an increase in market interest rates creates a positive event for the bondholder who has a coupon payment to reinvest, but creates a negative event for the bondholder who wants to sell a bond prior to maturity. The reverse is also true where a decrease in market interest rates creates a negative effect for the bondholder who has a coupon payment to reinvest, but creates a positive effect for the bondholder who wants to sell a bond prior to maturity.

When an investor's investment time horizon equals the duration of the bond portfolio, the investor's portfolio is immunized against parallel changes in the term structure of interest rates. The concept of *immunization* is a technique used by investors to shield the investor from interest rate risk. Bond immunization involves matching the duration of a bond or bond portfolio to the investor's cash-flow requirements.

Bond immunization can be used to create a bond portfolio with a duration equal to the investor's investment horizon or with a duration matching the investor's desired cash-flow requirements. The benefit comes from the ability to reduce interest rate and reinvestment risk.

MUTUAL FUNDS

Investment Return

The calculation of the investment return on a mutual fund takes into consideration any distributions paid to the investor. In most cases, distributions are reinvested and used to purchase additional shares, and this needs to be reflected in the calculation.

AMI

On January 1, Ami purchased 1,000 units of a mutual fund at $12 per unit, with a back-end load. During the year, the fund paid distributions of $0.25 per unit on each of March 31, June 30, September 30 and December 31. Each of the quarterly distributions were immediately reinvested and used to purchase additional units at the following unit values:

March 31 — $12.12

June 30 — $11.97

Sept 30 — $12.25

December 31 — $12.32

Using this information, we can determine that Ami's investment return on this mutual fund purchase was 11.3710% during the year.

Background:

⇨ Opening value on January 1 is $12,000 ($12.00 × 1,000 units)

⇨ Ownership of units

Date	No. of units purchased	Total units owned
January 1	1,000.0000	1,000.0000
March 31	20.6271	1,020.6271
June 30	21.3164	1,041.9435
September 30	21.2642	1,063.2077
December 31	21.5747	1,084.7824

We know that on January 1 Ami purchased 1,000 units, so on March 31, when the distribution was paid, Ami received a distribution of $250 ($0.25 × 1,000 units). This $250 was used to purchase 20.6271 units ($250 ÷ $12.12).

On March 31, Ami owned 1,020.6271 units (original 1,000 plus additional 20.6271 purchased with March 31 distribution). Ami received a distribution of $255.16 ($0.25 × 1,020.6271 units), which was used to purchase 21.3164 units ($255.15 ÷ $11.97) on June 30, for a new total of 1,041.9435 units.

On June 30, the 1,041.9435 units generated a $260.49 distribution, which purchased 21.2645 new units resulting in a new total of 1,063.2077 units on September 30.

continued . . .

---

continued . . .

And finally, on December 31, Ami received a $265.80 distribution ($0.25 × 1,063.2077 units), which purchased 21.5747 units for a year-end balance of 1,084.7824 units.

We know that at year-end the unit value was $12.32 and that Ami owned 1,084.7824 units for a total value of $13,364.52. This information and the opening balance are then used to derive the current yield.

Return

= (((Closing value) - (Opening value)) ÷ (Opening value)) × 100

= (($13,364.52 - $12,000) ÷ $12,000) × 100

= 11.3710%

STOCK VALUATIONS

Investors often compare the actual price of a stock with its "real" or intrinsic value. While there are many methods available to undertake this type of analysis, this section focuses on two different methods that are commonly used: one method is based on the dividends paid by the company and the other is based on the earnings of the company.

Dividend Discount Model

Investors often try to assess the intrinsic value of a share of common stock by discounting the expected flow of dividends at a rate of return appropriate for a security with a similar risk profile. This is a common technique used by fundamental analysts to capitalize the income associated with a stock and, therefore, predict its intrinsic value.

Dividends are defined as cash payments made by a corporation to its equity shareholders, including both preferred shareholders and equity shareholders. The dividend discount model focuses on the dividends paid to the residual owners of the company, the common shareholders. Dividends are commonly thought of as the partial distribution of earnings to the shareholders on a periodic basis, but, in reality, a company often pays dividends to its shareholders even during periods when it has a loss instead of a profit, in which case dividends are paid from retained earnings.

Companies are not required or obligated to distribute their earnings to shareholders in the form of a dividend. They are paid at the discretion of management, although many companies have a long history of paying dividends in good times and in bad. Many high technology companies are famous for not paying dividends to shareholders, even though both their profitability and cash on hand numbers are high. These companies need cash to finance strong growth, which is why they adopt the policy of reinvesting earnings instead of distributing earnings to shareholders in the form of dividends.

The *dividend discount model* (DDM) is based on the premise that the price investors will pay for a share of stock is driven by the future cash flows an investor expects to realize from that share, where the future cash flows will be realized in the form of dividends. In other words, the dividend discount model is a formula used to calculate the intrinsic value of a stock by discounting expected dividend payments.

The basic DDM is analogous to the *capitalization of income* approach for valuation. The basic formula is as follows:

$$P = (D_1 ÷ (1 + r)^1) + (D_2 ÷ (1 + r)^2) + (D_3 ÷ (1 + r)^3) + \ldots$$

Where,

P = intrinsic value of common stock

D_1 = expected dividend for period t

r = discount rate for cash flows of a similar risk

There is no maturity date associated with common stock, so the expected dividend flow has an infinite life. Since all dividends need to be accounted for in the model, the formula should be adjusted to reflect the infinite stream of dividends expected from the stock. To account for this, the formula can be adjusted to reflect a level of growth associated with the dividend.

Zero-Growth Model

In the *zero-growth* formula, it is assumed that the dividend is received in perpetuity and that the dividend remains constant, with no growth.

$P = D \div r$

where,

P = intrinsic value of common stock

D = constant dividend amount received in perpetuity

r = discount rate for cash flows of a similar risk

As the formula shows, to arrive at the intrinsic value of the stock this model uses the present value of all future cash flows, discounted at a rate that properly accounts for the risk of receiving the dividend.

GEORGE

George owns one share of ABC Company common stock that currently pays a dividend of $3 per year. Let's assume that George plans to hold the stock in perpetuity and that the stock will pay a dividend of $3 per year in perpetuity.

Further, assume that as an investor, George is compensated for the risk of receiving a dividend with a return of 12%. Using these assumptions, the formula calculates the intrinsic value of a share of ABC Company at $25.

$P = D \div r$

$P = \$3 \div 0.12$

$P = \$25$

In this situation, using the basic or zero-growth DDM approach, the intrinsic value of a share of ABC Company is $25.

The DDM value of a stock is equal to the present value of the cash flows (intrinsic value). Recall from Module 1 that the net present value calculation, sometimes called the discounted cash flow, is a well-accepted tool for assessing the financial business case for a potential investment. For an investment to make sense financially, it must generate a future cash flow such that the present value of that cash flow meets or exceeds the amount being contemplated as an investment. The guideline is that investments are made when the net present value of the future revenue stream meets or exceeds the original investment amount.

GEORGE (2)

If the current market price of ABC Company stock is $22 compared with an intrinsic value of $25, the DDM value per share is $3. In this case, the intrinsic value of ABC Company stock is greater than the current market price, which would lead to the conclusion that the share is undervalued by $3, so it would be a logical candidate for a buy recommendation.

An alternative method for using the dividend discount model is to solve for the internal rate of return (IRR) that equates the stock's current market price to the present value of the expected flow of dividends. This rate is then compared with the required rate of return for stocks with a similar risk profile.

The zero-growth model has limitations because it makes the assumption that the dividend paid on a common share will remain constant indefinitely, which is seldom the case. However, the model is quite practical when applied to preferred shares. With preferred shares, the steady flow of a fixed dividend is quite common, so the assumptions made in this model can work quite well for assessing the intrinsic value of a preferred share.

Constant-Growth Model

With the *constant-growth model*, assumptions are made that dividends grow at a constant rate from one period to the next. If the dividend paid during the previous year is D_0, then the dividend in the subsequent period is $D_1 = D_0 \times (1.0 + g)$ and each subsequent period is based on the previous period. The formula is:

$$P = D_0 \times (1.0 + g) \div (r - g)$$

where,

P = intrinsic value of common stock

D_0 = dividend amount in the first year

g = expected rate of growth for dividend

r = discount rate for cash flows of a similar risk

As with the zero-growth model, the assumptions are entered into the formula to derive an intrinsic value for the stock. The intrinsic value is compared with the current market price to determine the DDM value and ultimately whether or not the share is mispriced.

Note that a possible limitation of the constant growth DDM occurs if the anticipated dividend growth rate is higher than the discount rate. This would cause the price to become negative. The model has limitations and is not applicable in all circumstances.

GINA

If Gina owns stock of XYZ Ltd., which paid a dividend of $2 last year and the forecast is an indefinite increase of 3% annually, how much is the expected dividend for this year?

$P = D_0 \times (1.0 + g)$

$P = \$2 \times (1.0 + 0.03)$

$P = \$2 \times 1.03$

$P = \$2.06$

The dividend is expected to be $2.06.

Now, assume the discount rate is 9% and calculate the intrinsic value of the share.

$P = D_0 \times (1.0 + g) \div (r - g)$

$P = \$2 \times (1.0 + 0.03) \div (0.09 - 0.03)$

$P = \$2.06 \div 0.06$

$P = \$34.33$

If the current market price of the stock is $25, it would suggest that XYZ Ltd. is underpriced and therefore would result in a buy recommendation.

If the current market price of the stock is $39.55, it would suggest that XYZ Ltd. is overpriced and therefore would result in a sell recommendation.

Is it reasonable to assume a constant increase for dividends, year over year? Not likely. So like the zero-growth module, this formula also has limitations. Another model, the three-stage DDM, adapts the assumptions in the DDM to allow for changes in the growth rates, although it still requires assumptions relative to the forecasting of dividend patterns.

Three-Stage DDM

Many analysts use a DDM model, referred to as the *three-stage model*, because they believe it roughly corresponds to the three stages or phases that many companies experience: growth, transition, and maturity. During the growth phase, the company's earnings experience rapid growth as the competitive advantage that the company has developed is fully exploited. After that, the company enters the transition phase, where its additional size makes rapid growth more difficult; growth of the company slows, as do earnings and profitability. During the maturity phase, the company is expected to grow at levels that correspond to the growth of the economy as a whole and remains stable indefinitely.

Summary

Analysts use DDMs to determine the intrinsic value of a stock in order to compare the intrinsic value of the stock with the current market price. In this way, they can determine whether a stock is undervalued or overvalued. There are a variety of DDM models that make different assumptions. Regardless of the variables within the DDM model, predictions must be made relative to future dividends and each version of the model incorporates a variety of simplified assumptions.

The dividend discount model uses either a net present value or internal rate of return to determine if a stock is mispriced. If the outcome demonstrates that the stock is mispriced, the analyst would make either a buy or sell recommendation. While the DDMs might be useful in identifying a gap between the current price and the theoretical value of a stock, DDMs do not provide any insight on when the price of the stock might move to close the gap.

A negative of the DDM approach is the fact that it focuses entirely on the expected return of a single stock, without looking at the stock as part of a larger portfolio. As we learned in Module 15, the covariance of a stock's price movement with other stocks in the portfolio is a crucial element for lowering the risks of an investment. Looking at the expected return of the stock by anticipating price movements in response to DDM analysis, without examining the variance of the stock in the larger context of portfolio development, can be a short-sighted approach to investing.

Finite Holding Period

The DDM models discussed above make the assumption that the investor will hold the stock forever. The *finite holding period* model is another method of capitalizing income, but is adapted to incorporate the underlying premise that investors will not hold a stock in perpetuity, but will hold it for a finite period and then sell it. The expected sale price of the stock in the future is generally referred to as its *terminal price*, and it reflects the value of all the future dividends the company will pay after the future sale is transacted.

The model is expressed mathematically as:

$$= (D_1 \div (1 + r)^1) + (D_2 \div (1 + r)^2) + \ldots + (D_t \div (1 + r)^t) + (P \div (1 + r)^t)$$

Where,

P = intrinsic value of a common stock

D_t = expected dividend for each period through t

r = discount rate

P = terminal price of the stock in the future

In this model, the intrinsic value of the share is derived by discounting the dividends up to a defined point in the future and then adding the expected terminal price of the share. The fact that the terminal price reflects the discounted value of all future dividends means this model parallels the constant growth model.

Price-Earnings Based Valuations

An alternative, and more informal approach to stock valuation, is to look at the relationship between the earnings of a company and the price of the stock. Since common equity investors are the residual shareholders in a company, the earnings of the company, after all other obligations are met, accrue to them. Analysts will very often look at the specific relationship between price and earnings as they attempt to arrive at the value of a stock.

This approach begins with an analyst's estimate of the future price of the stock, which is derived from the product of his estimate of the anticipated earnings per share and his calculation of an expected price-earnings ratio for the stock. The combination of the future price of the stock and an estimate of the level of dividends generates an expected return for the stock. Forecasts and assumptions are incorporated, including a payout ratio for the expected earnings per share, to arrive at a mathematical model that allows the analyst to determine if a share is mispriced. This is achieved by comparing the share's expected price-earnings ratio to its actual price-earnings ratio. The type of assumptions incorporated in this model are much like those used for the DDM.

A share is considered underpriced if:

expected price-earnings ratio > actual price-earnings ratio.

A share is considered overpriced if:

expected price-earnings ratio < actual price-earnings ratio.

Note: > = greater than; < = less than

Zero-Growth Model

The *zero-growth model* is built on the assumption that earnings per share will always be a consistent fixed amount and that the payout ratio will always be 100%. The normal price-earnings ratio for a stock that is assumed to have zero growth is:

$1.0 \div r$,

where r is the discount rate.

Recall from Module 1 that the actual price-earnings ratio is:

P/E = (Current market price) ÷ (Net earnings per share)

HERB

Herb owns shares of O-Corp, whose shares have a current market price of $9 per share. The current dividends are $1.50 per share. Assuming a required rate of return of 8%, determine if O-Corp is mispriced.

Calculate expected price-earnings ratio:

$= 1.0 \div r$

$= 1.0 \div 0.08$

$= 12.50$

Calculate the actual P/E:

$= \$9.00 \div \$1.50$

$= 6$

Note: Under the zero-growth assumption, O-Corp has a 100% payout ratio, so the earnings per share are equivalent to $1.50.

O-Corp's expected price-earnings ratio is 12.50, which is greater than its actual price-earnings ratio of 6. This suggests that O-Corp's shares are underpriced and therefore would result in a buy recommendation.

Other Models

Similar to the DDM approach, the price-earnings ratio incorporates other assumptions to derive similar types of models. For example, the constant-growth model assumes that earnings grow at a steady, consistent rate into the future. There is also a multiple growth model that adapts the assumptions to allow for changes in the rate of growth of the earnings.

Summary

In summary, P/E ratios are calculated as the reciprocal of the earnings yield to allow analysts to compare a company to other companies in the industry. The P/E ratio of stock is driven by growth, and, to a lesser extent, risk. Companies in the growth phase of their business will often trade at higher P/E ratios in anticipation of that growth. Companies in the mature phase of their development will often have lower P/E ratios in recognition of their more stable expected-growth rates.

Unit 2
Analysis

INTRODUCTION

This unit covers the topic of security analysis, followed by a discussion regarding asset diversification and various models associated with active and passive investment styles. The development of any decisions relative to investment choices and options is best undertaken when there is a clear understanding of the individual's investment objectives. A review of the key investment objectives is followed by a discussion of other considerations that may influence decisions.

SECURITY ANALYSIS

Ideally, investors want to buy a common stock at a low price, and sell it after it appreciates in price. The key question is whether the stock is going to increase in price. Security analysis is the process of analyzing information related to securities for the purpose of predicting future price movements. The two major forms of security analysis are technical analysis and fundamental analysis.

Technical Analysis

Technical analysis is a long-standing process that is practiced by individuals known as technicians or chartists. Technicians believe that the price movement of stocks can best be explained through the mass psychology of investors, as opposed to the economic substance of the company issuing the security. In simple terms, *technical analysis* is a process of analyzing statistics generated by market activity, such as past price or trading volume, as a means to evaluate a security.

Technicians have little or no interest in the performance of the company issuing the stock. Instead, they believe that past price patterns of common stocks tend to continually repeat. In other words, they believe it is possible to predict future price movements of a stock by looking at the past price movements. Technical analysts use charts to identify these patterns, and are not concerned with measuring a security's intrinsic value.

Chartists spend time familiarizing themselves with the historical price patterns of individual stocks. They believe that historical patterns very often repeat themselves. Therefore, if they can find a current stock with historical price movements that imitate the first part of a well-known price pattern, they will be able to make money by knowing the (assumed) direction that the price of a stock is headed in the future. The specific patterns are well known to chartists.

Technical analysts look for factors such as trends, patterns, peaks or valleys in market activity that impact the price of a stock, and use this information as the basis on which to make buy and sell decisions. It is the patterns that technical analysts use as the basis for predictions because they believe that stocks move in predictable patterns that are consistently repeated. The concept of technical analysis is popular, with a tremendous number of claims that successful patterns or indicators have been identified.

Two terms, resistance and support, are frequently used by chartists. In situations where a stock has been rising in price but has trouble reaching or holding a specific price level, it is said to have met *resistance* at that price. Where the price of a stock has been falling but the price decrease stalls at a given price level, the stock is said to have *support* at that level.

The following is a discussion of two different tools used for technical analysis.

Moving Averages

One of the more simplistic analytical tools is the *moving average* that looks at the average price of the security over a period of time. Common time periods used for this analysis range from 20 to 200 days, where the closing price of a stock is tracked daily, using a fixed time span. The calculation involves a moving average: as each new day is added into the calculation, the oldest day is dropped from the calculation so only the specified number of days (i.e., 100-day average or 200-day average) in the time span are included. By using longer periods of time as the measuring span, it removes the volatility caused by daily pricing fluctuations. Alternatively, the shorter the time span, the more sensitive the graph will be to daily price movements.

There are a variety of strategies for using the information derived from this analytical tool. For example, one approach is that when the price of the stock crosses above the moving average and remains there for a target number of days, it is time to buy. Another approach may suggest that a buy signal occurs after the price of the security is at least 10% higher than the moving average.

Relative Strength Index

The relative strength index (RSI) is an indicator used in technical analysis to track and compare the patterns of the closing stock price where a comparison is made between the days the price closes higher and when it closes lower. RSI is calculated through a formula that results in a range of zero to one hundred. The formula is:

$$RSI = 100 - (100 \div (1.0 + RS))$$

where,

$$RS = (\text{Average of n-day up closes}) \div (\text{Average of n-day down closes})$$

n = days

The value of n can vary, but quite often is in the 9–15-day range.

The RSI value is the indicator on which a buy, sell or hold decision is based. For example, when the RSI exceeds the 70 range, or 80 during a bull market, it is suggested that a sell decision would be in order because the index indicates the market is stronger than what can be reasonably justified through the fundamentals. When the RSI falls below the 30 range, or perhaps 20 in a bear market, it is suggested that a buy decision would be in order because the index indicates the market is experiencing greater sales of the stock than is reasonably justified through the fundamentals.

Dramatic surges in the price of a stock will affect the RSI and could trigger false buy or sell decisions. Analysis through the RSI over longer periods of time, a year or more, will be helpful to the analysis, as it will identify historical RSI trends.

Moving averages and RSI are only two of the many different approaches that technical analysts may use to identify buy and sell decisions.

Fundamental Analysis

Another method for evaluating stocks is *fundamental analysis*, where the analyst measures the intrinsic value of a stock through studies of the economy, an industry and the financial condition and management of a particular company. Fundamental analysis is built on the premise of a relationship between the price of a stock and the health of a company, the state of an industry and the economy as a whole. The intrinsic value of a stock is the value based on perceptions. Fundamental analysis is used as a tool to identify mispriced securities.

Fundamental analysis has the same goal as technical analysis, but not the same methodology. The result of fundamental analysis is that investors are driven to buy undervalued stock and sell overvalued stock. They buy undervalued stock in the belief that it will rise to a price level consistent with its intrinsic value. They sell undervalued stock in the belief that it will fall to a price level consistent with its intrinsic value.

Technical analysts believe that there is an exploitable gap between the current price of a stock and its expected future price, based on historical price movements of the stock; fundamental analysts believe that there is an exploitable gap between the current price of a stock and its expected future price, based on the underlying intrinsic value of the stock (and company).

To conclude our parallel comparison: where technical analysts study historical price movements of the stock, fundamental analysts study the economy, industry and company to analyze the expected business performance of the underlying company.

Two approaches can be taken to the forecasting with fundamental analysis: top-down and bottom-up. Both approaches use a sequential approach, but the starting place differs. With the *top-down approach*, forecasts begin at the economic level, move through to the industry level and conclude with company-specific forecasts. On the other hand, the *bottom-up approach* begins with forecasts for a specific company, which lead into industry forecasts and finally conclude with economic forecasts. Often, fundamental analysts use a combination of both approaches.

The economic level of forecasting considers broad economic variables that may influence a particular industry. Predictions of the impact of various relationships between the broad economy and specific industries are carefully analyzed relative to the eventual impact on stock values within a particular industry.

At an industry level, analysts assess risk factors evident within the industry and consider different probabilities. The relationship between economic and industry variables is carefully considered and used to develop industry projections.

When analyzing at the company level, the analyst focuses on how well the company is expected to perform relative to industry projections. Financial statement analysis is a major component at the company level. A wide variety of ratio analysis that looks at areas such as revenue, liquidity, debt and profitability is used to make company-level predictions.

Analysts use the financial statements to assess the company's current status compared to potential changes, along with the probability of the potential change. Information used in the analysis is derived from many different sources, including company-prepared financial statements, securities filings, annual reports, documents sent to shareholders, proforma statements, interviews with key management, industry reports, and financial information collected and analyzed for internal company purposes.

In addition to the ratio analysis undertaken with the company's financial statements, analysts look at the company as a whole, including areas such as its history, management team and key business challenges.

With fundamental analysis, the objective is for the analyst to develop estimates of expected future earnings and dividends. If these estimates differ from the estimates of other analysts, but are viewed as likely more accurate, then the security would be viewed as mispriced. In this situation, if the analyst believes that the market price of a mispriced security will likely adjust, up or down, to reflect this new estimate, he would use this as an opportunity to suggest investors buy or sell the security, depending upon the expected price movement.

DIVERSIFICATION

Concept

The concept of diversification is built on the principle that diversification has a considerable impact on the composition and performance of an investor's portfolio. It is important to minimize portfolio risk by managing specific risk inherent to individual securities. The risk-return principle works on the premise that the greater the risk, the higher the return. However, this ties into the principle of diversification.

Investment diversification is the investor's attempt to follow that childhood dictum about not putting all our eggs in one basket. Recall that when the expected returns of a stock are considered, the risk of return is divided into its two component pieces: unsystematic or firm-specific risk and systematic or market-related risk. Unsystematic risk is said to be diversifiable because it is driven by events, which are independent. The idea behind diversification is that as we add more securities to the portfolio, the independent events will be both good and bad and will eventually cancel each other out, and thereby minimize the unsystematic risk.

The more investments in the portfolio, the more likely it is that random factors will cancel each other out and the expected return will be unaffected by random factors. From this, we can conclude that the first element of diversification is to have enough investments in our portfolio that we can minimize or eliminate firm-specific unsystematic risk.

The general principle of diversification is based on the premise that by combining securities into a portfolio, the risk associated with the total portfolio is reduced by an amount greater than the sum of average risk of each security. This principle builds on the assumption that by combining securities, good performing securities will help cancel out the poorer performing securities. The concept of asset allocation attempts to organize a portfolio with investments that will perform well, but are independent, at least to some degree, from each other. That is, their movements are not dependent on the same reasons, time or conditions as the other investments in the mixture.

Canceling out unsystematic risk through a sufficient number of investments can be augmented by choosing an asset allocation mix that further diversifies risk through asset allocation and security selection principles.

Diversification of assets can be approached on many different levels. The characteristics of financial instruments, such as debt versus equity, maturity dates, and liquidity are all a valid basis on which to develop diversification. Risk is another broad characteristic that allows for expansion of diversification. In the creation of a portfolio, the investor selects assets that are dependent on his risk and return preferences.

Yet, to manage the risk aspect, diversification is essential. Which countries should be chosen for an investment? Within each country, what percentage of portfolio assets should be invested in stocks, bonds, money market funds, and other assets? Within each of the major asset classes, what percentage of funds should be devoted to various bonds, listed stocks or perhaps over-the-counter stocks?

Types of Diversification

Asset Classes

In simple terms, the phrase *asset class* refers to the grouping of securities by specific common characteristics unique to that specific set of securities. On a broad level, when talking about asset classes within an investor's portfolio, experts may argue for hours about what is an asset class. The key is to group assets with similar characteristics into classes so that the asset classes can be combined into portfolios that provide the investor with expected rates of risk and return that meet the investor's objectives.

The discussion in the mutual fund section of Module 16 demonstrates the concept of asset classification. For example, with regard to mutual funds, the grouping of mutual funds by their investment objectives and the types of securities held within the fund's portfolio mix is an example of asset classification.

The risk associated with an asset class is dependent upon how variable the returns within the asset class are relative to their historic average (standard deviation), and also the extent to which the returns within the asset class vary from those of other asset classes (correlations). Consider, for example, an asset class that historically provides a low rate of return. This type of asset class may not fall within the investor's specific income objectives, but if returns within this asset class tend to move in the opposite direction as assets of other classes held within a portfolio, it could prove beneficial as an offset against the possible decline of returns from other asset classes held within a portfolio.

The heart of modern portfolio theory is that the risk of a portfolio of investments can be minimized, without affecting the return, by choosing assets or asset classes that have price movements that are negatively correlated with each other. As discussed in Module 15, if two stocks have an expected return of 12%, but the volatility of each stock has a perfectly negative correlation, when one varies in price in a positive direction, the other varies in a negative direction. The variability in expected return is effectively eliminated in the case of two securities, where the asset classes have a perfectly negative correlation with each other.

The combination of asset classes within a portfolio will generally sum to 100%. The effective use of asset classes in structuring a portfolio can play an important role in not only managing rates of returns on the portfolio but in the reduction of risk within the portfolio.

When considering the appropriate asset mix or asset allocation for a client, the factors to consider include the required returns, risk tolerance and the liquidity desired by the client. One popular approach to asset mix is the life-cycle theory of asset allocation. This theory postulates that the investment needs of an individual differ as a function of the stage of life. The investment needs and financial position of people in the retirement phase of the life cycle will, on average, differ from those who are just getting started in their 20s. According to this theory, an individual approaching retirement, for example, becomes more risk averse. Investors in their 40s, who are at the height of their earning power, are thought to have more of an appetite for higher-risk and higher-return investments.

Company Size

Within an investment portfolio, diversification can be enhanced by choosing stocks and bonds issued by companies of different sizes (market capitalization). Analysts will often diversify by investing in a combination of large public companies, smaller mid-market companies and even smaller companies trading in the over-the-counter market.

Company size can be an effective principle of diversification because the risks of larger companies tend to be associated with general economic conditions, while the risks of smaller companies tend to be centred more on technological and financial risk, which are somewhat independent of general economic factors. A portfolio diversification strategist is always looking for opportunities to combine assets with independent sources of risk. Company size can sometimes be a useful source of independent risk.

Industry

Different industries, another useful source of independent risk, can lead to positive or even negative correlation within a portfolio. By having several industry sectors represented in a portfolio, the diversification is enhanced. Investment managers prefer selecting industry sectors (i.e., telecommunications, oil and gas, health care, consumer goods, housing) that are subject to independent sources of risk.

Consider two sectors that may be independent sources of risk: housing compared with oil and gas. The profitability of the housing sector is highly dependent on housing starts, which is closely tied to the prevailing interest rate. On the other hand, the profitability of the oil and gas sector is driven by the price level that the commodities sell for, which in turn is driven by production output. Production output is often driven by political factors within the petroleum exporting countries. Of course, there is not perfect negative correlation between these two sectors, in that high interest rates tend to slow down economic output, which in turn would depress the demand for oil and gas, which would tend to lower its price. To the extent that these two industries might expect similar returns, but operate with less than perfect correlation in prices because of independent risk sources, there is some diversification achieved within the portfolio.

Geographic

Investment managers sometimes look to geography to help diversify a portfolio. Geographical diversification would be effective to the extent that the risks that cause price volatility in one geographic region would be unrelated to the risks that cause price volatility in another region. For this reason, portfolio managers will often build a portfolio that has a selection of investments from North America, Europe, Latin America and the Asian market in an attempt to create additional diversification in a portfolio. The problem with geographic diversification is that many of the world markets move together and have significant positive correlation in price movements. Without an independent source of risk, the diversification potential is greatly diminished.

Management Style

The management style of some investment managers can add to the diversification of a portfolio. For example, a contrarian style of investment management that focuses on buying when most are selling, and selling when most are buying, is designed to add diversification to a portfolio.

Fixed-Income Maturity Dates

Investment managers creating a bond portfolio will often diversify by choosing investments with a good variety of different maturity dates. Bonds with the same maturity date tend to be highly correlated. If the entire portfolio consisted of bonds that mature in 20 years, the probability is great that the price movement of one bond would be highly correlated with the price movement of every other bond. A diversified portfolio of bonds could consist of bonds with maturity dates of perhaps one to twenty years, because of the reduced likelihood that the price movement of bonds with different maturity dates would be strongly correlated with each other. Of course, longer-term bonds tend to have a higher rate of return, and it is likely that almost all bonds have some degree of positive correlation, but whatever added degree of independent risk can be sourced through the acquisition of bonds with different maturity dates, it adds to the level of diversification in the portfolio.

Credit Risk

As we discovered in Module 15, bonds are issued by organizations with different levels of creditworthiness. Bonds ranked AAA are considered prime debt by the ranking agencies. As the creditworthiness of the issuer declines, the ranking of the bonds also goes down. When bonds reach the level of BB+ they are considered speculative investments.

The price movements of different high-quality debt instruments will be highly correlated. The correlation is less when comparing bonds with different credit rankings, because of the independent risk factors that have eroded the credit ranking of the lower quality bonds in the first place. By creating a bond portfolio with bonds that have different credit risk, the diversification of the portfolio is enhanced.

Summary

In reality, it is very difficult to find investments with a perfectly negative correlation. However, portfolio managers will often look to a variety of diversifying principles to help build a portfolio of assets with as much negative correlation as possible.

INVESTMENT STYLES

Active Investing

We touched on the concept of active investing in the discussion regarding fundamental analysis. For investors who do not believe in the efficiency of the market (semi-strong form), active investing makes sense. Active investment refers to the process of buying stocks that are trading below their intrinsic value and selling stocks that are trading above their intrinsic value. Active investors believe they can exploit the difference between the intrinsic value of a stock and the price it is selling at. In other words, active investing attempts to locate mispriced securities and then purchase and sell these mispriced securities in an attempt to generate high returns.

For active investors to succeed, they must demonstrate a return that exceeds a benchmark portfolio, such as the S&P/TSX Composite Index or the S&P 500 Index. By necessity, active investors often have some of their investment funds sitting in cash.

Investors pursuing an active strategy have to assume that they possess some exploitable advantage relative to other market participants. These advantages could be better analytical or judgment skills, more current information, or the ability to take advantage of methods that institutional investors are unable to undertake, such as margin investing or short sales.

Many investors favour an active approach to stock selection and management because the potential rewards are very large. Investors feel confident that they can "beat the market". Actively managing a portfolio involves the constant selling and buying of securities, creating significant transaction costs. The inclusion of transaction costs into the calculation of overall net gain achieved through active portfolio management can have a significant impact on the net results.

Passive Investing

For those who believe in the efficiency of the market (weak and semi-strong form), passive investing makes sense. *Passive investing* acquires its name from the fact that no active selection of stocks is undertaken. Passive investors do not actively select some stocks and reject others; the investor merely attempts to construct a portfolio that mirrors the performance target, where the target is typically a well-diversified index. Once the passive investor acquires the specified mix of investments, the securities are retained for the long-term with little buy-sell activity, other than income reinvestment or moderate trading that results from the rebalancing of the portfolio.

Passive investors are satisfied that only random factors allow active investors to generate returns that exceed the returns of the market, and they are equally aware that those random factors could just as easily result in returns below that of the market. Passive investors are satisfied to see investments generate returns that mirror the market, with much lower fees being paid to the passive money managers.

A low number of transactions translates into minimal transaction costs for passive investors. These cost savings reduce overall expenses incurred through a passive investment style when compared with an active investing style, which means lower overall costs. This can prove beneficial because it means lower deductions from the fund's investment returns.

The advantage of passive investing is that returns seldom deviate from the returns of the benchmark — an event that happens quite frequently with actively managed portfolios. Passive investing also ensures that an investor is fully invested at all times, and will therefore never miss the "best days". The third advantage is that the fees an investor must pay a third party for managing a passive portfolio or mutual fund tend to be lower than what would be required if a third-party manager was managing an active fund.

Styles of Portfolio Development

The following is a discussion of various investment styles that are commonly used in the development of an investment portfolio. Some organizations prefer to use a single style, while others use elements or combinations of styles to derive what they feel is the optimal construction.

Security Selection

As the name suggests, *security selection* involves identifying the investments that are to be held within a portfolio and the proportion relative to the total assets. To derive the appropriate selection of securities, the investor considers tactics such as calculating the expected return, standard deviation and covariance on a breadth of obtainable securities. These simple tactics used in isolation are very time consuming and are not necessarily efficient in the selection of a security. However, when these tactics are used in combination with other investment styles, the construction of a portfolio becomes more effective.

Asset Allocation

Asset allocation involves the segmenting of funds into two or more different asset classes. Calculations, including expected return and standard deviation, are undertaken to determine the efficient portfolio mix.

The process of *strategic asset allocation* considers the division of the portfolio assets based on long-term forecasts for expected returns, variances and covariances, whereas the division of the portfolio's funds based on short-term forecasts using current market conditions is referred to as *tactical asset allocation.*

Tactical asset allocation involves the use of leading economic indicators as factors that influence adjustments to the asset allocation. The theory associated with a tactical approach is to benefit from the knowledge regarding upcoming changes to the business cycle. For example, leading indicators may suggest that the economy is heading toward a peak or trough. Based on historical studies, there are theories that suggest stock market prices act in a particular fashion in the period prior to changes in the business cycles, particularly peaks and troughs. As such, those who follow the tactical asset allocation approach would utilize the information of an upcoming peak or trough to make appropriate adjustments to portfolio holdings.

MANDY

Mandy supports the theory of asset allocation based on a tactical approach. Market indications suggest that the economy is approaching the end of a trough and there is clear movement toward a recovery/expansion phase.

Given this assessment, it is likely that production will begin to increase and employment will begin to expand as the economy begins to enjoy increased economic growth. As such, it is likely that Mandy will decrease the cash component of her portfolio that was held during the trough to minimize potential losses. In addition, during the trough Mandy may have lowered her proportion of stocks and would now consider expanding her corporate stock component to benefit from the improving business environment.

Strategic asset allocation relies on long-term forecast and involves periodic rebalancing of the portfolio to ensure that the targeted asset mix has not "slipped" — which will invariably happen over time as the investments appreciate. Conscientious investors make a concerted effort to incorporate a regular review of the asset mix on either a calendar basis or a threshold basis (when values exceed the allowable range) to determine if rebalancing is required.

Security selection helps identify specific securities to be held within the portfolio, while the split amongst asset classes helps determine the optimal combination within each class. Asset allocation is a process that can be used effectively under both active and passive portfolio construction models.

In summary, asset allocation refers to the diversification of an investment portfolio across multiple asset classes. Effective asset allocation works toward an appropriate mix of investments based on the investor's specific investment objectives that maximize the portfolio's performance potential while managing investment risk at a level within the investor's profile. The goal of asset allocation is to generate more consistent returns, lower volatility on the portfolio, and increase the chance of achieving financial objectives without skewing the risk factors to an unfavourable level.

Market Timing

Market timing is an active investment strategy whereby investors try to determine either from previous price history or fundamental analysis, that the stock (or market) is going to move one way or the other. In essence, market timing tries to exploit inefficiencies in the market.

Market timers try to buy during price troughs and sell during price peaks. While it sounds feasible, in practice it is exceedingly difficult to do. In simple terms, market timing involves the allocation of assets across different classes depending upon the portfolio manager's view of the economic or market outlook. Portfolios managed under this strategy often see significant swings between asset classes.

The other problem is that market timers are not fully invested at all times, which means that they are sometimes in cash as they deliberate on what investment to make next. Being in cash might be great if it helps market timers miss the bad days, but it can also be disastrous if the good days are missed as well. Predicting market movements is very difficult, particularly when identifying the entry and exit points. As such, there is great volatility in the returns under a market timing strategy.

Maturity Selection

In a bond portfolio, diversification is accomplished, in part, by selecting securities with different maturity dates. This can be a form of active investing in the bond market, as managers try to configure their maturity selection to take advantage of opportunities that they perceive to be developing.

Two types of passive strategies include a laddered and a barbell approach. A laddered strategy is commonly used for fixed-income securities, where the portfolio incorporates a selection of securities, such as bonds, that are equally weighted based on increasing levels of terms-to-maturity. The intention is to create a continuous cash flow, while reducing reinvestment risk. There could be some sacrifice of investment return depending upon the current interest rate environment, but the smooth cash flow helps to manage interest rate risk.

BOND PORTFOLIO

The following is an example of a bond portfolio that has been developed with an equal weighting of securities across four different maturity horizons.

Term to Maturity	Percentage
1 year	25%
3 year	25%
5 year	25%
10 year	25%
TOTAL	100%

While the example uses bonds, this same approach can be taken with most types of fixed-income securities.

Another strategy commonly used with bond portfolios is the barbell approach. The barbell approach is developed on the theory of holding primarily short-term and long-term bonds within the portfolio, with few, if any, intermediate term bonds. The intention of this structure is to allow one portion of the portfolio to benefit from higher yields while the other portion helps to moderate the risk.

Short Sales

Short selling is an integral part of active investing. When investors own a stock they are said to be long on the stock, and generally hope that the stock will rise in price, at which point they may sell. Investors who anticipate that a stock will fall in price can pursue a short selling strategy that allows the investor to profit from the falling price.

Short selling involves borrowing shares from the investor's stock broker's firm. The shares are sold, and the investor gets the proceeds from the sale. Eventually, the investor must close the short position by buying back the shares and returning them to the brokerage firm.

If the share price drops, the investor makes money by selling the shares at a higher value than the price he needs to repurchase the shares at. If the price of the shares rises, the investor has to buy them at a higher price, and will lose money.

Short selling is integral to active investing because it affords investors the opportunity to exploit what they feel are overvalued stocks, although many funds have rules that forbid more typical institutional money managers from taking a short position.

Style-Based Investing

The notion of style-based investing is an accepted part of the modern investment community. The underlying premise of style-based investing is that certain categories of stocks have similar defining characteristics and performance trends. In addition, the returns of stocks within a category tend to be highly correlated, but returns of stocks in different categories have low correlation levels. The two primary style types are: value and growth.

Value Stocks

An investment style that focuses on value stocks is one that targets stocks of companies where the stock is priced below average levels relative to historical prices when considering sales, cash flow, earnings or book value. The goal in this style is to identify undervalued stocks within a given universe, and, when found, they are purchased with the idea that eventually the stock will rise to the level of the target ratio of the universe to which it belongs.

There are three sub-styles that are found within the value category. The "low P/E ratio" manager concentrates on companies where the stock has a low P/E ratio relative to the P/E ratio for its universe. If the universe of stocks in this category is trading at a P/E ratio of 15, this kind of sub-style manager is trying to find a company within the category that is similar but is trading at a P/E ratio much lower than 15.

The contrarian manager focuses on the book value of a company and tries to identify companies that are trading at a low price relative to their book value. Typical companies in this mode might be depressed cyclical stocks or companies with little or no earnings or yield. Under this type of approach, a fund manager quite often seeks out companies where the market capitalization of the company is less than twice that shown under the net worth on the balance sheet.

And the final sub-style manager in the value style is the conservative-yield manager who focuses on identifying stocks that have above-average yields that are expected to stay high or even grow.

Growth Stocks

Whereas the value style manager is concerned with identifying undervalued stocks that will rise in value to be consistent with other stocks in that universe, the growth-style manager is concerned with identifying stocks with growth potential. A growth-oriented manager tries to identify stocks with a P/E ratio above the average in the universe, and where the earnings appear capable of continued, steady growth that will be reflected in the stock price.

There are two sub-styles found in the growth style of investment management. The first sub-style manager focuses on high-quality companies who have demonstrated consistent growth. These investment managers are known as consistent growth managers. The other sub-style is the earnings-momentum growth manager who is focused on finding more volatile stocks in terms of earnings, but who may be entering a period of above-average growth.

Indexed Portfolios

The most popular approach to passive investing is the *indexing strategy*. Portfolio managers who use an indexing strategy do not try to identify undervalued or overvalued stocks based on fundamental analysis, nor does the portfolio manager attempt to forecast any general or sector-based trends in the market. An indexing strategy is a purely passive approach that attempts to create a portfolio that tracks or mirrors the performance of an underlying benchmark index.

There are a couple of approaches a portfolio manager can take in constructing an indexed portfolio of stocks. The purest approach is to buy all of the stocks included in the benchmark index in proportion to their weightings. The other approach, sometimes called the capitalization approach, is to dedicate two-thirds of the investment funds to buying the top one-third of stocks in the index, ranked by capitalization. The remaining one-third of the funds is used to purchase the remaining two-thirds of the stocks in equal amounts. This is a simpler approach, and yet still generates returns that are very close to the returns generated by the benchmark index. *Exchange traded funds* (ETFs) operate under a similar way as indexed portfolios.

Buy and Hold

Buy and hold is considered another passive strategy, although it has an active element during the original selection of the stocks in the portfolio. Once the stocks are purchased, the buy-and-hold investor holds them until the end of the investment period, whatever that happens to be. This strategy ensures that the investor is fully invested for the entire period, but does not guarantee the investor that he will achieve the market return on the portfolio. A buy-and-hold strategy substantially reduces the fees that an investor would pay in a more actively traded portfolio.

PORTFOLIO INSURANCE

As the name implies, the phrase *portfolio insurance* refers to an investor's attempt to design the investment portfolio in order to avoid large losses and secure minimum favourable returns. Constant proportion portfolio insurance is a technique where the investor identifies a portion of the portfolio's assets for use in riskier investments. The riskier proportion of the assets is a constant multiple of an amount that exceeds a floor amount. As the total value of assets held within the portfolio changes, the investor adjusts his exposure between the risk-free and riskier assets to rebalance back to the constant proportion.

MARTIN

The total value of Martin's investment portfolio is $50,000. He would like to invest in common stock while utilizing a technique that provides portfolio insurance. If Martin applies the constant-proportion portfolio insurance technique and uses a floor of $45,000 along with a multiple of 4, he will initially allocate $20,000 (4 × ($50,000 - $45,000) to common stock and the remaining $30,000 will be allocated to a risk-free investment, such as treasury bills.

Assume $30,000 of Martin's initial $50,000 portfolio is invested in treasury bills that pay an annual nominal return of 3.25% and the remaining $20,000 is invested in common stock.

At the end of nine months, the risk-free portion of the portfolio is valued at $30,731. Assume that during this same nine-month period the common stock has risen to a market value of $21,000. Martin will adjust his market exposure to reflect $26,924 (4 × ($51,731 - $45,000)) in common stock with the balance of $24,807 ($51,731 - $26,924) remaining in treasury bills.

As the total value of Martin's portfolio shifts through time, he will continuously rebalance using the insurance portfolio technique. Martin is not confined to any specific time horizon when utilizing this technique.

INVESTMENT OBJECTIVES

While each investor will have his own set of objectives, specific to his personal circumstances, there will be consistent themes based on standard principles. An investor's circumstances will change as a function of age and station in life. Typically, an investor's objectives can be categorized into four main areas that emphasize one or a combination of:

- income;
- safety of principal;
- liquidity; and
- growth.

Income

Income is an important objective for investors who rely on their investment earnings to fund or supplement their living expenses. When income is a primary objective, appropriate investments will include different types of income-producing assets that align with the investor's risk tolerance. The level of return from the investment will obviously reflect the risk level of the investment. Income is produced from either the yield on debt instruments (i.e., guaranteed investment certificates, bonds, mortgages) or as dividends on equity investments such as preferred shares.

The frequency of income distributions also factors into the deliberation. Some investors prefer investments that provide monthly distributions, while others are satisfied with annual or semi-annual distributions. While income-type investments quite often represent a lower level of risk than growth-type investments, there are still various degrees of risk associated with different income-type investments, which means investors must consider the trade-offs relative to various levels of yield.

Income is frequently a key investment objective for individuals in the retirement phase of their life cycle. The emphasis on fixed-income securities to address this objective exposes the individual to significant inflation risk.

Safety of Principal

When there is not a zero-risk guarantee, risk management decisions are needed in order to ensure the selected asset, or combination of assets, aligns with the investor's risk tolerance. Safety of principal is a function of risk and is evaluated through consideration of the risk-reward issues.

Complete or nearly complete safety of principal means accepting a lower level of yield on an investment. As the risk factor increases, the safety of the investor's principal becomes more vulnerable, while the yield tends to increase.

When investors have safety of principal as their prime investment objective, it substantially reduces the number and variety of investments that can be considered. The universe of possible investments is very limited, as is the potential yield. On the other hand, there are few investors who do not have some level of concern with regard to the safety of their capital.

The risk-reward principle is an important guide for investors. Historical returns depict that while common shares tend to provide the highest return over the long-term, an investor must be prepared to cope with significant volatility relative to the returns and the risk of losing capital. At the opposite end of the spectrum is the basic T-bill where there is little volatility relative to the potential return and typically a risk-free situation for safety of capital. But, a T-bill also represents an investment that offers a very low level of return. Bonds fall into the middle of the spectrum where the potential for loss of principal is higher than a T-bill and typically lower than with common stock.

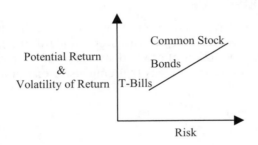

Liquidity

As discussed in Module 15, liquidity risk is the probability that an investment can ultimately be converted into cash, when needed. Investors, whose investment objectives include liquidity, typically are unwilling to consider investments that would put them in the position where there is a risk of substantial loss should they need to convert the investment to cash in a relatively short period of time.

The longer the term of an investment, the less liquid it is. For example, a treasury bill is highly liquid because of its very short-term nature. A one-year guaranteed investment certificate that is non-cashable may hold an acceptable liquidity risk for some, but not others. As the liquidity of an asset decreases, the yield on the investment tends to rise.

Liquidity is relevant when considering all types of investments. For example, investors may be penalized for liquidating fixed-term investments before a pre-determined maturity date, or simply may not be able to liquidate the investment until it actually matures. Real estate is a highly illiquid investment because of the complexity and extended time associated with the conversion of the asset into cash, at or near its true value.

The level of liquidity desired by an investor plays an important role in the selection of investments, as many investors will shun investments that have no secondary market or a thinly traded secondary market.

Growth

Some investors are willing to accept greater investment risk in exchange for the potential growth in the value of their investment over time. Similar to any of the other objectives, the risk-return model must be carefully assessed when looking at growth-type investments. There are investors who are willing to accept very high levels of risk in exchange for the potential of very high levels of growth, while other investors are quite satisfied to accept lower growth rates in return for more modest levels of risk. An investor's investment time horizon is an essential factor when considering growth as a primary objective.

Investors who seek growth-oriented investments should be distinguished from speculative investors who are also interested in high rates of return and are willing to accept high levels of risk to achieve it. Growth investors target equities and other securities that they feel have good inherent mid- to long-term growth prospects based on superior performance of the underlying entity. Speculative investors have more of a gambling mentality where they take the buy or sell side in a transaction in anticipation of short-term movements in the price of the underlying asset (i.e., options, futures, day trading).

Growth as an investment objective tends to align with individuals in the early and mid-years stages of the life cycle, because of the typically long investment horizon. However, for investments that have a short-term horizon, such as savings for a home or other consumable, growth would be nice, but increases the individual's exposure to market volatility without the benefit of a long investment horizon.

MARKETABILITY

The concepts of liquidity and marketability are interrelated and often the terms are used interchangeably. In simple terms, the phrase "marketable securities" refers to securities, such as cash equivalents, commercial papers and T-bills, that can be easily sold or converted into cash. Each type of investment possesses its own unique set of marketability characteristics.

Marketability can be an issue if there is a wide variance in the bid-ask price or rate for a particular security. If an investor is forced to liquidate a security unexpectedly, and if marketability of the security is an issue, the result can be a significantly lower return than originally anticipated, or even a potential loss.

In developing an investment portfolio, marketability issues must be looked at relative to the investor's overall portfolio and should be addressed in the selection of securities that meet the varied requirements of the investor.

The development of an investment portfolio will include a balance of securities where the selection of classes reflects an investor's requirement for liquid assets, even if the liquidity factor simply acts as a financial cushion. What is the investor's time horizon relative to the assets? What is the investor's ability to absorb unexpected losses that could arise if he is forced to liquidate investments during periods of market volatility? Answers to these types of queries will shape investment decisions.

BUSINESS CYCLES

As discussed in Module 15, Canada, like most other modern industrial economies, goes through significant swings or fluctuations in economic activity. There is a clear and obvious trend in the order in which the phases of a business cycle occur. Periods of recovery or expansion culminate in peak economic output, which is identified as a turning point, and is followed by economic contraction or recession. A recession ends in a trough, which is also, over time, recognized as a turning point. The economic flow continues the pattern and subsequently leads to another round of recovery.

Investments

For the most part, predicting economic phases and the potential timing is a challenge even for the most adept economist. Yet, given that there are obvious distinctions in the characterization of each phase, modifications to investment strategies can help minimize the impact of economic cycles on an investment portfolio.

Recovery/Expansion

During the recovery/expansion phase, there tends to be strong economic growth. This generates increased corporate earnings, which leads to increases in consumer confidence. Ownership of corporate stocks allows investors to take advantage of increased corporate success. Bonds tend to be less favoured because increasing interest rates push the price of the security downward.

Peak

During an economic peak, it is likely that short-term interest rates will not climb any further. Investors continue to hold stocks but with a shift toward an increased proportion of bonds. There is also a tendency for investors to increase their cash position.

Recession

Obvious and continued decline in output, employment and income signifies a depressed economy during a period of recession. Business activities show broad characteristics of contraction with all industries affected by the recession, some more than others. This leads to reduced consumer confidence and obvious contractions in corporate earnings, which suggests less emphasis on corporate stock. During this phase, ownership of long-term bonds may be attractive as interest rates decline causing bond prices to climb.

Trough

At this stage, output reaches its lowest point and the economy is preparing for recovery. Investors tend to move from bonds to stocks, as it is unlikely that bonds will appreciate significantly, while stocks become attractive, given the impending economic growth period that follows a trough.

HEDGING STRATEGIES

Hedging can be used to reduce the overall risk and volatility of an investment portfolio through diversification. There are a wide variety of hedging strategies, each with varying degrees of risk.

Selling Short

The concept of selling short involves the hope that the price of a security will fall in the future. An investor sells shares that he does not own, but anticipates that the price will drop in the future, at which time he will buy the shares in order to complete his transaction.

Options

Options involve a contract whose value is based on the performance of an underlying index, financial asset or other investment. An investor will use options as a means of insurance where the option is purchased by the investor as protection against a downturn in a particular stock. Using options, investors can cost effectively limit the downside associated with a particular investment while enjoying the full benefit of the upside.

Arbitrage

The concept of arbitrage revolves around an investor's expectation that he can exploit pricing inefficiencies. The purchase of a security on one market and then immediate resale on another market, with the objective of profiting from a price discrepancy, is an example of arbitrage.

Event Specific

Hedging can be as simple as making an investment based on the anticipation of a specific event taking place such as a spin-off, merger or acquisition.

LEVERAGED INVESTING

From an investment perspective, *leverage* means acquiring investments using borrowed funds. The use of a margin account, as discussed in Module 16, is a type of leverage. If an investor takes out a second mortgage on his residence and uses the borrowed proceeds to purchase a portfolio of mutual funds or stocks, this too is a form of leveraging.

Interest Deductibility

The ability to deduct the cost of borrowing can be an advantage to an investor who uses leveraging, although one must keep in mind that the tax-deductibility of borrowing costs does not negate the cost, it simply provides an enhanced benefit.

Tax-paying entities can typically deduct the interest on money borrowed to earn income from business or property, but there are a couple of caveats that must be kept in mind to ensure that the deduction applies.

For interest to be tax deductible, the money borrowed must be used for the purpose of earning income from a business or property. Interest on money borrowed is only deductible if the funds can be directly traced to the investment. Artificial arrangements to extinguish non-deductible interest on debt to replace it with tax-deductible interest on debt are not acceptable.

The last caveat is that money borrowed for an investment where the sole purpose is to realize a capital gain may also be non-deductible. The language in the applicable statute is quite exact: the money must be borrowed for the purpose of earning income from a business or property.

As well as the purpose test, interest must meet two other tests before it can be considered deductible. The interest must be paid or payable in respect of the year it is being deducted. And finally, a legal obligation to pay the interest must exist.

Magnification

There are a number of advantages and disadvantages of using leverage in an investment context. The primary reason that people use leverage is to increase the potential return on their investment.

BOB (1)

Bob uses cash to purchase 1,000 shares of XYZ Inc. for $10 per share. At the end of three years, Bob has earned a dividend of $1 per share each year for the 3 years. In addition, he sells the stock at the end of the 3 years for $12. (Disregard commissions and taxes.)

What is Bob's total return on his investment, expressed as a nominal percentage?

Total dividends received

= 1,000 × $1 × 3 year

= $3,000

Capital gain

= Proceeds of disposition - Purchase price

= (1,000 × $12) - (1,000 × $10)

= $12,000 - $10,000

= $2,000

The total dollar return is:

Dividends	$3,000
Capital gain	2,000
Total return	$5,000

The total nominal investment return

= Total dollar return ÷ Original investment

= $5,000 ÷ $10,000

= 50%

Now let's assume that Bob borrowed half of the money to purchase the XYZ Inc. shares. In other words, he put up only $5,000 of his own money. Over the 3-year period, Bob paid a total of $1,000 in interest costs on the $5,000 of borrowed funds.

continued . . .

---

continued . . .

Bob's total dollar return on the XYZ Inc. shares is:

Dividends	$3,000
Capital gain	2,000
Total return	5,000
Interest	(1,000)
Net Return	$4,000

The total nominal investment return

= Net dollar return ÷ Original investment

= $4,000 ÷ $5,000

= 80%

We can see that through the use of leverage, the percentage return on Bob's $5,000 investment increased by 60%; it changed from a 50% with no leverage, to an 80% return when Bob used borrowed funds to increase the size of his investment.

Without actually doing the calculations, it is also easy to see that if we borrowed even more, perhaps $8,000 instead of $5,000, the percentage return would be greater than 100% on the net amount of Bob's investment. When leverage is used and stocks increase in value, the return is magnified. If leverage has this kind of magical effect on returns, why do all investors not make use of leverage?

The reason, of course, is that leverage is a double-edged sword. It has the opposite effect when the price of a security falls below the original purchase price.

BOB (2)

Continuing the Bob SNAP, consider the impact if the market price of XYZ Inc. shares dropped from the original price of $10 to $6, during the 3-year holding period.

Without leverage, Bob's net loss would be $1,000 ($3,000 in dividends less a $4,000 capital loss). Based on the original investment of $10,000, the total return would be a 10% loss (-$1,000 ÷ $10,000).

If Bob borrowed half of the money ($5,000 of the total $10,000 investment), the net loss would be $2,000 ($3,000 in dividends less a $4,000 capital loss less $1,000 in interest costs). However, the total return would be a 40% loss (-$2,000 ÷ $5,000).

In addition to the 40% loss that Bob has experienced on his XYZ Inc. shares, he still owes $5,000 of borrowed funds, and regardless of the investment return, his $5,000 liability remains.

So while the advantage of leveraged investing is the magnification of the potential return, the exact opposite is true in that a negative return is magnified and can substantially change the balance of risk compared to when no leverage is utilized.

Other Considerations

When the concept of leveraging is used, the assessment becomes quite similar to other borrowing decisions. Two important considerations include the individual's ability to repay any borrowed funds and an assessment of how well the risks and costs of leveraging align with the individual's investment objectives.

Repayment Ability

When borrowed funds are used to make investment purchases, there is a risk that the market value of the investment will decline. In a margin situation, the investor must have the ability to meet any margin call, either through the availability of cash or other margin-eligible securities. Without readily available assets to meet a margin call, the dealer will be obliged to sell a portion of the securities to eliminate the margin deficiency.

If the investor has borrowed funds through a demand account, line of credit or other type of credit facility, he must have the funds to meet any payment schedule. While he may be relying on the assets purchased with the borrowed funds to increase in value, he is still obliged to repay any debt obligation regardless of any decline in market value.

DONNY

Donny took out a $40,000 loan, secured by the value in his home. The $40,000 was used to purchase a variety of stocks and bonds. Donny's repayment schedule required monthly payments over a five-year period. In this case, Donny needs sufficient regular income in order to make his monthly payments.

Investment Objectives

The use of leveraging should only be considered in light of the individual's investment objectives. Leveraging should never be the starting place, but rather can only be assessed after a complete review of the client's personal circumstances and, ultimately, his investment objectives. An evaluation of the investor's risk-return profile will help determine whether leveraging is an appropriate strategy.

Assessing the concept of leveraging relative to the investor's objectives should include a review of the investor's ability to understand both the short- and long-term issues associated with leveraging, as well as the impact of market volatility. How prepared is the investor, financially and psychologically, to withstand a downturn in the market value of the investment? Is leveraging the most cost-effective investment strategy, given the client's personal tax situation?

While leveraging has been used significantly in past markets, and is particularly attractive in a bull market, individuals must truly understand the risks and, in particular, the potential for capital losses. These types of risks can only be assessed through clearly developed investment objectives.

Application

For testing purposes, the CFP Education Program and CFP Exam utilize the financial calculator as the only tool to support any analysis. However, the calculator on its own has limitations, particularly when undertaking integrated financial planning solutions in your office on a day-to-day basis. Financial planners often utilize software packages as a valuable tool when working with integrated planning situations, such as a comprehensive financial plan. Good quality software allows the planner to enter a series of variables that reflect facts and assumptions relative to the client's specific situation, and then readily produces a variety of output that can be used in the analysis of case-specific issues.

CCH's Financial Planning Solutions (FPS) offers extensive software support for completing comprehensive and single-need planning. Using fully integrated workbooks with the spreadsheet format of Microsoft Excel, the software allows a planner to enter data, make assumptions and update assumptions in order to analyze the client-specific situation. The software produces output that is client-friendly. Appendix Two provides a SNAP that uses CCH's FP Solutions software to demonstrate the concept of leveraged investing. This SNAP is for information purposes only — for those who want to explore the concept in more detail; however, it is not required reading or testable.

FORMULA INVESTING

Concept

When an investor utilizes an investment strategy that is based on a specific set of rules, with no emotional implications, the approach is characteristically referred to as *formula investing*. Two common formula investing techniques include:

- a dividend reinvestment plan (DRIP), as discussed in the Module 16; and
- dollar-cost averaging.

A third technique, systematic withdrawal plans (SWPs) as discussed in Module 15, falls within the concept of formula investing. Although a SWP involves the withdrawal of investment funds, it is established based on a pre-determined, consistent withdrawal pattern (i.e., monthly or quarterly) and amount. This tends to moderate the impact of the withdrawals when compared with isolated independent withdrawals on a more sporadic basis.

Dollar-Cost Averaging

Dollar-cost averaging, also sometimes referred to as the *constant dollar plan*, is an investment strategy in which a set dollar amount is invested on a regular basis in a particular investment, regardless of whether the market is moving up or down. Investors use dollar-cost averaging to lower the overall cost per share, as it tends to remove the volatility. Instead of buying a substantial block of shares at irregular intervals, the investor buys smaller amounts of a particular security on a regular periodic basis, over an extended period of time. This is known as dollar-cost averaging.

The strategy is designed to take the guesswork out of trying to time the market. By investing a fixed amount of money at regular intervals, regardless of whether the market is high or low, the investor by default buys fewer shares when the prices are high and more shares when the prices are low. This strategy is also a good way for individual investors to maintain a regular investing pattern.

The relatively insignificant downside of dollar-cost averaging is that the transaction fees associated with more frequent purchases can erode the overall returns realized by the investor.

The opposite to formula investing is lump-sum investing, whereby a lump-sum amount is used to purchase securities, ideally when the investor believes the price to be low relative to its future direction. In other words, he expects the price of the security to rise. The advantage of lump-sum investing is derived from the potential gains, if indeed the price of the security rises. Overall, lump-sum investing tends to result in a higher expected long-term return than through dollar-cost averaging, because the money is completely invested in the market at all times. The downside of lump-sum investing is the potential volatility, which is much greater than with dollar-cost averaging.

REGISTERED VERSUS NON-REGISTERED

Capital Gains Issue

Investors often have the choice of investing in either a registered plan, such as a registered retirement savings plan (RRSP), or to use the funds for the purchase of a non-registered investment. The advantage of an RRSP is that the funds invested in the RRSP grow tax-sheltered while they remain within the registered vehicle and are only taxed when withdrawn from the plan. If the funds remain in the registered plan and are ultimately used for their original purpose, to provide a retirement income, the annuitant is typically in a lower tax bracket than when the funds were originally accumulated, so he benefits from a lower tax consequence.

The amount that can be invested into an RRSP is based on the taxable earnings of the taxpayer during the previous taxation year. The prevailing wisdom in terms of allocating funds between registered and non-registered plans has typically been to maximize investments in registered plans up to the allowable limits, while at the same time making sure that the investor has sufficient cash on hand, outside of the registered plan, to meet potential emergency obligations.

The lowering of the capital gains tax from 75% to 50% and the introduction of the Tax-Free Savings Account (TFSA) has changed the perception of some planners on the allocation of investments between registered and non-registered plans. Because funds held within the registered investment cannot benefit from the tax-preferred treatment associated with capital gains, some planners view this as a disadvantage that should be considered in the allocation of funds between registered and non-registered, or in the selection of specific assets.

A recent study found 76%[1] of people do not consider tax implications when they make investments. Interest-bearing investments, such as bonds and GICs, and foreign stock dividends, are taxed at the highest marginal tax rate of approximately 40%. In contrast, dividends, due to the dividend gross-up and tax credits, are taxed at marginal tax rates of approximately 16% to 25% for eligible and 28% to 34% for non-eligible dividends, depending on the province of residence. With the 50% capital gains exemption, capital gains are taxed at the lowest marginal tax rate of less than 25%.

In general, investors should put interest-bearing instruments and dividend paying foreign stocks into their RRSPs and TFSAs to shelter and defer the taxes on the income until the money is taken out. Canadian dividend paying stocks are better held outside RRSPs and TFSAs due the dividend tax gross-up and tax credits. Canadian stocks and foreign stocks that do not pay dividends that are mainly focused on capital gains growth should also be held outside RRSPs and TFSAs to benefit from the preferential capital gains scheme.

The actual allocation decision will differ from investor to investor, according to the specifics of each case.

	Interest Bearing (Bonds, GICs)	Canadian Dividend Stocks	U.S. and Foreign Dividend Stocks	Capital Gains
RRSP	Best	Good	Best	
TFSA	Best	Better	Best	Good
Non-Registered		Best		Best

Strip Bonds

While strip bonds do not provide the bondholder with interest from coupon payments, the bondholder is required to include in income, each year, a notional amount of interest income related to the bond. This annual accrual of a notional interest amount makes strip bonds a preferred investment for registered plans where there is no annual tax consequence on accruing investments.

MANAGING RISK

A portfolio is simply a mix of different assets where the selection of investments plays a critical role in the risk-return aspects of the portfolio. The return earned by the portfolio is dependent upon the mix of investments held. The greater the potential return, the higher the risk associated with the portfolio. Figure 2 shows four separate portfolios, each with a different risk-return profile. The conservative portfolio incorporates a mix of lower-risk assets that offer a lower potential return but also a modest impact relative to a period of market decline. At the opposite end of the spectrum is the speculative portfolio, which has

---

[1] Leger Marketing poll for BMO Nesbitt Burns, as quoted in "Outsmart the Grasping Hand", *Financial Post*, May 1, 2010, page FP9.

an asset composition that offers the greatest potential return, but is also the most vulnerable to periods of market decline.

Figure 2
Portfolio Positions

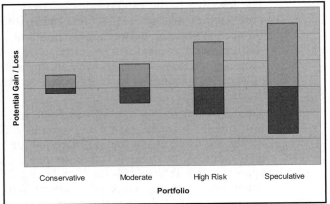

As an individual moves through the life cycle phases, it is inevitable that his personal goals will change and his risk-reward profile will evolve. The actual performance of his investment portfolio needs to be re-assessed regularly relative to prior assumptions. The following is a brief review of different types of risks and some of the issues relevant to investment decisions.

Business Risk

Business risk can be managed through diversification of the investor's portfolio. The selection of securities that cross multiple industries will lower a portfolio's overall risk. The use of rating services can help in the management of business risk when selecting financial assets.

When an investor holds financial assets that are connected to his place of employment, caution should be exercised relative to the proportional relationship between the individual's total investment holdings and holdings that are employer-related.

Professionally managed assets such as mutual funds and segregated funds can be valuable in the management of business risk, provided that there is a balance in the types and diversity of the holdings. For example, if an investor holds the bulk of his assets in mutual funds from four different fund companies, but the selected funds are all focused in a particular asset class, such as the health care industry, the diversification is very limited.

Market Risk

Investment assets with volatile prices tend to hold greater market risk than those investments where the volatility is more subdued. This type of risk needs to be considered in light of an investor's risk tolerance whereby some investors are simply not emotionally or financially able to handle the types of investments that experience significant price fluctuations.

While both common shares and government bonds fluctuate in price, the standard deviation of a common share depicts a much greater level of price volatility. Strip bonds are another example of investments that can be subject to significant market risk. If the investor plans to hold the strip bond until maturity, the market risk may not pose an issue; however, if there is a probability that the strip bond will be disposed of prior to maturity, market risk becomes an important consideration.

The use of options can be helpful to an investor in the management of market risk, whereas an investor's use of margin accounts can result in the magnification of losses, so will tend to increase risk. When market risk is of significant concern for an investor, he should avoid the use of margin or ensure the availability of sufficient liquid assets to cover any margin call.

The phrase "investing for the long term" can hold significant meaning for investors who are concerned about market risk. A short investment time horizon increases the probability that an investor will be faced with price fluctuations. Alternatively, when the investment time horizon is sufficiently long, it provides the investor with the opportunity to ride out the ups and downs that may occur within a market. A short investment time horizon is generally inconsistent with the purchase of speculative stocks and long-term bonds because of the potential for price sensitivity. These types of assets are more suited to an investor who is "investing for the long term".

Interest Rate Risk

Typically, bond prices are the most sensitive to interest rate risk. If interest rates in the general market are increasing, bonds held by the investor will be reduced in value. Typically, interest rate risk increases as the time to maturity increases. This means that a bond with a long period prior to maturity will experience greater price movement as interest rates change than a bond with a shorter period to maturity. During times of rising interest rates, longer-term bonds will experience a greater price drop than those bonds with shorter periods to maturity. Conversely, as interest rates drop, longer-term bonds will experience a greater price increase.

While fixed-rate term deposits provide the investors with the assurance of a certain rate of return for a fixed period, and therefore provide protection against falling interest rates, the investor may lose on the up-side because of a commitment to hold the investment until it matures, making the investor unable to take advantage of rising interest rates.

The selection of investment assets should align specifically with the investor's goals and objectives. For example, if an investor is 12 years from retirement and wants the security of a fixed-income investment, the selection of a 12-year corporate bond may shield the investor from the impact of interest rate and reinvestment risk.

Careful analysis of yield curves provides the investor with options to adjust the maturity of an investment in order to optimize the interest return. As well, the laddering of different maturity dates adds protection, so the portfolio holds investments with a variety of maturity dates and therefore corresponding interest rates.

Reinvestment Risk

Reinvestment risk should be considered when comparing potential investments of various maturities and various rates of return in a volatile market. As discussed in Module 15, if an investor's choice is between investment A, which pays 10% per year for two years, and investment B, which pays 9% per year for five years, the investor would examine the reinvestment risk associated with these investment choices before committing funds. If market interest rates are falling sharply, the case for investment B may be stronger, even though it returns less in the first two years. Reinvestment risk is one of the elements an investor considers as an integral part of selecting appropriate investments.

An investor also faces reinvestment risk when he receives a flow of income during the term of a fixed-income security. The annual income from a bond or preferred share is subject to reinvestment risk when the level of interest at which the income is reinvested is at a rate less than what is being paid on the security itself. Reinvestment risk also occurs when an investor receives a coupon or interest payment and simply leaves the income sit idle, even if only in the short term.

Automatic reinvestment programs, such as a DRIP, are helpful for managing reinvestment risk. The immediate reinvestment of income received from an asset reduces the time the income sits idle. The purchase of strip bonds is another approach for reducing reinvestment risk, although the investor will need to trade off the reduction of reinvestment risk with the potential for market risk.

Inflation Risk

The appearance of inflation risk is not always immediately obvious to an investor because erosion of purchasing power occurs over time. This type of risk is one of the most subtle and also one of the most complex to manage. There is little common agreement across advisors as to an optimum strategy for managing inflation. While stocks have traditionally been viewed as a typical hedge against inflation, the dramatic shifts in the equity markets during recent years highlights the risk trade-offs that an investor should consider carefully. Participation in an equity market means market risk, which may be inconsistent with the investor's investment goals and objectives. Issues such as liquidity and capital erosion are other relevant considerations.

When developing financial plans, particularly retirement plans, the implications of inflation need to be discussed thoroughly with a client and should be incorporated in the development of income strategies. While it is difficult for many to envision themselves 20 years into the future, time does not stop and the erosion of purchasing power is inevitable.

Individuals on a fixed income, such as those who have retired on a non-indexed company pension, face the erosion of their purchasing power because of inflation. An individual who retired 15 years ago with a company pension of $25,000 annually has less purchasing power today, even though he still receives the same $25,000 annually from the company pension plan.

The purchasing power of an individual's savings declines as inflation increases. This decline motivates some investors to seek substitute investments, such as gold, silver, precious stones or real estate, as a hedge against inflation.

Typically, real estate has been considered a valuable hedge against inflation, for both expected and unexpected inflation. Recall from Module 15 that expected inflation represents what economists and investors expect inflation will be over a given time frame, while unexpected inflation is the difference between actual and expected inflation.

The addition of real estate to an investment portfolio provides not only the opportunity to diversify the portfolio's overall investment structure, it also can provide inflation protection to a mixed-asset portfolio. However, because real estate is sensitive to economic growth, an investor should be cognizant of economic or business cycles when real estate is used as a hedge against the risk of rising inflation.

Application

The following SNAP uses CCH's FPS software as a support tool to demonstrate the concept of asset diversification.

KEITH

Keith, in his late forties, has always valued the advice that portfolio diversification is an important element of his investment strategy. Through effective diversification, Keith feels he will be better able to include some higher risk/higher return components for an improved overall return, while managing the risk relative to his total portfolio.

Let's look at output produced by CCH's FPS software, used to model the results derived from changing the asset mix within Keith's portfolio. See Appendix Three.

Item 1

This page sets out the current situation and the results derived from a change in the current diversification.

The top two pie graphs graphically illustrate the current and recommended investment mix. The current allocation is comprised of income arising from 50% interest income and 50% dividend income, both yielding 4% per annum. The recommended mix involves a one-third reduction of the assets that produce interest and dividends to be replaced with assets that produce capital gains.

continued . . .

---

continued . . .

The graph at the bottom of the page shows the financial results of these two different strategies.

Item 2

This page sets out a numerical comparison of the two investment portfolios, each on an after-tax basis, in order to identify the advantages of the recommended investment mix.

Item 3

The detail of the recommended investment mix is shown on this page.

Item 4

The detail of the current investment mix is shown on this page.

Item 5

This page highlights the differences between the current and recommended investment mix.

Item 6

Disclosure of the issues with respect to various investment strategies are detailed on this page along with a place for the client to sign an acknowledgement of the discussion that has taken place.

CONCLUSION

In this example, the recommended asset mix is shown to produce greater wealth over time. However, the financials are only one part of the analysis, and it is essential that Keith understand the risks associated with adjusting his asset mix before proceeding with any changes.

Note: For testing purposes, you are **not** responsible for using software to duplicate the results of this analysis. This SNAP is included for demonstration purposes only.

Unit 3

Module 17 Exercises and Case Study

MODULE 17 EXERCISES

1. Joan purchased a 90-day Canadian treasury bill for $97,500 with a maturity value of $100,000. What is the quoted yield on the T-bill?

2. Mary wanted to purchase a 180-day Canadian treasury bill with a quoted yield of 2.5% and a maturity value of $100,000. What is the purchase price of the T-bill?

3. Joan wanted to purchase a 180-day American dollar treasury bill with a quoted yield of 2.5% and a maturity value of US$100,000. What is the purchase price of the T-bill? What type of specific investment risk is Joan exposing herself to when she buys the investment? What is the key difference between yields on Canadian *versus* American T-bills?

4. Kam bought a 91-day T-bill for $9,750. Calculate the quote yield and the annualized effective yield on the T-bill.

5. Sandra is considering the purchase of a $25,000, 10% Alpha Corp bond. The bond was issued 20 years ago, but has only five years remaining. The current market rate of interest is 8%.

    a. What price should Sandra pay for the bond?

    b. What is the current yield on the bond?

    c. What is the yield-to-maturity on the bond?

6. Lyaca is considering purchasing preferred shares which have a par value of $80 and a dividend rate of 4.5%. If the prevailing market rate for similar types of investments is 5%, what is the current market price of the preferred shares?

7. Define the term duration and explain how is it used by portfolio managers.

8. How would an investor "immunize" his portfolio?

9. Ayesha owns one share of XYP common stock that currently pays a dividend of $4 per year that is forecast to increase 3% annually. Assume a discount rate of 9%. Calculate the intrinsic value under the constant-growth model and the zero-growth model.

10. Compare and contrast the technical and fundamental analysis approaches to security analysis.

11. Diversification can have a considerable impact on the performance of an investment portfolio. Identify five ways an investor can diversify his portfolio.

12. What are the four main categories of investment objectives?

13. Explain the term portfolio insurance.

14. What is the difference between active and passive investment styles?

15. Various investment styles are commonly used in the development of an investment portfolio. Explain the following styles: security selection, asset allocation, market timing and maturity selection.

16. Explain the differences between the value stock style and the growth stock style of investments.

CASE STUDY — ANN AND TOM NEWMAN: "WHERE FROM HERE?"

Ann and Tom Newman have been married for 25 years and currently live in Sometown, Canada. They have three children, all of whom depend fully on the couple for financial support. One daughter is entering her second year of university, while the other two daughters both attend a local, private high school. Dates of birth for each of the family members are:

	Date of Birth	**Position**
Tom	August 12, 1960	VP — Investment Banker
Ann	October 30, 1959	VP — Manufacturing Firm
Deanna	April 30, 1990	Second year university student
Christy	October 12, 1994	High school student
Ashley	July 10, 1995	High school student

Family is important to Ann and Tom and always takes priority. The Newmans estimate that they spend $25,000 annually on Deanna's education costs, including her tuition and residence. Christy and Ashley's attendance at a private school costs the Newmans about $45,000 annually.

Tom is an investment banker who earns $250,000 annually, and Ann earns $180,000 annually as the VP responsible for operations at an international manufacturing firm. Neither Ann nor Tom has any pension benefits, but both have RRSP assets. In addition, the couple have accumulated a wide portfolio of investment assets.

The Newmans' statement of net worth is shown in Appendix One. Additional information related to the couple's asset holding is as follows:

- Tom's cash equivalent holdings include two T-bills:
  - 180-day Canadian T-bill purchased for $9,704.43 with a maturity value of $10,000.
  - 60-day Canadian T-bill purchased for $19,950.50 with a maturity value of $20,000.
- Ann's bond portfolio is comprised of three sets of bonds:

Company	No.	Par Value	Coupon	Maturity Date	Market Value
ABC	500	$25.00	8.5%	June 30, 2011	$10,000
TUV	1,200	$18.00	6%	December 31, 2013	$18,600
XYZ	400	$25.00	5%	June 30, 2011	$9,000

Ann purchased the TUV bonds at par value.

- The equities held by Ann are common shares of her employer.
- The equities held by Tom are comprised of:

Company	Type	No.	Market Value	ACB
New Corp.	Common	2,500	$43,000	$45,000
Best Corp.	Common	1,200	$36,000	$15,000
Top Inc.	Preferred	1,500	$22,500	$19,000

The Top Inc. preferred shares have a 5% coupon and a par value of $10.

- Ann's mutual funds are invested in an Asian venture fund. Ann made the purchase one year ago when the unit value was $18 and it has now dropped to $10.
- The couple each own a universal life insurance policy on their respective life with the cash value invested in an indexed GIC based on the S&P/TSX Composite Index.

- The RRSP assets are currently sitting in an interest-bearing account that pays a variable rate each month. The account paid an amount based on an annual nominal rate of 2.85%. The couple moved the funds into this current structure in July in an effort to suppress any further loss of capital.

The Newmans own their single-family dwelling and have no mortgage or other debt. They make a practice of paying cash for their automobiles, as they do not want to pay unnecessary financing charges for leases or loans. Tom has indicated that he will likely purchase a new vehicle within the next six months. At that time, his vehicle will move to Ann and Ann's will move to Deanna.

In discussions with the Newmans, the couple have expressed their disappointment in the loss of capital in their RRSP portfolios during the first half of the year. As the couple was making RRSP deposits, the value of their funds was eroding and they were seeing an immediate loss. The couple is very risk averse and feel that safety of capital is an important priority. In addition, at their current age the couple feel now is the time to make some true gains on their asset holdings in preparation for retirement. With no pension available for either Tom or Ann, they will rely completely on their personal investments to fund their retirement lifestyle.

Tom is particularly focused on the concept of creditor protection. Although the family has no debt, Tom still feels strongly that if creditor protection were the only differentiating factor between two alternatives, he would always favour the option with this protection. Tom takes the lead in developing investment decisions for the family. He does not have a clear philosophy, but would view himself as a moderate believer in the efficient market, and would be satisfied with investment returns that mirror the market.

Other than the impending purchase of an automobile, neither Tom nor Ann foresee any large expenditures in the next five years that could not be easily funded out of their current cash flow.

Tom and Ann are both in the 45% marginal tax bracket, and the couple is open to suggestions as to how they could save taxes on their current investment holdings.

When answering the following series of questions, assume it is January 1, 2010, and disregard sales commissions unless otherwise noted.

Required

Address the following questions:

a. Calculate the quoted yield on Tom's 180-day T-bill.

b. Calculate the annual yield on Tom's 60-day T-bill.

c. What are the tax consequences of the earnings on Tom's T-bills if he holds them to maturity?

d. If Tom has 30 days remaining on each of his two T-bills, but opts to sell them now in order to help fund the purchase of his new vehicle, what is the income tax implication, if any?

e. If Tom were to use the funds of his maturing T-bills to purchase U.S. dollar T-bills, how might this affect his investment risk?

f. If Ann purchased her ABC bonds for their par value of $25,000 and she holds the bonds to maturity, what is her anticipated yield-to-maturity? (Disregard commissions.)

g. Assuming the price change on the TUV bonds is interest related, what has likely happened to interest rates since she made the purchase?

h. What is the current yield on Tom's Top Inc. preferred shares?

i. What is the risk profile of Ann's mutual fund holdings?

j. Tom has heard that strip bonds are a good long-term investment. He would like to add diversity to his non-registered portfolio by selling his Best Corp. shares and use the funds to purchase strip bonds. Comment on this strategy relative to the Newmans request for suggestions regarding tax savings.

k. Tom and Ann have suggested that they would like to move a portion of their non-registered investments to each of their children, in an effort to save income tax. What implications arise from this strategy?

l. If Tom believes in the efficient market theory, what type of investment approach should he consider?

m. How might the purchase of equity-based segregated funds align with Tom and Ann's investment objectives?

n. If the prevailing market rate for preferred shares is expected to rise to 6% later this year, calculate the market price of Tom's Top Inc. preferred shares at that time. In addition, calculate the prevailing market rate based on Tom's holdings of Top Inc. at the time of purchase.

o. Tom just realized that his TUV bonds are callable between the period of January 1, 2012 to May 31, 2012, with a $2.00 enhancement paid if the bond is called prior to maturity. What is Tom's effective yield-to-call?

p. Comment on the type of investment the Newmans have selected for the cash value of their universal life insurance policy.

Appendix One
Ms. Ann Newman and Mr. Tom Newman
Statement of Net Worth[1]
As of December 31, 2009

ASSETS	Ann ($)	Tom ($)	TOTAL ($)
Non-Registered Assets			
Cash and equivalents	8,500	30,000 (2)	38,500
GICs	4,000	22,000	26,000
Bonds	37,600	0	37,600
Equities	15,500	101,500	117,000
Mutual funds	2,000		2,000
Real Estate	0	0	0
Total Non-registered Assets	67,600	153,500	221,100
Registered Assets			
RESP			0
RPP			0
RRSP	168,000	184,000	352,000
Total Registered Assets	168,000	184,000	352,000
Other Assets			
Business Equity			0
CSV of life insurance	18,000	22,000	40,000
Total Other Assets	18,000	22,000	40,000
Personal Assets			
Home/Residence	275,000	275,000	550,000
Personal Effects	30,000	30,000	60,000
Cottage/Recreational Property	125,000		125,000
Vehicles	55,000	62,000	117,000
Total Personal Assets	485,000	367,000	852,000
TOTAL ASSETS	**$738,600**	**$726,500**	**$1,465,100**
LIABILITIES			
Credit cards/Consumer Debt	0	0	0
Loan - Vehicles		0	0
Business Loan			0
Investment loan	0	0	0
Mortgage	0	0	0
TOTAL LIABILITIES	0	0	0
NET WORTH	**$738,600**	**$726,500**	**$1,465,100**

Note: (1) Assets at market value could have income tax consequences that have not been accounted for in this Statement of Net Worth.

(2) T-bills entered at upcoming maturity value.

Appendix Two

Wendy SNAP

Investment Leverage

Application

For testing purposes, the CFP Education Program and CFP Exam utilize the financial calculator as the only tool to support any analysis. However, the calculator on its own has limitations, particularly when undertaking integrated financial planning solutions in your office on a day-to-day basis. Financial planners often utilize software packages as a valuable tool when working with integrated planning situations, such as a comprehensive financial plan. Good quality software allows the planner to enter a series of variables that reflect facts and assumptions relative to the client's specific situation, and then readily produces a variety of output that can be used in the analysis of case-specific issues.

CCH's *Financial Planning Solutions* (FPS) offers extensive software support for completing comprehensive and single need planning. Using fully integrated workbooks with the spreadsheet format of Microsoft Excel, the software allows a planner to enter data, make assumptions and update assumptions in order to analyze the client-specific situation. The software produces output that is client-friendly. This SNAP uses CCH's FP Solutions software to demonstrate the concept of leveraged investing. It is for information purposes only — for those who want to explore the concept in more detail; however, it is not required reading or testable.

WENDY

Wendy, a reasonably sophisticated investor, has a solid grasp of the concept of leveraged investing. She understands that leveraged investing is a means to create more wealth. However, she also recognizes that it is a double-edged sword; on one hand her investment growth can be magnified, yet conversely her current wealth can be eroded with a similar magnification, but in the reverse direction.

Wendy McCann is considering the option of borrowing $100,000, at a 6% rate of interest, and is committed to servicing the loan on a monthly basis. In order to assess whether the loan is an effective option, Wendy needs to establish a fair comparison basis. To do this, a second investment alternative is constructed where the same after-tax cash flow as that required to service the loan on option one is invested in a second portfolio to create option two.

For projection purposes, the following assumptions are made in respect of the two investment portfolios:

  ⇨   investment income is 1/3 capital gain, 1/3 dividend and 1/3 interest;

  ⇨   capital gains accrue at 8% annually;

  ⇨   dividends are paid at 4% annually; and

  ⇨   interest is earned at 4% annually.

The portfolio turns over regularly with 20% of the accrued gain realized annually.

This basic information has been input into the FPS software to create the output, as shown on the following pages, and which Wendy will use in her analysis.

Item 1

This page sets out the basic benefits and risks of leveraged investing. The first graph illustrates the results of the analysis. The second graph illustrates the debt position and servicing payments.

Item 2

Set out on this page is a numerical comparison of the two investment portfolios, each on an after-tax basis, in order to identify the advantages or disadvantages of the strategy.

continued . . .

---

continued . . .

Item 3

Details of the leveraged investing strategy are shown on this page. In this case, the loan is taken out in year one and repaid in year 11. Based on the analysis in the software, the loan is paid from the portfolio in year 11, which triggers more tax that year, $4,869. After the loan is repaid, the portfolio stands at $54,567.

Item 4

This item sets out the detail associated with the loan and the cost of servicing the loan. The after-tax interest payment is $3,215 per year.

Item 5

Next is a page that summarizes the detail of the comparison investment portfolio. This portfolio is built on an annual deposit of $3,215, which is the after-tax cash flow that would have been required under the leveraged strategy. After 11 years, the portfolio stands at $42,436.

This analysis of option two provides Wendy with a valid comparison against which she can assess the effectiveness of option one.

Item 6

Disclosure of the issues with respect to leveraged investing are detailed on this page, along with a place for the client to sign an acknowledgement of the discussion that has taken place.

CONCLUSION

In this example, option one, the leveraged investment strategy, provides Wendy with greater wealth than the strategy outlined in option two. However, the financials are only one part of the analysis, and it is essential that Wendy understands the risks of leveraged investing before proceeding with any decision.

Note: For testing purposes, you are **not** responsible for using software to duplicate the results of this analysis.

Investment Leverage

Borrowing to invest compared to making regular deposits

Prepared for: **Wendy McCann**

Prepared by:

Leverage investing is the process of borrowing money (going into debt) to purchase investments with the goal of magnifying the overall return once the debt is paid off. Rather than starting with a small amount and adding regular deposits to the investment, by borrowing you start with a larger sum of money and make regular payments towards the debt. It is important to note, however, that with a regular deposit strategy, if your ability to maintain the deposits changes, you can easily lower the amount being deposited. With a leverage strategy, although you can cash out some or all of the investment to pay against the debt, you are normally committed to the payment schedule.

Another aspect you have to consider is the effect the payments may have on your debt service ratio. If, with the leverage strategy, your total debt service exceeds 40% of gross annual income, you may have difficulty arranging future credit for personal use.

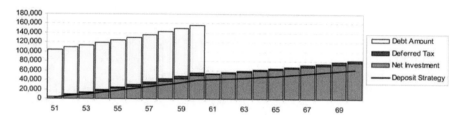

The above graph compares the value of the leverage strategy once all debt and deferred taxes have been paid, to the after-tax value of the deposit strategy. The following graph projects the future outstanding balance of any debt and the required annual payments.

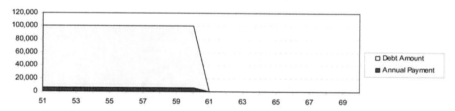

When considering whether borrowing to invest is appropriate for you, it is important that you understand how leverage can affect your returns, both positively as well as negatively. To illustrate leverage assume you have an investment you expect will earn 8% annually. For each $1,000 you have to invest, you borrow another $1,000 at 6%.

After one year you will have earned 8% on $2,000 and paid 6% on $1,000. Your return is $100 ($160 - $60) or 10% of the $1,000 you had to invest. Leverage provided you with a 25% increase on returns.

If, however, the investment had lost 8%, your total losses would be -$220 (-$160-$60) or -22% of the $1,000 you had to invest. In this case leverage had the effect of greatly magnifying your losses.

E. & O.E.

Page 4 of 9

Investment Leverage

Borrowing to invest compared to making regular deposits

Prepared for: **Wendy McCann**
Prepared by:

		Leverage Investment Strategy				Regular Deposit Strategy		
Year	Age	Year-end Balance	Deferred Tax	Outstanding Debt	After-tax Value	Year-end Balance	Deferred Tax	After-tax Value
1	51	104,515	533	100,000	3,982	3,275	7	3,268
2	52	109,149	1,077	100,000	8,072	6,695	32	6,664
3	53	114,015	1,634	100,000	12,381	10,270	75	10,196
4	54	119,129	2,206	100,000	16,923	14,009	137	13,872
5	55	124,504	2,795	100,000	21,710	17,923	220	17,703
6	56	130,158	3,403	100,000	26,756	22,021	323	21,698
7	57	136,108	4,032	100,000	32,076	26,316	450	25,866
8	58	142,371	4,684	100,000	37,687	30,819	600	30,220
9	59	148,968	5,363	100,000	43,606	35,545	775	34,770
10	60	155,919	6,069	100,000	49,850	40,506	976	39,530
11	61	54,567	2,380	0	52,187	42,436	1,197	41,239
12	62	57,021	2,598	0	54,423	44,470	1,425	43,045
13	63	59,606	2,827	0	56,779	46,615	1,662	44,953
14	64	62,330	3,069	0	59,261	48,878	1,908	46,969
15	65	65,201	3,325	0	61,877	51,265	2,165	49,100
16	66	68,230	3,595	0	64,635	53,786	2,433	51,353
17	67	71,425	3,881	0	67,544	56,448	2,713	53,735
18	68	74,797	4,183	0	70,613	59,261	3,007	56,254
19	69	78,356	4,504	0	73,852	62,233	3,316	58,918
20	70	82,115	4,844	0	77,271	65,376	3,640	61,736
21	71	86,086	5,205	0	80,881	68,700	3,981	64,719
22	72	90,282	5,589	0	84,694	72,216	4,341	67,875
23	73	94,718	5,996	0	88,722	75,938	4,722	71,217
24	74	99,409	6,429	0	92,979	79,878	5,123	74,755
25	75	104,370	6,890	0	97,480	84,050	5,548	78,502
26	76	109,619	7,380	0	102,238	88,469	5,998	82,471
27	77	115,174	7,902	0	107,272	93,152	6,475	86,677
28	78	121,054	8,458	0	112,597	98,114	6,980	91,134
29	79	127,282	9,050	0	118,232	103,375	7,517	95,858
30	80	133,877	9,680	0	124,197	108,954	8,087	100,867
31	81	140,865	10,352	0	130,513	114,871	8,693	106,178
32	82	148,271	11,068	0	137,203	121,148	9,337	111,812
33	83	156,121	11,832	0	144,289	127,810	10,021	117,788
34	84	164,444	12,646	0	151,798	134,880	10,750	124,130
35	85	173,271	13,514	0	159,756	142,386	11,526	130,860

E. & O.E.

Page 5 of 9

Investment Leverage

Value of investments using a leverage strategy

Prepared for: **Wendy McCann**
Prepared by:

Year	Age	Annual Deposit	Annual Withdrawal	Annual Growth	Weighted Return	Allowance For Tax	Year-end Balance	Deferred Tax
1	51	100,000	0	6,006	6.03%	1,591	104,515	533
2	52	0	0	6,307	6.07%	1,673	109,149	1,077
3	53	0	0	6,624	6.10%	1,757	114,015	1,634
4	54	0	0	6,957	6.14%	1,844	119,129	2,206
5	55	0	0	7,309	6.17%	1,934	124,504	2,795
6	56	0	0	7,681	6.20%	2,027	130,158	3,403
7	57	0	0	8,073	6.24%	2,124	136,108	4,032
8	58	0	0	8,487	6.27%	2,224	142,371	4,684
9	59	0	0	8,925	6.30%	2,328	148,968	5,363
10	60	0	0	9,388	6.33%	2,437	155,919	6,069
11	61	0	100,000	3,517	6.21%	4,869	54,567	2,380
12	62	0	0	3,391	6.25%	937	57,021	2,598
13	63	0	0	3,561	6.28%	976	59,606	2,827
14	64	0	0	3,742	6.31%	1,018	62,330	3,069
15	65	0	0	3,932	6.34%	1,061	65,201	3,325
16	66	0	0	4,134	6.37%	1,106	68,230	3,595
17	67	0	0	4,348	6.40%	1,153	71,425	3,881
18	68	0	0	4,574	6.44%	1,202	74,797	4,183
19	69	0	0	4,813	6.47%	1,254	78,356	4,504
20	70	0	0	5,067	6.50%	1,308	82,115	4,844
21	71	0	0	5,336	6.53%	1,365	86,086	5,205
22	72	0	0	5,620	6.56%	1,424	90,282	5,589
23	73	0	0	5,922	6.59%	1,486	94,718	5,996
24	74	0	0	6,242	6.62%	1,552	99,409	6,429
25	75	0	0	6,582	6.65%	1,621	104,370	6,890
26	76	0	0	6,942	6.68%	1,693	109,619	7,380
27	77	0	0	7,324	6.71%	1,769	115,174	7,902
28	78	0	0	7,729	6.74%	1,849	121,054	8,458
29	79	0	0	8,160	6.77%	1,933	127,282	9,050
30	80	0	0	8,617	6.80%	2,021	133,877	9,680
31	81	0	0	9,102	6.83%	2,114	140,865	10,352
32	82	0	0	9,618	6.86%	2,212	148,271	11,068
33	83	0	0	10,165	6.88%	2,315	156,121	11,832
34	84	0	0	10,747	6.91%	2,424	164,444	12,646
35	85	0	0	11,366	6.94%	2,539	173,271	13,514

E. & O.E.

Investment Leverage

Outstanding debt using a leverage strategy

Prepared for: **Wendy McCann**
Prepared by:

Year	Age	Debt Amount	Interest Rate	Annual Payment	Interest Portion	Interest Cumulative	Tax Savings	After-tax Payment
1	51	100,000	6.00%	6,000	6,000	6,000	2,785	3,215
2	52	100,000	6.00%	6,000	6,000	12,000	2,785	3,215
3	53	100,000	6.00%	6,000	6,000	18,000	2,785	3,215
4	54	100,000	6.00%	6,000	6,000	24,000	2,785	3,215
5	55	100,000	6.00%	6,000	6,000	30,000	2,785	3,215
6	56	100,000	6.00%	6,000	6,000	36,000	2,785	3,215
7	57	100,000	6.00%	6,000	6,000	42,000	2,785	3,215
8	58	100,000	6.00%	6,000	6,000	48,000	2,785	3,215
9	59	100,000	6.00%	6,000	6,000	54,000	2,785	3,215
10	60	100,000	6.00%	6,000	6,000	60,000	2,785	3,215
11	61	0	6.00%	0	0	60,000	0	0
12	62	0	6.00%	0	0	60,000	0	0
13	63	0	6.00%	0	0	60,000	0	0
14	64	0	6.00%	0	0	60,000	0	0
15	65	0	6.00%	0	0	60,000	0	0
16	66	0	6.00%	0	0	60,000	0	0
17	67	0	6.00%	0	0	60,000	0	0
18	68	0	6.00%	0	0	60,000	0	0
19	69	0	6.00%	0	0	60,000	0	0
20	70	0	6.00%	0	0	60,000	0	0
21	71	0	6.00%	0	0	60,000	0	0
22	72	0	6.00%	0	0	60,000	0	0
23	73	0	6.00%	0	0	60,000	0	0
24	74	0	6.00%	0	0	60,000	0	0
25	75	0	6.00%	0	0	60,000	0	0
26	76	0	6.00%	0	0	60,000	0	0
27	77	0	6.00%	0	0	60,000	0	0
28	78	0	6.00%	0	0	60,000	0	0
29	79	0	6.00%	0	0	60,000	0	0
30	80	0	6.00%	0	0	60,000	0	0
31	81	0	6.00%	0	0	60,000	0	0
32	82	0	6.00%	0	0	60,000	0	0
33	83	0	6.00%	0	0	60,000	0	0
34	84	0	6.00%	0	0	60,000	0	0
35	85	0	6.00%	0	0	60,000	0	0

E. & O.E.

Item 5

Investment Leverage

Value of investments using a regular deposit strategy

Prepared for: **Wendy McCann**
Prepared by:

Year	Age	Annual Deposit	Annual Withdrawal	Annual Growth	Weighted Return	Allowance For Tax	Year-end Balance	Deferred Tax
1	51	3,215	0	81	6.01%	21	3,275	7
2	52	3,215	0	279	6.05%	73	6,695	32
3	53	3,215	0	487	6.09%	128	10,270	75
4	54	3,215	0	708	6.12%	184	14,009	137
5	55	3,215	0	941	6.16%	243	17,923	220
6	56	3,215	0	1,187	6.19%	304	22,021	323
7	57	3,215	0	1,448	6.23%	368	26,316	450
8	58	3,215	0	1,723	6.26%	435	30,819	600
9	59	3,215	0	2,015	6.30%	505	35,545	775
10	60	3,215	0	2,324	6.33%	578	40,506	976
11	61	0	0	2,565	6.36%	634	42,436	1,197
12	62	0	0	2,701	6.40%	667	44,470	1,425
13	63	0	0	2,845	6.43%	700	46,615	1,662
14	64	0	0	2,998	6.46%	735	48,878	1,908
15	65	0	0	3,159	6.50%	772	51,265	2,165
16	66	0	0	3,330	6.53%	809	53,786	2,433
17	67	0	0	3,511	6.56%	849	56,448	2,713
18	68	0	0	3,703	6.59%	890	59,261	3,007
19	69	0	0	3,906	6.62%	933	62,233	3,316
20	70	0	0	4,121	6.65%	979	65,376	3,640
21	71	0	0	4,350	6.68%	1,026	68,700	3,981
22	72	0	0	4,592	6.71%	1,075	72,216	4,341
23	73	0	0	4,849	6.74%	1,127	75,938	4,722
24	74	0	0	5,121	6.77%	1,182	79,878	5,123
25	75	0	0	5,411	6.80%	1,239	84,050	5,548
26	76	0	0	5,718	6.83%	1,299	88,469	5,998
27	77	0	0	6,044	6.86%	1,362	93,152	6,475
28	78	0	0	6,391	6.89%	1,428	98,114	6,980
29	79	0	0	6,759	6.92%	1,498	103,375	7,517
30	80	0	0	7,150	6.94%	1,572	108,954	8,087
31	81	0	0	7,566	6.97%	1,649	114,871	8,693
32	82	0	0	8,008	7.00%	1,730	121,148	9,337
33	83	0	0	8,478	7.02%	1,816	127,810	10,021
34	84	0	0	8,977	7.05%	1,907	134,880	10,750
35	85	0	0	9,509	7.08%	2,003	142,386	11,526

E. & O.E.

Page 8 of 9

Investment Leverage

This document is not an estimate or guarantee of future performance

Prepared for: **Wendy McCann**

Prepared by:

Overview of concept:

This document compares two investment strategies, borrowing to invest (leverage) and making regular investment deposits. The amount invested in the regular deposit strategy is equal to the estimated after-tax loan payment of the leverage strategy with a similar deposit frequency.

In both cases the amount borrowed and the regular deposits are assumed to be invested in a portfolio of securities with similar allocation and return assumptions. Any taxes due on earnings including interest, dividends and realized capital gains are assumed to be deducted from the growth annually. All other assumptions including the marginal tax rate are similar for both strategies.

As stated on the summary page of this document, a leverage investment strategy magnifies losses as well as gains and as a result an investment made with borrowed funds involves a greater risk than an investment using cash resources only.

I acknowledge that:

I have fully reviewed and understand the illustrations and projections within this document. I recognize that this analysis is based upon numerous assumptions, and the ultimate performance of the proposed financial concepts and strategies will depend on but not be limited to:

- ■ **future investment performance,**
- ■ **the ultimate course of inflation,**
- ■ **evolving Federal and Provincial tax laws, and**
- ■ **the timing and amounts of any future investment deposits and withdrawals.**

I understand that inflation, interest rates and the performance of various securities can fluctuate significantly and that actual results will vary from those illustrated.

I acknowledge that this concept is an illustration only, and NOT a contract. I understand that there are no implied guarantees within this document.

Date: _____

_____
Signature of Wendy McCann

_____
Signature of

E. & O.E.

Appendix Three
Keith SNAP
Investment Strategies

Item 1

Investment Strategies

Recommended investment strategies compared to current strategies

Prepared for: **Keith Marino**
Prepared by:

Investment Allocation   **Recommended Strategies**   **Current Strategies**

◻ Cash
◼ Bond
◻ Equity

◻ Canadian
◻ Foreign

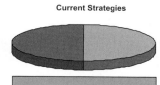

Diversification is an important element in any investment strategy, as it can help to reduce exposure to risk. A good investment plan should provide the best possible return for the degree of risk you are willing to assume. It must be kept in mind, however, that there are different kinds of risk. Market risk or volatility is not the only kind of risk. There is also the risk of declining interest rates as well as the potential for erosion of purchasing power due to inflation. Your investment plan must also take into account tax considerations. Certain types of investment returns are fully taxed at an investor's top marginal rate, while other types of returns feature significant tax advantages.

Interest is fully taxable each year at your top marginal rate.
Dividends are taxable as received, but those from Canadian companies are eligible for preferred tax treatment through the Dividend Tax Credit.
Capital Gains are only 50% taxable when realized. In the case of mutual funds, a percentage of gains must usually be reported each year even if shares are not disposed of, due to investment turnover within the fund.

The charts at the top of the page compare the composition of the current investment portfolio (including Canadian and foreign content) to that of the recommended investment portfolio.

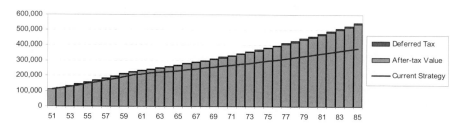

Although the allocation of the investment portfolio is used to determine the projected annual rate of return, there are a number of other planning strategies that can be utilized to further enhance the value of the plan. Deferral of income tax through the use of tax efficient investments, lowering portfolio turnover and the timing of the deposits and withdrawals all keep more of your hard-earned investment dollars working for you.

The above graph compares the projected value of the recommended investment strategies once all deferred taxes have been paid, to the after-tax value of the current strategies.

E. & O.E.   Page 4 of 9

Item 2

Investment Strategies

Recommended investment strategies compared to current strategies

Prepared for: **Keith Marino**
Prepared by:

		Recommended Strategies			Current Strategies			
Year	Age	Deposit / (Withdraw)	Net Growth	After-tax Value	Deposit / (Withdraw)	Net Growth	After-tax Value	Change In Value
1	51	6,000	5,150	109,550	6,000	4,120	108,549	1,001
2	52	6,180	5,681	119,657	6,180	4,466	117,493	2,164
3	53	6,365	6,244	130,351	6,365	4,827	126,847	3,504
4	54	6,556	6,841	141,660	6,556	5,205	136,627	5,033
5	55	6,753	7,473	153,618	6,753	5,600	146,849	6,769
6	56	6,956	7,945	166,058	6,956	6,013	157,525	8,533
7	57	7,164	8,627	179,194	7,164	6,444	168,678	10,516
8	58	7,379	9,347	193,056	7,379	6,895	180,326	12,730
9	59	7,601	10,111	207,683	7,601	7,365	192,488	15,195
10	60	7,829	10,921	223,116	7,829	7,856	205,183	17,933
11	61	0	11,320	230,938	0	8,207	210,261	20,677
12	62	0	11,772	239,089	0	8,410	215,467	23,622
13	63	0	12,243	247,582	0	8,619	220,803	26,779
14	64	0	12,737	256,434	0	8,832	226,272	30,161
15	65	0	13,253	265,661	0	9,051	231,879	33,782
16	66	0	13,507	275,001	0	9,275	237,618	37,382
17	67	0	14,034	284,719	0	9,505	243,501	41,218
18	68	0	14,591	294,841	0	9,740	249,531	45,310
19	69	0	15,174	305,387	0	9,981	255,713	49,674
20	70	0	15,785	316,377	0	10,229	262,049	54,328
21	71	0	16,094	327,506	0	10,482	268,535	58,971
22	72	0	16,718	339,084	0	10,741	275,183	63,901
23	73	0	17,380	351,141	0	11,007	281,998	69,143
24	74	0	18,073	363,702	0	11,280	288,984	74,718
25	75	0	18,800	376,791	0	11,559	296,145	80,646
26	76	0	19,169	390,047	0	11,846	303,474	86,573
27	77	0	19,912	403,836	0	12,139	310,987	92,849
28	78	0	20,700	418,197	0	12,439	318,689	99,508
29	79	0	21,525	433,156	0	12,748	326,584	106,573
30	80	0	22,391	448,745	0	13,063	334,676	114,069
31	81	0	22,830	464,533	0	13,387	342,959	121,574
32	82	0	23,715	480,956	0	13,718	351,450	129,506
33	83	0	24,653	498,059	0	14,058	360,154	137,905
34	84	0	25,636	515,875	0	14,406	369,075	146,800
35	85	0	26,666	534,441	0	14,763	378,221	156,220

E. & O.E.

Page 5 of 9

Investment Strategies

Value of investments utilizing the recommended strategies

Prepared for: **Keith Marino**
Prepared by:

Year	Age	Annual Deposit	Total Withdrawals	Annual Growth	Weighted Return	Allowance For Tax	Year-end Balance	Deferred Tax
1	51	6,000	0	5,150	5.03%	1,199	109,951	401
2	52	6,180	0	5,681	5.05%	1,382	120,431	773
3	53	6,365	0	6,244	5.08%	1,564	131,476	1,125
4	54	6,556	0	6,841	5.10%	1,747	143,126	1,466
5	55	6,753	0	7,473	5.12%	1,933	155,419	1,801
6	56	6,956	0	7,945	5.02%	2,132	168,187	2,129
7	57	7,164	0	8,627	5.04%	2,397	181,582	2,388
8	58	7,379	0	9,347	5.07%	2,587	195,721	2,665
9	59	7,601	0	10,111	5.09%	2,787	210,645	2,962
10	60	7,829	0	10,921	5.11%	2,997	226,397	3,281
11	61	0	0	11,320	5.02%	3,262	234,455	3,517
12	62	0	0	11,772	5.04%	3,391	242,835	3,746
13	63	0	0	12,243	5.06%	3,513	251,565	3,983
14	64	0	0	12,737	5.08%	3,639	260,663	4,229
15	65	0	0	13,253	5.11%	3,769	270,147	4,485
16	66	0	0	13,507	5.02%	4,067	279,586	4,585
17	67	0	0	14,034	5.04%	4,121	289,499	4,780
18	68	0	0	14,591	5.06%	4,251	299,839	4,998
19	69	0	0	15,174	5.08%	4,388	310,625	5,238
20	70	0	0	15,785	5.10%	4,533	321,877	5,500
21	71	0	0	16,094	5.02%	4,893	333,078	5,572
22	72	0	0	16,718	5.04%	4,931	344,865	5,781
23	73	0	0	17,380	5.06%	5,081	357,164	6,023
24	74	0	0	18,073	5.08%	5,241	369,996	6,294
25	75	0	0	18,800	5.10%	5,411	383,386	6,595
26	76	0	0	19,169	5.02%	5,841	396,714	6,667
27	77	0	0	19,912	5.04%	5,880	410,746	6,910
28	78	0	0	20,700	5.06%	6,057	425,389	7,193
29	79	0	0	21,525	5.08%	6,246	440,668	7,512
30	80	0	0	22,391	5.10%	6,447	456,612	7,867
31	81	0	0	22,830	5.02%	6,960	472,482	7,949
32	82	0	0	23,715	5.04%	7,004	489,193	8,237
33	83	0	0	24,653	5.06%	7,215	506,631	8,572
34	84	0	0	25,636	5.08%	7,440	524,827	8,951
35	85	0	0	26,666	5.10%	7,679	543,814	9,373

E. & O.E.

Page 6 of 9

Investment Strategies

Value of investments utilizing the current strategies

Prepared for: **Keith Marino**
Prepared by:

Year	Age	Annual Deposit	Total Withdrawals	Annual Growth	Weighted Return	Allowance For Tax	Year-end Balance	Deferred Tax
1	51	6,000	0	4,120	4.00%	1,571	108,549	0
2	52	6,180	0	4,466	4.00%	1,702	117,493	0
3	53	6,365	0	4,827	4.00%	1,839	126,847	0
4	54	6,556	0	5,205	4.00%	1,982	136,627	0
5	55	6,753	0	5,600	4.00%	2,131	146,849	0
6	56	6,956	0	6,013	4.00%	2,292	157,525	0
7	57	7,164	0	6,444	4.00%	2,456	168,678	0
8	58	7,379	0	6,895	4.00%	2,626	180,326	0
9	59	7,601	0	7,365	4.00%	2,804	192,488	0
10	60	7,829	0	7,856	4.00%	2,989	205,183	0
11	61	0	0	8,207	4.00%	3,129	210,261	0
12	62	0	0	8,410	4.00%	3,205	215,467	0
13	63	0	0	8,619	4.00%	3,283	220,803	0
14	64	0	0	8,832	4.00%	3,362	226,272	0
15	65	0	0	9,051	4.00%	3,444	231,879	0
16	66	0	0	9,275	4.00%	3,536	237,618	0
17	67	0	0	9,505	4.00%	3,622	243,501	0
18	68	0	0	9,740	4.00%	3,710	249,531	0
19	69	0	0	9,981	4.00%	3,800	255,713	0
20	70	0	0	10,229	4.00%	3,892	262,049	0
21	71	0	0	10,482	4.00%	3,996	268,535	0
22	72	0	0	10,741	4.00%	4,093	275,183	0
23	73	0	0	11,007	4.00%	4,192	281,998	0
24	74	0	0	11,280	4.00%	4,294	288,984	0
25	75	0	0	11,559	4.00%	4,398	296,145	0
26	76	0	0	11,846	4.00%	4,516	303,474	0
27	77	0	0	12,139	4.00%	4,626	310,987	0
28	78	0	0	12,439	4.00%	4,738	318,689	0
29	79	0	0	12,748	4.00%	4,853	326,584	0
30	80	0	0	13,063	4.00%	4,971	334,676	0
31	81	0	0	13,387	4.00%	5,104	342,959	0
32	82	0	0	13,718	4.00%	5,228	351,450	0
33	83	0	0	14,058	4.00%	5,354	360,154	0
34	84	0	0	14,406	4.00%	5,484	369,075	0
35	85	0	0	14,763	4.00%	5,618	378,221	0

E. & O.E.

Investment Strategies

Change in financial position by utilizing recommended strategies

Prepared for: **Keith Marino**
Prepared by:

Year	Age	Annual Deposit	Total Withdrawals	Annual Growth	Weighted Return	Allowance For Tax	Year-end Balance	Deferred Tax
1	51	0	0	1,030	1.03%	-372	1,402	401
2	52	0	0	1,216	1.05%	-320	2,937	773
3	53	0	0	1,417	1.08%	-274	4,629	1,125
4	54	0	0	1,636	1.10%	-234	6,499	1,466
5	55	0	0	1,873	1.12%	-198	8,570	1,801
6	56	0	0	1,932	1.02%	-160	10,662	2,129
7	57	0	0	2,183	1.04%	-59	12,904	2,388
8	58	0	0	2,452	1.07%	-39	15,395	2,665
9	59	0	0	2,745	1.09%	-17	18,158	2,962
10	60	0	0	3,065	1.11%	8	21,214	3,281
11	61	0	0	3,112	1.02%	133	24,194	3,517
12	62	0	0	3,361	1.04%	186	27,368	3,746
13	63	0	0	3,625	1.06%	231	30,762	3,983
14	64	0	0	3,905	1.08%	277	34,390	4,229
15	65	0	0	4,202	1.11%	325	38,267	4,485
16	66	0	0	4,232	1.02%	531	41,968	4,585
17	67	0	0	4,529	1.04%	500	45,998	4,780
18	68	0	0	4,851	1.06%	541	50,308	4,998
19	69	0	0	5,193	1.08%	588	54,912	5,238
20	70	0	0	5,557	1.10%	641	59,828	5,500
21	71	0	0	5,612	1.02%	896	64,543	5,572
22	72	0	0	5,977	1.04%	838	69,682	5,781
23	73	0	0	6,373	1.06%	889	75,166	6,023
24	74	0	0	6,794	1.08%	947	81,012	6,294
25	75	0	0	7,241	1.10%	1,012	87,241	6,595
26	76	0	0	7,323	1.02%	1,324	93,240	6,667
27	77	0	0	7,773	1.04%	1,254	99,759	6,910
28	78	0	0	8,260	1.06%	1,319	106,700	7,193
29	79	0	0	8,778	1.08%	1,393	114,085	7,512
30	80	0	0	9,327	1.10%	1,476	121,936	7,867
31	81	0	0	9,443	1.02%	1,856	129,523	7,949
32	82	0	0	9,997	1.04%	1,777	137,743	8,237
33	83	0	0	10,595	1.06%	1,861	146,477	8,572
34	84	0	0	11,230	1.08%	1,956	155,751	8,951
35	85	0	0	11,903	1.10%	2,062	165,593	9,373

E. & O.E.

Investment Strategies

This document is not an estimate or guarantee of future performance

Prepared for: **Keith Marino**
Prepared by:

Overview of concept:

This document compares the various investment strategies used currently with a number of recommended investment strategies. There are no limitations on the amount or type of strategies used and may include but are not limited to recommendations made in the following categories.

Asset Allocation of the investment portfolio including the amount invested in Canadian and Foreign content.
Tax Efficient Investing to maximize the long-term growth of assets through the deferral of income tax.
Management Expense associated with the various types of investment plans available.
Deposit and Withdrawal frequency to maximize the amount on deposit earning income.

The type of strategies recommended will depend on your particular circumstances and the goals and objectives you have set for yourself.

I acknowledge that:

I have fully reviewed and understand the illustrations and projections within this document. I recognize that this analysis is based upon numerous assumptions, and the ultimate performance of the proposed financial concepts and strategies will depend on but not be limited to:

- **future investment performance,**
- **the ultimate course of inflation,**
- **evolving Federal and Provincial tax laws, and**
- **the timing and amounts of any future investment deposits and withdrawals.**

I understand that inflation, interest rates and the performance of various securities can fluctuate significantly and that actual results will vary from those illustrated.

I acknowledge that this concept is an illustration only, and NOT a contract. I understand that there are no implied guarantees within this document.

Date: _____

_____
Signature of Keith Marino

_____
Signature of

E. & O.E.

Topical Index

CCH/ADVOCIS
EDUCATION PROGRAM

COURSE 4
WEALTH MANAGEMENT AND ESTATE PLANNING

MODULE 18
FINANCIAL MANAGEMENT

Module 18
FINANCIAL MANAGEMENT

Module 18
Financial Management

LEARNING OBJECTIVES

✓ Identify, explain and apply an in-depth knowledge of the planning process for educational needs, with a particular focus on the Registered Education Savings Plan (RESP).

✓ Demonstrate a solid comprehension and working knowledge of charitable giving strategies, including the tax implications.

✓ Demonstrate and apply a solid comprehension of the concepts and principles related to money management with particular attention on the budgeting process.

✓ Understand, explain and apply a working knowledge of debt management, including mortgages and different types of consumer credit.

OVERVIEW

The focus of this module is on topics that relate to the management of an individual's personal finances. The module begins with a discussion about planning for a child's education with a particular focus on Registered Education Savings Plans (RESPs) and the Canada Education Savings Grant (CESG).

A unit on debt and money management covers an array of topics, including different types of consumer credit, an in-depth discussion of the concepts associated with a mortgage and a comprehensive look at the budgeting process. And in the concluding unit, the issues, implications and various strategies for charitable giving are analyzed.

Unit 1
Education

INTRODUCTION

When a student has the abilities and initiative to attend post-secondary education, an important consideration for many, beyond being accepted into a program of choice, is the cost of education. Bursaries, scholarships, student loans and summer employment are a few of the ways a student can increase needed financial support. While these types of financial aids are helpful, advanced planning is an important element to ensure that sufficient funds are available for a child's education, when needed.

COST OF EDUCATION

It is truly impossible to identify a single target figure that applies in all situations when assessing the cost of higher education. When undertaking any type of planning, education costs tend to be estimates, where available information is translated into a comprehensive and rational analysis. To keep the process in perspective, education costs are often categorized into three main areas: tuition, textbooks and living expenses. Through this segmentation, it is easier to monitor and update assumptions. In addition, the cost of education can be substantial and the expense allocation is often a valued part of the communication process when describing how costs are derived.

The range for tuition fees in Canada is quite broad and fees for many programs have increased dramatically due to higher costs and the growth of privatization. Currently, annual fees tend to range from $4,000 to $12,000, for an undergraduate program at a Canadian institution. Graduate studies typically entail an even higher annual-fee structure. In addition, fees for a program of study outside of Canada normally exceed these levels, plus there is the added expense of foreign exchange.

In addition to tuition fees, there is the cost of textbooks and other educational resources. Again, there is a broad range of costs depending upon the program of study and number of courses.

The third major category captures living expenses while attending a post-secondary institution. This includes the cost of residence or an apartment, plus food and other expenses of daily living. When calculating daily living costs, allowances should be made for expenses that are often transparent when a student lives at home, but become quite apparent once the student is out on her own (i.e., telephone, laundry, cleaning). Typically, transportation costs are factored in here and would include public transportation on a daily basis and regular trips home.

All of these expenses are multiplied by the number of years associated with a program of study, which usually ranges from one to four years. A growing proportion of students are also pursuing additional areas of studies, such as teachers' college, graduate studies or a second diploma or degree beyond their initial program of study.

NED

Eighteen-year-old Ned has been accepted into an undergraduate program at QRT University. It is a four-year program with annual tuition currently pegged at $5,000 per year. Ned expects to spend $1,200 on textbooks each year and has chosen to live off-campus, which he feels will cost him $1,000 a month for eight months, and $600 a month during the four summer months. Ned's off-campus number includes allowances for daily living expenses.

Calculate the total cost of attending this four-year program.

Annual Cost	
Tuition	$ 5,000
Textbooks	$ 1,200
Living expenses	$10,400
Total	$16,600

Total four-year cost: $66,400 ($16,600 × 4 years)

Ned can expect to incur total costs of $66,400 during his attendance at QRT University, based on his current estimates for each of his major expense categories.

HANNAH

As part of their ongoing budgeting, Ed and Marian want to begin saving on a monthly basis to fund the education costs for their daughter, Hannah. Ed is Ned's uncle (from NED SNAP) so, using Ned as an example, Ed knows that the current cost for a four-year program is $66,400.

Ed is comfortable with this current cost estimate but realizes that Hannah is still quite young since she will only turn nine years old this year. He knows that the current cost estimate needs to be translated into future dollars, to reflect the expected cost at the time when Hannah begins her post-secondary studies.

How much will a four-year program cost 10 years from now, assuming costs increase by 3% per annum? (Disregard any cost increases during the term of the program.)

continued . . .

continued . . .

The four-year program that costs $66,400 today will cost $89,236.05 in 10 years, based on the given assumptions.

We know the following information:

- P/YR = 1
- xP/YR = 10
- I/YR = 3
- PV = -66,400
- PMT = 0

SOLVE FOR FV, which equals 89,236.0476

Ed and Marian plan to begin their savings plan on September 1, and will make contributions on the first of each month for the next 10 years.

Assuming an annual nominal investment return of 5%, compounded monthly during the accumulation period, how much does the couple need to contribute at the beginning of each month in order to have the full funding available after 10 years? (Disregard taxes and any grants.)

We know that the couple will require $89,236. On a regular savings program, the couple would need to set aside $572.29 at the beginning of each month, starting September 1, in order to achieve their savings objective.

We know the following information:

- P/YR = 12
- xP/YR = 10
- I/YR = 5
- PV = 0
- FV = 89,236
- MODE = BEG

SOLVE FOR PMT, which equals -572.2850

STUDENT LOANS

Student loan programs through the federal and provincial governments are normally available to students who demonstrate a financial need based on qualifying criteria. While it is nice to think about the possibility of obtaining a loan, the criteria typically involves an expectation that parents have a role to play in the cost of educating a child, so the parents' income forms an important part of the financial assessment. Whether a parent can truly afford the levels of support that the student loan criterion presumes, is dependent upon the facts of each situation.

While a number of students qualify for student loans, there are many who do not or who find that available loans are insufficient to cover actual expenses. An evolving trend relates to students who view loans as a last resort because of the financial burden of repayment that looms into the future.

A good starting place for access to student loan information is the Human Resources and Skills Development Canada (HRSDC) beginning at: http://www.hrsdc.gc.ca.

INCOME TAX

Students or former students who are in the repayment phase of a student loan are eligible to claim a non-refundable tax credit for interest paid during a taxation year, or during the previous five years if not already claimed, on a loan made under the *Canada Student Loans Act* or a similar provincial statute. The student as the debt holder is the only person who may claim the tax credit, although the actual loan payment can be paid by the student or by a person related to the student.

Only the interest portion of any payment is deductible, not the principal amount. If the student opts not to claim the deduction in a particular year, she does not immediately lose the credit but rather she can carry it forward for up to five years. Similar to almost all other federal non-refundable tax credits, this credit is also set at 15% (2009).

As discussed in Module 5, other types of common income tax considerations for students include:

(a) Deductions

- moving expenses if the student moved 40 kilometres or closer to school
- child care expenses
- *full-time students* — $400 education and $65 textbook credit per month
- *part-time students* — $120 education and $20 textbook credit per month

(b) Non-refundable tax credits

- interest paid on student loans
- tuition, and education and textbook amounts

REGISTERED EDUCATION SAVINGS PLAN (RESP)

Introduction

A *Registered Education Savings Plan* (RESP) is an educational savings program (ESP) registered with the Canada Revenue Agency (CRA) and designed specifically to assist with saving for a child's post-secondary education. A RESP involves three key roles: subscriber, promoter and plan beneficiary. In simple terms, the subscriber is the person who opens the RESP account and makes contributions into the plan. The promoter is the company that sells the plan to the subscriber. The beneficiary is the individual named under the plan who is intended to derive benefit from the RESP.

The rules for RESP contracts have evolved over the years and the government often permits existing plans to be administered on a *grandfathered* basis, when rule changes come into effect. The discussion in this unit will focus on the current rule structure, unless otherwise noted. In addition, throughout the module, the term *spouse* also refers to common-law partner, unless otherwise identified.

Types of Plans

There are three different types of RESP plans, including:

- non-family plan;
- family plan; and
- group plan.

The type of plan is an important distinction because while there are many rules that apply to all RESPs, there are also many rules that differ by plan type. Assessing an individual's objectives and needs relative to savings for education will help determine the most appropriate type of RESP given the specific circumstances.

Non-Family Plan

A *non-family plan* is one where there is a single beneficiary under the plan. The plan subscriber decides the amount and timing of contributions into the plan. With a non-family plan, there are no restrictions as to who can be the beneficiary under the plan, provided other qualifying criteria are met. In other words, the beneficiary and the subscriber do not have to be related.

Family Plan

As the name suggests, a *family plan* involves more than one beneficiary, where each beneficiary is related by blood or adoption to each living subscriber under the plan or to the deceased original subscriber. Similar to the non-family plan, the subscriber decides the amount and timing of any contributions into the plan.

Group Plan

A group plan is typically available through a non-taxable entity such as a foundation, and is administered on an age-group basis (i.e., all contracts for 12-year-olds are administered together). Actuaries calculate the contributions, where the amount and frequency remain the same provided the beneficiary is under the age of 18.

Roles

Subscriber

General Criteria

An individual who enters into a RESP contract with a promoter, makes contributions into the plan and has the authority to name the beneficiary(ies) is referred to as the *subscriber*. In other words, it is typically the person who opens and holds a RESP contract.

Quite often, a subscriber is one individual. However, under prescribed circumstances, a plan can have joint subscribers. The key here is that the subscriber must be an individual; trusts and corporations are not eligible to be the subscriber who initially establishes a RESP. It is important to note that an estate is defined as a trust within the *Income Tax Act* (the "Act") so does not qualify to establish a RESP.

Provided the structure of the RESP plan allows for it, the subscriber on a plan can be changed. So throughout this material, you will see terminology such as *original subscriber*, *deceased original subscriber* and *living subscriber*.

Residency

The Act does not dictate any residency requirement relative to the RESP subscriber, although the subscriber does require a Canadian social insurance number.

Age

The Act does not dictate any age restrictions relative to the RESP subscriber, although promoters may apply a minimum age restriction as it relates to the issue of its plans relative to contract law. For example, there is nothing in the Act that precludes a 10, 12 or 16-year-old child from being the subscriber of a RESP. However, a promoter who sells RESP contracts may have internal rules that prohibit such a sale, because of contract law.

Joint Subscribers

An individual and her spouse can be joint subscribers under a newly established plan, provided that at the time the contract is initiated, the couple meet the definition of a spouse as defined in the Act. Appendix One summarizes these definitions.

If a couple, who are joint subscribers under a plan, separate or divorce, the assets can remain in the plan and they can continue as joint subscribers because they met the criteria at the time that the plan was established. However, divorced couples cannot enter a plan as joint subscribers.

There are a number of plans currently in existence where two individuals other than spouses were the original joint subscriber at the time the plan was issued, under a different set of rules. The government has allowed these plans to continue through grandfathered provisions (i.e., son and father are joint subscribers); however, this type of arrangement could not be duplicated today for a newly established plan.

Changing Subscribers

Relationship breakdown and death are two scenarios under which a new subscriber may replace an original subscriber on a RESP, as outlined below.

(a) A spouse or a former spouse of the original subscriber can replace the subscriber on a RESP, as a result of a relationship breakdown and a subsequent court order or written agreement for the division of property.

(b) The death of a subscriber does not cause a plan to cease but rather allows for contributions to continue by an individual or the subscriber's estate, subsequent to the subscriber's death. The replacing individual or original subscriber's estate would become the new subscriber of the existing RESP. This provision applies to plans entered into after 1997, and where permitted under the terms of the promoter's contract. Note that while an estate cannot establish a RESP, these circumstances describe when the estate can become a subsequent subscriber on an existing plan.

When the plan's subscriber changes because of relationship breakdown or death, the new subscriber is considered to have made all contributions into the plan. Any subsequent tax consequences that arise due to excess contributions into the plan after 1997 are attributable to the new subscriber.

Multiple Plans

There are no restrictions as to the number of RESPs a subscriber may establish in relationship to one or multiple beneficiaries.

Employer-Sponsored Plan

While an employer may choose to sponsor a RESP plan for his staff, the employer's role is negligible in the actual contract provisions. The employer could facilitate the payment of contributions through payroll deductions, but the RESP remains a contract between the subscriber (the employee or employee's spouse) and the promoter. The employer has no role as a subscriber in the plan.

In cases where the employer makes contributions into a RESP on an employee's (subscriber's) behalf, any contributions are considered to be a taxable benefit and are included on the employee's T4 as income.

Promoter

The organization with which a subscriber holds a RESP contract is referred to as the plan *promoter*, and is typically the company that holds and manages the RESP and to whom the subscriber pays the RESP contributions.

Beneficiary

General Criteria

The term *beneficiary* is used to describe the individual who is named as the person who is to derive benefit from the RESP. With the exception of a family plan, there are no restrictions on who can be a beneficiary of a RESP.

A family plan allows the subscriber to name multiple beneficiaries, where each beneficiary must be related by a blood relationship or adoption to each living subscriber or deceased original subscriber. Family plans entered into after 1998 require that each beneficiary be less than age 21 at the time she is named as a beneficiary under the plan. If a family plan is transferred to another family plan, a beneficiary of the transferring plan who is age 21 or older is permitted under the receiving plan.

In order to receive payments from the RESP, a beneficiary must meet qualifying criteria at the time payments are made out of the plan.

Multiple Plans

There are no restrictions that limit the number of RESPs under which an individual may be a beneficiary. There is, however, a $50,000 lifetime maximum contribution limit that applies to each individual, regardless of the number of plans under which she is a beneficiary.

Multiple Roles

A non-family plan has no restrictions as to who can be a beneficiary so there are no limiting factors that would preclude a person from being both a beneficiary and a subscriber under the same plan. As such, a subscriber could fulfill the dual roles of subscriber and beneficiary under a non-family plan.

However, a family plan is subject to clearly defined criteria relative to the subscriber and her relationship to the plan beneficiaries. The restriction that necessitates that there be an adoptive or blood relationship between the subscriber and the beneficiary would preclude a person from fulfilling both roles under a family plan.

TOM

Tom is establishing two RESP contracts, one as a family plan and the other as a non-family plan. Under each of these two plans, Tom will be the subscriber. In addition, he can also be the beneficiary under the non-family plan. However, Tom cannot be included as one of the beneficiaries under the family plan.

Blood Relationship and Adopted

The definition of blood relationship is established according to the Act, and includes a parent and child or any other descendant of the parent including individuals such as grandchildren and great-grandchildren. In addition, the relationship of brother and sister is deemed to be a blood relationship, but does not extend further into nieces, nephews, aunts or uncles.

The definition of adopted includes a legal adoption and an adoption in fact. A legal adoption is pretty self-explanatory. For example, the adopted child of individual X is considered the child of X, and the grandchild of X's parents. An adoption in fact is assessed based on the facts of the situation, but is typically deemed to have occurred where the adopted child is wholly dependent on the adopting parent and is under the parent's custody and control. For example, the children of a common-law spouse could be considered adopted in fact where the spouse exercises effective parental care and guidance over the children on an ongoing basis.

HANK AND RHODA

Common-law partners Hank and Rhoda have lived together for five years. Rhoda's two young children, Nick and Nelly from a previous relationship, live with Rhoda and Hank on a full-time basis and have no contact with their biological father. Hank assumes a full-time parenting role in his relationship with Nick and Nelly, providing ongoing care and guidance. It is likely that Nick and Nelly would be viewed as having been adopted by Hank.

Changing Beneficiaries

The RESP guidelines established by the government allow for a beneficiary to be changed on a plan, although the design of the promoters' plan may or may not allow for such changes.

For purposes of the penalty tax on overcontributions into the plan, when a change of beneficiary is undertaken, any contributions made into the plan prior to the change are deemed to have been made at the original date relative to the new beneficiary. However, this rule is not applied in the following two situations.

    (a) The new and previous beneficiaries are:

- under age 21 at the time of the change;
- connected by a blood or adopted relationship to each other; and
- connected by a blood or adopted relationship to an original subscriber.

    (b) The new beneficiary is:

- under age 21 at the time of the change; and
- one of her parents is the parent of the previous beneficiary.

By not applying the deeming rule under the two scenarios outlined in (a) and (b) above, contributions made on behalf of the former beneficiary are not included when the lifetime contributions are calculated relative to the new beneficiary.

Contributions

Tax Implications

Contributions into a RESP plan are not tax deductible from the subscriber's income, but investment income is permitted to compound on a tax-sheltered basis, while retained within the plan.

Any interest paid on funds borrowed to make a RESP contribution is not tax deductible.

Limits

RESP contributions are subject to a lifetime contribution limit that is applied at a beneficiary level. For each beneficiary, the lifetime limit is $50,000; there is no annual limit.

In addition, contributions into family plans established after 1998 can only be made for beneficiaries who are under age 21 at the time of the contribution.

These limits exclude any payments made into the RESP from the Canada Education Savings Grant (CESG) program, which is discussed in a subsequent section, or the Alberta Centennial Education Savings Plan.

DAN

Dan established a RESP for his 12-year-old son Jonathon. He decided to contribute $2,000.

The following year, assuming no one else is contributing to any RESP under which Jonathon is a beneficiary, Dan can contribute any amount he wishes up to $48,000. Dan is not obliged to make any contribution into the plan but if he opts to make a contribution, he is subject to cumulative maximums that apply to Jonathon as beneficiary, not Dan as the subscriber.

Control of the contributions made into a RESP remains with the subscriber. When contributions are made into a non-family plan, the contribution is obviously allocated to the single beneficiary. However, under a family plan there are multiple beneficiaries, so as contributions are made, the subscriber must allocate contributions to specific beneficiaries. This is required in order to track contribution limits.

Contributions into a non-family plan can be made up to and including the 31st year of the plan's existence, whereas contributions into a family plan cannot be made after the year in which the beneficiary reaches age 31.

Overcontributions

When the total contributions made by all subscribers into all RESPs on behalf of a single beneficiary exceed the lifetime limit, an overcontribution is deemed to have occurred. Similar to overcontributions on a RRSP, the calculation is made at the end of the month and includes a prescribed penalty of 1% per month on the subscriber's share of the overcontribution. Tax on the overpayment is due no later than 90 days after the end of the taxation year in which the overcontribution occurred, and an overcontribution continues to exist until sufficient funds are withdrawn to realign the plan.

JENNY

Nine years ago, Rhonda established a non-family RESP under which her daughter Jenny is the beneficiary. For the past nine years, she has contributed $5,000 annually.

In May, Rhonda made a $6,000 contribution into the RESP she had previously established for Jenny.

It was not until October 15 that Rhonda realized that the $50,000 lifetime maximum is based on all contributions made into any RESP on behalf of Jenny as a RESP beneficiary.

Upon realizing the problem, Rhonda withdrew $1,000 from her plan on October 30. Rhonda is responsible for a penalty tax of $50.

The annual maximum was exceeded in May, and continued until late October. This represents 5 months (May to September inclusive).

Contributions

Rhonda's contribution	$6,000
Total contributions	$6,000
Maximum contribution for the year ($50,000 - (9 years × $5,000))	$5,000
Overcontribution	$1,000

Rhonda's overcontribution calculations: ($1,000 × 1% × 5 months) = $50.

While the withdrawal of funds will assist in realigning the contributions to eliminate an overcontribution penalty, the withdrawal does not re-establish contribution room relative to the beneficiary's lifetime maximum. In the Jenny SNAP, the $6,000 contributed will count toward the cumulative $50,000 lifetime maximum even though $1,000 was withdrawn to realign the plan.

Trustee Fees and Insurance Premiums

The payment for any insurance premium or trustee fees outside of the RESP does not affect contributions made into the plan. If, however, any fees are charged within the plan and deducted from contributions made, the fees are considered contributions into the plan. Reductions from the plan assets for fees and other charges will have a direct impact on the value of the plan.

Transferring a RESP

When the assets of a RESP are transferred from one plan to another under the following conditions, there are no income tax implications:

- The beneficiary under the transferring and receiving RESP is the same.
- The beneficiary under the transferring RESP is a sister or brother of the beneficiary of the receiving RESP and the receiving beneficiary is less than age 21 when the transfer is made.

In any other transfer situation, the calculation of the lifetime maximum may result in an overcontribution situation because the historical contributions under the transferring plan are applied to the calculations under the new plan.

A RESP plan with one subscriber can be transferred to a RESP with a different subscriber, where the beneficiary under both plans is the same individual. Where the beneficiary of the receiving plan, immediately before the transfer, is also a beneficiary under the transferring plan, the contribution history will not apply to the receiving plan when calculating excess contributions.

Qualified Investments

All property acquired by a RESP trust before October 28, 1998, is considered to be a qualified investment. Property acquired after October 27, 1998 must meet the criteria established for qualified RESP investments, which is specifically defined in the Act.

Qualified investments for a RESP are the same as those that qualify for a RRSP, with the exception of certain annuity contracts. The following list provides examples of a few of the more common qualified investments for RESPs:

- cash deposits and guaranteed investment certificate (GICs);
- shares of a corporation listed on a prescribed stock exchange in Canada or in a foreign country;
- bonds and debentures of the federal, provincial or municipal government or a Crown corporation;
- bonds and debentures of corporations listed on a Canadian or foreign stock exchange;
- units in mutual fund trusts; and
- segregated funds.

There are no restrictions on a RESP relative to the amount of foreign content that can be held within the plan.

It is also important to note that a RESP cannot be used as collateral for a loan.

Payments from a RESP

While the intention of a RESP is to help fund the beneficiary's cost of education, there are four types of payments that can be made from an RESP:

- payment of contributions to the subscriber or beneficiary;
- educational assistance payments (EAPs);
- accumulated income payments (AIPs); and
- payments to a designated educational institution in Canada.

Payment of Contributions

Contributions into an RESP can be returned to the contributor when the RESP contract ends or at any prior time. The return of contributions does not trigger any income tax reporting because it is simply a return of contributions.

The promoter can also pay contributions to the RESP beneficiary without triggering any tax consequence. This would normally occur in conjunction with an education assistance payment, as described in the next section.

Educational Assistance Payments

An *educational assistance payment* (EAP) is a distribution of money, comprised of accumulated income from within the RESP, Canada Education Savings Grant amounts, and Canada Learning Bonds (CLBs) to a beneficiary (student) under prescribed conditions. The purpose of the EAP is to help finance the cost of post secondary education.

For a payment to qualify as an EAP, at the time a payment is made to the beneficiary, she must:

- be enrolled in a full-time qualifying educational program at a post-secondary educational institution (attending the institution either on campus or through a distance education program); or

- The student has attained the age of 16 years and is enrolled part-time in a specified educational program.

A beneficiary is entitled to receive EAPs for up to six months after ceasing enrolment, provided that the payments would have qualified as EAPs if the payments had been made immediately before the student's enrolment ceased.

Limit on EAPs. For RESPs entered into after 1998, the maximum amount of EAPs that can be made to a student as soon as he or she qualifies to receive them is:

- *For full-time studies* — $5,000, for the first 13 consecutive weeks of full-time studies in a qualifying educational program. After the student has completed the 13 consecutive weeks, there is no limit on the amount of EAPs that can be paid if the student continues to qualify to receive them. If there is a 12-month period in which the student is not enrolled in a qualifying educational program for 13 consecutive weeks, the $5,000 maximum applies again; or

- *For part-time studies* — $2,500, for the 13-week period of enrollment in part-time studies in a specified educational program preceding the payment of an EAP.

Subject to the terms and conditions of the RESP, the promoter can supplement the $5,000 or $2,500 EAP by paying a portion of the contributions tax-free to the beneficiary.

Human Resources and Skills Development Canada has a policy under which they will review special situations, on a case-by-case basis, where a student requests consideration for an exception that allows her to exceed the $5,000 limit because the actual cost of tuition and related expenses are substantially higher than average.

A *qualifying educational program* is one that requires the student to spend 10 hours or more per week on courses or work in the program, and that lasts at least three consecutive weeks. Programs at a university, college or other designated educational institution in Canada must be at a post-secondary school level. The student is permitted to earn income from part-time or temporary employment intended to finance her education. However, if a student is receiving employment income and the program of study is connected with or is part of the student's employment, then the program will not be considered as a qualifying program.

A *post-secondary educational institution* includes:

- a university, college or other designated educational institution in Canada;

- a university, college or other educational institution outside of Canada that offers courses at a post-secondary level and provided the student is enrolled in a course that is at least 13 consecutive weeks; or

- an educational institution located in Canada that is certified by Human Resources and Social Development Canada as offering non-credit courses that develop or improve skills in an occupation.

An EAP can only be made to a qualifying student and cannot be made to the student's estate. An EAP is treated as taxable income to the receiving beneficiary, although the tax consequences tend to be quite low because the recipient generally is in a low-income tax bracket.

A subscriber may continue to make contributions into an RESP even after a beneficiary begins receiving EAPs, provided the timing does not exceed the maximum period during which contributions can be made.

Accumulated Income Payments

Description

An *accumulated income payment* (AIP) is an amount of income earned from the RESP that is paid out under the plan, most often to the subscriber. An AIP normally includes earnings on contributions into a plan and earnings on the CESG. An AIP does *not* include:

- a refund of contributions to the subscriber or to the beneficiary;
- EAPs;
- payments to a designated educational institution in Canada;
- transfers to another RESP; or
- repayments of CESG or any provincial program.

A RESP may allow for AIPs when the following conditions are met:

- the payment is made to, or for, a subscriber under the plan who is resident in Canada; and
- the payment is made to, or for, only one subscriber of the RESP; **and**

Any one of the following three conditions must also apply:

- the payment is made after the year that includes the ninth anniversary of the RESP and each individual (other than a deceased individual) who is or was a beneficiary has reached 21 years of age and is not currently eligible to receive an EAP;
- the payment is made after the year that includes the 35th anniversary of the RESP, unless the RESP is a specified plan in which case the payment is made after the year that includes the 40th anniversary of the RESP; or
- all the beneficiaries under the RESP are deceased.

Although these five criteria establish the framework, some leniency may be available when there is a reasonable expectation that the beneficiary could not pursue a post-secondary education because she suffers from a severe and prolonged mental impairment. A request for leniency is normally directed through the promoter and made to the Registered Plans Directorate.

An RESP must be terminated by the end of February of the year after the year in which the first AIP is paid.

Taxation of AIP

An AIP is reported on a T4A slip and must be claimed by the recipient for the year in which the payment occurs. The AIP is subject to regular income tax plus an additional 20% tax (12% for Quebec residents). The calculation of these two taxes is done in conjunction with the filing of the taxpayer's regular income tax return.

RRSP Relief

Under certain conditions, an individual can reduce the amount of tax payable on an AIP by making contributions into a Registered Retirement Savings Plan (RRSP). The AIP recipient can make contributions into a RRSP, where the recipient of the AIP is the subscriber or is the spouse of a deceased original subscriber (who has not been replaced with a subsequent subscriber on the plan) and where:

- the amount of the AIP (up to a maximum of $50,000) is contributed to the individual's RRSP or spousal RRSP during the year in which the AIP is received, or within the first 60 days of the following year; and
- the individual has a sufficient amount of RRSP contribution room available.

Where a RRSP contribution is made, the RRSP contributor claims the RRSP deduction for the year in which the payment is made. The contribution into the RRSP has the impact of lowering the individual's taxable income, which reduces her regular taxes but also reduces the amount of the additional tax to which an AIP is subject. If the RRSP contribution amount is equal to the amount of AIP, the net impact is no tax on the AIP.

When an AIP is made, the promoter normally applies tax withholding on any payment. However, there is no withholding required if both of the following apply:

- an AIP is transferred directly into a regular, spousal or common law RRSP; and
- the contributor has sufficient RRSP contribution room to permit the deduction of the contribution in the year it is made.

TORI (1)

Tori has met the criteria that allow her to receive an accumulation income payment from an RESP under which she is the subscriber. Tori realizes that the AIP represents taxable income that must be claimed in the year the payment is made from the plan and that the payment is subject to an additional 20% tax (she lives in a province other than Quebec).

Tori would like to minimize the income tax impact of the $30,000 AIP payment and has determined that she qualifies to have the AIP moved directly from the RESP and treated as a contribution into her RRSP. Tori has $30,000 of available RRSP contribution and plans to have the funds transferred directly into her RRSP, which will eliminate the need for the promoter to withhold income tax on the payment.

By making a $30,000 contribution into her RRSP, Tori realizes that she can reduce the amount of tax payable on the AIP, including the additional 20% tax normally applied to an AIP.

An individual cannot reduce the AIPs subject to tax if they become a subscriber because of the death of the original subscriber.

Alternative RRSP Strategy

If an individual subscriber is eligible for an AIP but does not have sufficient RRSP contribution room, she would normally lose the opportunity for the RRSP contribution as an offset. To avoid the loss of the RRSP contribution opportunity, it may be possible to restructure the plan's subscriber role to that of a joint subscriber. If the subscriber's spouse has adequate RRSP contribution room, she could be added as a joint subscriber to the RESP, which would allow the AIP to be paid to the spouse with sufficient contribution room.

TORI (2)

Continuing the Tori (1) SNAP, assume that Tori qualified to receive an AIP, but that she did not have any available contribution room under her RRSP. This would normally mean that Tori has no opportunity to minimize the tax implications associated with the receipt of the AIP.

However, if Tori's spouse has RRSP contribution room available, this could offer an alternative strategy to minimize the tax implications associated with the AIP. Tori could add her spouse to the RESP as a joint subscriber and then the spouse could apply for the AIP.

Plan Termination

All funds must be withdrawn from the RESP and the plan must collapse no later than the last day of the 35th year following the year in which the plan was established. Assets from the collapsing RESP can be:

- transferred to another RESP;
- used to fund an EAP;
- used to refund the CESG;

- used to make an AIP; or

- used to make a payment to a designated educational institution.

RESP Summary

- A non-family RESP may have only one beneficiary and there are no restrictions as to who can be the beneficiary under the plan, provided other qualifying criteria are met.

- A family RESP can have any number of beneficiaries but requires that the beneficiaries meet relationship criteria relative to the subscriber.

- A maximum contribution of up to a lifetime maximum of $50,000. Where the same individual is a beneficiary under more than one plan, the total contributions across all plans cannot exceed the applicable limits.

- Contributions are not tax deductible, so they may be withdrawn at any time without triggering any tax consequence.

- Contributions into a non-family plan can be made up to and including the 31st year of the plan's existence, whereas contributions into a family plan cannot be made after the year in which the beneficiary reaches age 31.

- Investment earnings accumulate tax-free and are typically paid out to the qualified beneficiary as an EAP.

- The plan must be collapsed by the end of the 35th year in which it was established.

- To qualify for EAP payments under a plan, the beneficiary must meet specific qualifying criteria relative to the program of study and institution.

- If a beneficiary does not pursue post-secondary education, she may be replaced with a new beneficiary.

- If a beneficiary does not pursue post-secondary education and there is no replacement beneficiary, the contributor may withdraw the earnings under prescribed conditions.

- Figure 1 provides an overview of the key players involved in a RESP, and introduces the CESG program, which is covered in the following section.

Figure 1
RESP Overview

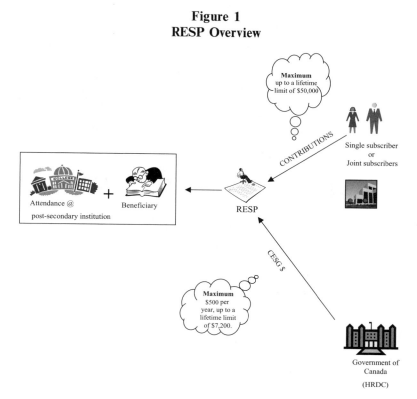

Note: Participation in the CESG program is discussed in the following section.

CANADA EDUCATION SAVINGS GRANT

Introduction

The *Canada Education Savings Grant*, commonly referred to by the term *CESG*, is a grant paid by Human Resources and Skills Development Canada to the RESP trustee for deposit into an account on behalf of a specific beneficiary.

In simple terms, the program involves a bonus payment from the federal government, designed as an incentive for Canadians to save for a child's post-secondary education, and is calculated based on the annual amount subscribers contribute into an RESP on behalf of an eligible beneficiary.

For each year a child is resident in Canada, beginning in 1998 and continuing up to and including the year she reaches age 17, the child accumulates $500 of CESG contribution room, but it can only be triggered based on RESP contributions under prescribed conditions. The maximum amount of grant paid under the CESG program is $7,200 per lifetime per single child.

> *SANDRA AND JOE (1)*
>
> Sandra and Joe are the children of Emily and Doug Parson who live in XYZ Province. The family's qualifying income of $79,000 exceeds the threshold for additional CESG on the first $500 of contributions. Using Sandra and Joe as examples, let's see how much CESG room they have each accumulated.
>
> Sandra was born in 1996. It is now 2010, so Sandra has $6,500 of CESG room available for her credit ($500 for each of 1998 through to 2010).
>
> Joe, who was born in 2001, begins to accumulate CESG room starting the year he was born. It is now 2010 and Joe has $5,000 of CESG room available for his credit ($500 for each of the years between 2001 and 2010).

Amount and Calculation

HRSDC pays a basic CESG of 20% of annual contributions made to all eligible RESPs for a qualifying beneficiary to a maximum CESG of $500 in respect of each beneficiary ($1,000 in CESG if there is unused grant room from a previous year), and a lifetime limit of $7,200.

HRSDC will also pay an additional CESG amount for each qualifying beneficiary based on net family income. For 2010, the additional CESG rate on the first $500 contributed to an RESP for a beneficiary who is a child under 18 years of age is:

- 40% (extra 20% on the first $500, up to $200) if the child's family has qualifying net income for the year of $39,065* or less; and

- 30% (extra 10% on the first $500, up to $150) if the child's family has qualifying net income for the year that is more than $39,065* but is less than $78,130*.

Note: These amounts are updated each year based on the rate of inflation. The qualifying net income of the child's family for a year will generally be the same as the income used to determine eligibility for the Canada Child Tax Benefit (CCTB). Beneficiaries qualify for a grant on the contributions made on their behalf before the end of the calendar year in which they turn 17 years of age.

Canada Learning Bond

To assist low-income families, the Canada Learning Bond (CLB) will provide an initial $500 to children born on or after January 1, 2004 in families entitled to the National Child Benefit Supplement (NCBS) for each child, followed by up to 15 annual $100 entitlements for each year the family is entitled to the NCBS supplement for the child. Contributions do not necessarily have to be made to the RESP in order to receive the CLB.

To cover the cost of opening as RESP for the child, HRSDC will pay an extra $25 with the first $500 bond. If the beneficiary does not pursue post-secondary education, the CLB is returned to the federal government.

> *SANDRA AND JOE (2)*
>
> Emily and Doug Parson are joint subscribers of two non-family RESPs. Sandra is the beneficiary under one plan and Joe is the beneficiary under a second plan.
>
> Every year, Sandra and Joe each earn new CESG room of $500. This $500 of available grant can only be accessed if contributions are made into an RESP on behalf of Joe and Sandra.
>
> If the Parsons contribute $2,500 into Sandra's RESP, she will qualify for the full $500 of grant (20% of $2,500).
>
> If the Parsons contribute only $1,500 into Sandra's RESP, she will qualify for only $300 of grant (20% of $1,500).
>
> *continued . . .*

> *continued . . .*
>
> If the Parsons do not make any contributions into Sandra's RESP, the grant is not available, but the unused grant room ($500) can be carried forward into future years.

If RESP contributions are not made in a particular year, but the child has accumulated grant room under the CESG program, unused room is carried forward and can be used in a future year, under prescribed conditions. The grant that applies to any single grant year is normally $500, which is calculated as 20% of the RESP contributions made on behalf of an RESP beneficiary, up to a maximum RESP contribution of $2,500 (20% × $2,500) each year. If there is carryforward grant room, the maximum is $1,000 in CESG (current year $500, plus one carryforward year of $500). If the family's qualifying net income is less than $78,130 a CESG grant amount to a maximum of $600 ($500 × 40% + $200 × 20%) ($1,200 if there is carryforward CESG room) is possible.

SANDRA AND JOE (3)

Assume that Emily and Doug first established RESPs for their children in 2010 and that it is the first year in which they have ever made any RESP contributions.

If 2010 was the first year for RESP contributions, Sandra will have CESG carryforward room equal to $6,000, which is derived from $500 for each year from 1998 to 2009.

If the Parsons contributed $4,000 into Sandra's RESP, she would qualify for the grant under the CESG ($500), based on the first $2,500 of RESP contributions. The second $1,500 can be used to pick up grant carryforward room. In this case, the Parsons could use the $1,500 to apply for carryforward of the grant room that has not yet been used ($300 calculated as 20% of $1,500).

This same scenario applies to Joe. Joe will have $4,500 of grant carryforward room, which is attributed to 2001 to 2010 ($500 × 9), plus $500 available for the current year. A $4,000 contribution into Joe's RESP can be used to claim the grant and the grant from a previous year, not yet claimed. Therefore, Joe would qualify for $800 of grant ($500 current year plus one year carryforward) ((4,000 - 2,500) × 20% = $300).

Note that the total grant available is subject to a lifetime maximum of $7,200.

If the Parsons contribute $4,000 into Sandra's RESP next year, she will again qualify for $800 of grant based on next year and one year of carryforward room. Each successive year, the Parsons can pick up carryforward room until the earlier of when:

— there is no carryforward balance remaining;
— the beneficiary no longer qualifies to receive the grant; or
— the lifetime maximum limit has been reached.

The grant is available only up to the end of the calendar year in which the beneficiary reaches age 17, and the accumulation of all grant payments applicable to any single beneficiary (child) is subject to a lifetime maximum limit of $7,200.

SANDRA AND JOE (4)

The last year in which a grant under the CESG program can be claimed for Sandra is the year in which she turns age 17, assuming she has not previously reached her lifetime limit of $7,200.

Normally, the grant is paid by the end of the month following the qualifying RESP contribution.

Contributions made into any RESP prior to 1998 are not eligible for the grant. If the beneficiary does not pursue post-secondary education the CESG is returned to the federal government.

Eligibility

An RESP beneficiary is eligible for the CESG up to the end of the calendar year in which she reaches age 17, provided she:

- is a resident of Canada at the time the RESP contribution is made; and
- has a valid social insurance number.

In addition, to be eligible for the grant, RESP contributions must have been made after 1997 and before the end of the year in which the beneficiary reaches age 17. And, if the beneficiary is age 16 and 17, other special conditions apply as described in the next paragraph.

RESP beneficiaries age 16 and 17 are only eligible for the grant, if:

- a minimum of $2,000 of RESP contributions were made with respect to, and not withdrawn from, the beneficiary's RESP before the year in which the beneficiary reached age 16; or
- a minimum of $100 annual RESP contributions were made with respect to, and not withdrawn from, the beneficiary's RESP in any four years prior to the year in which the beneficiary reached age 16. The contributions do not have to be made in consecutive years.

If one of the above two criteria is not met, the beneficiary aged 16 or 17 is not eligible for the grant.

Payments

When there have been grants from the CESG program paid into a RESP, a portion of each EAP is attributable to CESGs paid into the plan. The CESG portion of an EAP is calculated using a ratio of CESGs contributed to the plan relative to the plan's investment earnings, and will reduce the remaining balance in the plan's CESG account.

If the beneficiary is non-resident when an EAP is made, no grant can be paid.

Grant Repayments

Once a grant has been paid into an RESP on behalf of a beneficiary, the funds are not immediately vested but rather there are ongoing conditions that must be met in order to retain the grant money. Repayment of the grant will be required in the following circumstances:

- plan is collapsed or registration of the RESP is revoked by the CRA;
- an AIP is made to the subscriber or a payment is made to a designated educational institution directly;
- a beneficiary is replaced, except if the replacement beneficiary is less than age 21 and a sister or brother of the beneficiary of the former beneficiary; or both the old and new beneficiaries are under age 21 and related to the subscriber; or
- an ineligible transfer is made from one RESP to another RESP.

The lifetime maximum CESG ($7,200) is applied at a beneficiary level. The following are examples of applications that limit the maximum payment of CESG money out of a plan:

- If a family plan has multiple beneficiaries, the total amount of CESGs paid to any single beneficiary cannot exceed $7,200. For example, if a plan has three beneficiaries and the plan received $20,000 in grants under the CESG program, but only two beneficiaries pursue post-secondary education, only $14,400 of the CESG can be paid to the two beneficiaries. The remaining $5,600 must be repaid to the government.
- If an individual is a beneficiary under multiple RESPs, that single individual is entitled to a total of $7,200 of CESGs. An individual who receives a sum that exceeds the $7,200 limit will be required to repay the excess.

APPLICATION

NINA AND SPENCE

Nina and Spence established a RESP for the benefit of their son Tom, who turned age 5 in 2010. After investigating their options, the couple has decided to be joint subscribers on a non-family plan purchased through ABC Insurance Company.

Based on their qualifying income, they will receive 20% CESG on contributions. Nina and Spence would like to optimize all RESP contributions and available grants under the CESG program each year, beginning with their first RESP contribution on January 1, 2010.

For the following series of questions, assume Tom is not a beneficiary under any other RESP and that the couple follows the strategy outlined in the previous paragraph.

(a) Calculate the sum of the annual contributions the couple can make into a RESP on Tom's behalf, beginning in 2010 and concluding in the year in which Tom reaches age 18.

Nina and Spence can contribute $50,000 during this period and can maximize the CESG at $7,200.

SOLUTION BACKGROUND

When analyzing a CESG situation, it is helpful to create a chart, similar to Table 1. This allows for easy summary of the annual and lifetime RESP contributions, as well as the annual and lifetime limits for the CESG.

Table 1
Maximize RESP Contributions

Tom — date of birth 2005

Year	Age	Annual RESP ($)	Lifetime RESP ($)	Annual CESG ($)	Carryforward CESG ($)	Lifetime CESG ($)
2010	5	5,000	5,000	500	500 re - 2009	1,000
2011	6	5,000	10,000	500	500 re - 2008	2,000
2012	7	5,000	15,000	500	500 re - 2007	3,000
2013	8	5,000	20,000	500	500 re - 2006	4,000
2014	9	5,000	25,000	500	500 re - 2005	5,000
2015	10	5,000	30,000	500		5,500
2016	11	5,000	35,000	500		6,000
2017	12	5,000	40,000	500		6,500
2018	13	5,000	45,000	500		7,000
2019	14	5,000	50,000	200		7,200
2020	15	0	50,000	0		7,200
2021	16	0	50,000	0		7,200
2022	17	0	50,000	0		7,200
2023	18	0	50,000	0		7,200

Table 1 depicts the RESP contribution pattern and corresponding grants that assumes maximization of the RESP contribution beginning on January 1, 2010.

On January 1 of each year from 2010 through to 2019 inclusive, Tom's parents will contribute $5,000 into the RESP and claim a $500 grant for the current year's contributions, plus a $500 grant from carryforward room (2005 to 2009).

When the CESG carryforward room is used up after the January 1, 2014 contribution, the RESP will have acquired grants totaling $5,000. This leaves $2,200 ($7,200 lifetime limit less $5,000 acquired), of grant still available.

For the next five years, 2015 to 2019 inclusive, the couple will claim the standard grant ($500 annually), while making RESP contributions of $5,000. On January 1, 2020, the grants received will reach the lifetime maximum of $7,200, and RESP contributions will reach the lifetime maximum of $50,000. Total contributions plus all grants represent $57,200.

On January 1, 2020, there is no opportunity to contribute any additional funds into Tom's RESP because the lifetime limit was reached during the previous taxation year.

(b) Calculate the total value of the RESP assets on December of the year Tom turns age 18, using the following assumptions:

continued . . .

continued . . .

— **all contributions and corresponding grants are made on January 1 of each year, starting the year Tom turns age 5;**

— **the annual nominal rate of interest is 6%, compounded annually; and**

— **there are no withdrawals made from the plan.**

The total value of the RESP at December 31, 2023 is $108,185.09.

Solution Background

The calculations required to solve this question involve four separate time frames:

— 2010 to 2014, when contributions are $5,000 and grants are $1,000;

— 2015 to 2019, when contributions are $5,000 and grants are $500; and

— 2020, when there are no contributions, but current assets continue to accumulate.

1a. The value at December 31, 2014 of $6,000 deposited January 1 for the periods 2010 to 2014 is $35,851.91.

We know the following information:

- P/YR = 1
- xP/YR = 5
- I/YR = 6
- PV = 0
- PMT = -6,000
- MODE = BEG

SOLVE FOR FV, which equals $35,851.91

1b. The value at December 31, 2019 of $35,851.91 received on January 1, 2015, and five contributions of $5,500 (January 1 of 2015 to 2019) is $80,842.19.

We know the following information:

- P/YR = 1
- xP/YR = 5
- I/YR = 6
- PV = -35,851.91
- PMT = -5,500
- MODE = BEG

SOLVE FOR FV, which equals 80,842.19

1c. The value at December 31, 2023 is $108,185.09.

We know the following information:

- P/YR = 1
- xP/YR = 5
- I/YR = 6
- PV = -80.842.19
- PMT = 0

SOLVE FOR FV, which equals 108,185.09

Unit 2
Debt Management and Budgeting

INTRODUCTION

Understanding personal credit, debt and money management is integral to the process of financial planning. Effective use of income and credit can be a powerful tool that allows individuals to optimize all available resources and minimize unnecessary expenses. While retirement and investment planning are important to the outcome of a family's personal financial goals, these types of planning initiatives are most successful when integrated into the family's debt and budget management process. Generally, it is best to pay off the debt that has the highest interest rate first, instead of the largest debt amount.

CREDIT ASSESSMENT

Overview

Normally, any time an individual attempts to borrow money, the lending institution will automatically undertake a credit assessment, which involves an evaluation of the applicant's ability to repay the borrowed funds. Current income, payment history on previous or current loans, assets, outstanding liabilities and ability to meet the required payment schedule are all elements considered in any credit evaluation. The extent of the questions and required documentation will vary depending upon the type of credit being applied for and any associated collateral.

Two key ratios used in the course of credit evaluation are the:

- total debt service ratio; and
- gross debt service ratio.

Total Debt Service Ratio

The most widely accepted guideline for estimating how much of an individual's income can be allocated to a monthly loan payment is derived through a mathematical equation referred to as the *total debt service ratio* (TDSR). This ratio calculates the proportion of all debt obligations relative to the borrower's gross income. Debts include housing costs such as a mortgage payment, property taxes and heating as well as other liabilities such as credit cards, car loans and other personal loans. The TDSR is calculated as:

$$\text{TDSR} = \frac{(\text{Monthly housing costs}) + (\text{All other monthly debt payments})}{(\text{Gross monthly income})} \times 100$$

The lower the ratio, the more likely an individual has sufficient income to meet her current debt obligations. The typical rule of thumb is that this ratio should be managed at a level that does not exceed 40%. When the number rises above 40%, it is likely that a lender will decline an application for credit until the debt and income structure falls below the 40% range.

Keep in mind that this calculation is based on gross income and has not factored in taxes, which in fact is an additional liability. The use of this ratio in credit assessment is intended to ensure that individuals do not become over-extended to the point that they become high-risk candidates for default on their debt.

HENRY

Henry has applied for a car loan, which would allow him to purchase a new vehicle. As part of the lender's credit assessment, Henry's total debt service ratio was evaluated using the following information.

continued . . .

---

continued . . .

Monthly debt obligations:

- a regular $400 payment being used to reduce outstanding credit card balance;
- a $300 student loan; and
- housing costs of $1,500.

In addition, the monthly payment on the car loan will be $600.

Henry's gross monthly income is $7,900.

TDSR

= ((Monthly housing costs) + (All other monthly debt payments)) ÷ (Gross monthly income) × 100

= ($1,500 + $300 + $400 + $600) ÷ ($7,900) × 100

= 35%

Based on this calculation, Henry's TDSR falls within the target range of less than 40% and would likely be considered acceptable by most lending institutions.

Gross Debt Service Ratio

Most mortgage lenders use the *gross debt service ratio* (GDSR) to evaluate an applicant's ability to service her mortgage debt. Included in the calculation are monthly payments associated with the mortgage principal, mortgage interest and property taxes. In addition, an estimate of monthly heating costs is commonly added to the liability side of the equation by many lending institutions. When the mortgage involves a condominium, condominium fees often become part of the equation. The GDSR is calculated as:

$$\text{GDSR} = \frac{\text{(Monthly mortgage payment) + (Property taxes) + (Heat)}}{\text{(Gross monthly income)}} \times 100$$

JOAN (1)

Joan has applied for a mortgage on her new home that will require a monthly payment of $900, including principal and interest. Taxes on the property are expected to be $250 per month and monthly heating costs are estimated at $25. Joan's gross annual income is $60,000. Using this information, we know that Joan's GDSR is 23.5%.

GDSR

= ((Monthly mortgage payment) + (Property taxes) + (Heat)) ÷ (Gross monthly income) × 100

= (($900 + $250 + $25) ÷ ($60,000 ÷ 12)) × 100

= ($1,175 ÷ $5,000) × 100

= 23.5%

There is no single maximum number for the GDSR, but rather the rule of thumb tends to be a range, 25% to 35%, depending upon the institution and its specific policies. When the outcome from the calculation of this ratio is higher than the company's prescribed maximum, a lender will normally decline to issue a mortgage. The thought is that the lower the ratio, the more likely an individual will be able to service her debt associated with mortgage, taxes and heat.

JOAN (2)

At 23.5%, Joan's gross debt service ratio is actually below the suggested maximum range of 25% to 35%, so she is well within the acceptable standard for most institutions.

It is important to note that, although this is a primary ratio, lenders still look at the total debt picture. Even though a borrower's GDSR ratio may not be high, she likely has other types of debt obligations that are not included in this ratio. If total debt obligations are excessive, the lender may decline the mortgage application until total debts are within a more manageable level.

Collateral

When tangible assets are pledged by the borrower as security for a loan, the assets are referred to as *collateral*. If a borrower goes into default on a secured loan, the lender has the right to seize and sell the asset to raise funds in order to recover the outstanding debt. Examples of tangible assets that might be used to secure a loan could include an automobile, property, investments or equipment. When a loan is secured by collateral it is referred to as a *secured loan*, which differs from an *unsecured loan* where no assets are pledged as security.

BILL

Bill has been approved for a $15,000 car loan to assist him with the purchase of a new car. The lender has explained to Bill that they will secure the loan by holding the car as collateral. If Bill defaults on the loan, the lender has the right to seize and sell the car to raise funds to pay off Bill's outstanding debt obligation.

CONSUMER CREDIT

Credit Cards

Today, credit cards play a vital role in the daily purchasing habits of most Canadians. Through a credit application, a consumer applies for a credit card and, upon approval by the financial institution, she receives a credit card that can be used to make purchases up to a specific limit.

Approval of the application is one aspect of the credit application, while the decision as to the amount of credit is a second aspect. Two individuals may both qualify for a credit card, but their credit limit on the card could vary substantially. A student with limited resources might only qualify for a $500 credit limit, whereas an individual with a clean credit history and a steady source of income might be awarded a $5,000 limit.

Quite often, credit card companies monitor a cardholder's pattern of payments and will automatically increase credit limits. In addition, increases to credit limits can typically be acquired through a credit assessment undertaken over the telephone. It is this easy access to credit that can lead to financial problems for some people who are less skilled at managing their personal financial resources.

Normally, purchases can be made on a credit card and no interest applies until the cardholder is billed for the purchase and the bill becomes due. If the bill is paid in full on or before the due date, the cardholder will not be charged any interest. If, however, the balance on the credit card is not paid in full, interest charges are applied based on the original purchase dates.

The majority of credit cards allow a cardholder to carry an outstanding balance, provided she makes the required minimum monthly payment. By allowing the balance to carry forward, the credit card company makes money on the interest paid by the cardholder. Interest rates charged on outstanding balances tend to be some of the highest rates in the credit market. This means that a cardholder is paying incredibly high fees for the use of the institution's funds. It is almost always advisable to pay off any credit card balance when it falls due, to avoid costly interest charges.

It is normally in the cardholder's best financial interest to eliminate credit card balances as quickly as possible. When a credit card balance begins to roll over month after month, and the cardholder is making limited progress in the reduction of the outstanding balance, she should pursue options to eliminate the outstanding balance. This can be achieved through the use of other, less expensive credit options such as:

- available liquid assets;
- funds from a line of credit; or
- possibly a personal loan.

However, using one of these methods to restructure the outstanding debt and then allowing the credit card balance to slip right back up again does not accomplish any valuable outcome. In fact, it simply creates additional debt that the individual is responsible for servicing and could compound current problems.

Line of Credit

A line of credit is simply that; the borrower has access to a specific amount of credit from which she can borrow and repay as needs arise, without seeking credit approval each time that she uses the credit facility. Typically, the financial institution will calculate a minimum monthly payment when there is any outstanding loan balance.

Similar to any other type of credit process, an applicant for a line of credit completes a credit application. Once approved, the lending institution provides an available line of credit based on a specific maximum (e.g., $15,000). Interest charges only apply when there is an outstanding balance.

This type of loan facility has become very popular and is often used as a means of liquidity to address emergency issues or to simply fill in the financial gaps between paycheques. There is no restriction as to how the funds can be used, and some other common uses include home decorating, tuition or a special vacation.

Single Purpose Personal Loans

Borrowing funds to purchase a car, sometimes referred to as a car loan, is an example of a single purpose personal loan. Other types of single purpose loans might include a loan to fund home renovations or a loan used to pay off a multitude of financial obligations in an effort to consolidate debt into a single payment.

The terms established for a personal loan could include a fixed rate of interest and a fixed monthly payment schedule. Alternatively, the loan could incorporate a variable rate of interest that fluctuates with changes to the prime rate, and includes a feature that allows conversion to a fixed rate, at the borrower's option. In today's credit market, there tends to be tremendous breadth in the types of products and features, so borrowers should treat the process of borrowing like any other purchase — seek products that suit their specific needs.

Investment Loan

For interest on the investment loan to be tax deductible, the money borrowed must be used for the purpose of earning income from a business or property and directly traceable to the investment. The interest must be paid or payable in respect of the year it is being deducted and a legal obligation to pay the interest must exist.

Money borrowed for an investment where the sole purpose is to realize a capital gain may not be tax deductible.

Insurance Loan

If an individual holds an insurance policy such as a whole life policy with a cash value, they may borrow from the cash value of the policy. Interest rates are usually established on a floating basis. The benefits include easy, immediate access to cash. There is no repayment schedule, although interest charges apply as long as the loan is outstanding.

Company Loan

A company may issue loans to employees to assist them in purchasing a home or relocation loans to a new place of work. The tax impact of each loan is as follows:

Home Loan to Purchase a Home

Taxable interest benefit uses the lesser of the prescribed interest rate at the time of the loan and prescribed rate for each quarter.

If the term of the loan exceeds five years, the home loan's prescribed interest rate is reset every five years.

Interest benefit = Prescribed interest rate × Loan amount × Time period

Home Relocation Loan

A *home relocation loan* is a loan to an employee that moves at least 40 kilometres closer to work. The employee reports the total interest benefit, but can claim a deduction equal to the taxable benefit charged on the first $25,000 for five years.

REFINANCING AND DEBT CONSOLIDATION

Refinancing is an activity where an individual uses a new source of debt to pay off an existing source of debt. For example, a homeowner who has an open mortgage may be able to negotiate a new mortgage at a lower interest rate. They will use the new mortgage to pay off the higher interest rate mortgage.

Debt consolidation involves negotiating a new source of debt and then paying off the various other sources of debt one has. For example, an individual has $1,000 in credit card debt at 28% and a $5,000 car loan at 10%. They would be better off negotiating a line of credit of $6,000 at 6% and then paying off the credit card and car loan debt. As a result, they will be paying a lower rate of interest of 6% instead of 28% and 10%.

MORTGAGES

A home represents one of the largest purchases an individual will make in her lifetime. After the decision is made as to the type of home to buy, the selection of a mortgage becomes the next most important step because of the significant financial implications.

The majority of people utilize a mortgage to help finance a home purchase. A large array of innovative mortgage products are available in the marketplace, which, combined with the keen interest of mortgage lenders to attract a continuous flow of new customers, makes the mortgage market a very competitive environment.

Simplistically, a mortgage is money lent by a financial institution to a borrower who is purchasing real estate and requires additional financial resources to complete the purchase of the property. The mortgage becomes a debt of the borrower, and is secured against the real estate on which the mortgage is held.

In 2010, the federal government introduced three new mortgage rules to increase the stability of the Canadian housing market. All borrowers need to be able to qualify for a five-year fixed mortgage rate even if they choose a shorter mortgage term or other interest rate. Existing homeowners are only able to refinance up to 90% (from 95%) of the value of their homes. Finally, investors must have a minimum 20% down payment (from 5%) to obtain government-backed mortgages on non-owner occupied properties. The new rules will not affect the majority of homeowners.

Basics

Amortization

The term *amortization* refers to the period over which the payments associated with the repayment of a debt, including interest and principal, is based. The length of the amortization period is an important element in the calculation of the monthly payments. The longer the amortization period, the lower the payment amount; however, this causes the principal amount of the mortgage to be outstanding longer and, therefore, increases the total amount of interest paid on the mortgage. Conversely, the shorter the amortization period and the higher the payment, the sooner the principal amount is repaid and the lower the total amount of interest paid on the debt.

When a first-time homebuyer seeks a new mortgage, a 25-year amortization period is quite common. This means that the repayment schedule for the debt is based on repayment of the principal over a 25-year period. A borrower is under no obligation to use a 25-year amortization schedule, and may select payments based on a shorter period, 15 or 20 years, if she can afford the resulting payments.

MILA

Mila is scheduled to take possession of her new home at the end of next month, and will borrow $175,000 to assist in the financing of her home. To help Mila in the selection of an amortization period that suits her financial needs, the lender has prepared the following comparison, which uses a 5% rate of interest.

Amortization Period (Years)	Monthly Payment ($)	Total Payments Over Amortization Period ($)
25	1,017.81	305,343
20	1,149.97	275,993
15	1,379.22	248,260

For comparison purposes, Mila can see that a 25-year amortization schedule would offer the lowest monthly payment, while a 15-year schedule would increase her payment by 36%. However, an important note for Mila is that to the extent that her total payments exceed the original mortgage balance, the difference is all interest expense.

Mila knows that she will borrow $175,000 and under the 25-year amortization schedule her payments will total $305,343. This represents $130,343 of interest expense ($305,343 - $175,000).

For comparison, the interest cost under the 15-year amortization schedule is $73,260 ($248,260 - $175,000). And using a 20-year amortization schedule, the interest cost falls in the middle at $100,993 ($275,993 - $175,000).

Mila would review her monthly cash flow to determine which amortization schedule best fits her situation. She would also be aware of the fact that the shorter the amortization period, the higher the monthly payment, but the lower the total cost of interest.

Term

The phrase *mortgage term* is the period during which the lender extends funds to the debtor. The interest rate associated with the mortgage is a function of the current mortgage term. Mortgage terms range from as short as six months to as long as ten years, although terms longer than five years are not commonly used. Throughout the period during which a mortgage is held on a property, the borrower will move through several terms.

When a mortgage is first acquired, the debtor selects a term, which is the period during which the lender will extend funds. The term is also important because it is the period for which the interest rate conditions are established. At the end of the term, the mortgage is considered to have matured and the debtor must either renew the mortgage or repay the outstanding balance. For example, if a debtor has a three-year term, she has the opportunity to lock in the interest rate for the term, in this case three years.

Interest Rates

Overview

The market interest rate charged on mortgages will vary depending upon the term selected by the debtor. In addition to the term, there may be other features that affect the rate of interest charged on the loan and would need to be considered in a competitive assessment, such as the method by which interest is calculated or financial incentives paid directly to the consumer.

All lending institutions post their interest rates, but the majority of major financial institutions have some flexibility. Quite often, it is to the debtor's benefit to negotiate with the financial institution rather than simply accepting the posted interest rates. While a few institutions have a policy to post their best rate and stipulate that there is no room for negotiation, the majority of lenders have flexibility, especially when lending to individuals with a strong credit rating.

Fixed Rate Mortgage

A *fixed rate mortgage* is one where the rate of interest applied over the term of the mortgage is locked in and will not change. This is a choice the borrower makes each time a mortgage term begins. For example, an individual could lock in the interest rate available on a six-month term, and for that six-month period, the rate will not change. The borrower might decide that there is greater comfort in fixing the guaranteed rate of interest for a longer period of time, so might choose a fixed rate of interest on a five-year term. This would result in a guaranteed rate of interest over the five-year term.

A fixed rate of interest provides the comfort of a guarantee that the interest rate will remain stable and, subsequently, the required payment schedule is fixed for the period of the term selected. A combination of a fixed interest rate and a longer term provides the borrower with greater certainty as to her financial commitments.

The downside of a fixed interest rate is the inability to benefit from dips to interest rates during the term. If rates decline during the term of the mortgage, the borrower may be locked in with no ability to make changes, or if changes are permitted, there may be a financial penalty that outweighs the benefit.

Variable Rate Mortgage

A *variable rate mortgage* is one where the interest rate applied during the term of the mortgage will vary based on changes to the Bank of Canada rate or other similar posted rate, referred to as the index rate. The lender establishes the starting rate of interest and defines the criteria as to how the rate of interest will move relative to changes in the index rate.

The financial risk resulting from the changing rate of interest creates a level of uncertainty that many Canadians find unattractive. A variable rate mortgage is typically best suited for individuals who have a high risk threshold and expect interest rates to remain relatively stable or decline during the term of the mortgage. Quite often, the lending institution provides the borrower of a variable interest mortgage with the opportunity to lock in a fixed rate of interest at any time during the term of the mortgage. This type of feature helps manage the risk associated with a variable rate mortgage.

Conventional versus High Ratio

When an individual takes out a mortgage, the size of the debt is assessed relative to the value of the property against which the debt will apply. When the debt represents an amount that is less than 80% of the property's appraised value or purchase price, whichever is less, it is considered a *conventional mortgage*.

The opposite of a conventional mortgage is a high ratio mortgage. As the name suggests, it is one where the amount of the mortgage represents a high proportion of the value of the home. When a mortgage exceeds 80% of the value of the home, where value is defined as the lower of the appraised value or the purchase price, the mortgage is described as a *high ratio mortgage*. In this case, the down payment on the property would be an amount that represents less than 20% of the value of the home. A high ratio mortgage may also be referred to as a *non-conventional mortgage*.

The distinction between a high ratio and a conventional mortgage is important because, in Canada, a high ratio mortgage is insured by the Canada Mortgage and Housing Corporation (CMHC) or a private insurer. As one might surmise, there is greater risk of default on a high ratio mortgage than on a conventional arrangement, so the addition of CMHC insurance provides protection for the lender. The high ratio mortgage insurance premium (based on the loan-to-value ratio) ranges from 1% to 3.4% of the new mortgage amount. The one-time premium is generally added the approved new mortgage amount.

Features

Open Mortgage

A mortgage where the debtor has the complete freedom to pay off the entire outstanding balance or any portion, at any time, without penalty, is referred to as an *open mortgage*. Normally, open mortgages are available for only shorter terms, such as 6 months and one year. This means that for the term of the mortgage, such as six months or one year, the mortgage remains open and the borrower may repay any portion of the outstanding balance without penalty.

Interest rates on open mortgages tend to be somewhat higher than on an equivalent closed mortgage because the lender runs the risk that the funds will be repaid and a new borrower of the funds must be sought.

Closed Mortgage

In the past, a *closed mortgage* referred to one where the borrower was committed to the repayment schedule negotiated for the term of the mortgage, and was not permitted to make any additional payments against the outstanding balance during the term of the mortgage. In some cases, repayment was only permitted if the home was sold.

Today, the breadth of features available on mortgage products makes it more difficult to provide a specific definition of a closed mortgage that applies across all lenders. In reality, different features available on a closed mortgage have become important distinguishing characteristics that increase the attractiveness of one lender's offerings compared to that of another lender. In general terms, a *closed mortgage* is defined as one where the borrower does not have the complete freedom to pay off the entire outstanding balance or any portion that she so chooses, during the term of the mortgage.

Many mortgages allow the individual to pay down or prepay up to 10%–15% of the mortgage each year without any penalties. If the mortgage is a closed mortgage, the individual may have to pay up to three months interest penalty or an interest rate differential (IRD) penalty for early payment of the full mortgage. The IRD is the difference between the borrower's stated interest rate and the rate at which the lender could currently loan money for an equivalent term.

IRD formula = (((Mortgage interest rate - Current interest rate) $\times$ Outstanding balance) $\times$ (Remaining months) $\div$ 12)

BETH

Beth has 6 months left on her 5-year, 6% mortgage. The principle is $50,000 and the current interest rate on 6-month mortgages is 4%. The penalty would be:

$$IRD = [((6\% - 4\%) \times 50,000) \times (6 \div 12)$$
$$= 2\% \times 50,000 \times 0.5$$
$$= \$500$$

When taking out a closed mortgage, it is important to evaluate features of the mortgage relative to the borrower's specific needs. While no one has a crystal ball to predict the future, if there is a chance the borrower may want to sell her home during the term of the mortgage, can the mortgage be paid off? What is the financial penalty? What types of pre-payment options are available?

Portability

Portability is a feature that has grown in popularity over the past decade because it provides the borrower with the ability to sell her current property and move the existing mortgage to a replacement property. While the new home will have to be assessed relative to the lender's criteria, portability allows the borrower to retain the features and benefits of the existing mortgage. If additional mortgage funds are required, the borrower will have to qualify financially for the additional funds, and the old and new mortgage amounts will normally be blended into a revised payment schedule based on a blended interest rate.

Costs

Administration

It is common for lenders to charge borrowers an administration fee for setting up a mortgage and for processing each renewal. While the administrative fee for renewals may be small, such as $100 to $250, it can add up when an individual opts for shorter terms, such as six months, and affects the total cost borne by the debtor.

TAMMY

Tammy feels that market interest rates will move in ebbs and flows throughout the next three years so plans to opt for six-month renewals on her mortgage. This means that for each six-month period, the interest rate will remain fixed at a pre-established rate and the rate may be higher or lower at each renewal.

The one area of concern for Tammy is the $200 administration charge that her lender applies for processing each renewal. While Tammy hopes to optimize the interest charges on her loan by using six-month renewals, each time she renews there is a $200 charge. Over a three-year period the charges will amount to $1,200 (6 renewals at $200 each). This type of extra charge increases Tammy's overall cost associated with the mortgage debt, so she has negotiated with the lender to have the renewal fee waived.

Similar to the discussion regarding interest rates, it can be in the borrower's best interest to discuss administrative fees prior to selecting a mortgage lender and request that such fees be waived. For very credit-worthy customers, these types of exceptions are often the norm but only if requested.

Even with an open mortgage, it is common for a lender to charge administration fees when a mortgage is paid out. There is no commonality across the fee structures of the various institutions so, when assessing a mortgage prior to any commitment, it is valuable to look at all types of costs and fee structures, not simply the pure interest rate.

Payment Schedule

In years gone by, a mortgage repayment schedule was typically built based on a single monthly payment, with 12 payments per year. Today, most lending institutions offer a variety of schedules. In addition to monthly payments, other common schedules include weekly, bi-weekly and semi-monthly.

RALPH

Ralph is renewing his mortgage and has selected a 3-year-term at a 5.2% fixed rate of interest and a 15-year amortization schedule. The outstanding balance on his mortgage is $122,000. Ralph has the opportunity to accept a weekly, bi-weekly or monthly payment schedule. His mortgage lender has prepared the following table that details the payment amount under each of the different options.

Frequency	Payment Amount ($)	Total Payments Over 15-Year Amortization Period ($)
Monthly	973.98	175,316.40
Bi-weekly	449.01	175,113.90
Weekly	224.39	175,024.20

In reviewing his choices, Ralph would consider a payment schedule that best fits his cash flow. The total of all payments under each of the frequency options is roughly the same because the required payment was calculated taking into account the frequency option.

However, Ralph might decide that while his cash flow best matches the weekly payment schedule, he can afford to pay $250.00 per week, which is roughly one-quarter of his scheduled monthly payment. By increasing his weekly payment to $250 rather than the $224.39 required under this schedule, Ralph could reduce his principal sooner than scheduled. In this case, a $250 weekly payment would reduce his amortization period by 2.3 years (total savings of $9,778 over the entire amortization period).

Note that the calculation of these payment options is beyond the scope of this material and your course calculator.

Application

The breadth of incentives and features available on mortgage products make it quite difficult to undertake a comprehensive apples to apples comparison of the actual costs between different lenders. Individual features provide benefits that can be looked at in isolation, but it is also important to consider some features in relationship to others, and to consider the suitability of the product as a whole relative to the borrower's specific circumstances.

DAWN

Dawn is financially secure and her mortgage payments represent a low percentage of her monthly income. She has the financial means to withstand a substantial increase in her mortgage payment, and is very interested in the opportunity to save interest costs. Dawn does not foresee any significant increase to mortgage interest rates over the next few years, so she has opted for a six-month closed mortgage at a 4% fixed rate of interest.

This means that during the six-month term, Dawn will be charged interest at 4%. At the end of the six-month term, Dawn will be obliged to either renew the mortgage at the then current interest rate on whatever new term she selects, or she can repay the outstanding funds. Dawn is in a sufficiently secure financial position and is willing to take the risk that interest rates might fall and she could benefit from a lower interest rate at the renewal. The risk is that the renewal rate may be higher.

> *ROBERT*
>
> Robert's current finances are quite tight and he has very little disposable income because of his commitment to funding his daughter's skating ambitions. Robert relies on the fact that he knows his mortgage payment is a set amount and will not change for quite some time.
>
> Robert's mortgage is up for renewal. While Robert feels interest rates will continue to shift up and down over the next few years and he would like to benefit from any interest savings, his financial position does not afford him this opportunity. Robert is willing to lock in a 5-year interest rate as it will provide him with a guaranteed mortgage payment for that period, and he will not succumb to any risk that his required payment could jump to a level he could not afford.

Reverse Mortgages

For many Canadians, a significant portion of their savings is tied up in the value of the home in which they live. A reverse mortgage allows an individual to access the equity in her home while still living in it. The individual must be at least 62 years old and can access between 10% and 40% of the home's appraised value.

Nature of a Reverse Mortgage

With a traditional mortgage, an individual takes out a mortgage to buy a home and makes regular payments to the financial institution against the debt obligation represented by the mortgage. With a reverse mortgage, the individual uses the equity portion of her property for collateral on a loan that only becomes due when she dies, or sooner if she sells her home. As with a regular mortgage, the individual who takes out a reverse mortgage continues to own her home but there becomes a debt obligation on which interest accumulates, although no payments are required until the debt obligation becomes due at death or when the house is sold.

Types of Reverse Mortgages

Reverse mortgages are relatively new in Canada and have not caught on as a significant trend; generally, there is very low public awareness. The three main types are: reverse annuity mortgage, line of credit reverse mortgage, and a fixed term reverse mortgage.

With a reverse annuity mortgage, a lump-sum amount is borrowed and invested in an annuity with monthly income payments for the rest of the homeowner's life. The mortgage is repaid upon death of the homeowner or sooner if the home is sold.

A line of credit mortgage allows the homeowner to borrow funds as needed from a line of credit secured by the value of the home. Interest only accumulates when the funds are withdrawn.

A fixed term reverse mortgage provides funds to a homeowner for a fixed period of time, often five to ten years. The repayment of the borrowed funds and accumulated interest occurs at end of the fixed term.

Taxation

According to the CRA, simple reverse mortgage payments and lines of credit are not taxable since they are equivalent to loan advances from a traditional mortgage. The income generated by a reverse mortgage annuity is not taxable.

When reversed mortgages are used for investment purposes, the accruing mortgage interest is tax-deductible against any investment returns generated by the mortgage proceeds, providing individuals with a stream of tax-sheltered income.

Leases

Leasing is similar to renting an item for a period of time. Examples of items leased include automobiles, furniture and equipment. The main benefit of leasing is that an individual gets to use the item without incurring a large upfront cost. They pay for the items through periodic payments over the term of the lease.

The term of the lease varies based on the life of the item being leased and may be a fixed term. The interest rate, initial payment and residual value of the item are used in the calculation of the monthly lease payment.

INSOLVENCY AND BANKRUPTCY

Overview

A person whose liabilities are greater than her assets is considered to be financially insolvent. And when a person is financially insolvent with no foreseeable means of meeting outstanding credit obligations, *bankruptcy* is the legal process that allows the individual to be released from most of her debts to creditors and begin fresh.

When a person defaults on debt payments, creditors who are owed money would normally seek repayment from the borrower through the use of collection agencies and, ultimately, by suing the debtor. The process of bankruptcy is performed under the federal *Bankruptcy and Insolvency Act*, and involves the assignment of all assets, except those exempt by law, to a trustee in bankruptcy who arranges for an orderly distribution of the proceeds from the assets as compensation to creditors. Through the legal process of bankruptcy, the overburdened debtor is relieved of most debts and any further legal proceedings underway from most creditors.

Asset Assignment

The process of bankruptcy requires the assignment of a debtor's assets to the trustee. This assignment involves all assets that the debtor owns with the general exception of essential needs, such as basic furniture and tools of a trade. Exceptions will vary by province.

Non-Released Debts

While an individual is released from many debts through the process of bankruptcy, it is not all-inclusive. Rather, the following list of debts owed by the bankrupt individual are not released through bankruptcy:

- debts which included a co-signer or guarantee of another individual;
- student loans if the bankruptcy occurs while the debtor is still a student;
- student loans if the bankruptcy occurs within seven years after having ceased to be a student;
- claims for alimony;
- spousal or child support payments;
- debts related to any involvement with fraud;
- court fines; and
- damages owed to another individual due to an assault.

> **BEN**
>
> Ben filed for bankruptcy and was relieved of $44,000 of debt including a car loan, personal bank loan, outstanding balance on a line of credit and credit card balances.
>
> At that time, Ben also owed $12,000 in child and spousal support to his former spouse. This $12,000 debt was not released through bankruptcy and Ben remains responsible for its payment.

Credit Rating

An individual's credit rating plays a vital role in her ability to acquire most types of credit, including credit cards. As such, the notation of bankruptcy on an individual's credit rating will directly impact future applications for credit.

Tax Filing

When an individual files for bankruptcy, she completes two income tax returns for that taxation year: one for the period from January 1 to the date of bankruptcy and a second return for the post-bankruptcy period during the remainder of the year.

Consumer Proposal

There is an alternative to filing for bankruptcy called a *Consumer Proposal*. A consumer proposal is a legal procedure available to people living in Canada who are insolvent and experiencing financial difficulties, but can still afford to repay a portion, usually more than 50%, of their unsecured debts. A licensed trustee will meet with the debtor and work out a payment plan, and then present that plan to all of her creditors. In most cases, she agrees to repay a portion of the unsecured debts instead of filing for bankruptcy. A proposal is better for the creditors because even though they may not get all of their money, they are getting more than they would get in a bankruptcy. If the proposal is accepted, it becomes a legally binding settlement of the unsecured debts.

A consumer proposal is suitable if:

- debts are over $5,000, but not over $250,000 (not including the home mortgage).
- Debtor has good job, and can afford to make some payments each month, but she can not afford to repay everyone in full with interest.
- Debtor can't get a debt consolidation loan because their debts are too high, even with her steady income.
- Payer does not want to file for bankruptcy.

There are several advantages of a consumer proposal for the consumer. The debtor can negotiate to repay only a portion of the debt they owe with all to their creditors and they usually get to keep their house and other unsecured assets. All of the unsecured debts are included (credit cards, bank loans, payday loans, and income taxes), except for support, alimony, and student loan obligations. Interest stops accumulating and all collection activities by creditors stop (except for support, alimony, and student loan obligations) at the date a consumer proposal is filed. The maximum repayment period is five years and the effect on a person's credit rating is less severe than a bankruptcy.

DEBT MANAGEMENT

The process of debt management involves optimizing the structure of an individual's serviceable debt to allow for the most effective use of available funds. There is no single strategy but rather it involves an analysis of the situation taking into account assets, cash flow and personal requirements.

The interest-free period on credit card purchases is an excellent source of short-term money. Using the lender's funds for this interim period frees up dollars that can be used in other ways. However, when the use of credit cards flows into the interest payment phase because the cardholder carries an outstanding balance, the cost of the borrowing skyrockets to one of the highest levels of interest in the marketplace.

Money borrowed to purchase an automobile or other short-term durable good should generally not be financed through an addition to a mortgage because of the long-term nature of a mortgage. It is often not wise to use long-term debt and long periods of amortization to finance shorter-term assets. Rather, a single-purpose loan or a line of credit tend to be more appropriate sources for financing.

Another strategy that aids in effective debt management is to optimize deductible interest where possible, rather than non-deductible interest. Deductible interest involves the ability to deduct the interest payment from the borrower's income and lower the borrower's income tax liability. If, for example, an individual has an outstanding loan balance where the interest is non-deductible and also has available cash that she would like to use for investment purposes, it could be to the individual's advantage to consider using the available cash to pay off the debt and then borrow funds to make a subsequent qualifying investment.

As discussed in the prior modules, the interest on funds borrowed for investment purposes may qualify as tax deductible, provided that the funds meet established criteria. To meet the spirit of the rules, available cash would be used to pay off debt and then future investment decisions may involve the use of borrowed funds. Of course, this type of strategy should always be looked at relative to the individual's overall investment strategy.

Reducing a mortgage as quickly as possible is another debt management strategy. The use of additional lump-sum payments and shortened amortization periods will help to accelerate elimination of the mortgage debt. In addition, it is better to pay down debt with the highest interest rate first, instead of the largest amount of debt.

MONEY MANAGEMENT

Overview

The concept of money management is an integral part of financial planning because financial goals can only be established on solid ground if there are sufficient resources to support the planned outcome. Financial goals can be optimized through the use of money management strategies, and the concept of money management ties closely to that of debt management.

Debt is inevitable at some point in most people's lives. Without a mortgage, the ability to purchase a home would be unthinkable for the majority of people. Similarly, debt is an important resource that allows individuals to acquire assets to achieve a particular lifestyle. However, when debt becomes overwhelming it impacts lifestyle, either financially or emotionally. When debt is in a controlled state, money management becomes achievable.

Budgeting Process

Personal money management involves the prioritization of the cash flows in and out of a family unit in an effort to achieve desired financial goals. This can be accomplished through budgeting, which involves advanced planning for a systematized allocation of expenditures of net income.

> *The financial statements referred to in the MAX AND SHARON WEST series of SNAPs are located in Appendices Two through Five.*

> **MAX AND SHARON WEST (1)**
>
> Sharon and Max West, a married couple who live in XYZ Province, know that saving for retirement is important; and while they feel they can safely set aside $20,000 each year, it is simply a guess at this point in time. The couple is unsure as to when they can safely invest available funds so they do not create ongoing short-term liquidity problems, which has been a nagging problem in the past.
>
> The couple has provided income and expenditure data to their financial advisor, Sara, who has created a projected cash flow statement for 2010, as shown in Appendix Three.

Income

Income from all sources is summarized to derive the total amount of money available to support expenditures. The timing of cash inflows forms an important part of this analysis. There should be a distinction made between regular inflows of cash (i.e., monthly salary) and lump sum amounts that are received on an infrequent basis (i.e., dividend income). Variance in the timing of cash inflows should be reflected in the allocation of income across the monthly cash flow statement.

> **MAX AND SHARON WEST (2)**
>
> From the cash flow statement we know that the Wests expect to have net income of $107,200. But this information on its own is insufficient because discussions with the Wests indicate that the income is not evenly distributed throughout a 12-month period.
>
> Using information provided by the Wests, Sara created an income projection for each month, as shown in Appendix Four. From this monthly projection, it becomes more obvious that there are income disparities between different months. For example, April has the lowest net income ($7,088) and December has the highest ($14,927).

Expenses

Similar to the income section, the timing of expenses should be incorporated into a monthly projection, recognizing ongoing monthly and lump-sum amounts. The types of expenses will differ by family, but the important matter is to ensure that all expenses are captured and accounted for, as is best possible. The budgeting exercise involves estimates, as information is not always known in advance. Estimates should be based on all realistic information available when the projection is created. As new information arises, it can be integrated through a revision process.

> **MAX AND SHARON WEST (3)**
>
> The middle portion of the family's cash flow statement lists all expenses that the Wests anticipate. Using 18 categories of expenses that have meaning to this couple, the information depicts that the family anticipates expenses of $76,800 during the year (Appendix Three).
>
> Using information provided by the Wests, Sara created a monthly summary of the expected cash outflows as shown in Appendix Five. This monthly allocation reveals a very sporadic outflow of cash from a high of $9,450 in July to a low of $4,533 in October.

Net Income Available for Saving

Once the income and expenses have been entered into a monthly projection, the third step is to use this information to identify the net income available for savings. This is achieved by subtracting the expenses from the net income. Few people experience an equal flow of income and expenses through each month, and the picture on a monthly basis often looks quite different than on an annual basis. When the result is positive, it indicates that there are funds available for savings, whereas a negative result indicates that expenses in that month are greater than income and a shortfall will occur. To address a shortfall, the family will need to access additional cash, perhaps from available savings or a line of credit.

MAX AND SHARON WEST (4)

At a macro level, Max and Sharon have substantial resources available for savings on an annual basis, and this year they will have $30,400. The couple thought they should be able to save $20,000, but through the analysis (Appendix Six), it is clear that they have an additional $10,400 ($30,400 - $20,000) available.

Discussions between Sara and the couple indicated that they would like to increase their savings to $25,000 and retain a cushion of $5,400 to allow for any variances in their budget estimates.

During preliminary discussions, the couple indicated that they have experienced a nagging problem with ongoing short-term liquidity. When looking at the cash flow on a macro level, there appears to be sufficient funds, which indeed there are. However, the short-term lack of funds only becomes truly apparent when the cash flow is examined at a micro level.

In January and July, there is a negative cash flow, which means expenses exceed available cash inflows. In February, the net result is positive, but only by a small margin (Appendix Six).

The net available cash for savings is a calculation made before any funds are allocated for investment purposes. Depending upon the amount of funds directed toward investments, the couple could find themselves in a deficiency throughout many months of the year. If the deficiency is funded through a line of credit, the couple may be incurring unnecessary interest costs. In addition, the couple may find they are taking out loans for their RRSP contributions, which could easily be eliminated by using the cash flow analysis to guide the timing of investment purchases.

With this information, Sara has demonstrated to the Wests that they actually have 50% more available resources for savings than they originally estimated. Together Sara and the Wests can work through the timing of investments so that the couple does not feel that they are constantly in a catch-up mode.

Emergency Fund

Everyone will experience the need for unexpected cash at some point in their life; some just experience it more often than others. The concept of an emergency fund is one where there are sufficient readily accessible liquid funds.

In the past, a standard rule of thumb was that a family should have 10% of their gross income set aside in a liquid asset that could be used to finance emergency needs. The growth in popularity of a line of credit has had some impact on this rule of thumb.

If a family has an available line of credit that is not constantly in use or often in the upper limit, then some planners feel that the amount of money set aside as an emergency fund could be managed downward, to an amount below the 10% rule. Every family should still have some available funds that can be easily accessed (i.e., savings account, Canada Savings Bonds, modest size cashable GIC) for emergency purposes, but the amount will vary depending upon other easily accessible resources.

Conclusion

The process of budgeting causes individuals to examine information at a detailed level. This type of examination is important if a family wants to optimize available resources and minimize excess interest costs. Even when there are abundant funds available, the process of cash management can increase the effectiveness of how the funds are used, reducing unnecessary costs.

The analysis also provides a great guide as to how the family's resources are being spent. Once the budget is complete, the monitoring of actual expenses will help assess whether the budget estimates are reasonably accurate. Variances should be assessed and any pertinent information incorporated into subsequent projections.

SPECIAL NEEDS PLANNING

Introduction

The care and understanding of special needs situations is part of the financial planning process. Examples of special needs situations include:

- disabled children;
- dependent adults; and
- a terminally ill person.

Disabled Children

A key concern for families with disabled children often relates to the financial well-being of the disabled child after the passing of her parents. While parents are alive and well, they quite often play an important role in the child's welfare — personally, emotionally and financially. Careful planning for the estate of a parent with a disabled child is important to minimize any impact on support from government bodies, for which the child may qualify. This concern and solution is discussed further in Module 19, "Estate Planning".

Dependent Adult

The personal, emotional and financial care of a dependent adult often starts quite gradually as one or more adult children take on increasing responsibility for the care of an elderly parent. The responsibility gradually increases, and the adult child begins to play a vital role in the dependent adult's life. The actual relationship can differ but it often involves an elderly relative and an adult child, grandchild, niece or nephew.

An increasing number of people want to include provisions for a dependent adult as part of their personal financial plan. To address this need, a series of questions should be incorporated in the fact-finding stage of the engagement, which allows the planner to fully explore the issues and opportunities relative to the dependent adult. This type of exploration would examine areas such as:

Personal care — the amount of involvement the client has in the personal care of the dependent adult; the involvement of others in the dependent adult's care; alternative arrangements that may be available; consequences of this care not being available due to death or disability of either the client or other caregivers.

Emotional support — amount of involvement the client has in the emotional care of the dependent adult; the involvement of others in the dependent adult's care; alternative arrangements that may be available; consequences of this care not being available due to death or disability of either the client or other caregivers.

Financial support — amount of financial support provided by the client; financial support provided by others; consequences and resulting issues of the financial support disappearing.

This list is not all-inclusive and should certainly be customized to the needs of the situation. Nonetheless, the questions should gather sufficient qualitative and quantitative data that will allow for a thorough review of alternatives and recommendations, relative to the dependent adult.

Terminally Ill

Financial planning for a terminally ill individual will generally focus on the organization of the individual's personal affairs in preparation for her passing. This will certainly involve a discussion of the individual's testamentary wishes and level of preparation relative to the distribution of her estate. For example, does she have a current and valid will, and, if so, does it reflect her current testamentary wishes? If she does not have a current and valid will, does this need to be addressed? Are there actions that should be undertaken while the individual is capable of making sound decisions relative to beneficiary designations, trusts or asset ownership structure?

A second key area is the level of preparedness relative to the individual's declining state of health. Does the individual have a valid power of attorney for property and for personal care? If not, does this need to be addressed? As you will note in the following module, proper legal documentation is essential if someone else is to manage an individual's legal and financial affairs, which often becomes necessary with the declining health of a terminally ill person. Similar legal documentation is necessary relative to personal care and health-related decisions.

Unit 3
Charitable Giving

INTRODUCTION

Many times an individual will have charitable intentions and the only way to meet her objectives effectively is to ensure that her charitable gifts become part of her larger financial plan. Understanding the options and associated tax rules will allow for complete integration of the charitable gifts into the individual's comprehensive financial plan.

BASIC TAX RULE

Federal Non-Refundable Tax Credit

Generally, charitable donations may be claimed up to a limit of 75% of the taxpayer's net income (line 236). Any charitable donation amount that a taxpayer cannot or does not claim in the taxation year can be carried forward and used in any of the subsequent five years. In the year the taxpayer dies, charitable donations may be claimed up to a limit of 100% of the taxpayer's net income. Amounts that a deceased taxpayer cannot claim in the year of death, because of the net income maximum, can be carried back one year and claimed as a credit, up to 100% of net income.

RACHEL

Rachel inherited a substantial estate and decided to donate $75,000 to the local hospital. Rachel's net income was $60,000. The maximum amount that Rachel can claim for charitable donations is $45,000 (75% of $60,000). The balance can be carried forward and claimed on her return in any one of the next five years.

WAYNE

Wayne donated $50,000 to the local hospice. That same year, his net income totaled $31,000. If Wayne died, how much of the $50,000 donation can his executor claim for charitable donations?

The executor can claim $31,000 (100% of his net income) for his current year tax return and the remaining $19,000 ($50,000 - $31,000) can be carried back to his return for the prior year.

Optimizing Credit

Charitable donations are different from other federal tax credits in that two separate tax rates apply to calculate the amount of the tax credit. The first $200 of donations is converted to a federal tax credit by multiplying the amount donated (up to $200) by the lowest federal tax rate, which is currently 15% (2009). For donations above $200, the donation amount (up to the taxpayer's income maximum), less the first $200, is multiplied by the federal tax rate from the highest bracket (currently 29%) to arrive at a second amount that is deducted from the federal taxes payable. The result is that low-income taxpayers actually receive an enhanced tax benefit from donations of more than $200, because the tax rebate uses 29%, which may be more than the taxpayer's marginal tax bracket.

If charitable donations are made in a year in which the donation tax credit cannot be used because the taxpayer has zero tax to pay, the charitable donation amount can be carried forward for up to five years.

With charitable donations, the CRA's administrative practice has been to allow the donations to be claimed by either the taxpayer or the taxpayer's spouse or common-law partner. In other words, they have allowed the donations made by a couple (spouses or common-law partners) to be combined and claimed by either spouse or common-law partner. Because the first $200 of donations uses only a 15% tax credit, it is more advantageous for a couple to combine their donations so that only $200 will attract the 15% rate, rather than $200 for each spouse. In addition, it is generally more advantageous for the higher-income spouse to claim the charitable tax credit, if the province of residence has surtaxes.

KIM AND KYLE

Common-law partners Kyle and Kim had receipts for charitable donations that totaled $900, which was comprised of $400 donated by Kyle and $500 donated by Kim. While Kim and Kyle have receipts that indicate their respective donation amounts, by combining their donations onto one partner's return they can maximize the available credit.

The table below shows the calculations of option 1, where Kyle and Kim each claim their own donations, which results in a total tax credit of $206, compared to option 2 where the amounts are combined and claimed by one spouse, resulting in a tax credit of $233.50.

	Option 1a Kyle	Option 1b Kim	Option 2 Combined
Total charitable gifts:	$400.00	$500.00	$900.00
Federal non-refundable credit			
• First $200 @ 15%	$ 30.00	$ 30.00	$ 30.00
• Remaining portion @ 29%	$ 58.00	$ 87.00	$203.00
Total	$ 88.00	$117.00	$233.00

By combining the charitable donations onto one tax return, Kyle and Kim can save $28.00 in federal taxes. If they live in a province that applies a surtax, it may be advantageous to have the higher income partner make the claim.

Gifts in Kind

While many donations are based on cash, a charitable gift can also be completed as a non-cash charitable donation, which is referred to as a gift in kind. A *gift in kind* refers to property other than cash, such as a capital property and personal-use property, including listed personal property. Examples of a gift in kind include stocks, bonds, land, building or a valued piece of art.

The CRA has rules that direct how a gift in kind is valued, which often includes independent appraisal of the item to determine an appropriate fair market value.

Gifts of capital property or depreciable property result in a disposition of the property at fair market value. This fixes both the amount of the proceeds and the size of the donation.

SPECIAL CIRCUMSTANCES

The earlier section describes the basic rule for federal non-refundable donation tax credits; however, there are a number of exceptions to the basic rule.

Gifts in the Year of Death

In the year the taxpayer dies, charitable donations may be claimed up to a limit of 100% of the taxpayer's net income. Amounts that a deceased taxpayer cannot claim in the year of death, because of the net income maximum, can be carried back one year and claimed as a credit, up to 100% of net income.

Ecological Gifts

Ecological gifts are an exception to the basic rule in that a charitable donation credit may be claimed for amounts up to 100% of the taxpayer's net income.

Cultural Property

Gifts of cultural property may be claimed for amounts up to 100% of the taxpayer's net income. In addition, capital gains on qualifying donations are exempt from taxation.

Capital Property

General Rule

As outlined earlier, the basic rule for the federal non-refundable tax credit limits the claim for charitable gifts to 75% of net income. This limit is increased when taxable capital gains and/or recaptured depreciation are realized on the disposition of capital property to a charity.

- For capital gains resulting from the donation of publicly traded securities made after May 1, 2006, the inclusion rate is zero. Publicly traded securities are defined as shares traded on a prescribed stock exchange in Canada and a number of foreign countries, as listed in the Income Tax Regulations.

- As noted earlier, qualifying donations of cultural property are exempt from taxation.

The intent of this exception is to provide the taxpayer with full tax relief on any income caused by the gift of capital property.

Shares Acquired Through Stock-Option Plan

When an individual donates shares of a publicly listed corporation that were acquired through her employer's stock-option plan, she can claim an additional 50% of the employment benefit resulting from the exercise of the stock option. The intent is to offset the employment benefit triggered by the disposition of the shares. To qualify for this additional deduction:

- the shares must be donated within 30 days of having been acquired and within the same year as having been received; and

- the taxpayer would otherwise be entitled to claim the stock option deduction on line 249 of the T1 General.

Gifts to U.S. Charities

Generally, when an individual has U.S. income, she can claim any donation to a U.S. charity that would normally be allowed on a U.S. return. The charitable donation may be claimed up to a limit of 75% of the taxpayer's net U.S. income. Where a taxpayer commutes to work or business in the U.S. and that activity is her main source of income, she may be able to claim the donation up to 75% of her net world income.

LIFE INSURANCE

Faced with ever increasing costs, charitable organizations rely heavily on planned gifts from individuals, and the use of life insurance can play a valuable role in an individual's gifting strategy. There are three primary methods for utilizing a life insurance policy to plan a charitable gift. The first method is through an absolute assignment of the policy to the charity, while the second involves retaining ownership but designating the charity as beneficiary. A third method is to use the insurance policy to fund a bequest made within a will.

While the outcome of each method results in benefits for the charity, the process and tax consequences differ. Only by assessing the facts of each unique situation is one able to judge the overall effectiveness.

Absolute Assignment

Through the completion of an absolute assignment, the owner of a life insurance policy can transfer the policy to the charity. The charity then becomes the owner and names itself as beneficiary. Upon the death of the life insured, the charity will receive the benefit proceeds from the policy. Once the policy is assigned, the charity becomes the new owner and is responsible for the payment of premiums. However, the donor may continue to pay the premiums on behalf of the charity, although she is under no obligation to do so.

(a) If the policy has a cash surrender value, such as a whole life or universal life policy, the donation will be valued as the sum of the cash surrender value plus any dividends on deposit less any outstanding loans. The donation of the policy is treated as a disposition and any income gain upon disposition is taxable to the policy owner (donor).

If the donor of the policy continues to pay policy premiums, each premium payment is treated as a charitable donation for tax purposes.

(b) If the policy has no cash value and there are no dividends on deposit (i.e., term life insurance or a universal life policy with no cash value), while the policy has been transferred through an absolute assignment to the charity, there is no corresponding tax receipt. Instead, if the donor continues to pay the policy premiums, each premium payment is treated as a charitable donation, for tax purposes.

KENNETH

Kenneth had two life insurance policies that he no longer requires as part of his estate plan; however, he is very charitable minded and has decided to donate the policies.

Policy A — 10-year term insurance with a face value of $100,000

Policy B — Universal life policy with a cash surrender value of $52,000

Kenneth transferred policy A to the local woman's shelter, through an absolute assignment of the policy. The policy transfer did not entitle Kenneth to claim a charitable donation because the policy was a term insurance policy and, as such, did not represent any immediate value. However, if Kenneth continues to pay the $3,000 annual premium, the premium payment represents a charitable donation by Kenneth in the year the payment is made.

The absolute assignment of policy B to the hospital constitutes a donation because it had a $52,000 cash surrender value. Ken will receive a receipt for a $52,000 donation. In addition, any premium payments that he continues to make on the policy will be treated as a charitable donation in the year the payment is made.

Beneficiary Designation

The second method by which life insurance can be used in gift planning is for the individual to retain ownership of the policy and name the charity as the beneficiary. The payment of the death benefit to the charity upon the death of the life insured is considered a donation made by the policy owner in the year of death. Some people prefer this method because they continue to retain full control of the policy and the freedom to adjust the strategy if warranted by future circumstances.

Where one person owns a life insurance policy on another person's life and names the charity as the beneficiary, the payment of the death proceeds to the charity will not be treated as a donation. Instead, the policy owner could name herself as the beneficiary, and use the death proceeds to make a direct contribution to the charity.

Will Planning

When an individual wants to fund a charitable bequest through the use of life insurance, rather than naming the charity as beneficiary directly on the policy, she could vary this approach. An alternative is to create a charitable bequest in the testator's will and use life insurance to fund the bequest.

Under this alternative, the testator's estate is named as beneficiary of the life insurance policy, and, upon her death, the proceeds are paid to the estate. The estate uses the proceeds to fund the charitable bequest, and receives a donation receipt that can be used in the year of death or carried back one year.

It is important to note that the payment of the life insurance proceeds into the estate makes them subject to probate and inclusion in the calculation of applicable probate fees. In addition, because the proceeds of the policy become an asset of the estate, they are subject to the claims from creditors of the estate.

CONCLUSION

A taxpayer should be cautious in that charitable donations may only be claimed if the charitable institution to which the taxpayer made the donation is registered with the Department of National Revenue. It is the responsibility of the taxpayer to ensure that the charity is registered. There is no relief for a taxpayer who makes a donation to a non-registered charity. The CRA maintains a list of registered charities on its Web site at http://www.cra-arc.gc.ca/charitylists.

Unit 4
Self-Test Questions

QUESTIONS

The following background should be used with questions 1 through 4, inclusive.

Sam Watson is a single dad whose son, Ned, turns age 10 in May 2011. Sam hopes Ned will follow in his footsteps and attend the same university he did, which is located in another province. Current cost estimates suggest it will cost $90,000, as of 2010, to fund four years of Ned's post-secondary education. He estimates that the total cost of Ned's education will increase by 3% annually by the time Ned begins school in nine years at age 18. Sam's income is $81,000 per year.

As of September 1, 2010, Sam will have $23,000 set aside in Ned's education fund.

Question 1

Based on Sam's inflation factor, how much will Ned's university program cost when he begins at age 18?

    a. $87,420

    b. $112,337

    c. $117,430

    d. $120,925

Question 2

If Sam saves an additional $600 at the beginning of each month, beginning September 1, 2010, what annual nominal rate of return, compounded monthly, must he earn in order to have $120,000 in Ned's education fund by August 31 of the year Ned reaches age 18?

    a. 3.63%

    b. 5.27%

    c. 9.44%

    d. 12.5%

Question 3

If Sam makes maximum annual contributions into Ned's RESP beginning September 1, 2010 until he reaches the lifetime maximum, and applies to maximize the grant available under the CESG program, which one of the following statements regarding the CESG program is true?

    a. He will receive only $500 annually for nine years.

    b. He will receive $1,000 annually for the first four years and $500 annually for the next five years.

    c. He will receive $1,000 annually for the first eight years and $500 for one year.

    d. He will receive $1,000 annually for nine years.

Question 4

With regard to a RESP for Ned, which of the following statements is/are true?

1. Sam could optimize his $23,000 of current savings by using the full amount as an immediate contribution into a RESP on Ned's behalf.

2. If Ned begins university on September 1, 2019, the last contribution that Sam can make into a RESP on Ned's behalf is August 31, 2019.

3. If Sam makes maximum RESP contributions on Ned's behalf beginning September 1, 2010, it will allow Ned to qualify for the lifetime maximum CESG.

4. If Sam becomes short of funds, he is eligible to receive a return of contributions without triggering any tax consequences.

5. Ned will automatically qualify to receive an educational assistance payment from the RESP, beginning on his 18th birthday.

    a. 4 only

    b. 1 and 3 only

    c. 2 and 4 only

    d. 2, 3 and 5 only

Question 5

Sally established a family RESP under which she is the subscriber and her three minor grandchildren are beneficiaries. The plan has total assets of $62,000, of which $48,000 is from direct contributions, $9,600 is grants received from the CESG program and the balance is interest on the contributions and grants. Sally has encountered an unexpected emergency and wants to access money from the plan. She currently has $25,000 of available RRSP contribution room. Given this scenario, which one of the following statements is true?

    a. Sally will require consent from the guardian of each beneficiary before she can access any funds in the plan.

    b. Sally is entitled to withdraw $48,000 without triggering any tax consequence.

    c. The maximum amount Sally can withdraw is $25,000, without triggering any tax consequence.

    d. Sally could collapse the plan and $4,400 will qualify as an AIP.

Question 6

Randy and Dianne Kendall are in the process of purchasing their first home and plan to make a $45,000 down payment. An appraisal shows the home is valued at $228,000, the same amount as the couple has agreed to pay. The Kendalls have opted for a closed mortgage based on a six-month term with a 4.9% fixed rate of interest, and a 20-year amortization schedule. Given this scenario, which of the following statements are true?

1. The Kendalls have a high ratio mortgage.

2. The Kendalls have a non-conventional mortgage.

3. The Kendalls have locked in a 4.9% rate of interest for the next 20 years.

4. The Kendalls have established a variable rate mortgage.

5. If the Kendalls had selected a longer period of amortization, their total interest costs would have been higher than under the current arrangements.

    a. 1 only 4 only

    b. 3 and 5 only

    c. 1, 2 and 5 only

    d. 2, 3 and 4 only

Question 7

Twenty-six-year-old Sherri finished school two years ago with $23,000 of debt from government-issued student loans. Sherri has not been able to find work in her field so has been working on a part-time basis earning minimum wage. She has accumulated credit card debt of $4,700 and is now three months behind in payments on a car loan that has an outstanding balance of $19,000, and which her father co-signed. Sherri feels that her only way out from under the mountain of debt is to file for bankruptcy. Other than her car, Sherri owns no assets. Based on this scenario, which one of the following statements is true?

    a. Filing for bankruptcy would alleviate only $4,700 of Sherri's debt.

    b. Filing for bankruptcy would alleviate only $23,700 of Sherri's debt.

    c. Filing for bankruptcy would likely alleviate all of Sherri's debt and allow her to begin fresh.

    d. If Sherri files for bankruptcy, it is unlikely that it would affect her credit rating.

Question 8

Doreen has completed a monthly breakdown of her anticipated expenses, and has divided the expenses into 15 meaningful categories that her financial planner pre-established. Doreen's planner will use this information to prepare a detailed cash flow statement. For which of the following purposes will this information be useful?

    a. To prepare Doreen's Net Worth Statement.

    b. To calculate Doreen's total assets.

    c. To optimize the timing of discretionary purchases.

    d. To maximize Doreen's total interest expenses.

Question 9

Which of the following scenarios would typically be considered a debt management strategy?

1. Consolidate ongoing credit card balances into a single purpose personal loan to reduce the total cost of interest.

2. Use a home mortgage as a means to finance an automobile purchase.

3. Optimize deductible interest opportunities where permitted rather than non-deductible interest.

4. Use additional lump-sum payments to accelerate the reduction of the outstanding mortgage balance.

    a. 2 only

    b. 1 and 3 only

    c. 2 and 4 only

    d. 1, 3 and 4 only

Question 10

Edward was thrilled to hear that he will fully recovery from a recent heart attack, which could have been fatal. He attributes his survival to outstanding care and is anxious to demonstrate his gratitude through a $5,000 donation to the hospital. With regard to Edward's donation, which of the following factors would be required to determine Edward's tax savings?

1. Lowest federal tax rate

2. Marginal tax rate

3. Highest federal tax rate

4. Edward's taxable income

    a. 1 and 2 only

    b. 1 and 3 only

    c. 2 and 4 only

    d. 1, 3 and 4 only

QUESTIONS & SOLUTIONS

The following background should be used with questions 1 through 4, inclusive.

Sam Watson is a single dad whose son, Ned, turns age 10 in May 2010. Sam hopes Ned will follow in his footsteps and attend the same university he did, which is located in another province. Current cost estimates suggest it will cost $90,000, as of 2010, to fund four years of Ned's post-secondary education. He estimates that the total cost of Ned's education will increase by 3% annually by the time Ned begins school in nine years at age 18. Sam's income is $81,000 per year.

As of September 1, 2010, Sam will have $23,000 set aside in Ned's education fund.

Question 1

Based on Sam's inflation factor, how much will Ned's university program cost when he begins at age 18?

    a. $87,420

    b. $112,337

    c. $117,430

    d. $120,925

Answer: c

   ⇨ $117,430

Solution:

   ⇨ P/YR = 1

   ⇨ xP/YR = 9

   ⇨ PV = 90,000

   ⇨ I/YR = 3

   ⇨ PMT = 0

   ⇨ Solve for FV

Reference: Page 18-7

Question 2

If Sam saves an additional $600 at the beginning of each month, beginning September 1, 2010, what annual nominal rate of return, compounded monthly, must he earn in order to have $120,000 in Ned's education fund by August 31 of the year Ned reaches age 18?

    a. 3.63%

    b. 5.27%

    c. 9.44%

    d. 12.5%

Answer: b

    ⇨ 5.27%

Solution:

    ⇨ P/YR = 12

    ⇨ xP/YR = 9

    ⇨ PV = -23,000

    ⇨ PMT = -600

    ⇨ FV = 120,000

    ⇨ MODE = BEG

    ⇨ Solve for I/YR

Reference: Page 18-7

Question 3

If Sam makes maximum annual contributions into Ned's RESP beginning September 1, 2010 until he reaches the lifetime maximum, and applies to maximize the grant available under the CESG program, which one of the following statements regarding the CESG program is true?

    a. He will receive only $500 annually for nine years.

    b. He will receive $1,000 annually for the first four years and $500 annually for the next five years.

    c. He will receive $1,000 annually for the first eight years and $500 for one year.

    d. He will receive $1,000 annually for nine years.

Answer: c

    ⇨ He will receive $1,000 annually for the first eight years and $500 for one year.

Reference: Pages 18-20 to 18-25

Question 4

With regard to a RESP for Ned, which of the following statements is/are true?

1. Sam could optimize his $23,000 of current savings by using the full amount as an immediate contribution into a RESP on Ned's behalf.

2. If Ned begins university on September 1, 2019, the last contribution that Sam can make into a RESP on Ned's behalf is August 31, 2019.

3. If Sam makes maximum RESP contributions on Ned's behalf beginning September 1, 2010, it will allow Ned to qualify for the lifetime maximum CESG.

4. If Sam becomes short of funds, he is eligible to receive a return of contributions without triggering any tax consequences.

5. Ned will automatically qualify to receive an educational assistance payment from the RESP, beginning on his 18th birthday.

    a. 4 only

    b. 1 and 3 only

    c. 2 and 4 only

    d. 2, 3 and 5 only

Answer: a

    ⇨ If Sam becomes short of funds, he is eligible to receive a return of contributions without triggering any tax consequences.

Reference: Integrated throughout the module.

Question 5

Sally established a family RESP under which she is the subscriber and her three minor grandchildren are beneficiaries. The plan has total assets of $62,000, of which $48,000 is from direct contributions, $9,600 is grants received from the CESG program and the balance is interest on the contributions and grants. Sally has encountered an unexpected emergency and wants to access money from the plan. She currently has $25,000 of available RRSP contribution room. Given this scenario, which one of the following statements is true?

    a. Sally will require consent from the guardian of each beneficiary before she can access any funds in the plan.

    b. Sally is entitled to withdraw $48,000 without triggering any tax consequence.

    c. The maximum amount Sally can withdraw is $25,000, without triggering any tax consequence.

    d. Sally could collapse the plan and $4,400 will qualify as an AIP.

Answer: b

    ⇨ Sally is entitled to withdraw $48,000 without triggering any tax consequence.

Reference: Pages 18-14 to 18-17

Question 6

Randy and Dianne Kendall are in the process of purchasing their first home and plan to make a $45,000 down payment. An appraisal shows the home is valued at $228,000, the same amount as the couple has agreed to pay. The Kendalls have opted for a closed mortgage based on a six-month term with a 4.9% fixed rate of interest, and a 20-year amortization schedule. Given this scenario, which of the following statements are true?

1. The Kendalls have a high ratio mortgage.

2. The Kendalls have a non-conventional mortgage.

3. The Kendalls have locked in a 4.9% rate of interest for the next 20 years.

4. The Kendalls have established a variable rate mortgage.

5. If the Kendalls had selected a longer period of amortization, their total interest costs would have been higher than under the current arrangements.

      a. 1 only 4 only

      b. 3 and 5 only

      c. 1, 2 and 5 only

      d. 2, 3 and 4 only

Answer: c

     ⇨ 1. The Kendalls have a high ratio mortgage (less than a 20% down payment).

     ⇨ 2. The Kendalls have a non-conventional mortgage.

     ⇨ 5. If the Kendalls had selected a longer period of amortization, their total interest costs would have been higher than under the current arrangements.

Reference: Pages 18-30 to 18-35

Question 7

Twenty-six-year-old Sherri finished school two years ago with $23,000 of debt from government-issued student loans. Sherri has not been able to find work in her field so has been working on a part-time basis earning minimum wage. She has accumulated credit card debt of $4,700 and is now three months behind in payments on a car loan that has an outstanding balance of $19,000, and which her father co-signed. Sherri feels that her only way out from under the mountain of debt is to file for bankruptcy. Other than her car, Sherri owns no assets. Based on this scenario, which one of the following statements is true?

      a. Filing for bankruptcy would alleviate only $4,700 of Sherri's debt.

      b. Filing for bankruptcy would alleviate only $23,700 of Sherri's debt.

      c. Filing for bankruptcy would likely alleviate all of Sherri's debt and allow her to begin fresh.

      d. If Sherri files for bankruptcy, it is unlikely that it would affect her credit rating.

Answer: a

     ⇨ Filing for bankruptcy would alleviate only $4,700 of Sherri's debt.

Reference: Pages 18-36

Question 8

Doreen has completed a monthly breakdown of her anticipated expenses, and has divided the expenses into 15 meaningful categories that her financial planner pre-established. Doreen's planner will use this information to prepare a detailed cash flow statement. For which of the following purposes will this information be useful?

    a. To prepare Doreen's Net Worth Statement.

    b. To calculate Doreen's total assets.

    c. To optimize the timing of discretionary purchases.

    d. To maximize Doreen's total interest expenses.

Answer: c

    ⇨ To optimize the timing of discretionary purchases.

Reference: Pages 18-38 to 18-40

Question 9

Which of the following scenarios would typically be considered a debt management strategy?

1. Consolidate ongoing credit card balances into a single purpose personal loan to reduce the total cost of interest.

2. Use a home mortgage as a means to finance an automobile purchase.

3. Optimize deductible interest opportunities where permitted rather than non-deductible interest.

4. Use additional lump-sum payments to accelerate the reduction of the outstanding mortgage balance.

    a. 2 only

    b. 1 and 3 only

    c. 2 and 4 only

    d. 1, 3 and 4 only

Answer: d

    ⇨ 1. Consolidate ongoing credit card balances into a single purpose personal loan to reduce the total cost of interest.

    ⇨ 3. Optimize deductible interest opportunities where permitted rather than non-deductible interest.

    ⇨ 4. Use additional lump-sum payments to accelerate the reduction of the outstanding mortgage balance.

Reference: Page 18-37

Question 10

Edward was thrilled to hear that he will fully recovery from a recent heart attack, which could have been fatal. He attributes his survival to outstanding care and is anxious to demonstrate his gratitude through a $5,000 donation to the hospital. With regard to Edward's donation, which of the following factors would be required to determine Edward's tax savings?

1. Lowest federal tax rate

2. Marginal tax rate

3. Highest federal tax rate

4. Edward's taxable income

     a. 1 and 2 only

     b. 1 and 3 only

     c. 2 and 4 only

     d. 1, 3 and 4 only

Answer: b

     ⇨ 1. Lowest federal tax rate

     ⇨ 3. Highest federal tax rate

Reference: Pages 18-43 and 18-44

Unit 5
Module 18 Exercises and Case Study

MODULE 18 EXERCISES

1. List the common income tax considerations or deductions available for students.

2. Define the three key roles — subscriber, promoter and plan beneficiary — of a RESP.

3. Explain the differences between the non-family plan, family plan and group plan for RESPs.

4. What are the conditions under which it is possible to change the subscriber of a RESP?

5. What is the lifetime maximum limit and tax implications of making RESP contributions? What is the tax penalty on overcontributions?

6. What are the four types of payments that can be made from a RESP?

7. Explain the difference between educational assistance payments (EAP) and accumulated income payments (AIP).

8. List the five prescribed conditions under which an AIP payment can be made.

9. Explain the criteria used for Canada Education Savings Grants (CESG). What are the yearly and lifetime maximums?

10. Explain the difference between the total debt service ratio and the gross debt service ratio.

11. What is the significance of having a high-ratio mortgage?

12. Bankruptcy is the legal process that allows an insolvent person to be released from most of her debts to creditors. Identify five types of debt owed by a bankrupt individual that are not released through bankruptcy.

13. Outline the basic federal non-refundable tax credit tax rule for charitable donations.

14. Explain the tax implication of donations in the year of death, ecological gifts, cultural property and capital property donations.

15. Comment on Sharon and Max West's Net Worth and Cash Flow Statements (Appendices Two to Five). Identify five recommendations for the West family.

CASE STUDY — JOAN AND CLEM LI

Joan and Clem Li approached you recently to talk about how to pay for their children's education. The Lis have two children, Liam and Qi, ages eight and four. They expect both of their children to pursue post-secondary school when they reach the age of 18. Liam wants to be a mechanical engineer, and Qi wants to be a teacher. Joan and Clem heard a radio advertisement recently that stated the government has a Registered Education Savings Plan (RESP) that could help them save today for the future costs of post-secondary education, and they want to learn more about the program from you. They are mainly concerned about paying for Liam's future education.

Specifically, they want you to answer the following questions:

a. What amount of money would they need to have for Liam when he starts his post-secondary education in 10 years if it currently costs $96,000 for four years of university and costs are rising by 2% annually? (Disregard any increases during the term of the program.)

b. What monthly amount will the Lis have to personally save at the beginning of each month to accumulate the amount needed for Liam's education described in part a., assuming they do not set up a RESP? Assume a 7% interest rate.

c. What type of RESP would you recommend they establish?

d. What is the lifetime maximum contribution? Is there a maximum age up to which contributions can be made?

e. Calculate the sum of the annual contributions the couple can make into a RESP on Liam's behalf, beginning in 2010 and concluding in the year he turns age 17.

f. Calculate the total value of the RESP assets in December of the year Liam turns 17 using the following assumptions:

— all contributions and corresponding grants are made on January 1 of each year, starting the year Liam turns age eight;

— the annual nominal rate of interest is 7%, compounded annually; and

— there are no withdrawals from the plan.

Appendix One

Income Tax Terminology

Terminology	Definition of Spouse	Definition of Common-Law Partner
Spouse and Common-law partner	Legally married.	A person of the same or opposite sex, living in a conjugal relationship with the taxpayer: • for the previous 12-month period; or, • who is the natural or adoptive parent of the taxpayer's child.
Separated spouse and Separated common-law partner	A spouse who is separated due to marriage breakdown.	A common-law partner, separated from the taxpayer, for less than 90 days due to a conjugal relationship breakdown.
Former spouse and Former common-law partner	A spouse becomes a former spouse when the divorce becomes final.	A common-law partner becomes a former common-law partner on the first day after a 90-day separation. Reconciliation after the 90-day separation results in common-law partner status once again, but without the need to repeat the 12-month cohabitation requirement.

Appendix Two
Ms. Sharon West and Mr. Max West
Statement of Net Worth
As of December 31, 2010

ASSETS	Sharon ($)	Max ($)	TOTAL ($)
Non-Registered Assets			
Cash and equivalents	8,500	4,000	12,500
GICs		12,000	12,000
Bonds			
Equities	15,500	8,000	23,500
Mutual funds	2,000		2,000
Stock options (vested)			
Real Estate			
Life Insurance CVS			
Total Non-Registered Assets	26,000	24,000	50,000
Registered Assets			
RESP	3,300		3,300
RPP		44,000	44,000
RRSP	28,000	12,000	40,000
Total Registered Assets	31,300	56,000	87,300
Other Assets			
Business Equity			
CVS of Life Insurance		8,000	8,000
Total Other Assets		8,000	8,000
Personal Assets			
Home/Residence		265,000	265,000
Personal Effects	5,500	7,800	13,300
Cottage/Recreational Property	125,000		125,000
Vehicles	6,000	10,000	16,000
Other	1,000	1,000	2,000
Total Personal Assets	137,500	283,800	421,300
TOTAL ASSETS	194,800	371,800	566,600
LIABILITIES			
Credit Cards/Consumer Debt	2,300	7,100	9,400
Loan — Vehicles		9,000	9,000
Business Loan			
Investment Loan	2,000	4,000	6,000
Mortgage		220,000	220,000
TOTAL LIABILITIES	4,300	240,100	244,400
NET WORTH	190,500	131,700	322,200

Note: Assets at market value could have income tax consequences that have not been accounted for in this Statement of Net Worth.

Appendix Three
Ms. Sharon West and Mr. Max West
Projected Cash Flow Statement
For 12 Months Ending December 31, 2010

	Sharon	Max	Total
INCOME			
Salary	54,200	98,500	152,700
Self-employment earnings	12,000		12,000
Dividend income		1,200	1,200
Interest income		500	500
Other/Miscellaneous	800		800
Less source deductions: Income tax	17,000	35,000	52,000
Less source deductions: CPP/QPP	1,500	2,800	4,300
Less source deductions: E.I.	1,200	2,500	3,700
Total Net Income	**47,300**	**59,900**	**107,200**
EXPENSES			
Mortgage		28,000	28,000
Property Taxes		4,000	4,000
Utilities	1,000		1,000
Food	4,000		4,000
Day Care	1,200		1,200
Education			
Vehicle - Loan/Lease		4,800	4,800
Vehicle - Gasoline & Repair	1,500	3,000	4,500
Insurance - Life	1,200	1,500	2,700
Insurance - General	800	1,500	2,300
Insurance - Vehicle	1,400	2,200	3,600
Personal	2,500	3,000	5,500
Entertainment	900	1,000	1,900
Vacations		4,000	4,000
Consumer Debt	2,500	2,500	5,000
Donations	500	500	1,000
Recreational property expenses		2,300	2,300
Other/Miscellaneous	500	500	1,000
Total Expenses	**18,000**	**58,800**	**76,800**
NET INCOME AVAILABLE FOR SAVINGS	**29,300**	**1,100**	**30,400**
Non-registered savings	2,000	4,000	6,000
RRSP contributions	7,000	12,000	19,000
RESP contributions			
Total Savings & Reinvestment	**9,000**	**16,000**	**25,000**
UNALLOCATED CASH FLOW	**20,300**	**-14,900**	**5,400**

Appendix Four

Ms. Sharon West and Mr. Max West

Monthly Income

For 12 Months Ending December 31, 2010

	Jan	Feb	Mar	Apr	May	June	July	Aug	Sept	Oct	Nov	Dec	Total
INCOME													
Salary	12,725	12,725	12,725	12,725	12,725	12,725	12,725	12,725	12,725	12,725	12,725	12,725	152,700
Self-employment earnings			3,000			3,000						6,000	12,000
Dividend income	125	200	225	30	300	60	150	50	25			35	1,200
Interest income												500	500
Other/Miscellaneous					400					400			800
Less source deductions: Income tax	4,333	4,333	4,333	4,333	4,333	4,333	4,333	4,333	4,333	4,333	4,333	4,333	52,000
Less source deductions: CPP/QPP	717	717	717	717	717	717							4,300
Less source deductions: E.I.	617	617	617	617	617	617							3,700
Total Net Income	**7,183**	**7,258**	**10,283**	**7,088**	**7,758**	**10,118**	**8,542**	**8,442**	**8,417**	**8,792**	**8,392**	**14,927**	**107,200**

Appendix Five

Ms. Sharon West and Mr. Max West

Monthly Expenses

For 12 Months Ending December 31, 2010

	Jan	Feb	Mar	Apr	May	June	July	Aug	Sept	Oct	Nov	Dec	Total
EXPENSES													
Mortgage	2,333	2,333	2,333	2,333	2,333	2,333	2,333	2,333	2,333	2,333	2,333	2,333	28,000
Property Taxes	667	667	667				667	667	667				4,000
Utilities	83	83	83	83	83	83	83	83	83	83	83	83	1,000
Food	333	333	333	333	333	333	333	333	333	333	333	333	4,000
Day Care		250			250						700		1,200
Education													
Vehicle - Loan/Lease	400	400	400	400	400	400	400	400	400	400	400	400	4,800
Vehicle - Gasoline & Repair	375	375	375	375	375	375	375	375	375	375	375	375	4,500
Insurance - Life	1,500		1,200										2,700
Insurance - General	800					1,500							2,300
Insurance - Vehicle	1,800		1,200				600						3,600
Personal	389	389	389	389	255	389	800	300	300	300	300	1,300	5,500
Entertainment	150	150	150	150	250	250	250	100	100	100	100	150	1,900
Vacations		1,000					3,000						4,000
Consumer Debt	417	417	417	417	417	417	417	417	417	417	417	417	5,000
Donations		250		100		50						600	1,000
Recreational property expenses	192	192	192	192	192	192	192	192	192	192	192	192	2,300
Other/Miscellaneous			250			250			250			250	1,000
Total Expenses	9,439	6,839	7,989	4,772	4,888	6,572	9,450	5,200	5,450	4,533	5,233	6,433	76,800

Appendix Six

Ms. Sharon West and Mr. Max West

Projected Cash Flow Statement

For 12 Months Ending December 31, 2010

	Sharon	Max	Total	Jan	Feb	Mar	Apr	May	June	July	Aug	Sept	Oct	Nov	Dec
INCOME															
Salary	54,200	98,500	152,700	12,725	12,725	12,725	12,725	12,725	12,725	12,725	12,725	12,725	12,725	12,725	12,725
Self-employment earnings	12,000		12,000			3,000			3,000						6,000
Dividend income		1,200	1,200	125	200	225	30	300	60	150	50	25			35
Interest income		500	500												500
Alimony/Child Support	800		800					400					400		
Other/Miscellaneous															
Less source deductions: Income tax	17,000	35,000	52,000	4,333	4,333	4,333	4,333	4,333	4,333	4,333	4,333	4,333	4,333	4,333	4,333
Less source deductions: CPP/QPP	1,500	2,800	4,300	717	717	717	717	717	717						
Less source deductions: E.I.	1,200	2,500	3,700	617	617	617	617	617	617						
Total Net Income	**47,300**	**59,900**	**107,200**	**7,183**	**7,258**	**10,283**	**7,098**	**7,758**	**10,118**	**8,542**	**8,442**	**8,417**	**8,792**	**8,392**	**14,927**
EXPENSES															
Mortgage		28,000	28,000	2,333	2,333	2,333	2,333	2,333	2,333	2,333	2,333	2,333	2,333	2,333	2,333
Property Taxes		4,000	4,000	667	667	667				667	667	667			
Utilities	1,000		1,000	83	83	83	83	83	83	83	83	83	83	83	83
Food	4,000		4,000	333	333	333	333	333	333	333	333	333	333	333	333
Day Care	1,200		1,200		250			250						700	
Education															
Vehicle - Loan/Lease		4,800	4,800	400	400	400	400	400	400	400	400	400	400	400	400
Vehicle - Gasoline & Repair	1,500	3,000	4,500	375	375	375	375	375	375	375	375	375	375	375	375
Insurance - Life	1,200	1,500	2,700	1,500		1,200									
Insurance - General	800	1,500	2,300	800					1,500						
Insurance - Vehicle	1,400	2,200	3,600	1,800		1,200				600					
Personal	2,500	3,000	5,500	389	389	389	389	255	389	800	300	300	300	300	1,300
Entertainment	900	1,000	1,900	150	150	150	150	250	250	250	100	100	100	100	150
Vacations		4,000	4,000		1,000					3,000					
Consumer Debt	2,500	2,500	5,000	417	417	417	417	417	417	417	417	417	417	417	417
Donations	500	500	1,000		250		100		50						600
Recreational property expenses		2,300	2,300	192	192	192	192	192	192	192	192	192	192	192	192
Other/Miscellaneous	500	500	1,000			250			250			250			250
Total Expenses	**18,000**	**58,800**	**76,800**	**9,439**	**6,839**	**7,989**	**4,772**	**4,888**	**6,572**	**9,450**	**5,200**	**5,450**	**4,533**	**5,233**	**6,433**
NET INCOME AVAILABLE FOR SAVINGS	**29,300**	**1,100**	**30,400**	**-2,256**	**419**	**2,294**	**2,316**	**2,870**	**3,546**	**-908**	**3,242**	**2,967**	**4,258**	**3,158**	**8,493**
Non-registered savings	2,000	4,000	6,000												
RRSP contributions	7,000	12,000	19,000												
RESP contributions															
Total Savings & Reinvestment	**9,000**	**16,000**	**25,000**												
UNALLOCATED CASH FLOW	**20,300**	**-14,900**	**5,400**												

Topical Index

CCH/ADVOCIS
EDUCATION PROGRAM

COURSE 4
WEALTH MANAGEMENT AND ESTATE PLANNING

MODULE 19

ESTATE PLANNING

Module 19
ESTATE PLANNING

Module 19
Estate Planning

LEARNING OBJECTIVES

✓ Demonstrate and apply a solid comprehension of the concepts and principles related to the taxation of a deceased taxpayer, including the final income tax return, the rights or things return, deemed dispositions, charitable donations upon death and spousal trusts.

✓ Understand, explain and apply a working knowledge of probate, testamentary trusts and an estate freeze.

✓ Identify, explain and apply an in-depth knowledge relative to intestacy, the importance of a will, clauses in a will, beneficiary designations and the appointment of an executor and trustee.

✓ Demonstrate a solid comprehension and working knowledge of a power of attorney for property and for personal care.

✓ Understand, explain and apply an in-depth comprehension of the estate planning process relative to an orderly distribution of an estate, methodologies to minimize tax, issues relative to the financial support of dependents, *inter vivos* trusts and attribution rules.

OVERVIEW

Estate planning is a comprehensive process undertaken to ensure that loved ones are well cared for after the death of an individual, the transfer of assets to intended beneficiaries takes place according to the deceased's wishes, and that income taxes are minimized without compromising the deceased's intentions.

Actions an individual undertakes while alive have a direct impact on the smooth transition of his estate. This includes the structuring of asset ownership, the creation of a will, establishing buy-out arrangements where appropriate and even the establishment of charitable arrangements.

The concept of estate planning is not just for the wealthy or those with significant assets. After all, the definition of significant assets is highly dependent upon an individual's personal perspective. For some individuals, $50,000 or $100,000 may represent significant assets, while others may feel that significant assets really only begin at some much larger number, such as $500,000 or $1 million. The dollar amount of an individual's estate should not be the deciding factor relative to whether estate planning is a valued strategy.

Estate planning provides an individual with the opportunity to align the distribution of his estate with his intended wishes. It is important that each strategy used in the estate planning process be assessed relative to the individual's particular circumstances and that forward thinking be used as part of that analysis. Otherwise, an individual could unknowingly expose his assets, either in a pre- or post-mortem situation, to the proceedings of a divorce, lawsuit or judgment, related to his personal situation or perhaps to that of an intended heir.

Estate planning is not a singular all-encompassing module, but rather significant concepts, important to the process of estate planning, have been covered throughout numerous other modules. As a student who has completed the prior 18 modules of this education program, you already have a significant foundation in the topic of estate planning. While some material taught in previous modules will be repeated as it relates to estate planning, you are responsible for understanding issues and concepts, even if they are not repeated in this module. For some students, it may be wise to revisit each of the previous modules to ensure that you have a sound foundation of core principles, particularly as they relate to the death of an individual.

In Module 1, time value of money calculations looked at how much money an individual needs given specific factors. This relates to estate planning because when an individual predeceases a spouse, or financially dependent children, it is important that there be sufficient financial resources to address the surviving family's needs. The topic of life insurance and the calculation of capital needs analysis utilized these concepts in Module 10.

In Module 4, a variety of government-sponsored benefit programs were examined relative to the death of the recipient. The topic of income tax was discussed in Modules 5 and 6, including many issues related to the death of a taxpayer. Trusts, different forms of asset ownership and holding companies, as they relate to an estate freeze, were discussed in Module 7. Modules 11 to 14 looked at retirement planning and discussed numerous issues that fall into the field of estate planning. The strategy of named beneficiaries was explored in several modules. All of these topics are important to the process of estate planning and are assumed to be a prerequisite foundation to this module.

Reference in this material will focus on the common law provinces, and will address Quebec, which operates under civic law, only where specifically noted.

Unit 1
Power of Attorney

INTRODUCTION

Many people are unaware that an individual does not automatically have the right to handle his spouse's legal and financial affairs in the event that the spouse is not able to because of illness or simply because she is unavailable (i.e., traveling out of the country). Without the proper legal documents, when a spouse becomes ill, the healthy spouse will have to apply to the courts for permission to act on behalf of the incapacitated spouse. Without proper legal documentation, one spouse cannot act on behalf of the other spouse as it relates to legal or financial affairs.

While many people are familiar with the concept of a will, which addresses issues after an individual dies, a power of attorney is not nearly as well understood by the general population. A power of attorney addresses the issue of who has decision-making authority (known as an attorney or agent) on another individual's behalf (referred to as grantor or donor), under specific circumstances, while the grantor is alive.

Powers of attorney are subject to provincial jurisdiction and each province has its own laws and procedures. Specific terminology related to a power of attorney may differ depending upon the provincial jurisdiction, but the concepts and applications are similar. The term attorney, in this situation, does not refer to a lawyer, but rather refers to a person who is legally appointed to act on another's behalf. The attorney, or agent, must be at least age 18 or 19, depending upon the jurisdiction, and mentally competent.

In most jurisdictions, a grantor may appoint a single individual or corporation, such as a trust company, to act as his attorney. Or, the grantor may appoint multiple attorneys, depending upon the terms established through the grantor's document.

There are two primary types of power of attorney: one related to a person's property and another related to a person's personal care. The powers granted under the power of attorney document are defined within the document itself, or by what is not defined in the document. When a power of attorney is created, provided it meets the requirements set out by the provincial jurisdiction in which it is created and executed, it will be a valid and legal document in that particular jurisdiction; it may or may not be a valid and legal document in other jurisdictions.

POWER OF ATTORNEY FOR PROPERTY

A *limited power of attorney* can be drafted where the grantor authorizes the attorney to make decisions and commitments on the grantor's behalf, relative to a specific or defined task. For example, when an individual is out of the country for a prolonged period of time, he may authorize one of his children to manage his bank account, which gives the child the authority to write cheques, pay bills or undertake any other transaction that the grantor could perform on his own, relative to the bank account.

BARRY

Barry recently retired and plans to spend the upcoming winter in Arizona. The significant distance from home makes it difficult for Barry to manage the payment of his bills.

To address this issue, Barry completes a power of attorney that provides his son, Carl, with the authority to transact on Barry's bank account, at a specific banking institution.

Typically, banks have their own power of attorney forms that apply to accounts at that specific institution.

BARBARA

Barbara is the sole shareholder and manager of Cards Inc., a greeting card business that she established six years ago in the province of XYZ. Barbara is planning a buying trip that will take her out of the country for four weeks. During her absence, she would like to appoint her sister to make any decisions or commitments on her behalf, relative to her business affairs.

To accomplish this, Barbara would use a limited power of attorney that specifies the purpose and time frame during which her sister would handle the business affairs of Cards Inc. The power of attorney will provide Barbara's sister with the legal right to deal with Barbara's assets, located in XYZ province, where the document was executed (assuming the document was created to meet the jurisdictional requirements).

A *general power of attorney* for property typically provides the appointed attorney with the power to make any decision or commitments that an individual can make on his own, with the exception of making a will or a power of attorney. This means that, provided the grantor has the authority to undertake the transaction in the first place, the appointed attorney could undertake the sale of investments, purchase of investments, or perhaps the sale or purchase of an automobile. While there may be specific limitations established under provincial jurisdictions, the attorney normally has unlimited access to the grantor's property and has the authority to deal with it as he chooses.

A general power of attorney is effective immediately, once it is signed and witnessed. The document terminates automatically, if:

- the grantor dies;

- the attorney dies (unless there is a subsequent attorney or multiple attorneys who continue to have ongoing authority); or

- the grantor becomes incapacitated due to mental infirmity.

A grantor may specifically revoke the authority, in writing, and he is typically responsible for advising those with whom the attorney might have dealings. For the most part, it is the grantor's responsibility to ensure that others are made aware that the power of attorney has been revoked.

COLLEEN (1)

Fifty-year-old Colleen, the mother of four children, has been widowed for two years. Colleen's two older children, Agnes age 23 and Darrin age 25, live in a city about 20 miles from Colleen. Her two younger children, a pair of twins, are in grade nine and live with Colleen.

Colleen has granted her oldest two children as power of attorney for property and will designate that they work jointly, requiring both signatures, to undertake any transaction. While the twins still live with Colleen, they are too young to assume the role of attorney.

A *continuing* or *enduring power of attorney for property* is commonly used as a legal means to provide an individual with the authority to act on the grantor's behalf, in the event that the grantor becomes incapacitated due to illness, injury or senility. As noted earlier, a general power of attorney terminates if the grantor becomes incapacitated due to mental infirmity. However, the addition of an enduring or continuing clause within the power of attorney results in the ongoing validity of the power of attorney, even if the grantor becomes mentally infirm.

Without a valid enduring or continuing power of attorney, provincial authorities through the public guardian and trustee office typically assume responsibility for the incapacitated individual's affairs. Alternatively, a family member or friend of the incapacitated individual may apply to assume responsibility for the individual's affairs, but it is a legal and time-consuming process that may not result in the outcome that the incapacitated individual had intended.

COLLEEN (2)

Colleen was surprised to learn that if she were to become mentally incapacitated, perhaps in an accident, Agnes and Darrin would not have the authority to act on her behalf. This surprised Colleen because she thought she had a valid power of attorney.

Colleen's new lawyer explained that she indeed has a valid power of attorney but that it does not have an enduring or continuing provision that allows the powers to remain in effect after she suffers a loss of capacity.

There are typically two types of enduring powers of attorney:

- the general power of attorney that incorporates the continuing or enduring clause; and

- an enduring power of attorney that becomes effective when triggered by a specific event, such as the mental incapacity of the grantor (often referred to as a contingent or springing power of attorney).

A contingent power of attorney, which becomes effective based on a triggering event, may not be recognized in some provincial jurisdictions.

Given the broad authority granted to the attorney under a power of attorney, the selection of a trusted individual is essential. It is important that the person selected acts in the best interest of the grantor and has sufficient skills and knowledge to deal with the grantor's property. In most situations, the power of attorney can be one or more individuals or can be a financial institution.

A continuing or enduring power of attorney does not provide the authority to deal with an individual's estate, as the attorney's authority is limited to the period while the grantor remains alive, and the document remains valid.

POWER OF ATTORNEY FOR PERSONAL CARE

In general terms, a *power of attorney for personal care* is a legal document through which the grantor appoints an attorney (name of the role can vary by jurisdiction) to make binding decisions regarding the grantor's medical or personal care during the grantor's lifetime, but only when the grantor is unable to do so because he is incapacitated due to illness, injury or senility.

This type of document may be referred to by a variety of names such as a health directive, advance directive, durable power of attorney for medical care or personal directive living will, depending upon the jurisdiction. The key issue relates to the fact that the power of attorney for personal care is relevant only during the grantor's lifetime and only when he is incapacitated and unable to make decisions for himself. Normally, the attorney's power to act becomes effective only when the grantor's health-care providers judge the grantor as being incapacitated from making his own decisions.

Typically, this document can be general or specific in nature. A general document leaves decisions to the attorney, although the grantor may provide some specific direction. Alternatively, the document can relay specific directions on issues important to the grantor, such as organ donations, blood transfusions or heroic efforts to extend life. It is important that any instructions in the document be clear and easily interpreted.

A power of attorney for personal care does not provide the attorney with any powers or authority relative to the grantor's property, but is solely related to decisions regarding health and personal care. The attorney appointed for health and personal care may be the same person as that appointed for property; or the grantor may select a different individual. Nonetheless, the two different types of powers of attorney, property and health care, normally each require separate documents. The existence of a power of attorney for property does not extend the attorney's authority to issues related to the health of an individual.

CALLI

Sixty-five-year-old Calli has a power of attorney for her personal property, but recently became aware that this document does not address any issues related to her personal health. As a widow with three children, Calli feels it is wise to prepare a power of attorney for her personal care.

Callie is very close to her youngest daughter, Carrie. Callie feels Carrie truly understands how she thinks and feels and, as such, would be an ideal person to appoint as the attorney for Calli's personal care. While Carrie is also the attorney for Calli's power of attorney for property, a separate document will be created to address this issue relative to Calli's personal care.

Unit 2
Estates and Wills

INTRODUCTION

The definition of estate normally includes all real and personal property. The *net value of the estate* is the value of the estate after payment of any charges to the estate, debts and expenses.

In broad terms, all real estate and personal property owned wholly by an individual normally forms part of the individual's estate, except for select assets that are structured to pass outside of the estate to a named beneficiary. In addition, any portion of property, real or financial, owned by an individual as a tenant in common forms part of the individual's estate.

BASICS OF A WILL

Nature

A person who makes a will or dies leaving a will is referred to as a *testator*, if he is male, and *testatrix*, if female.

A *will* is a legal document completed as a means to legally communicate a testator's directions relative to the distribution of his estate after his death. Jurisdiction over wills is a provincial matter, with each province having its own specific legislation. To be valid, a will must comply with the respective provincial Wills Act.

A will is often viewed as the cornerstone of an individual's estate plan. To be enforceable, the language used in the will for the distribution of assets must be mandatory in nature. Statements must be clear, precise and use binding language rather than statements that are suggestive in nature.

LAURA

In Laura's will she uses the statement, "I recommend to him that he deposit the moneys so received in a Registered Retirement Savings Plan of his own or that he use it to purchase a single premium annuity on his life". While this statement provides Laura's beneficiary with an understanding of her preference, the beneficiary is under no obligation to act in this manner because it is only suggestive in nature.

A will is effective from the date of the testator's death.

Types of Wills

English Form Will

While each province has its own laws and statutes relative to wills, the most common type of will used in Canada, with the exception of Quebec, is referred to as an English form will, which simply means that it has British roots. This type of will may also be referred to as a *witnessed will* because it requires the signature of two witnesses.

An English form will must be a written document (most often typed, although hand-written is acceptable, as opposed to verbal) and must be signed by the testator. The testator must sign the document in the presence of two witnesses or acknowledge in their presence that it is his signature, as the testator of the will. The witnesses, who must be the age of majority, must sign the will as having witnessed the testator's signature. A beneficiary named in the will cannot be a witness to the will, nor can the spouse of a beneficiary. A beneficiary acting as a witness does not cause the will to become invalid, but rather any bequest made to the individual who acted as a witness will be denied.

Notarial Will

A *notarial will* is one drawn up by a notary and is commonly used in Quebec. Under Quebec civil law, a notarial will does not have to be probated because of the significant formality associated with its original creation.

This type of will incorporates the date and place that the will was made and is read by the notary to the testator, although the witness need not be present when this reading takes place. The testator signs the will, in the presence of a witness, to acknowledge that the document reflects his intentions. In most circumstances, a single witness is sufficient. The notary retains the original copy of the will.

International Will

An *international will* is one prepared in a form that meets specific standards that are valid in jurisdictions that are party to the 1973 Convention Providing a Uniform Law of an International Will. When a testator owns assets outside of his country of residence, this type of will is a valid estate planning consideration.

Holograph Will

A will written solely in the personal handwriting of the individual whose signature it bears is referred to as a *holograph will*. Each province recognizes a holograph in some form or substance, although the specific criteria may differ. Typically, this handwritten document is signed and dated.

In the past, store-bought will kits did not typically qualify as a holograph will because the typed portions of the pre-printed form did not meet the criterion that the will must be written solely in the handwriting of the testator. However, there is a case precedent in Newfoundland that under some circumstances a fill-in-the-blank-type of will could qualify as a holograph will. While wills in general can be the source of contention, holograph wills tend to be more problematic and are not recommended.

Mirror Wills

The term *mirror will* is used to describe the situation when two wills are drafted, quite often for spouses, and each testator is the beneficiary of the other's residuary estate.

Joint Will

A *joint will* is one where two or more people execute one will intended to serve as the will for any or all of the parties. A joint will is typically used to address a contractual situation and was more common prior to the computer age. A joint will is seldom recommended but rather the process of estate planning can be used to develop appropriate strategies to address complex needs, most often leading to distinct wills for each party.

Mutual Will

A *mutual will* is commonly used with two spouses who execute separate but related wills. Where two documents are prepared as mutual wills, the two wills will mirror each other. For example, in simplistic terms, John leaves all of his assets to his spouse Betty, and Betty leaves all of her assets to her spouse John. John and Betty have mutual wills that mirror each other. Mutual wills may also involve some type of contractual arrangement, but this need not be the case.

Simplistically, a mutual will might be used in a second marriage where two spouses have agreed that they will each bequest all of their respective property to the other and, upon the surviving spouse's death, the remaining property from the first spouse's death will be left to his children. The couple creates this type of agreement through the establishment of mutual wills. However, while the couple may have an agreement not to revoke either will, or to arrange their future affairs in a manner that matches the original will, a party to the agreement may well revoke his/her will. The intent is that a constructive trust is imposed by a mutual will, and a third party (a beneficiary under the mutual will but not under the subsequent will) could request the court's intervention.

Purpose

A will typically communicates the testator's directions relative to issues such as:

- how the testator's assets are to be divided;

- appointment of an executor;

- recommendation for the preferred guardian of any minor children; and

- specific powers entrusted to the executor or any trustees.

While some wills are used to give instructions relative to the testator's burial, this is often a mistake because a will may not be examined until after the funeral. Instructions for a funeral may be better served in a letter separate from the testator's will, but should also be communicated in advance to the testator's executor and family.

Use of a will is fundamental to estate planning as it minimizes expense and delay in the transfer of assets upon the testator's death. A will has no binding implications on the testator during his lifetime. Even if a will notes that the wishes outlined in it are irrevocable, a will can always be changed. A will should be treated as a dynamic document that is updated as a testator's circumstances change throughout life.

While a will communicates the testator's intentions, there may be provincial legislation that must be considered when drafting a will, such as the *Family Law Act* in Ontario. If applicable legislation is not considered and if a will contravenes relevant legislation, there is the probability that the final distribution of assets will differ from that outlined in the will.

Creation

If a testator makes a valid will while residing in one province and later relocates to a new province, normally the laws of the new province will govern the rules applicable to the testator's will, intestacy, dependant responsibility and family law. A change of provincial jurisdiction warrants a comprehensive review of an individual's estate plan, including his will.

The discussion from this point forward will focus on issues specific to the English form of will, unless otherwise specified.

Testator

While some provinces require that an individual be at least the age of majority in order to create a will, others permit younger persons to make a will. In all provinces, the individual must be mentally competent. If a will is made under duress, it will not be considered a legal will.

ESTATE FUNDAMENTALS

Legacy/Bequest

The terms *legacy* and *bequest* are used interchangeably to describe a gift passed through a will. There are four classifications of a legacy, which is also referred to as a testamentary disposition under a will. These include:

- specific;

- demonstrative;

- general; and

- residual.

A *general* bequest is a legacy of monetary value paid out of the general assets of the estate, whereas a *specific* bequest is one that is an explicit and identifiable asset such as "my cottage" or "my antique automobile collection".

A *demonstrative* bequest is typically a monetary legacy where there is a direction that the bequest be satisfied from the proceeds of a specific asset or property. For example, "$10,000 from my GICs held at XYZ Bank". In this situation, the beneficiary may receive the full $10,000, if the specific assets from which the funds are drawn can support this amount. If at the time of the testator's death, the GICs at XYZ Bank no longer exist, there is ademption.

Alternatively, if the asset cannot support the full $10,000 bequest, but the asset still exists — perhaps its value is only $5,000 because of withdrawals prior to the testator's death — then there is abatement, whereby the beneficiary will receive only $5,000. Only the assets specifically named in the bequest can be used to fulfill the bequest; the beneficiary's gift cannot be fulfilled through other assets held within the estate.

A *residual* bequest is one based on the assets remaining in the estate after all other bequests have been satisfied.

Ademption

The term *ademption* refers to the removal of a bequest within the will because the asset is no longer in the estate at the time of the testator's death. While the asset existed when the testator created the will, it no longer exists within the estate so it is removed as a bequest.

When ademption occurs, and there are no subsequent directions, the intended beneficiary is left with nothing. To avoid situations of this nature, it is important that the testator include a statement in his will that addresses the possibility that the specific item is no longer in the estate. If the particular asset is already disposed of:

- the testator may well intend that the beneficiary receive nothing; or

- the testator may want to provide a substitute item.

By following through with an explanation, the testator adds clarity and avoids ambiguity.

Abatement

The term *abatement* applies to the situation where a bequest is made but there are not sufficient assets available to satisfy the full bequest, so the amount is lowered or adjusted to reflect a reduced amount. In simple terms, abatement is a proportionate reduction due to insufficient funds.

Lapse

Where a gift cannot be made under a will because the intended beneficiary has predeceased the testator, and where there is no contingent beneficiary relative to the specific gift, the gift is considered to have failed or *lapsed*. Typically, the lapsed gift reverts into the residual clause of the will, but if there is no residual clause, the gift would be an intestacy.

The testator has the power to name contingent beneficiaries for any gift within the will. This process is also referred to as a *gift-over provision*. A specific person may be named as the contingent beneficiary in which case the gift-over provision would apply in the event that the first beneficiary predeceases the testator. Alternatively, a statement could be made that the gift passes through the residual clause if the named beneficiary predeceases the testator. Either way, clarity is achieved through the inclusion of an explanation as to the consequence of the gift, if the beneficiary predeceases the testator.

Exoneration

When an asset is bequeathed to a beneficiary, the will should address any outstanding debts against the specific asset. If the debt is not addressed, the gift will pass to the beneficiary free of debt and the testator's estate will be required to address the debt obligation. The will should expressly indicate how debts against specific gifts are to be addressed: is the debt exonerated, and if so, to what extent?

Residue

The residual estate, also referred to as *residue*, is the remainder of the estate after debts, expenses, taxes and legacy distributions.

BILL AND BOB

Bill and Bob were the only beneficiaries of their mother, Ethel's, estate. A widow for many years, Ethel's will provided for Bill to inherit the cottage and for Bob to inherit the residue of her estate.

The cottage had an outstanding mortgage of $75,000, but this was not specifically addressed in the will.

Upon taking control of the estate, the executor transferred title of the cottage to Bill (a market value of about $350,000) as stated in the will. He then proceeded to liquidate Ethel's other assets and pay off her debts.

Ethel's other assets consisted of a small RRIF, a small savings account and a condo in the city. The executor wound up with about $450,000 of cash from the liquidation of Ethel's assets (other than the cottage) and proceeded to pay her final expenses, taxes owing on her terminal tax return and the mortgage on the cottage. After payment of these liabilities, the executor was left with about $200,000, which he subsequently paid to Bob as beneficiary of the residual estate.

Because Ethel's will provided a specific bequest to Bill and did not address the issue of the mortgage, the cottage passed to Bill in whole and the mortgage was paid as a debt from the assets of the estate.

The structure of bequests under Ethel's will resulted in inequitable distributions, which may not have been what she had intended.

Per Stirpes versus Per Capita

Two important phrases, *per stirpes* and *per capita*, are commonly used in a will to govern the distribution of assets to successive generations when death within a beneficiary generation occurs prior to the death of the estate owner. In many senses, these two phrases are opposite in nature.

The term *per stirpes* follows a system where the children of a deceased parent share in the inheritance that their parent would have received had he survived the recently deceased descendant. In essence, the children claim a share by representing their parent. Per stirpes involves the division of property based on degrees of kinship.

Per capita refers to an alternative system of inheritance where named descendants of the deceased share equally in the size of the share that each inherits regardless of degree of kinship. Per capita refers to an equal amount per head, for all who inherit.

MADELINE (1)

Fifty-six-year-old Madeline has three children, Bob, Carl and Don. In Madeline's will she leaves her estate to her three sons, in equal shares, but should any of her sons predecease her, Madeline's will provides for the deceased son's share to pass to his surviving children in equal shares *per stirpes*. In simple terms, the *per stirpes* means the respective children of the deceased child will share equally in the inheritance that their father would have received.

Let's consider a series of different circumstances that could evolve. Assume Madeline dies July 1, leaving a net estate of $300,000.

1. All children survive Madeline

If all three of her children are alive, each son (Bob, Carl and Don) will receive $100,000. Any children of Bob, Carl and Don will not be beneficiaries under Madeline's estate because each of the primary beneficiaries are alive to receive their legacy.

2. Bob predeceases Madeline

On July 1, Carl and Don are both alive but Bob has predeceased Madeline. Bob's surviving children are Etienne and Frank.

Madeline's estate will be distributed to her two sons, Don and Carl, who will each receive $100,000, and her two grandchildren, Etienne and Frank, who will each receive $50,000.

Don and Carl's children will not receive any funds from Madeline's estate, nor will Bob's spouse. The share intended for Bob will be distributed *per stirpes* to his surviving children Etienne and Frank.

3. Bob and Carl predecease Madeline

On July 1, Don is alive, but Bob and Carl have predeceased Madeline. Bob's surviving children are Etienne and Frank while Carl never had any children.

Madeline's estate will be distributed as follows:

- $150,000 to her son Don;
- $75,000 to each of Etienne and Frank (Bob's children).

In this case, because Carl predeceased Madeline and because he did not have any children onto whom his share could pass as outlined in Madeline's will, the estate is split equally between the surviving beneficiaries.

Bob's children, Etienne and Frank, are contingent beneficiaries specifically identified in Madeline's will. There is no contingent beneficiary eligible to receive Carl's share of Madeline's estate.

4. Bob, Carl and Don all predecease Madeline

On July 1, all three of Madeline's sons have predeceased her. The following describes the surviving children of the three sons:

- Etienne and Frank (Bob's children);
- Georgina, Hans and Iggy (Don's children); and
- Carl never had any children.

continued . . .

---

continued . . .

Madeline's estate will be distributed as follows:

- $75,000 to each of Etienne and Frank (Bob's children);
- $50,000 to each of Georgina, Hans and Iggy (Don's children).

Since Carl predeceased Madeline and did not leave any children to whom his share could pass as outlined in Madeline's will, the estate is shared between Bob's surviving children and Don's surviving children. The *per stirpes* allocation means that the grandchildren will share in their respective father's share of Madeline's estate. As an outcome, Bob's two children receive a larger inheritance (two children share $150,000) than Don's three children (three children share $150,000).

MADELINE (2)

On July 1, Madeline dies leaving a net estate of $300,000. Madeline's will leaves her estate to her three children (Bob, Carl and Don) and her five grandchildren (Etienne, Frank, Georgina, Hans and Iggy) in equal shares per capita.

In simple terms, the per capita means that if any of Madeline's beneficiaries predecease her, his/her share will be divided amongst the remaining beneficiaries.

Let's consider a series of different circumstances that could evolve. Assume Madeline dies July 1, leaving a net estate of $300,000.

1. All children and grandchildren survive Madeline

If all 8 of her beneficiaries are alive, each will receive $37,500.

2. Bob predeceases Madeline

On July 1, Carl and Don are both alive, but Bob has predeceased Madeline. Bob's surviving children are Etienne and Frank.

Madeline's estate will be distributed equally among her two surviving sons (Don and Carl) and her five grandchildren with each beneficiary receiving $42,857.

3. Bob and Carl predecease Madeline

On July 1, Don is alive but Bob and Carl have predeceased Madeline. Madeline's estate will be distributed to her one remaining son (Don) and five grandchildren, with each receiving $50,000.

4. Bob, Carl and Don predecease Madeline

On July 1, all three of Madeline's sons have predeceased her. The following describes the surviving children of the three sons:

- Etienne and Frank (Bob's children); and
- Georgina, Hans and Iggy (Don's children);
- Carl never had any children.

Madeline's $300,000 estate will be divided equally amongst the five grandchildren, as follows:

- $60,000 to each of Etienne and Frank (Bob's children);
- $60,000 to each of Georgina, Hans and Iggy (Don's children).

EXECUTOR

Selection

An *executor* is the person named within the will to carry out the instructions described in the testator's will. The title applied to this position can vary by jurisdiction. For example, in Ontario this role is now referred to as an *estate trustee*. The term executor is a male version of the word, whereas a female in this role is referred to as an *executrix*.

The testator may appoint a single individual, or perhaps a trust company, to act as his executor. Or, the testator may appoint multiple executors. Multiple executors are typically expected to make decisions on a unanimous basis, unless the terms established through the will provide otherwise, such as the inclusion of a majority-decision clause. A majority decision clause, with an odd number of executors, eliminates the possibility that the executors could become deadlocked on an issue. Alternatively, there are other ways to structure the voting provisions to ensure flexibility and continuity. The key issue is to ensure that the structure is functional and addresses the testator's objectives.

Selection of the executor is an important decision that should be carefully considered. While some estates are viewed as simple and straightforward, there is still work and responsibility associated with the role of executor. Some individuals prefer to have an independent executor, such as a lawyer or trust company, whereas others prefer to name a family member or friend. The executor should be someone whom the testator feels will act in the estate and the beneficiaries' best interest.

The selection of the executor should consider the complexity of the estate and the type of skills the executor might have to demonstrate. Will the executor undertake the majority of work on his own or will he have the authority to hire individuals to assist? Is there a possibility of contention within the family that might be better managed by appointing a non-family member as executor?

Where is the executor located? If the executor is located in an eastern province and the testator lives in British Columbia, how effectively can the executor fulfill his role across the distance? If multiple executors are appointed, how close are they located to each other and what type of decision-making authority will they have? For example, if two executors are required to work jointly and one lives in New Brunswick, while the other lives in British Columbia, and the estate is located in Ontario, the process may become quite complex.

While a witness to the will cannot be a beneficiary under the will, an executor can be a beneficiary. The naming of an alternate executor will address the possibility that the first named executor may be unable or unwilling to act as executor at the time of the testator's death.

It is common practice for the testator to appoint an alternate executor, or even two alternates, to provide for the possibility that the intended executor is unable or unwilling to fulfill his role. If the will fails to appoint an executor, an application must be made to the courts for the appointment of an estate administrator.

Role

The role of the executor includes:

- gathering and accounting for assets of the estate;
- payment of outstanding debts, including any income taxes triggered by the death of the deceased;
- distribution of estate assets; and
- completion of the personal and estate income tax returns.

The executor is eligible to be paid a fee for his role in the estate. When the executor is a friend or family member, quite often he may decline any compensation. A professional executor, such as a trust company, will require compensation.

Powers

Provincial laws necessitate that the executor is obligated to follow the instructions set out in the will by the testator, subject of course to any limitations imposed by the law.

The role of the executor is to act as a trustee for the beneficiaries of the estate and, as such, in most situations, the executor takes legal title to the property that is to ultimately move from the deceased to the beneficiaries. The property would typically move from the deceased, to the executor, to the beneficiaries, where the executor holds the property in trust until it can be distributed to the beneficiaries. This process would not apply to property that passes to a beneficiary automatically upon death, such as an insurance policy with a named beneficiary or property held in joint title with the right of survivorship.

DISTRIBUTION OF ESTATE

Creditors

Creditors of the deceased must be paid before any distributions can be made to the beneficiaries of the estate. If prior distributions are made to beneficiaries that deplete the assets of the estate to the point that creditors are left unpaid, the estate executor or administrator can be held personally liable. It is important to note that income tax is a debt of the estate and must be paid, or provided for, before any distributions to the beneficiaries.

Priority Order

While the distribution of the estate assets falls to the estate executor or administrator, provincial legislation stipulates that the assets of an estate must be prioritized for payment. This really only becomes an issue when the expenses of the estate exceed the assets, in which case it would be referred to as an *insolvent estate*. The priority of items differs by provincial jurisdiction but examples of expenses that frequently receive higher priority include such items as:

- funeral expenses (typically first in priority order);
- income taxes (typically immediately following funeral expenses);
- taxes payable under provincial estate/probate legislation (typically very high in priority order);
- solicitor's costs;
- liabilities incurred by the personal representative in respect of the administration of the estate;
- commissions/fees payable to the personal representative in respect of the administration of the estate; and
- payment of other debts.

Heirs

Amount

The testator has the sole authority to decide on the size of bequest left to each beneficiary. While there are many situations where it makes good sense to leave equal amounts of net assets to each of the testator's children, there are certainly reasons the testator might chose to differ the size of the bequest left to each heir.

MEINSINGER FAMILY (1)

When Don Meinsinger died last month, his three children were surprised to discover that the distribution of assets was not done equally amongst the three children. Don had bequeathed his youngest child, Ami, $100,000 more than he had bequeathed to the older two children, Michelle and Nancy.

continued . . .

---

continued . . .

Michelle and Nancy were both finished their post-secondary education and were becoming well established in their respective careers. Ami had just finished her final year of high school and had every intention of attending university.

Don felt that $100,000 was a close representation of the amount he had spent on post-secondary education for Michelle and Nancy. An additional $100,000 for Ami was his way of providing for her education, on an equitable basis.

Timing

The timing of payments under the bequest can differ. For example, where the amount of money is sizeable, a testator might opt to have payments made in multiple instalments — one at age 18, a second at age 25 and a third at age 30 — rather than as a single lump sum amount.

MEINSINGER FAMILY (2)

Continuing the Meinsinger family SNAP, not only did Don's bequest amount differ between the children, so did the timing.

Twenty-five-year-old Michelle received her full bequest immediately, whereas 23-year-old Nancy was eligible to receive half of her bequest immediately and the remaining half when she reaches age 25. In Ami's case, she is entitled to receive half of the bequest when she reaches age 18 and the remaining half at age 25. All funds not distributed immediately were held in separate testamentary trusts, for the benefit of each respective beneficiary.

Other Considerations

The choice of leaving specific property to certain heirs, or requiring the sale of specific property and then distributing the cash, are different options that should be looked at relative to the testator's intended outcome for testamentary dispositions.

A second marriage or a common-law relationship creates the situation where two parties may bring separate estates, separate families and separate issues into the picture. Estate planning provides the opportunity to address issues such as providing for the second spouse or common-law partner while perhaps structuring the estate plan to have the remainder of the assets flow through to the testator's children from his first marriage. These types of issues need careful discussion and consideration to ensure that the asset flow occurs as the testator intends.

The naming of alternate beneficiaries is a strategy that can address the event where an heir predeceases a testator. Perhaps a child predeceases his father but leaves three children. Is it the father's intention that the three grandchildren inherit their deceased parent's portion of the estate? If so, has the will been structured to address this issue or is it an outstanding concern?

There are times where an intended heir is viewed, by the testator, as having incredibly poor skills in financial management and he may be unwilling to leave a bequest without adequate provisions to address this dilemma. This type of concern can be dealt with through estate planning, as can a broad range of other important vulnerabilities, such as providing adequately for physically or mentally disabled heirs.

Assets of the estate will be distributed according to the will; so all bequests should be clearly listed in the will. When a bequest is made to a beneficiary, and there is no provision in the bequest that specifies that the funds are to be used for another individual's benefit, the beneficiary is free to utilize the inheritance at her sole discretion.

JANICE

When Janice died, her daughter, Amanda, was the sole beneficiary of Janice's estate. Prior to her death, Janice had discussed the idea of using $100,000 of assets to make RRSP contributions for each adult grandchild ($25,000 each), although there was no mention of this in Janice's will.

Amanda is under no obligation to make RRSP contributions on behalf of the adult grandchildren. If Janice had wanted each of the adult grandchildren to receive an RRSP bequest, such a legacy must be identified within her will.

If Amanda decides to give each grandchild $25,000, she is free to do so, but is not obliged. Any amount given to the grandchildren would be treated as an *inter vivos* gift from Amanda to the grandchildren and would be subject to any income tax consequences and attribution rules related to an *inter vivos* gift.

Special Needs Beneficiaries

Minor Children

Children under the age of majority may inherit property, but the law requires that someone over the age of majority act as trustee and assume responsibility for the management of the inherited property during the child's minority years. Where such arrangements have not been made in the will, provincial laws dictate the appointment of provincial authorities to act in this capacity.

It is best to plan for minor children through specific directions set out in a will. This can be accomplished through the creation of a testamentary trust where the trustee is obliged to act in the best interest of the beneficiary of the trust and to follow the settlor's directions. When a bequest is made to the minor children of the testator, he may decide to establish a single trust for each child; or alternatively, a single trust for all children. The topic of multiple trusts is explored further under the testamentary trust section.

When life insurance is purchased with the intention of using the funds to provide for the care of minor children and/or to provide funds as an inheritance that will last into adulthood, the policy owner needs to arrange for the funds to be managed on the children's behalf. This can be achieved by naming the trust as beneficiary of the policy and establishing the details of the testamentary trust in the deceased's will.

If a single life insurance policy is to provide funds to more than one child, the policy owner needs to specify the percentage split of funds amongst the beneficiaries, if it is anything other than equal.

Educational Costs

Parents often provide financial support for their children's education well beyond their minor years. The cost of education is not an insignificant expense and should be considered as a unique issue in the planning process. For example, a parent may establish a separate pool of assets to cover educational needs for all of his children prior to the distribution of any subsequent bequest. Alternatively, the will could provide a separate inheritance for each child, and it is the child's responsibility to fund his educational costs from the inheritance. While the testator is not limited to any single strategy, the magnitude and importance of educational costs is worthy of special consideration.

Disabled Child

The ability to provide for the ongoing special needs of a disabled child, whether because of physical or mental limitations, often creates significant concern for parents when they are preparing their estate plan. Not only do the parents, or perhaps an older sibling, provide direction and emotional support to the disabled child, there is typically an essential monetary element that ensures the child is well cared for.

Unfortunately, government programs designed to assist disabled individuals with a variety of services and financial support tend to complicate the process of estate planning, because these programs frequently pull back on services or financial support when a disabled individual's income or assets exceed prescribed limits.

While parents are alive and active in their disabled child's life, the parent recognizes the financial issues relative to a comfortable standard of living and is able to find ways around government limitations, without causing the disabled child to be disqualified for support. However, upon the parent's demise, a bequest from the parent to the disabled child could unwittingly impact the child's qualification for benefits of a financial or service nature, from government-sponsored programs.

Government financial support for a disabled individual falls into provincial jurisdiction. As such, issues and dollar limits will vary by province, so the magnitude of the problem will differ depending upon the provincial jurisdiction. A tested solution to this potentially significant concern is the use of an absolute discretionary trust, often referred to as a Henson trust. The term Henson is used in recognition of Audrey Henson, a disabled individual from Guelph, Ontario whose father's will utilized an absolute discretionary trust to provide for her after his demise. The case has been tested in the courts and upheld as a valid planning technique.

The concept is to provide financially for the disabled child's lifetime without impacting any provincial benefits for which the disabled individual may qualify. A discretionary trust provides the trustee with the authority to use his discretion in the management of the trust. Through the use of trustee discretion, the trust is established so the disabled person does not have absolute rights to the property.

While the trust could be funded with existing assets from the estate, it is quite common and economical to fund the trust with life insurance (i.e., the trust is established as the beneficiary of the life insurance policy). A trust of this nature would not be subject to claims from the creditors of the settlor or the beneficiary.

These types of arrangements require careful planning and an essential understanding of the impact of any bequest on the child's qualification for provincial benefits.

CHRIS

Two years ago, when Chris's parents passed away unexpectedly, he assumed responsibility for his younger sibling, Evan, who is severely disabled and receives provincial benefits because of his disability. Now, at age 30, Chris feels it is essential that he establish plans to ensure that Evan is financially cared for, should Chris die prematurely.

In Chris's will, he has planned for the creation of a testamentary trust that will be structured as an absolute discretionary trust with Evan as the beneficiary. Chris has purchased a life insurance policy with a $1,000,000 face value, where he is the policy owner and life insured. Chris has named the trustee as beneficiary of the insurance policy.

Upon Chris's death, the proceeds of the life insurance policy will be used to settle the testamentary trust. The trustee will have full and complete discretion over the trust, deciding when any income or capital is distributed to Evan, as beneficiary of the trust. The trustee will handle the funds from the trust in a manner so not to impede any provincial benefits for which Evan qualifies.

By combining the trust arrangement and the use of an insurance policy, Chris is able to create an effective plan that provides for Evan financially, in the event that he should predecease Evan.

Releases and Passing of Accounts

It is the estate executor or administrator's responsibility to bring closure to the estate through one of two methodologies. The executor/administrator may obtain releases from the beneficiaries or alternatively may apply to the courts for the passing of accounts.

To provide valid *releases*, beneficiaries or their representatives must have the appropriate authority to do so. When all of the beneficiaries are competent adults over the age of majority, they are typically considered in a position to provide a valid release. When the beneficiary is a minor, his guardian or trustee will normally be in a position to provide a valid release.

The *passing of accounts* involves the executor/administrator's presentation of the estate's accounts to the courts with a request for approval. While the passing of accounts is not typically a necessity, an executor often chooses this method because it is viewed as a more prudent approach that provides protection to the executor against further claims. Alternatively, a challenge by a beneficiary who questions the management of the estate accounts could force the trustee to apply for a passing of the accounts.

In managing the accounts of the estate, the executor's role increases in complexity when the estate involves capital and income issues relative to the beneficiaries. If both income and capital are issues within the testator's will, the executor must track and account for capital and income separately. This type of tracking would typically be required in the situation where one beneficiary receives a bequest that involves a life interest in a property while another beneficiary is to ultimately receive the capital property.

DEPENDANTS' RELIEF

While an individual has the right to distribute his estate as he wishes, it typically does not remove his responsibility to provide adequately for his dependants. These types of issues fall into provincial jurisdiction, with each province free to establish its own parameters. Most provinces have legislation, often in the area of dependents' relief, succession or family law, that allows a spouse, common-law partner or children to make a claim against the estate if adequate provisions have not been taken to meet the deceased's financial obligations.

The definition of dependant will differ by provincial jurisdiction and typically includes a spouse or common-law partner and children. Other times, it may also include a parent or a sibling of the deceased where the deceased was contributing to the financial support of that parent or sibling, either voluntarily or under legal requirements, immediately prior to the death of the deceased.

SPOUSAL RIGHTS

In some jurisdictions, such as Ontario, the surviving spouse has options that could circumvent the outcome of the testator's original intentions. In Ontario, for example, a marriage is treated as an economic partnership, and upon the cessation of the partnership there is an entitlement to an equalization payment from the deceased spouse to the surviving spouse. The death of one spouse represents an event that would entitle the surviving spouse to an equalization of net family property.

As such, a spouse in Ontario has the opportunity to choose between taking an equalization payment or receiving the inheritance set out in the deceased's will. The surviving spouse has a six-month window during which he can make this decision; no payments can be made from the estate until the earlier of the expiration of the six-month period or until a written election is made by the surviving spouse.

A similar type of claim for equalization of net family property upon the death of a spouse or partner is also available in Manitoba.

Typically, a divorced spouse cannot claim or dispute the arrangements under a testator's will, except to the extent of the continuation of support payments.

CLAUSES IN THE WILL

Introduction

The content of a will is important because it sets the foundation relative to a broad array of issues. Items not addressed in a will are typically subject to provincial jurisdiction. The complexity of a will is certainly dependent upon the testator's personal circumstances and testamentary intentions.

The remainder of this section is focused on a discussion regarding a variety of clauses used within a will. The will of Ashley Thomas is shown in Appendix One, and forms the basis for this discussion. The reference to an item (i.e., Item A) indicates there is a corresponding denotation in Ashley's will.

ASHLEY THOMAS (1)

Forty-year-old Ashley Thomas is married to Donald Thomas, and together they have three children, Deanna (age 19), Christy (age 15) and Scott (age 14).

The Thomases have been married 24 years, and live in ABC City, in XYZ Province. In 1992, they had their lawyer prepare new wills, to which no changes of any nature have been incorporated since that time. The couple have mirror wills where Ashley leaves her entire estate to Donald, and Donald leaves his entire estate to Ashley. Otherwise, the provisions within each of their wills are identical.

This is a first marriage for both Ashley and Donald and neither had any common-law relationship with another individual prior to their marriage.

Prior to this 1992 will, Ashley and Donald had prepared wills in 1979 when they were first married.

Identification

Typically, the initial clause in the will identifies the testator and provides added clarity through the inclusion of her full name and residency. (See Item A.)

ASHLEY (2)

The identification of the testator in this will is:

Ashley Christine Rachel Thomas, of the City of ABC, in the Regional Municipality of DEF, and in the Province of XYZ.

Revocation of Previous Wills

This clause is intended to clearly revoke all former wills, codicils and testamentary dispositions, establishing that the current document is declared as the last and most current will. (See Item B.)

ASHLEY (3)

Ashley's will, prepared in 1992, is her most current will, and clearly revokes all former wills, codicils and other testamentary dispositions.

Although it has been several years since Ashley's will was prepared, it remains current and valid in the province of XYZ because, as noted earlier, she has not completed any subsequent will or codicils.

Appointment of Executor

The will includes the appointment of an executor, who becomes responsible for managing the estate. In addition, the testator names a trustee who is charged with responsibility for carrying out any testamentary trust arrangements established through the will. Frequently, the same person is named as both the executor and trustee, although this does not need to be the case. (See Item C.)

Without the incorporation of contingency arrangements for an alternate executor, the courts would need to become involved if the appointed executor was unable or unwilling to fulfill the role. This same process applies to the role of a trustee. If a trustee is required but is not named in the will, provincial jurisdiction would dictate how an appointment would be handled, which would typically necessitate court involvement.

ASHLEY (4)

Ashley's will appoints her husband Donald as the sole executor and trustee of her estate. She also incorporates contingency arrangements should Donald be unwilling or unable to assume the role. The contingent executor and trustee is Darlene Wiley, and should Darlene be unwilling or unable to perform the role, Jack Darling is appointed as executor and trustee.

In each case, Ashley has appointed a single individual to act as executor and trustee, but with contingency arrangements.

Registered Money Rollover

Ashley's will includes a clause that directs any funds received by the estate as a refund of premium are to be paid to her spouse as beneficiary. Ashley recommends that Donald roll the funds into another registered plan, but there is no prescribed requirement that necessitates that Donald follow this recommendation. (See Item D.)

ASHLEY (5)

Over 18 years have passed since Ashley prepared her will in 1992. It is quite likely that she has participated in a RRSP or pension plan during that time, and may have signed beneficiary designations. This clause in Ashley's will simply addresses the issue of funds that are received as a refund of premium by the estate. The clause does not impact any named beneficiary designations.

Payment of Debts

Death does not eliminate a testator's financial obligations, as all debts are still payable. A clause in the will directs the executor to pay appropriate debts. (See Item E.)

> *ASHLEY (6)*
>
> This clause directs the executor of Ashley's estate to pay any debts owing including any funeral and testamentary expenses.

Bequests

A bequest is a gift of real or personal property and there are many ways in which bequests can be worded. When preparing a will, the majority of married couples leave everything to each other under the premise that the surviving spouse will provide for the care and needs of their children, as is the case in Ashley's will. This sample will incorporates three sets of clauses to establish the terms and circumstances of the bequests. (See Items F, G and H.)

When creating a bequest, there are some legal limitations. Examples include:

- A bequest cannot be contingent on a marriage or divorce.

- A general bequest such as, "I leave the family cottage to Emily, if and when she goes to university", is very general in nature and leaves many unanswered issues.

- An animal cannot be the recipient of a bequest. A favoured pet is best cared for by bequeathing the animal to a specific individual and providing funds for the animal's care.

Arrangements for the long-term care of someone with special needs, such as a disabled child or aging parent, are best achieved through the establishment of a trust that is created to address a specific, clear purpose.

Included in this sample will is a clause that is commonly referred to as a *common disaster clause*; the requirement that a specific beneficiary survive the testator by a period of at least 30 days in order to qualify to receive the inheritance. While there is no magic to the use of a 30-day number, a clause of this nature is commonly used to reduce a number of concerns that could otherwise arise. If both the testator and the beneficiary were in the same accident, and died within minutes, hours or a few days of each other, it may not be the testator's intentions to have her assets flow immediately to her beneficiary and then immediately onward to the beneficiaries of her beneficiary's estate. The common disaster clause reduces this possibility and also minimizes the likelihood of double probate that would arise in a flow-through situation.

> *ASHLEY (7)*
>
> Ashley has arranged that all assets pass to her husband Donald after the payment of any debts and expenses of the estate, provided that Donald survives her for a period of 30 days. By requiring a 30-day survival period, Ashley lowers the possibility that her wishes will not be fulfilled as intended.

> *ASHLEY (8)*
>
> If Ashley's estate does not pass to Donald, the alternate heirs are Ashley's children. The children (Deanna, Christy and Scott) would share equally in the estate, based on prescribed circumstances. The children would share equally if they are alive, and if one of the children is not alive but has left surviving children (Ashley's grandchildren), the surviving issue of Ashley's deceased child are entitled to the share to which his/her parent would have been entitled if living (equal shares *per stirpes*).

ASHLEY (9)

If Ashley's estate does not pass to Donald, and if Ashley has no children or surviving issue, then Candice Sherman is the beneficiary of Ashley's estate.

Trustee Powers

A clause that identifies the powers of the trustee is important to avoid the situation where a trustee's ability to act is limited to the powers established through provincial jurisdiction. Without clear direction in the will, the powers of the trustee typically default to provincial standards, which tend to be very limited. (See Item I.)

ASHLEY (10)

Ashley has provided full power and authority to her trustee whereby she states, "... to the full and same extent I could do as owner were I alive, including the power to execute all deeds, conveyances and other documents required from time to time in the administration of my estate".

Trustee for Minor Beneficiaries

Minor children cannot assume responsibility for the management of any assets, so asset transfers through a will to minor children need to include the appointment of a trustee who becomes responsible for managing the assets until the children reach age of majority. Without the appointment of a trustee, the provincial authorities become involved. (See Item J.)

ASHLEY (11)

Ashley's will sets out provisions for the handling of any share of her estate that passes to any person who has not yet attained the age of majority. The clause provides direction that conveys absolute sole discretion to the trustee. The will directs that the assets pass to the child upon reaching the age of majority.

If circumstances prevailed that caused Ashley's estate to pass to her children today, Deanna's share would be paid directly to her because she has passed the age of majority. The amounts payable to Christy and Scott would be held in trust for each of them, with the trustee having absolute sole discretion over the funds. Upon their reaching the age of majority, the funds would move from the trustee to Christy and Scott.

Releases on Behalf of Minor Beneficiaries

This clause provides the trustee with the authority to make payments to the parent or guardian of any minor beneficiary, or to any person the trustee considers to be a proper recipient on behalf of the minor. It further stipulates that the trustee can accept a release for the funds from the person acting in a trustee capacity, on behalf of the minor. (See Item K.)

Qualification of Beneficiary

This type of clause stipulates that any reference to a person in terms of a relationship determined by blood or through marriage does not include someone who was born outside of marriage. The intention is to preclude claims from any individual who may be a child of the testator but who was not born in wedlock. Without this clause, the broad use of terms, such as "children", would include all children of the testator, not simply those born within wedlock. (See Item L.)

ASHLEY (12)

Ashley's three children — Deanna, Christy and Scott — are eligible to share in Ashley's estate based on the terms of this will. If Ashley had a child outside of her marriage to Donald, this clause is intended to preclude that child from making a claim against Ashley's estate as one of her children.

Special Provision

This statement is intended to stipulate that a bequest under the will should not be treated as community property between the beneficiary and his/her spouse and that the inheritance should not form part of the beneficiary and his/her spouse's family property. (See Item M.)

Guardianship

A person who has legal custody of a child is referred to as a guardian. In a will, a testator would normally nominate the preferred individual(s) to become guardian and assume responsibility for the testator's minor children. Where there is a surviving spouse, the issue of guardianship is not typically an issue. A discussion of the implications that arise when a deceased spouse does not want the surviving spouse to have custody is beyond the scope of this material.

It is advisable to always name the preferred guardian of the children, as this addresses the issue for single parents, as well as the possibility that both parents might die in a common disaster. To avoid conflict, both parents should preferably nominate the same person to become guardian. Where a guardian needs to be put in place, a judge will normally appoint the nominee provided he views it to be in the best interest of the child(ren). The topic of "best interest of the children" is obviously subjective but could consider such questions as:

- moral habits and conduct of the nominated guardian;
- the child's relationship to the guardian;
- the child's preference, particularly with older children; and
- who can provide the greatest stability and best meet the child's needs. (See Item N.)

ASHLEY (13)

Ashley's will appoints Darlene Wiley as guardian of Ashley's minor children in the event that Donald has predeceased her. The will also includes a backup, Candice Sherman, in the event that Darlene is unwilling or unable to fulfill the role.

If circumstances prevailed where Ashley were to die today and Donald had predeceased her, Christy and Scott are minors who would need a guardian. Deanna is over the age of majority so a guardian is not of concern.

Date and Signatures

The will concludes with a date and required signatures. The date is important for assessing whether the will is indeed the most current copy. (See Item O.)

> *ASHLEY (14)*
>
> In this case, the will states how the signatures were affixed, "SIGNED, PUBLISHED AND DECLARED by the above-named Testatrix, ASHLEY CHRISTINE RACHEL THOMAS, as and for her last Will and Testament, in the presence of us, both present at the same time, who at her request, in her presence and in the presence of each other, have hereunto subscribed our names as witnesses."
>
> Ashley has signed the will and Darrin Rogers and Emily Pythe have signed as witnesses to Ashley's signature.

Other Clauses

There is a wide array of clauses that can be incorporated into a will, depending upon the specific circumstances. A few examples of other clauses not yet discussed include:

Power to borrow, lend or renew debt obligations — These types of clauses specify the powers available to lend, borrow or renew debt obligations. Without these specific clauses, the estate executor or trustee is limited to provincially prescribed arrangements.

Will drafting in contemplation of marriage — Because marriage automatically revokes a will, a special clause is inserted when a will is drafted in contemplation of a specific marriage to a specified individual.

TESTAMENTARY TRUSTS

Integration

A *testamentary trust* is a trust created on the day a person dies. The terms of a testamentary trust are established by the deceased person's will or by law if there is no will, or by a court order under provincial legislation.

The assets of the deceased's estate pass into a testamentary trust by way of the testator's will. Where there is no will, the assets pass into a testamentary trust by court order under provincial legislation. The estate is administered as a testamentary trust.

Testamentary trusts may be used as part of a will for a variety of purposes, including:

- hold assets for minor children;

- provide ongoing income for minor children;

- provide for a disabled child or relative;

- provide for a spouse or common-law partner; or

- provide for a wide variety of special needs.

Testamentary trusts are very useful to assist in the management of assets when it is not possible or it may be inappropriate to have distributions made directly to a beneficiary. Through the establishment of a testamentary trust, the settlor has control over the assets that would not be possible if the assets passed directly to the beneficiary. It is important to note, however, that an executor does not have the power to establish a testamentary trust after the demise of a testator; the testator must make provisions for the testamentary trust prior to his death.

Types of Trusts

While a testamentary trust is a trust created on the day an individual dies, it is not uncommon to see a variety of names applied to the trust. From an income tax perspective, testamentary trusts fall into one of two categories: a spousal trust and all other non-spousal trusts.

Spousal Trust

A testamentary *spousal or common-law partner trust* is a trust created at the time of the testator's death in which the surviving beneficiary spouse or common-law partner is entitled to receive all income that may arise during his/her lifetime and is the only person who can receive or access use of any income or capital of the trust during his/her lifetime.

A spousal trust is commonly used as an estate planning tool that allows for the settlor to provide for the needs of his surviving spouse during her lifetime while maintaining control of the assets. The provisions within the spousal or common-law partner trust document will dictate whether the trust is viewed as a qualified spousal trust.

For a spousal trust to meet the requirements of a qualified spousal trust, the trust must have been created by the deceased taxpayer for the benefit of his spouse or common-law partner such that only the spouse or common-law partner may receive or use any of the income or capital of the trust, prior to the beneficiary spouse or common-law partner's death. As well, the trust must be resident in Canada and the property must vest indefeasibly in the trust within 36 months. If for any reason the trust does not meet this qualifying criteria, the trust is treated as a tainted spousal trust and is not eligible for any benefits specific to a qualified spousal trust. A tainted spousal trust becomes a non-spousal trust.

BERNIE

Bernie and Maxine Smith were residents of Alberta when Bernie passed away. Bernie's will provided for the establishment of a spousal trust upon his death, with $1,500,000 of assets to be held by the trust. The trust document named Maxine as the income beneficiary under the trust and the Smith's two children as the capital beneficiaries who are eligible to receive the property only after Maxine's death. Maxine has full and complete use of all income from the assets held within the trust during her lifetime. Under these arrangements, the trust is treated as a qualified spousal trust.

If the trust included provisions that allowed anyone other than Maxine to potentially receive income or assets from the trust during Maxine's lifetime, the trust would be viewed as a tainted spousal trust. Examples of circumstances that would taint the trust include:

— if the trust provided for either of the Smith's children to receive a portion of the trust assets upon reaching age 21; or

— if the trust provided for the children to receive some or all of the capital in the event that Maxine were to become fully incapacitated or perhaps remarry.

The simple inclusion of these types of provisions in the trust is sufficient to taint a spousal trust; the actual events described above need not happen in order to taint the trust.

The primary benefit of a qualified spousal trust is the special tax treatment afforded to the trust, such as spousal rollovers, while allowing the trust to maintain control of the assets. The secondary benefit is the fact that the trust is not subject to a deemed disposition of its assets every 21 years.

In order for the spousal rollover provisions to apply to the assets moving from a deceased spouse to a qualified testamentary spousal trust, the following conditions apply:

- the property becomes indefeasibly vested in the spouse or common-law partner or trust within 36 months of the taxpayer's death;
- the trust must be resident in Canada; and
- the property is transferred from the taxpayer to his spouse as a consequence of the taxpayer's death.

Non-Spousal Trust

If a testamentary trust is established and it does not meet the definition of a qualified spousal trust, it falls into the category of a non-spousal testamentary trust for income tax purposes.

A testamentary trust may be established for the benefit of minor children, a disabled child or perhaps even an elderly parent. All of these examples of testamentary trusts have a different purpose, but all meet the definition of a testamentary trust created on the day that the settlor dies and all are treated similarly for tax purposes.

HANNAH

When fifty-nine-year-old Hannah died suddenly, most of her assets passed into testamentary trusts. These included:

- a qualified spousal trust established for the benefit of her husband Hank;
- separate trusts established for each of Hannah's three minor children (from a previous marriage);
- a trust established to retain ownership and ongoing control of the family cottage; and
- a trust established to provide for the ongoing care of her elderly father.

Hannah is the settlor of each of these testamentary trusts, created upon her death. The spousal trust provides for Hank as the income beneficiary throughout his life. Upon Hank's death, the capital of the spousal trust passes to Hannah's three children, but prior to Hank's death the children have no rights to access any assets of the trust.

Separate trusts for each of Hannah's three minor children provide sufficient structure that the trustee of each trust assumes responsibility for management of the assets, so there is no possibility of government intervention. Each child is the sole beneficiary of his/her respective trust.

The trust established to retain ownership of the family cottage is separate from the other trusts, and has its own trust document that sets out the provisions of the trust.

And finally, Hannah has established a trust under which her elderly father is the sole beneficiary. The purpose of the trust is to provide financial support for her elderly father during his lifetime. Upon her father's death, the remaining assets in the trust will be distributed to Hannah's adult siblings.

Out of the six testamentary trusts established through the provisions of Hannah's will, one trust is considered a qualified spousal trust while the remaining five are considered non-spousal testamentary trusts, for income tax purposes. These classifications are important because they establish the tax provisions that will apply to the trusts.

Assets moved into the qualified spousal trust will qualify for rollover treatment, which is not the case for the other trusts.

The executor of Hannah's estate has no opportunity to establish any additional testamentary trusts that have not been provided for initially, based on the terms of Hannah's will.

The phrase *family trust* is often used to describe a trust that is established for beneficiaries who have a family relationship to the settlor of the trust, but this type of arrangement is really no different from any other testamentary trust. In some situations, the beneficiaries may include the testator's surviving spouse, children and perhaps even grandchildren. In other situations, it may involve only children or perhaps only grandchildren. There is no unique definition of the term family trust, although it is a commonly used term. The terms of the trust can differ depending upon on the needs of the intended beneficiaries and the testator's wishes.

A testamentary trust is commonly used to hold assets that are to be retained and managed over an extended period, such as a family cottage.

ERIN

Erin owns a cottage that has become a treasured family asset. With four children, Erin is concerned as to how she should deal with the cottage after her death. While Erin is very well off financially and each of her children will receive a substantial inheritance, Erin is very uneasy as to her options relative to the cottage.

Each of Erin's four children is married and three of the couples have children of their own. Erin could not bring herself to bequeath the cottage to only one child because it would be viewed as favouring that selected child, even if the remaining three children received an equal and offsetting value in their inheritance.

Erin could leave the cottage to her four children as tenants in common, but given the different lifestyles each of the children have and different priorities, she feels that this will cause severe rifts relative to ongoing maintenance costs. While Erin could sell the cottage and simply allocate the value back to the children as a bequest, this is not an option that Erin wants to pursue.

Erin is financially sound and has sufficient assets that would allow her to create a testamentary trust in which she could hold the cottage, along with other assets that could be used to fund the ongoing maintenance and expenses associated with the cottage. The trust could own the cottage and manage it based on the provisions of the trust document.

Types of Interest

In the trust document, the settlor of the trust can grant a *fixed interest* in the trust property to which the beneficiary is entitled; or, the settlor can grant a *discretionary interest* to the beneficiary in which case the trustee is given authority to determine if and when the beneficiary is to receive proceeds of the trust property and if so, the amount.

The trust document defines what entitlements the beneficiaries have in the trust, as discussed in Module 7.

Trustee

The selection of the trustee should consider the role and responsibilities of the trustee. When a trust for children is involved, the person appointed as trustee can also be the same person who is guardian of the children, but there is no requirement that dictates this as a necessity. Circumstances may suggest that one person may be ideal as guardian for the children, but may not be appropriate relative to the skills and decisions required for management of the trust, depending upon the size of the trust left to the children. In other situations, the testator may include the guardian as one of the trustees but in addition may appoint a second or third individual who together with the guardian all assume the role of trustees.

Undertaking the role of a trustee creates a fiduciary relationship between the trust and beneficiaries. While the role of the trustee is defined in the trust document, a trustee is legally obliged to:

- act in the best interest of the beneficiaries;

- act impartially between different beneficiaries; and

- act with reasonable and prudent judgment.

Provincial legislation sets out the statutory powers, duties and obligations of a trustee, which are dictated by the province in which the trust is established. Because the scope and authority of trustees can be severely restricted by provincial legislation, it is valuable for the settlor to confirm and expand on the statutory provisions in the trust document.

While all aspects of authority can be important, of particular interest is the investment powers afforded to the trustee. Provincial legislation is quite specific and limiting in the types of investments permitted, so expansion of authority in the trust document will ensure that the trustee is empowered to invest in a way that meets the needs and objectives intended by the settlor.

Taxation

Trust Income

Testamentary trusts are taxed at the same marginal tax rates as those for personal income tax. All income received by the trust is initially reported by the trust, but income tax is only paid at the trust level on income retained by the trust. The earnings retained by the trust is the balance remaining after income allocations have been made (or are payable) to the beneficiaries.

If income were allocated from the trust to a beneficiary, the beneficiary would include the income on her tax return and pay the income tax on the income. In this situation, the trust does not have a tax liability in respect of allocated income. However, the trustee may decide to have the income taxed to the trust, rather than to the beneficiary. Even if the income is taxed in the trust, the money can still be paid out to the beneficiary. In other words, either the trust or the beneficiary will pay the tax, but not both.

If a beneficiary of the trust is in a low marginal tax rate, there may be no advantage to having the trust pay tax on the income. However, if the beneficiary is in a high marginal tax rate, and the trust is in a low marginal tax bracket (i.e., lower than the beneficiary), having the income taxed to the trust could produce tax savings.

TANYA

Eighteen-year-old Tanya is the only beneficiary of a testamentary trust established by her uncle. The trust has assets of $1,500,000 earning 5% interest, which results in taxable income of $75,000.

What are the results of taxing all of the income in the trust versus all of the income to Tanya (assuming she has no other income)? As well, consider the results of splitting the income equally between the trust and Tanya.

continued . . .

---

continued . . .

Table 1
Income Tax Review

	Review of Options			
	Option A **Taxed in Trust**	*Option B* **Taxed to Beneficiary**	*Option C* $\frac{1}{2}$ **Taxed in Trust and** $\frac{1}{2}$ **Taxed to Beneficiary**	
Taxable Income	$75,000	$75,000	$37,500	$37,500
Taxes Payable	$22,170	$20,223	$ 7,106	$ 8,792

Note: While this table shows three different options, the trust is not limited simply to three alternatives; rather, the split of income between the beneficiary and the trust can be any amount as the trustee deems appropriate, provided the choice does not impede any provisions established by the settlor in the trust document.

Table 1 shows three different methodologies for allocated income between the trust and Tanya as the beneficiary of the trust. In option A, total income tax payable is $22,170 compared with $20,223 under option B, and $15,898 under option C. All taxes payable amounts are assumed amounts.

If the trustee opts to have Tanya take the income on her tax return only (option B), there is a lower tax consequence than when the trust takes the full amount into income (option A). This difference results because Tanya is entitled to a personal non-refundable tax credit, which the trust is not.

However, by splitting the income between Tanya and the trust (option C), the total tax bill is even less. This lower tax liability results because of the utilization of the personal non-refundable tax credit and the maximization of the lower marginal tax rates.

The establishment of multiple testamentary trusts can provide a tax planning mechanism for income splitting. There is a cost associated with the establishment and ongoing retention of a trust (i.e., legal, accounting and trustee), so for small amounts held within the trust the offset between the total cost of operating the trust and tax savings may not warrant multiple trusts. Typically, this issue should be addressed through the estate planning process, relative to each individual's personal circumstances. Multiple trusts make good financial sense in a broad number of situations, but it is important to ensure that an analysis occur if the funds are limited and the cost of administering the trust might outweigh the benefit.

MARIE

Marie established a separate testamentary trust for each of her four grandchildren with the proceeds of her significant estate being divided equally across the four trusts. By establishing separate trusts, capital could be sprinkled among the four trusts, thereby setting the stage for income to be divided amongst eight taxpayers (four trusts and four individuals).

The results of such a plan can be observed from the Tanya SNAP, where the tax liability was reduced by $4,325 by splitting income between two taxpayers.

Property Transfers

Property is transferred by the deceased's estate into the testamentary trust. Since the transfer is from the estate, the property has already been subject to the deemed disposition rules upon death. This means that the estate has an adjusted cost base (ACB) equal to the fair market value (FMV) of the property, except in the case of spousal rollovers.

Property transferred into a testamentary trust is deemed to have been acquired by the trust at the estate's ACB (equal to FMV) at the time of the transfer, with the exception of spousal rollovers, which is at the deceased's ACB. Future capital gains or allowable capital losses are based on the difference between the proceeds of disposition at the time the property is sold, and the property's ACB.

Property transferred from a testamentary trust to a beneficiary of the trust may be transferred to the beneficiary at the trust's ACB, and therefore rolls tax-free at the time of transfer. This does not negate tax on the capital gain but simply defers it until the beneficiary later disposes of the property. The trust could elect out of this rollover treatment. The elect-out decision would depend on the facts of the situation, including such items as the taxpayer's tax attributes, the powers of the trustee and the implications to other beneficiaries.

Multiple Trusts

Where more than one trust exists, but where a single person contributed substantially all of the property into the trusts and the income accrues for the benefit of the same beneficiary or class of beneficiaries (i.e., children, grandchildren), the Canada Revenue Agency (CRA) may group these separate trusts and treat them as a single trust. To avoid grouping of the trusts by the CRA, advance planning would involve making the trusts as distinct as possible. For example, if each trust is for the benefit of a different child, then multiple trusts may be treated separately.

ADMINISTRATIVE ISSUES

Multiple Wills

It is common for individuals to prepare multiple wills where each will deals with different property, in different jurisdictions. This type of arrangement may be undertaken to reduce the probate fees. An important consideration is to ensure that the arrangement is structured so that the existence of more than one will does not revoke any others, when each is intended to address separate issues.

Retention of a Will

Once a will is created, the original copy is quite often retained at the lawyer's office, although, with the exception of a notarial will, this is not a requirement. It is highly recommended that a copy be maintained in a safe, secure location such as a safety deposit box. The will should be safe from fire or water damage.

Updating a Will

Timing

A will should never become a static document. It should be reviewed regularly and updated to reflect changes in a testator's personal circumstances. A will is part of any estate plan and while the idea of estate planning may seem too complex for many people, a will should not be ignored. As part of the estate planning process, the will should be reviewed and updated, where appropriate, at least every two to three years and whenever there is any major change or event in the testator's life. This includes events such as:

- birth or adoption of a child;
- marriage;
- undertaking of a common-law relationship;
- separation from a spouse or common-law partner;

- receipt of an inheritance;
- death of a child;
- relocation to a new province of residence;
- if changes occur to the provincial legislation;
- illness or death of an executor or trustee named in the will; or
- illness or death of a significant beneficiary.

Codicil

A new will can be created at any time but, if only a single or few simple items need updating, this change can be accomplished through the creation of an additional document referred to as a *codicil.* The legal requirements for a valid codicil are the same as those for a will including the witnessing of the document but, in addition, the codicil must clearly refer to the will document and note that it is an amendment to it. A codicil should be retained together with the original will.

Cancelling a Will

Typically, when a new legal will is created it automatically cancels any previous will. This result needs to be carefully managed when an individual opts to use multiple wills as an integral part of his estate plan. In addition, most wills normally include a revocation clause, which is intended to clearly invalidate all previous wills.

A will may also be cancelled simply by destroying the original version, although it is also wise to destroy any copies. A signed written document, with the signature of two independent witnesses, may also be used to cancel a will but it is important that the document clearly identify the document it is intended to cancel.

In all provinces except Quebec, the will of a testator is automatically cancelled if he marries (or remarries) after the date on which a will is signed, unless the will is written in contemplation of the marriage and this is noted in the will itself. This is an important consideration and one that is not obvious to many people. In the situation where an individual has married or remarried and dies without having created a new will subsequent to the marriage, his estate will be distributed according to the rules of intestate succession.

MAX AND AUDREY

For three years Max and Audrey lived in a common-law arrangement. During that time, they prepared wills that addressed their joint circumstances and provided for each other in the event that either should die prematurely.

Two months ago, Max and Audrey were married. The wills that the couple prepared while living common-law were automatically revoked upon their marriage. In the event that either of them should die, their respective estate will be distributed according to the rules of intestate succession in the province where they reside.

Issues specific to a provincial jurisdiction may also affect the validity of a will. For example, in Ontario, a decree absolute of divorce revokes provisions in a will relative to a former spouse unless the will prescribes otherwise. The separation of a married couple residing in Ontario does not affect the terms of a will.

Unit 3
Intestate

INTRODUCTION

The word *relationship* has many meanings, but there is a clearly definitive standard that is used to define a legal connection between individuals. This unit explores this definitive standard followed by a discussion of the issues and resulting implications of an individual dying without a valid will.

RELATIONSHIPS

While individuals have the freedom to select their friends, this is not the case with relatives. Definitive standards are used to define any legal connection between relatives.

The term *descendant* refers to a person whose lineage can be traced to a particular individual. Alternatively, the term *ascendant* simply refers to the person from whom one is descended. *Consanguinity* refers to a relationship connection, by blood.

Lineal consanguinity exists between descendants where one is directly descended from another such as a mother, daughter and granddaughter. Accordingly, this relationship is also a direct ascending lineal relationship upward from granddaughter, to daughter to mother. The terms descendant and ascendant include natural children as well as adopted children, with no distinction.

AMELIA

Amelia was born in 1900 and married Aaron in 1917. Together they had three children: Alexis, Arby and Arial. As well, Amelia and Aaron adopted Ashem. In 1934, Aaron died prematurely. Amelia subsequently married Austin and together they had two children: Alison and Avril.

Alexis, the daughter of Amelia and Aaron, married Bing and together they had two children, Bob and Betty. At age 21, Bob married Carey and together they had one child: Calvin.

A direct lineal relationship exists between Amelia and her children: Alexis, Arby, Arial, Ashem, Alison and Avril.

A direct lineal relationship exists between Amelia, Alexis, Bob and Calvin. In this case, Alexis, Bob and Calvin are descendants of Amelia. Alternatively, Amelia is an ascendant to Calvin.

Figure 1 displays these relationships in pictorial terms.

Figure 1
Lineal and Collateral Relationships

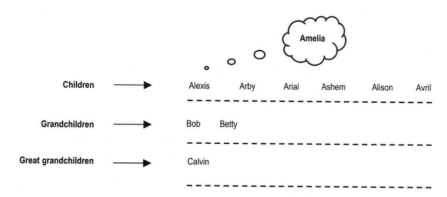

Collateral consanguinity is a phrase used to describe individuals who have a common ancestor but have descended from a different line. The concept of a tree is often used to describe collateral relatives where the relatives arise from the same root but through different branches. Examples of collateral relatives are bothers, sisters, nieces and nephews, where there is a common ancestor but there is not a direct lineage. In the Amelia SNAP, Amelia's six children are collateral relatives. Similarly, Betty and Bob (Alexis's children) are collateral relatives of Arby, Arial, Ashem, Alison and Avril because they are a niece and nephew.

There is a definitive standard for determining the degree of consanguinity between two individuals, as shown in Figure 2.

Figure 2
Consanguinity
Blood Relationships Radiating from "X"

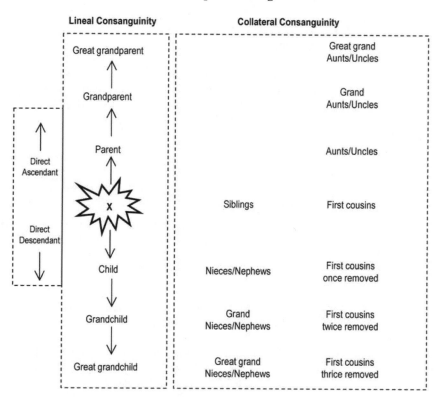

Note that the addition of the term *step* to a relationship, such as stepmother, indicates a close legal relationship due to a remarriage, but there is no blood relationship. As well, the addition of the term *in-law* to a relationship identifies a relationship connected through marriage, but it is not a blood relationship.

OVERVIEW OF INTESTACY

When the deceased does not leave a legal will, he is considered to have died *intestate.* Provincial legislation determines the distribution of the deceased's estate and simply put, the government dictates who becomes a beneficiary of the estate through very strict rules referred to as the *rules of intestacy*. An individual who does not leave a will, or whose will is determined to be invalid, is considered to have died intestate.

Each province develops and administers its own intestate legislation. For this reason, terminology, specific definitions and application of definitions may differ. The explicit details of intestate legislation, by province, are beyond the scope of this material, but it is important to understand the broad and common conceptual aspects. In addition, you are encouraged to investigate and review, on your own, legislation relative to your own provincial jurisdiction. For those who will practice in this area of financial planning, it is important to remain abreast of the topics that are relevant to your provincial jurisdiction.

A very important note relative to dying intestate is the fact that, in the past, most provinces did not necessarily recognize the common-law status under the rules of intestacy. A claim against the estate by a surviving opposite-sex common-law spouse quite often was limited to support as a dependant of the deceased, which is also covered by provincial legislation. In many provinces this remains the case; however, a number of provinces have updated or are considering changes to legislation, which provides greater rights to a common-law partner (opposite and same-sex). Much of the rapid change to legislation that is underway has been in response to court rulings that have found current laws to be unconstitutional.

In 2002, Alberta legislation came into effect that fundamentally changed how common-law partners are treated when one of the partners dies intestate. The new legislation provides that where an adult independent person lives with a partner, either of the same or opposite sex, in a conjugal relationship for more than three continuous years immediately before the death of the deceased, or in a relationship of some permanence immediately prior to death and where there is a child, by birth or adopted, the surviving partner is now entitled to share in his intestate partner's estate similar to a spouse, which is defined as a married partner.

In Alberta, if an individual dies intestate and is survived by both a spouse and an adult interdependent partner, the surviving adult interdependent partner is treated as the surviving spouse and the deceased's spouse has no role in the estate. The government of Alberta has a specific definition for the term, *relationship of interdependence.*

New legislation in Quebec became effective in 2002 that created a new institution known as a civil union. Same-sex couples now have the option of a civil union, which is intended to provide similar rights, privileges and obligations as those afforded through marriage or a *de facto* union. Upon a breakdown of the union, there is a specific process that must be followed in order to dissolve the union.

The *Common-Law Partners' Property and Related Amendments Act* (2002), made common-law partners residing in Manitoba eligible to share in the estate of a spouse who dies intestate. While it is common that individuals live together for a required period of time to be considered common-law partners, the new legislation includes a registry system in which a couple may register their relationship without the need to wait the statutory period. The process that follows upon a breakdown of the relationship differs depending upon whether the relationship was registered or unregistered.

Saskatchewan's intestate laws recognize same-sex and opposite sex common-law partners, and treat them equivalent to a surviving spouse.

Provincial laws are changing rapidly, so it is important that an advisor understand the changes and implications of the changes in their provincial jurisdiction.

DISTRIBUTION OF ESTATE

Overview

When an individual dies intestate, his estate is distributed according to the provincial laws of intestacy. The legislation typically makes reference to the word *issue*, which is normally defined as all lineal descendants, born inside and outside of marriage, as well as those adopted.

Most provinces recognize a posthumous birth under their intestate laws. Where a descendant or relative is conceived prior to the intestate's death but is born subsequent to the death, the individual is treated as if he had been born during the lifetime of the intestate and survived the intestate.

The following discussion summarizes the general strategy used for distribution of an estate, across the various provincial jurisdictions, when the deceased dies intestate (without a will). Unless otherwise noted, references in this section do not include Quebec.

In all provinces except Quebec, if the intestate dies leaving only a spouse and no children, the spouse normally is eligible to inherit the net value of the estate. Similarly, if the intestate dies leaving his children but no surviving spouse, the children are normally eligible to inherit the net value of the estate.

A common misconception is that the surviving spouse automatically inherits the full estate from the intestate. While there may be circumstances when this is true, there are many situations where this simply is not the case.

Preferential Share

Many provinces utilize the notion of a *preferential share* where a specific dollar amount of the net estate is directed first toward the surviving spouse, if one exits. If the net value of the estate is below the pre-established preferential share amount, which differs by province, the full amount of the estate passes to the surviving spouse. If the net value of the estate exceeds the preferential share amount, the surviving spouse receives the preferential share amount and then shares in the residue with the intestate's children. The age of the children is not considered, but rather eligibility to share in the estate is based simply on relationship.

The amount of the preferential share differs by province from a low of $40,000 in Alberta to a high of $200,000 in Ontario. While Manitoba utilizes a preferential share, if the intestate dies leaving a spouse and issue, and if all of the issue are also issue of the surviving spouse, the entire intestate estate goes to the surviving spouse. If, however, one or more of the intestate's issue are not also issue of the surviving spouse, then the preferential share comes into play.

Table 2 summarizes the status of each provincial jurisdiction, relative to the notion of preferential share.

Table 2
Preferential Share
Provincial Summary

	Preferential Share for Spouse	Preferential Share ($)
Alberta	Yes	First $40,000
British Columbia	Yes	First $65,000
Manitoba	Yes	Depends[1]
New Brunswick	No	
Newfoundland	No	
Northwest Territories	Yes	$50,000
Nova Scotia	Yes	First $50,000
Nunavut	Yes	$75,000
Ontario	Yes	First $200,000
Prince Edward Island	Yes	First $50,000
Quebec	No	
Saskatchewan	Yes	First $100,000
Yukon	No	

Note: (1) If there is a surviving spouse and issue, and all of the issue are also issue of the surviving spouse, the entire estate goes to the surviving spouse. If there is a surviving spouse and issue, and one or more of the issue are not also issue of the surviving spouse, the surviving spouse receives the first $50,000 plus one-half of any remainder.

Beyond Preferential Share

The net value of the estate that exceeds the preferential share is shared between the surviving spouse and the intestate's issue. Typically, the distribution between the spouse and the child(ren) is based on simple criteria:

- where there is a spouse and one child; or
- where there is a spouse and more than one child.

The residue distribution is defined by the provincial jurisdiction. Where there is one spouse and one child, the majority of the provinces provide for the net value of the estate, beyond the preferential share, to be distributed one-half to the spouse and one-half to the child, where the child's half is distributed *per stirpes* to his issue if he is predeceased.

Where there is a spouse and more than one child, the distribution between the spouse and the children (after the preferential share) differs by jurisdiction, generally with one-half to one-third going to the spouse, and the remainder going to the children in equal shares *per stirpes*. Again, the age of the children is not considered, but rather eligibility to share in the estate is based simply on relationship. In most provinces, the children's share is distributed *per stirpes*, but there are situations where the interpretation for application of *per stirpes* may vary by province.

Table 3 provides an example of how a province might prescribe the distribution of the remaining estate, after the preferential share has been distributed.

Table 3
Sample Distribution After Preferential Share

	Distribution that applies after payment of preferential share:	
	Surviving Spouse and One Child	Surviving Spouse and More Than One Child
ABC Province	• 1/2 to spouse • 1/2 to child	• 1/3 to spouse • 2/3 to children of the intestate in equal shares *per stirpes*.

• *Note:* Distribution is based on net estate value.

ADAM (1)

For purposes of this example, assume ABC province's intestate distribution provides for a preferential share of $100,000 and the remainder of the intestate estate is to be distributed according to the example in Table 3.

Adam, age 55, died suddenly. Surviving Adam are his wife Barbara and his three children Cam, Donna and Ellen. Three years before Adam's death, his eldest son, Farooq, died in a car accident, leaving his wife Shelly to raise their three young children on her own. Farooq's three children are Tom, Sara and Paul.

Unfortunately, Adam did not leave a will. The net value of Adam's estate was $600,000.

Using the intestate laws of ABC province, calculate how Adam's estate will be distributed.

⇨ Because ABC province provides for a preferential share, Barbara will be entitled to the first $100,000 of Adam's net estate value.

⇨ After allowing for payment of the preferential share to Barbara, the remaining net value of Adam's estate is $500,000. This $500,000 will be split as follows:
- $166,667 to Barbara (1/3 of $500,0000);
- $333,333 to Adam's children.

⇨ The $333,333 will be distributed *per stirpes* to Adam's children, resulting in the following payments:
- $83,333 to Cam;
- $83,333 to Donna;
- $83,333 to Ellen; and
- $83,334 to Farooq's children.

⇨ The $83,334 to Farooq's children will be distributed as follows:
- $27,778 to Tom;
- $27,778 to Sara; and
- $27,778 to Paul.

ADAM (2)

For this SNAP, let's use all of the same facts as described in the Adam (1) SNAP, except with regard to Farooq. Assume that Farooq was Adam's fourth child, but died when he was a young child so he did not have any children.

continued . . .

continued . . .

How would this change the estate distribution?

⇨   Barbara's share of Adam's estate would be unaffected by this change.

⇨   If Farooq died as a young child and left no issue, Adam's three surviving children, Cam, Donna and Ellen would share the $333,333 equally among only the three of them. This would result in payments of:

- $111,111 to Cam;
- $111,111 to Donna; and
- $111,111 to Ellen;

ADAM (3)

For this SNAP, let's use all of the same facts as described in the Adam (1) SNAP except with regard to Farooq. Assume that Farooq predeceased his father, but at the time of Farooq's death he was married to Shelly, but the couple had no children and he had no children from any other relationship.

How would this change the estate distribution?

⇨   Barbara's share of Adam's estate would be unaffected by this change.

⇨   If Farooq died without leaving any issue, Adam's three surviving children, Cam, Donna and Ellen, would share the $333,333 equally among only the three of them. This would result in payments of:

- $111,111 to Cam;
- $111,111 to Donna; and
- $111,111 to Ellen.

Shelly would not be eligible to receive any inheritance from Adam's estate.

No Preferential Share

In the provincial jurisdictions where there is no preferential share for the surviving spouse, there is a sharing arrangement similar to that discussed above, but without the spouse being allocated a favoured or preferential amount prescribed by provincial regulation. New Brunswick, Newfoundland and Yukon are examples of provinces/territories that do not utilize a preferential share.

Table 4 provides an example of how a province might prescribe the distribution of the estate, where the province does not provide for a preferential share for the surviving spouse.

Table 4
Sample Distribution in a Province with No Preferential Share

Distribution of intestate's estate:				
	Surviving Spouse Only (no issue)	**Children Only (no surviving spouse)**	**Surviving Spouse and One Child**	**Surviving Spouse and More Than One Child**
XYZ Province	• 100% to spouse	• 100% to children	• 1/2 to spouse • 1/2 to child	• 1/3 to spouse • 2/3 to children of the intestate in equal shares *per stirpes*

- *Note:* Distribution is based on net estate value.

ELLY (1)

For purposes of this example, assume XYZ province's intestate distribution follows the information outlined in Table 4.

Emily, age 45, died after a lengthy illness and is survived by her immediate family which includes:
— her 47-year-old husband Bob; and
— her two children, Thelma (age 23) and Thomas (age 25).

In addition, Thelma has a 2-year-old child, Joyce, and Thomas has four-year-old twins, Tim and Tanya.

The net value of Emily's estate is $125,000.

Using the intestate laws of XYZ province, explain how Emily's estate will be distributed.

⇨ XYZ province does not provide for a preferential share, so the distribution immediately falls to the right-hand column of Table 4. Emily's estate will be divided so that one-third of the net value of the estate ($41,666.67) goes to Bob with the remaining $83,333.33 to be distributed equally between Emily's children, Thelma and Thomas ($41,666.67 to each of them).

⇨ Since Thelma and Thomas are both living, their children will not share in the distribution of Emily's estate.

Other Heirs

Up to this point, the discussion has focused on the distribution of an estate when an intestate leaves a surviving spouse and/or children. In many situations, individuals will die and not leave a spouse or child, in which case provincial intestate legislation dictates that the estate is distributed to ascendants and collateral heirs according to a prescribed schedule unique to each provincial jurisdiction. Again, each province has the legislative authority to set the prescribed distribution schedule and while many provinces follow very similar structures, details within the structure, terminology and application may differ by province.

In all provinces, with the exception of Quebec, when the intestate dies without having left a surviving spouse or issue, the net value of the estate passes to the intestate's parents in equal shares. If there is only one surviving parent, that surviving parent inherits the full estate.

Where there is no surviving parent, in most of the provinces, the intestate's estate passes equally between the brothers and sisters of the intestate. In most provinces, children of a deceased sibling are eligible to receive their parent's share. Where there are no surviving siblings, typically nieces and nephews share equally in the estate. And, where there is no surviving niece and nephew, the estate is typically distributed equally amongst the intestate's next of kin of equal degree of consanguinity. When the estate is distributed to the next of kin, kindred is computed by counting upward from the intestate to the nearest common ancestor and then downward to the relative. For the most part, kindred of the half blood inherit equally with those of whole blood in the same degree.

Escheat

If a person dies intestate and without an heir, each province has legislation that provides for the estate to pass to the Crown through a process referred to as *escheat.*

PARTIAL INTESTATE

The situation of partial intestate may arise when an individual who has a valid will dies, but for some reason his will does not deal with the whole estate or a segment of the will is considered invalid. The part of the estate that is not disposed of by the will is distributed in accordance with the provincial *Intestacy Act.*

When partial intestacy occurs, it is typical for many jurisdictions to integrate, in some way or another, the benefits that a spouse is eligible for under the will of the deceased and the maximum entitlement the spouse is eligible to receive under the provincial intestacy rules.

APPOINTMENT OF AN ADMINISTRATOR

When an individual dies without a will, an application must be made to the courts for the appointment of an *estate administrator.* The administrator becomes responsible for the distribution of the deceased's property according to provincial intestate laws. A number of provinces have regulations associated with the posting of a bond by the administrator. Once appointed, the administrator is responsible for managing all aspects of the deceased's estate, including identification and management of all assets, payment of the deceased's debts and distribution of the estate assets in accordance with relevant provincial legislation.

The order of preference followed by the courts when appointing the estate administrator quite often follows an established norm. Assuming the candidate is appropriately suited, the order typically follows:

- spouse;
- children;
- grandchildren;
- great-grandchildren;
- parents;
- siblings; and
- grandparents.

The courts are not obliged to follow this norm, although quite often they do. Prior to the appointment of the administrator by the courts, no one has the power to transact on behalf of the estate.

Without a valid will, no one has the immediate authority to represent the estate or deal with the deceased's assets. This presents an array of concerns relative to the surviving family of the intestate. The surviving spouse does not have the authority to access bank accounts or to deal with assets held in the deceased's name. An application to the courts for the appointment of an estate administrator takes time, creates costs and could be challenged by others. An intestate estate is left in limbo until the court appointment of an administrator.

MEGAN

When Megan died this week, her spouse, Harold, thought he could automatically step into her shoes and continue running her magazine publication firm. Unfortunately, Megan died without a will and Harold now has to apply to the provincial court to become administrator of her estate.

In the meantime, Harold has come to realize that he has no authority to deal with the company bank account, suppliers or those business activities. Harold is unable to deal with any assets registered in Megan's name.

Unit 4
Probate

INTRODUCTION

Once an individual dies, there is a process of administration that is typically followed. Probate is part of this administration process.

PROCESS

Letters Probate

The process known as *probate* is a legal process undertaken, following the testator's death:

- in order to have the will of the testator declared as valid and effective by the court; and
- to have the executor named in the will formally appointed to the role.

Probate falls within provincial jurisdiction. Upon receiving satisfactory proof of the will's validity, the courts will issue a document entitled *Letters of Probate.*

Letters of Administration

The term *administration* is used to describe the process undertaken to appoint a legal representative of the deceased person when an individual dies without a valid will, when the will fails to appoint an executor or when the executor named in the will is not available to fulfill the role either by choice or because he is deceased. Administration is a legal process by which the courts provide the appointed administrator with the same legal capacity as that of an executor. The court will issue a document entitled, *Letters of Administration*, which is formal proof of the administrator's legal power to act as the legal representative of the deceased person.

Legal Representative

The phrase *legal representative* is commonly used to describe the roles of the estate executor and administrator.

Documentation

The process of probate involves the completion of an extensive series of forms and preparation of documents; seldom is an actual court appearance necessary. Included in the requirements is a complete inventory of the deceased's assets. Probate may involve the payment of fees and these fees differ by provincial jurisdiction. More importantly, the process of probate involves the loss of privacy because a probated will becomes open to public view.

Recall from earlier discussions that under Quebec civil law, a notarial will does not have to be probated because of the significant formality associated with its original creation.

PROBATABLE ASSETS

The structure under which an asset is owned plays a significant role in determining whether an asset is subject to probate. Assets that were wholly owned by the deceased or that were owned as a tenant in common are typically subject to the probate process.

When an asset is owned as tenants in common, each of the co-owners has ownership and control of his respective share of the property and, upon the death of one co-owner, the property passes through the deceased co-owner's estate.

Probate legislation in each province identifies the assets that are subject to probate, as well as the formula for calculating the value of the applicable estate subject to probate. When valuing the estate for purposes of probate, some provinces exclude specific assets, such as personal property or real estate owned outside of the province of residence. These definitions differ by province.

FEES

There may be a fee levied on the estate by the provincial court that grants the letters probate. Each provincial jurisdiction establishes:

- their applicable fee schedule; and
- the rules as to how the estate assets are valued relative to the application of any applicable probate fees.

The data shown in Appendix Two provides an overview of provincial probate fees. Ontario and British Columbia have the highest fee schedules, while Alberta's schedule is quite minimal.

PROBATE PLANNING

Confidentiality

The process of probate exposes the deceased's will to public view, resulting in the loss of personal and family privacy. This result is often a driving force for some individuals to structure their personal affairs in a manner that minimizes the amount of information that needs to be revealed through their will. The process of estate planning provides the opportunity to consider a variety of probate planning opportunities, and thereby reduces exposure of the estate to public scrutiny.

Probate planning techniques that achieve a greater degree of confidentiality include:

- the use of an *inter vivos* trust because the assets do not form part of the deceased's estate;
- select use of named beneficiary designations; and
- appropriate use of joint title with the right of survivorship for asset ownership.

Cost versus Benefit

While some people view the cost of probate as expensive, this cost should not be the primary motivation that influences decisions a testator makes relative to the distribution of his estate. An even more important reason individuals wish to avoid probate often involves the loss of personal privacy.

Avoiding probate fees may be a valid consideration in any estate planning decision, but it should be only one of a number of factors considered when structuring any plan.

Developing the Plan

The organization of an individual's estate plan should reflect important issues, including the testator's wishes, estate planning objectives, pre- and post-mortem considerations relative to asset control, implications of asset disposition, and testamentary intentions.

- **Wishes** — The individual's personal wishes should be fully explored and used to develop objectives for the estate plan that become the benchmark against which decisions are tested and assessed.
- **Objectives** — The objectives of the estate plan must be a primary consideration to ensure the chosen structure is designed to reflect the individual's desired outcome for estate distribution.

- **Asset control considerations** — While the planning objectives are a priority, the ultimate plan should not inadvertently infringe upon the issues or needs of the individual during his lifetime. This is a very important consideration because there are estate decisions and structures that may appear valid under the immediate circumstances, but which could infringe on the individual's lifestyle or cause the loss of control, either unknowingly or perhaps because of changing circumstances. The estate should be structured to withstand the test of time and the changes that can occur within a family and within an individual's personal circumstances.

- **Disposition** — Does the probate plan cause a deemed disposition of the asset during the individual's lifetime and, if so, what is the cost? Does the individual understand the implications of a deemed disposition? Does he have the liquidity to handle the resulting tax consequences? Does the disposition fit with his long-term intentions for the asset?

- **Testamentary intentions** — It should be easy to identify the individual's testamentary intentions when reviewing the overall estate plan. The plan should be well structured so changes to circumstances within the individual's personal life or within the life of the beneficiaries or other family members will not cause the estate plan to unwittingly fall offside. While an estate plan needs to be dynamic and updated as personal circumstances change, how bulletproof is the plan relative to unplanned changes? For example, the movement of an asset from a parent's single ownership into joint title with right of survivorship, between a parent and child, could expose the asset to potential issues relative to divorce, creditors or the death of a joint owner.

Influence of Residency

If an individual's sole objective is to minimize probate fees, one strategy is to relocate to a province with a modest probate schedule. For example, Alberta's $400 maximum means that the upper limit an individual will pay is $400. Alternatively, if the individual resides in Quebec and completes a notarial will, his estate would not be subject to probate.

Multiple Wills

A growing number of individuals are beginning to use the concept of multiple wills. Multiple wills are commonly used as a convenience for individuals who maintain assets in different jurisdictions. The testator simply completes an original will for each jurisdiction in which he owns assets; and when the testator dies, the will is easily submitted to the appropriate court without any dependency on the other will(s). There may be some complexity to ensure that the strategy is created to meet the needs of each jurisdiction and that one will does not inadvertently revoke another. This type of strategy should involve a testator working with a professional advisor who specializes in this field.

The types of issues that need to be carefully managed include:

- The assets of each will should be clearly identified and worded so that the will deals only with those assets within the specific jurisdiction.

- One will should not inadvertently revoke the other.

- Each will should be drafted to meet the unique rules of the specific jurisdiction, including powers of the trustee.

- Appropriate wording should be used in each of the wills relative to the payment of debts, so that it is clear as to which will takes the primary role or how this issue is addressed across the multiple wills.

- If a legacy is dealt with in only one will, there should be sufficient liquid assets available to address the legacy.

Non-Probate Assets

Assets that do not form part of the deceased's estate are not subject to probate. In addition to the financial savings that may arise because of the reduced size of the estate subject to probate fees, non-probate assets are not open to public view.

Joint Tenancy

Assets held in joint tenancy with the right of survivorship are considered non-probate assets. Each of the joint tenants has an equal, undivided interest in the whole property, but before using this strategy as a means to avoid probate, the implications need to be considered. It is unwise to transfer assets into joint tenancy with the right of survivorship simply to avoid probate. Such a strategy can be fraught with disaster. Prior to undertaking a transfer of an asset into joint tenancy, an individual should truly understand and assess the implications relative to the benefits.

Ownership transfer of an asset from single to joint ownership with the right of survivorship:

- creates potential income tax consequences and can trigger an immediate tax liability;
- exposes the property to potential creditors and family law claims of the new joint owner;
- could disrupt the flow of the property relative to the original intentions; and
- could trigger implications relative to provincial legislation (i.e., matrimonial home to someone other than a spouse in the province of Ontario).

Property transferred from sole ownership to ownership as a joint tenant triggers a disposition and resulting tax consequences (with the exception of spousal rollovers).

DAVID

Seventy-six-year-old David owns a family cottage that was acquired in 1988 at a cost of $45,000. The cottage has a current market value of $345,000. David is considering the transfer of ownership of the cottage into joint title with his two adult daughters, Tina and Tammy, as he feels it would save him probate fees and reduce the amount of work required at the time of his death.

The value of David's home has grown substantially since it was first purchased, and the plan is to use the principal residence exemption to offset the gain on the home.

What financial consequence should David consider before changing the ownership structure?

If David transfers ownership of the cottage into joint tenancy with himself, Tina and Tammy, he will trigger a capital gain that must be accounted for at the time of transfer. In this case, David is transferring two-thirds of the property so he will trigger $66\frac{2}{3}$% of the gain. The outcome is a taxable capital gain of $100,000, calculated as $66\frac{2}{3}$% × (($345,000 - $45,000) × 50%).

While David may be able to utilize the principal residence exemption to offset some or all of the gain, he still incurs a taxable capital gain, which must be reported.

This type of change should consider the question: Does David understand the financial consequence of this change in ownership; and, if so, does he have the financial means and liquidity to meet the tax liability that arises?

What other issues should David consider before changing the ownership structure?

Once David makes the transfer, he loses the ability to control the asset. David will require both of his daughters to sign any documents in respect of legal decisions related to the cottage.

Named Beneficiary

The use of named beneficiary designations can be valuable in structuring circumstances where assets pass directly to the beneficiary and do not form part of the deceased's estate. For example, this type of approach can be used for registered assets such as Registered Retirement Savings Plans (RRSP), Registered Retirement Income Funds (RRIF) and registered pension assets. As well, life insurance and segregated fund policies can also be structured to accomplish a similar outcome.

TONY

Tony was the owner and life insured of two life insurance policies. Policy #1 provided a death benefit of $1 million with Tony's estate named as policy beneficiary. Policy #2 had a $500,000 death benefit and Tony's spouse, Eleanor, was named as beneficiary. Eleanor was the sole beneficiary of Tony's will.

Upon Tony's death, Eleanor received the $500,000 of benefit proceeds directly from the insurance carrier, and the proceeds did not pass through Tony's estate. As such, the $500,000 did not attract any probate fees.

The insurance company paid the $1 million of proceeds from Policy #1, $1 million death benefit, directly to Tony's estate and it therefore was subject to probate fees.

Other

The use of successive owners for life insurance and segregated fund policies are examples of other strategies that can be effective for purposes of probate planning.

For example, if the life insured and owner of a life insurance policy differ, the death of the policy owner will not trigger payment of the death benefit proceeds, but instead the policy remains a valid asset of the owner. By naming a successive owner the policy can pass to the new owner without becoming an asset of the deceased's estate. Without a successive owner, the policy becomes an asset of the estate, is subject to probate and is dealt with through the deceased's will.

This same life insurance policy could be rolled to the spouse on a rollover basis, thereby deferring any immediate tax consequence. This outcome is possible provided the spouse is named as a successor owner or where the policy passes to the spouse through a bequest in the will. By using the successor owner route, the policy does not form part of the deceased's estate and can pass to the spouse without attracting probate.

Similar outcomes are possible in the structuring of a segregated fund policy, as discussed in Module 16.

An *inter vivos* trust is another means by which an individual can use advance planning to minimize probate concerns, and is discussed in Unit 5, "Wills Substitutes".

APPLICATION

TERRI

Sixty-year-old Terri is a recent widow who is in the process of reviewing her personal estate plan, following the recent death of her husband.

Terri has a monthly income flow of $3,000 per month that consists of government benefit programs and registered pension benefits. Terri's deceased husband owned a life insurance policy on Terri's life with a face value of $350,000, which has now passed to Terri as the successor owner. The beneficiary of the policy is listed as Terri's estate. As well, Terri's estate is listed as the beneficiary of her RRSP.

Terri owns the following assets, all registered in her name.

⇨ $245,000 — personal residence
⇨ $350,000 — cottage
⇨ $100,000 — bond portfolio (non-registered)
⇨ $150,000 — stock portfolio (non-registered)
⇨ $350,000 — RRSP assets
⇨ $50,000 — personal assets including home furnishings, etc.
⇨ $50,000 — vehicle

continued . . .

---

continued . . .

The adjusted cost base (ACB) of select assets is as follows:

- ⇨ $83,000 — personal residence
- ⇨ $180,000 — cottage
- ⇨ $72,000 — bond portfolio (non-registered)
- ⇨ $48,000 — stock portfolio (non-registered)

Terri is very young at heart and has longevity in her family, so she expects to live for many more years. With three single children, ages 23, 34 and 35, Terri wants to ensure that each of the children inherit equally and should one of her children predecease her, she wants the remaining children to share equally. In addition, Terri would like to structure her estate to minimize any costs associated with probate but in doing so she does not want to expose herself or her estate to any long-term issues.

Terri lives in ABC province where the probate schedule is:

- ⇨ $6.00 per $1,000 for the first $50,000; and
- ⇨ $12.00 per $1,000 or part thereof on the value that exceeds $50,000,

where probate applies to the gross value of the estate and includes all personal property and all Canadian real estate holdings.

1. Under the current ownership structure, which of Terri's assets are subject to probate?

All of the following assets are typically subject to probate:

- ⇨ $245,000 — personal residence
- ⇨ $350,000 — cottage
- ⇨ $100,000 — bond portfolio (non-registered)
- ⇨ $150,000 — stock portfolio (non-registered)
- ⇨ $350,000 — RRSP assets
- ⇨ $50,000 — personal assets including home furnishings, etc.
- ⇨ $350,000 — insurance
- ⇨ $50,000 — vehicle

TOTAL $1,645,000

2. How might Terri quite easily restructure her estate using named beneficiaries?

Terri could name her three children as beneficiaries to her life insurance policy and her RRSP assets. The three children could be named as equal beneficiaries.

3. If Terri names the three children as beneficiaries of her life insurance policy and RRSP, how does this impact the assets typically subject to probate?

By naming the children as beneficiaries of the life insurance and RRSP, the proceeds from these assets will pass directly to the children in equal shares upon Terri's death. The proceeds would not form part of Terri's estate and, as such, would not be subject to probate.

4. What implications, if any, should Terri be cognizant of when using the strategy of naming a beneficiary?

While the strategy of using a named beneficiary is a valid estate planning strategy, Terri should fully understand that the estate would be subject to any income tax consequences that result from the disposition of the asset upon her death.

For example, while the three children would receive the proceeds of her RRSP assets, $116,666.67 each ($350,000 ÷ 3), the estate faces a potential tax bill of approximately $157,500 (45% × $350,000, where the 45% represents Terri's marginal tax rate, at the time of her death).

In Terri's case, she has a substantial pool of assets, which would quite easily cover the tax consequences associated with the disposition of the RRSP. However, Terri should be aware of this consequence relative to the total estate plan.

5. Terri has three children and three significant assets — the cottage, a RRSP and a life insurance policy — that are each individually worth $350,000. Since one of the children would like the cottage and the other two have no interest in the cottage, what are the implications of naming one child as the beneficiary of the life insurance policy, a second child as the beneficiary of the RRSP, and bequeathing the cottage to the third child through the will?

As discussed in number four above, the estate is subject to any income tax consequences that result from the disposition of the assets upon Terri's death. In addition to the tax bill of approximately $157,500 associated with the RRSP, the estate will be faced with the tax consequences associated with the disposition of all assets owned by Terri.

continued . . .

continued . . .

Terri is single, so there is no opportunity for the rollover of any assets in order to minimize the income tax consequences upon Terri's death. Many of her assets will trigger tax consequences upon her death. For example, the bond and stock portfolio could trigger a combined capital gain of $130,000 (bond $28,000 and stock $102,000). This represents a taxable capital gain of $65,000 (50% × $130,000) and tax of about $29,250. This $29,250 of tax combined with the $157,500 tax liability on Terri's RRSP, means a potential tax bill of $186,750.

Next, there is a capital gain triggered either through the cottage or principal residence, depending upon how the principal residence exemption is applied.

The calculation of potential income taxes is critical to the overall estate plan, because if Terri leaves bequests of the life insurance to one child and the RRSP to another child, they will each receive property valued at $350,000. However, there is the potential that the estate may not have sufficient assets remaining to cover the required income tax consequences without cutting into the value of the cottage.

6. Assuming that Terri lives in ABC Province and using the probate schedule information outlined earlier, calculate Terri's cost of probate based on the facts outlined in the original case and compare with the cost of probate assuming that Terri utilizes a named beneficiary strategy on the life insurance policy and RRSP.

Based on the facts of the case, the total value of Terri's assets is $1,645,000 (personal residence, cottage, bond portfolio, stock portfolio, RRSP assets, personal assets, and new vehicle). In ABC Province the cost of probate is $19,440, derived as follows:

$300 ($6 × $50,000 ÷ 1,000)

plus

$19,140 ($12 × (($1,645,000 - $50,000) ÷ 1,000))

equals

$19,440

By naming the children as beneficiaries of the life insurance policy and RRSP, the gross value of the estate is reduced by $700,000 to $945,000, resulting in probate costs of $11,040, derived as follows:

$300 ($6 × 50)

plus

$10,740 ($12 × (($945,000 - $50,000) ÷ 1,000))

equals

$11,040

The estate saves $8,400 in probate fees if Terri utilizes a named beneficiary for the RRSP and life insurance.

7. What is the implication for Terri if she were to move some of her assets into joint ownership with the right of survivorship?

While the transfer of select assets into joint ownership with the right of survivorship could reduce the cost of probate for Terri's estate, there are broad implications to this strategy that should be carefully explored.

The RRSP cannot be moved to joint tenants because the owner and annuitant must be the same. The transfer of the home, cottage or investment assets into joint tenants would trigger a deemed disposition, creating immediate tax consequences. Does Terri want to pay the tax now and, if so, does she have sufficient liquidity to fund the required payment?

Changing ownership of the assets would directly impact Terri during her lifetime because she would require permission of the joint owner in order to sell or dispose of the asset. With an annual income of $36,000, it is likely that Terri will want to access capital over the remainder of her lifetime. Assets owned as joint tenants can only be disposed of with the permission of all owners.

If Terri's personal circumstances should change and she should want to remove one of the children as a joint owner, she could not do so without that joint owner's permission.

The jointly owned asset will become exposed to the creditors of the joint owners, and should one of her children incur a liability, the debtor could potentially access the jointly owned asset to satisfy the debt. In addition, the jointly owned asset could become exposed to family law issues should the joint owner marry or enter a common-law relationship or have a child.

Unit 5
Will Substitutes

INTRODUCTION

There are a variety of estate planning strategies that can serve as a substitute to a will, allowing an individual to do much of what he wants without the asset having to pass through his estate. Through advance planning, an individual has the opportunity to assess the pros and cons of the various strategies relative to his personal circumstances and estate objectives. This section takes a further look at the concept of joint tenancy with the right of survivorship, followed by a review of a named-beneficiary strategy. The concept of *inter vivos* trusts is explored and builds on information from earlier modules.

JOINT TENANCY OWNERSHIP

Ownership as joint tenants is created only through an express agreement. This type of ownership is unique because of the right of survivorship. The death of one of the joint tenants causes the deceased tenant's share to pass immediately upon death to the surviving tenant. The deceased tenant's share does not pass to his estate nor is it governed by his will.

Property owned through joint tenancy automatically passes to the surviving co-tenant(s) in equal shares under the right of survivorship when a co-owner dies and the property does not become part of the deceased's estate. A joint tenant cannot sever his share of a piece of property through his will because property held as joint tenants passes automatically to the surviving joint tenant(s) and does not come under the administration of the estate. This approach is considered a valid strategy that allows the deceased's share of a piece of property to pass to a surviving owner without passing through probate. The use of joint ownership is a commonly used strategy for married couples, particularly when assets are to pass to the surviving spouse.

Before implementing a joint tenancy strategy, an individual should understand the pre- and post-mortem implications, many of which were discussed in the previous unit.

When property is owned as joint tenants, it is subject to the creditors of any of the joint tenants. For example, if a married couple own a cottage as joint tenants and the creditors of one of the spouses seeks restitution for a debt owed, the creditor could take the entire property to satisfy the judgment. If a parent transfers his home to joint tenancy with a child, that child's spouse could potentially include the home as part of a divorce or family law claim. As well, the creditors of that child could use the home as an asset to satisfy a judgement against the child. Joint ownership creates vulnerability that needs to be carefully assessed prior to any structural changes.

Upon the death of one of the joint tenants, the asset passes automatically and with that ownership transfer, the surviving tenant attains full control of the asset. The surviving tenant has full control of the property and is under no obligation to provide for the heirs of the deceased tenant.

ADAM AND BOB

Adult brothers, Adam and Bob, inherited their parent's cottage just three months ago and now own it as joint tenants with the right of survivorship.

After a courageous battle with cancer, Bob died this past week. Ownership of the cottage passes automatically to Adam without passing through Bob's estate. The cottage does not form part of Bob's estate and Bob's family has no say or ownership in the property.

BENEFICIARY DESIGNATIONS

Using a named beneficiary designation can be a useful strategy to:

- eliminate issues that can arise due to probate;
- ensure that the deceased's testamentary wishes are fulfilled; and
- minimize the possibility of substantial assets becoming caught in lengthy delays brought about by challenges to the will.

However, there are circumstances when it makes good planning sense to have the asset flow into the estate rather than using a named beneficiary approach. For example, when an estate needs liquidity to fund debt and tax liabilities or to address immediate financial needs it can be quite appropriate and is advisable to ensure that sufficient liquid assets move directly into the estate.

When using a named beneficiary strategy, the asset owner needs to be aware of any changes that could impact the designation or circumvent the owner's intended wishes. Many times, individuals do not connect the naming of a beneficiary as part of their estate plan, so beneficiary designations on policies are often overlooked when a regular estate review is undertaken. The owner should be conscious of any beneficiary designation and respond to a triggering event that may impact his wishes.

If a named beneficiary predeceases the asset owner, does the policy have a successor beneficiary named under the policy? If the named beneficiary predeceases the owner and there is no living successor beneficiary named in the policy, the assets will form part of the asset owner's estate when he dies.

If the asset owner wants to leave the asset to his children, does the designation need updating with the arrival of a new child? If the asset owner has divorced and intends for the proceeds to pass to someone other than his former spouse, has the beneficiary designation been updated to make this change? It is not unusual to find one or both parties who have divorced still have the ex-spouse appearing as the named beneficiary on an asset, when this is not the spouse's intention. A separation or divorce does not automatically sever a named beneficiary designation on a life insurance policy or RRSP.

While the annuitant of a registered retirement savings plan (RRSP) or registered retirement income fund (RRIF) has the ability to name a beneficiary on his plans, the implications to his estate should be carefully considered as part of the overall estate plan.

SIGFRID

Fifty-six-year-old Sigfrid is a widower with two adult children, Yoshi and Willis. Yoshi is located in British Columbia while Willis resides in Ontario. Sigfrid has only two major assets: a RRSP with a current value of $100,000 and GICs valued at $110,000.

For simplicity, Sigfrid has structured his estate plan to provide what he estimates as $100,000 to Willis and a similar amount to Yoshi.

⇨   Sigfrid names Yoshi as the beneficiary of the RRSP. Upon Sigfrid's death, the RRSP proceeds will pass directly to Yoshi, as the named beneficiary of the policy.

⇨   Sigfrid names Willis as the only beneficiary of his estate, which he estimates to be $110,000 of GIC assets.

continued . . .

---

continued . . .

Because the GICs will pass through probate, Sigfrid feels the extra $10,000 in the GIC will offset any probate fees and, for the most part, the two children will receive an equal inheritance.

While Sigfrid feels he has created a fair and equal distribution of his estate, this is not the case.

The estate will have an income tax liability based on the value of the RRSP. This means that the GIC that passes through the estate will have to fund this tax liability, leaving Willis with an amount substantially less than the $100,000 Sigfrid anticipated.

INTER VIVOS TRUSTS

Uses of an Inter Vivos Trust

Instead of leaving an estate at the time of death, some individuals opt to make a transfer of assets into a trust during their lifetime. Use of an *inter vivos* trust can be beneficial if there is a threat of the will being challenged by an heir or non-heir. When trusts are established during the settlor's lifetime, they are referred to as an *inter vivos* trust. A transfer of assets into a trust provides the settlor with the opportunity to establish the terms of the trust in the trust document, thereby allowing some measure of control. Use of an *inter vivos* trust provides the settlor with flexibility over the timing and quantity of assets distributed to the trust's beneficiaries.

The use of trusts in an estate planning engagement may appear to increase the complexity of the plan; but should not be overlooked as a valid and increasingly common mechanism for asset management prior to an individual's death. An *inter vivos* trust is not a separate legal entity but is treated by the *Income Tax Act* (the "Act") as a taxpayer and, therefore, is required to file a separate annual income tax return.

The following is an overview of how an *inter vivos* trust may be used as an integral element of an individual's estate plan.

- An *inter vivos* trust can be established in advance of a parent's death in anticipation of providing for the maintenance and financial well-being of children in a wide variety of circumstances. For example, an *inter vivos* trust could be used to provide for children from a previous marriage; or to ensure for the financial care of a disabled child.
- An *inter vivos* trust can be established for the benefit of a spouse or common-law partner, or ex-spouse or ex-common-law partner.
- The use of a trust can provide for the maintenance and financial well-being of elderly family members.
- A trust can be valuable for retaining control of business interests.
- Trusts can be established to maintain and administer a cottage or vacation property for the benefit of future generations.
- The only reporting requirement for an *inter vivos* trust is with the CRA, so there is a significant element of privacy associated with the use of a trust. For this reason, trusts are commonly used to ensure privacy in the estate planning process and the distribution of assets. A trust offers privacy and confidentiality in moving assets because trust documents have no public accountability, except in tax reporting to the CRA.
- In some circumstances, trusts can enhance creditor protection of assets.

Establishing an *inter vivos* trust can eliminate concerns associated with succession provisions that may arise from the use of wills and the public process of probate.

Donatio Mortis Causa

A unique form of an *inter vivos* transfer is one referred to as a *donatio mortis causa*, whereby a seriously ill person, who anticipates that his death is near or pending, gives a gift to an individual, conditional upon his death. The legacy resulting from a *donatio mortis causa* is incomplete during the ill person's lifetime, and as such remains revocable.

To constitute a valid *donatio mortis causa*, the gift must be:

- of personal property, and not real property such as real estate;
- made by the donor in peril of death; and
- is only complete if death should occur as a result of an impending illness.

TREVOR

Trevor and his long-term girl friend, Sherri, were backpacking across Canada when Trevor stumbled and fell several hundred feet into a ravine near their campsite. Trevor was rushed to the hospital with life-threatening injuries.

With Sherri by his side, Trevor realized that he would likely succumb to his injuries so he told Sherri that if he did not survive, he wanted her to have his rare baseball card collection.

This type of gift from Trevor to Sherri is referred to as a *donatio mortis causa* because it was made while Trevor was near death, was contingent on his death, involved personal not real property, and ownership of the property would not change hands unless Trevor succumbed to his injuries resulting from the fall.

If Trevor succumbs to his injuries from this accident, the rare baseball card collection becomes Sherri's and does not form part of his estate.

If Trevor does not succumb to his injuries from this accident, he retains ownership of the baseball cards and there is no further pending gift. Should he later die, from causes unrelated to the accident, Sherri would not be entitled to the baseball cards.

As an *inter vivos* transfer, a *donatio mortis causa* gift does not form part of the deceased's estate, so is not subject to probate fees.

Taxation

Income

Inter vivos trusts are taxed at a rate equal to the top marginal tax rate (federal and provincial combined). This is an important distinction between a testamentary and *inter vivos* trust. This high level of taxation can be a deterrent for individuals when considering the use of an *inter vivos* trust as an estate planning strategy. However, these costs need to be offset against the estate planning benefits derived from the use of trusts. A cost-benefit analysis typically is not simply a numerical calculation but involves a broad assortment of softer, non-quantifiable benefits.

Property Transfers

For property transferred into an *inter vivos* trust, there is a deemed disposition of the property by the settlor of the trust at the time that the property is transferred. Therefore, the settlor will realize any accrued capital gain with the result of a possible income tax liability. There are a few exceptions to this rule, as outlined in the following paragraph.

Transfers to a spousal or common-law partner trust are deemed to have occurred at the settlor's ACB, resulting in a tax-deferred transaction. Property transfers into an *alter ego* or joint partner trust are also deemed to have occurred at the settlor's ACB, therefore deferring the realization of any accrued capital gain. The settlor of any of these types of trusts has the opportunity to elect out of the rollover.

Property transferred from an *inter vivos* trust to a beneficiary of the trust may be transferred to the beneficiary at the trust's adjusted cost base, so therefore the asset rolls tax-free at the time of transfer. This does not negate tax on the capital gain but simply defers it until the beneficiary later disposes of the property.

A disposition of property will occur where property is sold or disposed of by the trust and not rolled to a beneficiary of the trust. If the trust incurs a capital gain or allowable capital loss, the trustees could allocate the capital gain to a beneficiary or choose to retain the gain/loss on its tax return.

Deemed Disposition

A deemed disposition of the trust's capital property will occur every 21 years starting 21 years after the trust was initially settled. This deemed disposition needs to be taken into consideration when the trust is designed in order to ensure that the cash flow required to fund the resulting income tax liability has been appropriately taken into consideration.

Income Attribution

When a trust is established as revocable, the *Income Tax Act* disallows certain tax provisions that are otherwise available to an irrevocable trust. With a revocable trust:

- all income and capital gains is taxed to the settlor; and

- the tax-free roll-out to beneficiaries, other than the settlor, is denied.

If the settlor is one of the discretionary capital beneficiaries of an irrevocable trust, the trust is viewed as a revocable trust for tax purposes. While there is a loss of certain tax preferences, the structure achieves other non-tax objectives, including isolating the assets outside of an individual's estate holdings so that the assets would not be subject to probate.

ALEX

Alex considers himself fairly well off but not rich. He really wants his children and grandchild to benefit from the assets that he has accumulated, while still retaining full control of the assets during his lifetime. Alex did not want the bulk of his assets to pass through his estate, so he began to consider what arrangements could be made during his lifetime to address these two issues.

Alex decided to establish a discretionary trust with a settlement of $3,000,000. He named himself along with his adult children as the income and capital beneficiaries, and himself a sole trustee.

In this situation, the trust would be considered a revocable trust because the capital of the trust could revert to Alex. As such, all income and capital gain from the trust is attributable to Alex during his lifetime. Upon Alex's death, the assets would not form part of his estate and would be distributed based on instructions in the trust indenture.

Special Trusts

Two types of *inter vivos* trusts that are eligible for special tax treatment are an *alter ego* trust and a joint partner trust. Transfers of property to a trust typically constitute a disposition of property at fair market value, which triggers the realization of any accrued capital gain and ultimately creates a tax liability. Of course, an exception to this rule is the rollover of property to a spousal trust. The concept of an *alter ego* trust and joint partner trust is an extension of the exception to this disposition rule.

Alter Ego Trust

Using an *alter ego trust*, an individual can transfer capital property to a trust without the transfer being considered a disposition at the fair market value for tax purposes. Disposition will be deemed to take place upon the death of the transferor of the trust, at the property's fair market value at that time. In addition, the sale of an asset by the trust will cause a disposition. To qualify as an *alter ego* trust, all of the following conditions must be met:

- the transferor has to be at least age 65 at the time of the trust's creation;
- the trust must be created after 1999;
- only the transferor is entitled to all of the trust income during the transferor's lifetime; and
- no other person is entitled to the capital of the trust during the transferor's lifetime.

A trust that meets these criteria may elect out of the *alter ego* designation by filing an election with the trust's first tax return.

Joint Partner Trust

Specific to spousal situations, a *joint partner trust* can be established by an individual for his personal benefit plus that of his spouse (including a common-law spouse). The property contributed to such a trust will be permitted a tax-free rollover, thereby deferring the realization of any accrued capital gain until the disposition of an asset by the trust or the death of the second of the two spouses.

To qualify as a joint partner trust, all of the following conditions must be met:

- the transferor must be at least age 65 when the trust is created (the age of the spouse is not taken into consideration);
- the trust must be created after 1999;
- only the transferor and his/her spouse are entitled to all of the trust income (but note that attribution rules will continue to apply to the income); and
- no other person is entitled to the capital of the trust during the transferor's or the spouse's lifetime.

A trust that meets these criteria may elect out of the joint partner designation by filing an election with the trust's first tax return.

Taxation of Alter Ego or Joint Partner Trust

When an *inter vivos* transfer of property takes place from a taxpayer to an *alter ego* or joint partner trust, the rollover provision applies automatically unless the taxpayer specifically elects to opt out of the rollover provision.

The tax consequences of the rollover provision are:

- the transferor is deemed to have disposed of the property at its adjusted cost base or undepreciated capital cost in the case of depreciable property; and
- the trust that acquires the property assumes the taxpayer's adjusted cost base for the property.

The rollover treatment results in no capital gain or loss for the transferring spouse on the disposition of the property. The receiving trust takes ownership of the property, assuming the taxpayer's adjusted cost base on the property and tax on the capital gain is deferred until the trust disposes of the property at some time in the future. The capital gain is not eliminated, but rather tax on the capital gain is deferred into the future.

It is important to note that while this rollover provision exists, attribution rules take precedence and could preclude a rollover if the attribution rules are not followed. In addition, it is important to note that while a rollover can occur relative to the capital property, income attribution rules will continue to apply to the property transferred through rollover.

If the taxpayer specifically elects out of the rollover provision, the tax treatment on the property follows the basic capital gains process with capital gains treatment.

Tax planning considers the economic results of opting out of the provision compared with the results of the rollover. Some situations where opting out may be more economically viable include:

- the transfer of property at fair market value to eliminate continued income attribution;
- if the taxpayer has a current capital loss or a capital loss carryforward, triggering a capital gain at the time of transfer could permit an offset; or
- the taxpayer may have a capital gain exemption under which the gain can be sheltered.

Spousal or Common-Law Partner Trust

An *inter vivos* "spousal" or "common-law partner trust" is one established by a spouse, during his lifetime and where the beneficiary spouse or common-law partner is entitled to receive all income that may arise during his/her lifetime and is the only person who can receive or access use of any income or capital of the trust during his/her lifetime.

In addition, the settlor and the beneficiary must both be residents of Canada in order for the transfer to take place on a rollover basis, and the property must vest indefeasibly, as discussed in other sections of this module.

Living or Family Trust

A common use of an *inter vivos* trust is to create what is quite often referred to as a *living trust* or *family trust*. There is no magic to the terms living trust or family trust, as it is simply an *inter vivos* trust. Quite often it is a revocable trust, which is created by the settlor who is often named as the trustee. Through the structure of the trust document and by naming himself as trustee, the settlor can retain control over the assets during his lifetime.

The non-public nature of an *inter vivos* trust is a definite attraction to many people, because it avoids the necessity of assets passing through probate and allows for the retention of complete privacy because there are no documents open to public view.

The trust documents can be drafted to provide the settlor with exclusive rights to the assets placed in the trust, and upon his death the assets pass directly to the individuals named as beneficiaries of the trust without passing through the estate. This type of arrangement can be beneficial when the beneficiaries are below the age of majority, as the trust can establish the provisions under which the assets will be held and managed until such time as the trust provides for the assets to be distributed to the beneficiaries.

Unit 6
Taxation

INTRODUCTION

The final personal income tax return (T1) filed for a deceased taxpayer is commonly referred to as a *final* or *terminal* income tax return. When a taxpayer dies, it causes an immediate year-end for tax purposes where the final or terminal return covers the period beginning January 1 in the taxpayer's year of death up to and including the taxpayer's date of death. The final return is required and not optional. The estate reports income earned after the date of death.

Recall from Modules 5 and 6 that death causes a deemed disposition relative to capital property owned by the deceased taxpayer. Any taxable income resulting from this deemed disposition that does not pass through an eligible rollover is included in the deceased's final return along with regular income. As well, the final return would include any applicable recapture of capital cost allowance (CCA) that arises from the deemed disposition of depreciable property.

In addition to a final return, there is the opportunity to elect to file three additional returns on behalf of the deceased. The elective returns allow for specific types of income to be reported through separate income tax returns. If the elective return is not filed, the income that would otherwise be reported is reported on the terminal return. The typical reason to opt for the filing of additional returns, where possible, is to lower the marginal tax rate associated with the relevant income, increase access to multiple tax credits or to better use tax credits that might otherwise be lost (i.e., medical tax credit).

The three elective returns are associated with income related to:

- rights or things;
- proprietor or partnership business income; and
- a testamentary trust.

The discussion in this unit assumes you have a good understanding of Canadian income tax law.

ELECTIVE RETURNS

Rights or Things Income

Income which was owed to the deceased but not paid at the time of his death, and which would have been included in his income had he not died, can be reported on a *rights or things return*. If an election is made to file a rights or things return, then all income that falls into the rights or things category must be reported on that return; there is no option to split the income between the rights or things return and the final return.

Income included on a rights or things return can be divided into:

- employment rights or things; and
- other rights or things.

Employment rights or things include moneys owing from the employer to the deceased employee such as commissions, salary, vacation pay and retirement allowance. These types of employment income can be reported on the rights and things return provided that the income was owed to the deceased on the date of death and it is for a pay period that ends prior to the date of death.

Income that falls within the other rights or things category includes items such as:

- uncashed matured bonds;
- bond interest payable that was earned up to a period prior to death but not yet paid or reported in a prior year;

- declared and unpaid dividends, if the ex-dividend date (or date of record if no ex-dividend date) is prior to the date of death; and

- Old Age Security benefits due and payable on a date prior to the deceased's death.

The rights or things return **cannot** include items such as:

- income from registered retirement plans such as a RRSP or RRIF;

- period accumulations such as bank account interest;

- bond interest accumulated between the last payment date prior to the deceased's death and the date of death; or

- capital property and eligible capital property.

The income tax liability for items that fall within the rights or things return may be transferred to a beneficiary within the time frame permitted for filing a return for rights or things. The beneficiary then becomes responsible for reporting the income on his personal income tax return for any amounts transferred from the rights or things. A partial transfer of rights or things income to a beneficiary is possible.

When filing a rights or things return, full personal tax credits may be claimed on this return. This includes medical expenses and charitable donations, provided that the amounts have not been claimed on other returns.

MAHOOD (1)

Upon Mahood's premature death, he was entitled to a $15,000 dividend that was declared by the private company that he owned. The $15,000 dividend was declared, yet not payable at the time of Mahood's death.

The $15,000 dividend can be declared on a separate rights or things tax return. As an eligible dividend, the $15,000 would be grossed up to create a taxable dividend and Mahood would be entitled to federal and provincial tax credits.

If this were Mahood's only item on the rights or things return, there would likely be no tax liability because of Mahood's ability to declare the non-refundable personal tax credit.

Mahood's executor will report these dividends on Mahood's final tax return or on his rights or things return. If the executor opts to file a rights and things return for other items, he has no choice but to include this dividend income on the rights and things return. Similarly, if the legal representative opts to include these dividends on a rights or things return, then all other income that falls into the rights or things category must be reported on that return.

Proprietor or Partnership Income

If the deceased was a sole proprietor or partner in a business, and if the business operated on a fiscal year other than a calendar year, an optional return may be filed if the deceased dies subsequent to the end of the fiscal year but prior to the end of the calendar year in which the fiscal period ended. This return captures business income for the period between the end of the fiscal year and the date of death, which is often referred to as a *stub period*. If this separate return is not filed, all business income is reported on the final return.

MAHOOD (2)

At the time of Mahood's premature death on July 31, he was a partner in a partnership that had a January 31 year end.

Income allocated to Mahood at the January 31 year end of the partnership must be reported on his final tax return. His legal representative is entitled to claim income from February 1 to July 31, the stub period, on a separate tax return, if he so chooses.

Testamentary Trust Income

If the deceased was an income beneficiary of a testamentary trust that operates in a fiscal period other than the calendar year, an optional return may be filed if the deceased dies subsequent to the end of the fiscal year but prior to the end of the calendar year in which the fiscal period ended. This return captures income for the period between the end of the fiscal year and the date of death, which is often referred to as a stub period. If this separate return is not filed, all income from the trust is reported on the final return.

MICK

Thirty-six-year-old Mick died suddenly on September 1. He was an income beneficiary from a testamentary trust established upon his father's death, ten years ago. The trust's year end is March 31.

The trust allocated $10,000 of interest income to Mick on March 31. In addition, it allocated an additional $2,500 of interest income to Mick's estate as his share of the trust, up to his date of death.

Mick's legal representative will report $10,000 of interest income on Mick's final tax return and has the option to claim the $2,500 payment on a separate tax return.

INTEGRATION OF RETURNS

The completion of income tax returns relative to the deceased should be carefully managed in order to minimize the overall income tax liability. While there are a total of four income tax returns that can be filed on behalf of a deceased taxpayer, there is important integration that needs to be considered across the returns. The following four sub-sections highlight items that can be:

- claimed on each return;
- divided between returns;
- claimed against specific income; and
- claimed on the final return only.

Full Claim on Each Return

The following non-refundable tax credits may be claimed in full on each of the four returns filed on behalf of the deceased:

- basic personal amount (line 300);
- age amount (line 301);
- spouse or common-law partner amount (line 303);
- amount for an eligible dependant (line 305);
- amount for infirm dependants age 18 or older (line 306); and
- caregiver amount (line 315).

Divided Claim Permitted

There is a series of non-refundable tax credits that may be split across the four returns, provided the total amount claimed for each credit does not exceed the amount that would be allowed if only the final return was filed. These credits include:

- disability amount (for deceased);
- disability amount transferred (from a dependent);
- interest paid on certain student loans (for deceased);
- tuition and education amounts (for deceased);
- tuition and education amounts (transfer from a child);
- charitable donations (up to net income reported on the return);
- cultural, ecological and Crown gifts; and
- medical expenses (with a reduction equal to the lower of the annual limit or 3% of total net income on all returns).

Claim Against Specific Income

There is a series of deductions and non-refundable tax credits that may be claimed only if the return includes related income. These include:

- employee home-relocation loan deduction;
- stock options and share deductions (line 249);
- vow of perpetual poverty deduction;
- other employment expenses;
- Canada/Quebec Pension Plan contributions;
- Employment Insurance premiums;
- pension income amount; and
- social benefits repayment (line 235).

Eligible for Final Return Only

If eligible, the following items may be claimed as amounts on the deceased's final return, but not on any of the elective returns:

- RRSP and RPP contributions;
- professional, association and union dues (line 212);
- child care expense (line 214);
- attendant care expense (line 215);
- allowable business investment losses (ABILs) (line 217);
- moving expenses (line 219);
- support payments (paid) (line 220);
- carrying charges & interest expense (line 221);
- losses from other years;
- capital gains deduction (line 254); and
- amounts transferred from your spouse/common-law partner (line 326).

ADMINISTRATIVE ISSUES

Filing Dates

Normally, the final income tax return for a deceased taxpayer is due the later of:

- six months after the date of the taxpayer's death; or
- April 30 of the year following death.

If a deceased taxpayer was self-employed or was the spouse or common-law partner of a self-employed individual and:

- if death occurred on or between January 1 and December 15, the tax return filing due date is June 15 of the year following death; or

- if death occurred on or between December 16 and December 31, the tax return filing due date is six months after the date of death.

The due date for the balance of taxes owing on a final return for a deceased taxpayer is:

- April 30 of the year following death, if the taxpayer died on or between January 1 and October 31; or

- six months after the date of death, if the taxpayer died on or between November 1 and December 31.

If *testamentary debts* are being handled through a spousal or common-law partner trust, the due date for filing the final return is extended to 18 months after the date of death, although taxes owing are generally due by the normal dates for deceased taxpayers.

Also worth noting is that if a person dies after December 31, but on or prior to the filing due date for the previous taxation year, and if he has not filed that return, the return and any balance owing is due within six months after the date of death.

The idea behind these rules is that the legal representative of the deceased should have at least six months before being required to submit a return. If the taxpayer dies on December 30, the return would have to be filed by June 30 at the latest. This represents a maximum 15-day extension if the individual or individual's spouse was self-employed (normal deadline June 15) or a maximum 45-day extension if the individual or individual's spouse was not self-employed (normal deadline April 30).

Table 5 summarizes the filing and payment due dates for a deceased taxpayer.

Table 5
Due Date Summary for Deceased Taxpayer

Final Income Tax Return — Due Dates	*Comments*
Normally*, the later of: • six months after death; or • April 30 of the year following death. For self-employed or a spouse of a self-employed person: • if death occurred January 1 to December 15, the due date is June 15 of the year following death; or • if death occurred December 16 to December 31, the due date is six months after the date of death. *If testamentary debts are being handled through a spousal or common-law partner trust, the due date for the final return is extended to 18 months after the date of death, although taxes owing are generally due by the normal dates outlined in this section.	If death occurred January 1 to October 31, the balance of taxes owing is due by April 30 of the year following death If death occurred between November 1 and December 31, the balance of taxes owing is due six months after the date of death.

ROBERTA

Roberta, a retired individual, died on June 18, 2010. Her 2010 income tax return is due April 30, 2011.

RAYMOND

Raymond, a single individual, died on December 9, 2010. Raymond was an employee of Justin Manufacturing where he had worked for 20 years. His final return is due June 9, 2011, six months after death.

HELGA

Helga, a 58-year-old widow and employee of EZ Appliances, died January 3, 2010. Her 2009 income tax return had not yet been filed. Helga's 2009 return is due by July 3, 2010, while her final return for 2010 is due by April 30, 2011.

DEATH OF A TAXPAYER

General Tax Treatment

An individual is deemed to have disposed of all of her capital property at fair market value immediately prior to her death. The individual who acquires the capital property upon the taxpayer's death is deemed to have received the property at a cost equal to the fair market value (FMV).

Spousal Rollover

An exception to this deemed disposition rule occurs when the property is left to a spouse or common-law partner or to a trust created for the benefit of the spouse or common-law partner. This exception is commonly referred to as a spousal rollover.

Qualifying Criteria

To qualify for a spousal rollover:

- the deceased and the deceased's spouse must have been resident in Canada immediately prior to the deceased's death;
- the property must vest indefeasibly in the spouse or trust created for her benefit within 36 months after the deceased's death (an extension may be possible if requested during the 36-month period by writing to the Minister and assuming it is viewed as reasonable in the circumstances); and
- if a trust is involved, the trust must be resident in Canada immediately after the time the property vests indefeasibly in the trust.

Tax Consequences

Assuming the above conditions are met, the spousal rollover provision applies automatically when capital property is left to the surviving spouse or common-law partner or a spousal trust, resulting in the following tax treatment:

- the deceased taxpayer's capital property is deemed to be disposed of at the property's adjusted cost base or undepreciated capital cost in the case of depreciable property; and

- the spouse who acquires the property assumes the deceased taxpayer's adjusted cost base or undepreciated capital cost for the property.

Through utilization of the spousal rollover tax treatment, the deceased spouse incurs no capital gain or loss on the deemed disposition of the property. The receiving spouse takes ownership of the property; assumes the deceased taxpayer's adjusted cost base on the property (or undepreciated capital cost if it is depreciable property); and tax on the accrued capital gain is deferred until the receiving spouse disposes of the property at some time in the future. The capital gain is not eliminated, but rather tax on the accrued capital gain is deferred into the future. The receiving spouse assumes the tax liability.

Electing Out of a Spousal Rollover

The legal representative of the deceased may make an election to opt out of the spousal rollover provision, in which case:

- the deceased taxpayer's deemed disposition would occur at the fair market value of the capital property; and

- the adjusted cost base of the property would be set at fair market value for the receiving spouse.

An election to opt out of the rollover provision would normally be made if an assessment of the options (rollover, no rollover, or partial rollover) indicated it was beneficial to the tax situation of the deceased taxpayer or her spouse. It should be noted that the election is in respect to each property. A partial rollover is available by electing out of the rollover on some pieces of property and not others.

FRED

When Fred passed away earlier this year, he owned 10,000 shares of CatSmart Co. with an ACB of 10 cents per share and fair market value of $2,000,000 in total. The executor of the estate worked with Fred's surviving spouse to assess various tax planning strategies as shown in Table 6

Table 6
Assessment of Rollover Options

	OPTIONS		
	A	B	C
	Full rollover	No rollover	Partial rollover
# of shares rolled	10,000	0	7,500
# of shares elected as not rolled	0	10,000	2,500
Deemed proceeds of disposition	0	$2,000,000	$500,000
Less: adjusted cost base	0	$1,000	$250
Capital gain	0	$1,999,000	$499,750

Under option A the executor could defer Fred's full accrued capital gain and pass the accrued liability onto Fred's surviving spouse. In this case, Fred's estate would incur no tax liability because it has been deferred until his spouse disposes of the assets (actual or deemed disposition).

continued . . .

---

continued . . .

Under option B, the executor could trigger Fred's full-accrued capital gain on the final tax return. This may be desirable if Fred has a net capital loss carried forward from previous years or other deductions that would potentially be lost and which could be used to offset the gain.

Under option C, the executor could trigger $499,750 of Fred's accrued capital gains on the final return. This may be desirable if Fred had the enhanced capital gains exemption available.

Property Owned as Joint Tenants

General Treatment

While property owned as joint tenants is unique because of the right of survivorship, capital property is still subject to capital gains at the time of disposition. The death of one of the joint tenants causes the deceased tenant's share to pass immediately upon death to the surviving tenant. This transfer is viewed as a deemed disposition for tax purposes and must be considered in the calculation of capital gains for the deceased taxpayer.

The tax consequences are:

- the deceased taxpayer is deemed to have disposed of her interest in the property at fair market value immediately prior to death; and
- the remaining tenant who acquires the interest in the capital property is deemed to have received the interest in the property at a cost equal to the fair market value.

The disposition is based on the deceased taxpayer's share in the property. For example, if two individuals own the property as joint tenants, the calculation is based on a 50% share of the capital gain at the time of death; or, if three individuals owned the property as joint tenants, the calculation is based on one-third of the capital gain, unless other evidence can be provided to substantiate a different split.

JOYCE AND GAIL

Sisters, Joyce and Gail, owned shares of Sugar Inc. as joint tenants. When Gail died, the shares passed to Joyce through the right of survivorship. The Sugar Inc. shares were originally purchased by Joyce and Gail in 1989 for $75,000 and had a fair market value of $230,000 at the time of Gail's death.

Gail's death triggers a deemed disposition attributable to her estate, creating a $38,750 taxable capital gain, calculated as 50% of (($230,000 - $75,000) × 50%). Note that a taxable capital gain is triggered on only half of the asset and is attributable to Gail only.

After Gail's death, Joyce has 100% ownership of the property with a fair market value of $230,000 and an ACB of $152,500 (50% of $75,000 and 50% of $230,000).

Spousal Rollover

When spouses meet the qualifying criteria for spousal rollover and when they own property together as joint tenants, the spousal rollover provision applies automatically in the event of the death of one spouse. The deceased's legal representative must elect out of the rollover provision, if she does not want the provision to apply.

If an election is not made, the rollover provision applies, resulting in the following tax treatment:

- the deceased taxpayer's portion of the joint property is deemed to be disposed of at the property's adjusted cost base or undepreciated capital cost in the case of depreciable property; and

- the receiving spouse acquires the deceased's portion of the property at the deceased spouse's adjusted cost base or undepreciated capital cost in the case of depreciable property.

The tax treatment results in the deferral of the capital gain on the property until the surviving spouse disposes of the property at some point in the future.

Electing Out of Spousal Rollover

If an election is made to opt out of the rollover provision, the resulting tax treatment is the same as described above under Property Owned As Joint Tenants — General Treatment.

Capital Gains

Deemed Disposition

The death of a taxpayer results in a deemed disposition of capital property, which will trigger a capital gain or capital loss unless the property qualifies under the provisions of a spousal rollover.

Treatment of Allowable Capital Loss

An allowable capital loss from the disposition of capital properties can generally be offset against taxable capital gains, with certain exceptions. If, however, a taxpayer has an allowable capital loss and no taxable capital gains, the allowable capital loss cannot be claimed against any other type of income. There is an exception to this rule in the taxpayer's year of death. Where a capital loss is realized in the year of death or a capital loss is carried forward into the year of death, the allowable portion is deductible against any type of income realized in that year.

Principal Residence

A comprehensive discussion of the topic of principal residence was examined in Module 6, so it will not be repeated here.

Transfer of Farm Property at Death

The Act permits the transfer of farm property from a taxpayer to his child, at the taxpayer's death, on a tax-free rollover basis. The following is a list of rules that must be met.

- The property must be located in Canada and must have been used as a farm on a regular and continuous basis by the transferor, transferor's spouse or common-law partner, or the transferor's children immediately prior to the transfer.

- The property is transferred from the taxpayer to the child as a consequence of the taxpayer's death.

- The recipient child was resident in Canada immediately prior to the taxpayer's death.

- The property becomes indefeasibly vested in the receiving child within 36 months of the taxpayer's death.

The formula for calculating the application of capital gains treatment for the transfer of farm property was discussed extensively in Module 6, so it will not be repeated here.

Alternative Minimum Tax

Alternative minimum tax is not applicable in the year of a taxpayer's death, although any previous carryforward amount may be used to reduce a regular tax liability in excess of the minimum on the taxpayer's terminal return.

Attribution

Attribution rules no longer apply when there is a change in specific circumstances. As such, attribution no longer applies after the death of a taxpayer (i.e., no attribution beyond the grave).

Estate Property

Capital losses and terminal losses realized by the estate on the disposition of capital property and depreciable property, during the first taxation year of the estate, can be carried back and claimed on the terminal tax return for the deceased.

Summary — Death of a Taxpayer

- An individual is deemed to have disposed of all of her capital property at fair market value immediately prior to her death. The individual who acquires the property is deemed to have received the property at a cost equal to the FMV. This is the general tax treatment at death.

- When property is left to a spouse, there is a spousal rollover provision that provides an exception to the general tax treatment.

- The spousal rollover provision has qualifying criteria that includes a residency and a vesting requirement.

- If the spouses meet the qualifying criteria for a spousal rollover, the rollover applies automatically when capital property is left to the surviving spouse.

- Under the spousal rollover provision, the deceased taxpayer is deemed to dispose of the property at the property's ACB, or UCC in the case of depreciable capital property; and, the receiving spouse assumes the deceased spouse's ACB or UCC for the property.

- The deceased taxpayer's legal representative may elect out of the rollover provision.

- Property owned as joint tenants is subject to capital gains at the time of disposition. The disposition is based on the deceased taxpayer's share of the property.

- For property owned as joint tenants that passes through the right of survivorship, the general tax treatment results in proceeds of disposition for the deceased taxpayer equal to the FMV of the deceased's share.

- When spouses own property as joint tenants, the spousal rollover applies automatically if the qualifying criterion is met. The deceased's legal representative can elect out of the rollover provision.

- Capital losses and terminal losses realized by the estate on the disposition of capital property and depreciable capital, during the first taxation year of the estate, can be carried back and claimed on the terminal tax return for the deceased.

Death of a RRSP Annuitant

General Terms

Upon the death of the annuitant, if the assets of the unmatured RRSP pass to someone other than a spouse/common-law partner or a qualified child or grandchild, the fair market value of the plan assets, immediately before death, must be included in the annuitant's income for the year of death.

If there is a decrease in the value of an unmatured RRSP or a RRIF between the date of death and the date of final distribution to the beneficiary or estate, the legal representative for the deceased person can request the amount of the decrease to be deducted on the deceased's final return. This applies where the final payment from the RRSP or the RRIF occurs after 2008.

If the assets of the unmatured RRSP pass to the annuitant's spouse/common-law partner, or a dependent child or grandchild, there is no tax consequence for the deceased taxpayer's estate but rather responsibility for the tax consequence passes to the receiving individual. The receiving individual becomes responsible for the taxation associated with the RRSP assets, which must be treated as an income inclusion in the year of receipt. In order to qualify for special tax treatment that allows for the deferral of the income tax consequences, the amount transferring from the deceased annuitant to the beneficiary must meet the definition of a refund of premiums.

Refund of Premiums

A *refund of premiums* is defined as any amount paid out of or under a RRSP to the spouse or common-law partner of the deceased annuitant, prior to the plan's maturity. In addition, an amount paid from the RRSP to a dependent child or grandchild is also considered a refund of premium.

To qualify under the term *dependent*, a child or grandchild of the deceased annuitant must have been financially dependent on the deceased at the time of her death, where financially dependent is defined as having earned an income amount that is less than the basic personal amount in the year preceding the annuitant's death.

This definition is extended even further if a child or grandchild of the deceased was financially dependent on the deceased at the time of her death, by reason of mental or physical infirmity. In this case, financially dependent is defined as having earned an income amount that is less than the annual disability income amount in the year preceding the annuitant's death.

In general terms, a refund of premiums is terminology used to define assets from an unmatured RRSP resulting from the death of the RRSP annuitant and which are paid to a qualified beneficiary under specific conditions. Generally, qualified beneficiaries fall into three categories:

1. the deceased annuitant's spouse or common-law spouse;
2. the deceased annuitant's financially dependent child or grandchild; or
3. the deceased annuitant's financially dependent child or grandchild who is mentally or physically disabled.

Qualified beneficiaries may receive the refund of premiums directly as a consequence of a named beneficiary designation on the RRSP account. Alternatively, the funds could be received indirectly as a bequest through the estate. An indirect receipt of a refund of premiums can arise where the deceased annuitant fails to name a beneficiary on the RRSP account and consequently the RRSP assets flow through the estate. In order for an indirect receipt to qualify as a refund of premiums, the qualified beneficiary must be an heir under the will and, together with the administrator of the deceased annuitant's estate, they must file a joint election.

Spouse or Common-Law Spouse

The assets may transfer directly into another qualified plan without creating an immediate tax consequence; or, the spouse may receive the assets personally and subsequently elect to contribute the funds to another qualified plan. If the funds are received personally, subsequent contributions into another qualified plan must be made during the year in which the funds are received or within 60 days after the end of that year, in order to continue the tax-deferral feature. If a subsequent contribution is not made within the specified time frame, the full amount of the refund of premium will be treated as taxable income to the receiving spouse in the year that the funds were received.

A refund of premium may be transferred from a RRSP to another type of plan without attracting immediate tax consequences as described above, provided the funds are applied under the new plan as follows:

- into a RRSP;
- into a RRIF; or
- to acquire a qualifying annuity.

These indirect transfers must be made in the year in which the income inclusion arises, or within 60 days thereafter.

Financially Dependent Child or Grandchild

If the beneficiary of the deceased annuitant's RRSP assets is a financially dependent child or grandchild, the recipient becomes responsible for payment of the tax associated with receipt of the RRSP benefit. The child or grandchild has the option to transfer the amount into a term certain to age 18 annuity, which spreads out the tax consequences.

The RRSP assets may transfer directly into the term certain to age 18 annuity or the individual may receive the assets personally and subsequently elect to contribute the funds to the annuity. If the funds are received personally, subsequent contributions into the annuity must be made during the year in which the funds are received or within 60 days after the end of that year in order to continue the tax deferral feature. If a subsequent contribution is not made within the specified time frame, the full amount of the refund of premium is included as taxable income to the recipient in the year that the funds were received.

Financially Dependent Child or Grandchild (Disabled)

If the beneficiary of the deceased annuitant's RRSP assets is a financially dependent child or grandchild who is dependent by reason of mental or physical infirmity, the recipient becomes responsible for payment of the tax associated with receipt of the RRSP benefit.

The beneficiary has the opportunity to defer tax on the receipt of the benefit whereby the refund of premiums may be transferred from the deceased's RRSP to another type of qualified plan, without attracting immediate tax consequences, as described above, provided the funds are applied under a new plan as follows:

- into a RRSP;
- into a RRIF; or
- to acquire a qualifying annuity.

These indirect transfers must be made in the year in which the income inclusion arises, or within 60 days thereafter.

RRSP Contributions After Death

A taxpayer's legal representative can make contributions to a spousal RRSP on behalf of a deceased taxpayer in the year of the taxpayer's death or within 60 days after the end of the taxation year in which the taxpayer dies. The deceased taxpayer is considered the contributing spouse and the deceased taxpayer's surviving spouse is the plan annuitant.

Contributions cannot be made to a deceased taxpayer's RRSP after her death, but contributions to the spousal RRSP are permitted and provide the opportunity for a RRSP deduction on the deceased taxpayer's final income tax return up to her available RRSP deduction limit.

Death of the RRIF Annuitant

General Terms

Upon the death of the annuitant, if the assets of the RRIF pass to someone other than a spouse/common-law partner or a qualified child or grandchild as a designated benefit, the fair market value of the plan's assets, immediately before death, must be included in the annuitant's income for the year of death. Both the value of the assets and the value of any payments received from the RRIF during the year are reported on the deceased's final return.

Designated Benefit

A *designated benefit* is defined as any amount paid out of a RRIF to the spouse or common-law partner of the deceased annuitant, or an amount paid to a financially dependent child or grandchild of the deceased annuitant.

Designated benefits include:

- fair market value of the RRIF at date of death; and
- income earned in the RRIF from the date of death, until December 31 of the year after the year of death.

Any income earned by the RRIF after December 31 of the year following the year of death, until the proceeds are distributed, does not qualify as a designated benefit.

In general terms, a designated benefit is terminology used to define assets from a RRIF resulting from the death of the RRIF annuitant and which are paid to a qualified beneficiary under specific conditions. Generally, qualified beneficiaries fall into three categories:

1. the deceased annuitant's spouse or common-law spouse;
2. the deceased annuitant's financially dependent child or grandchild; or
3. the deceased annuitant's financially dependent child or grandchild who is mentally or physically disabled.

The definitions of qualified beneficiaries mirror those discussed under the previous RRSP section. Similarly, the tax consequences associated with a designated benefit mirror those discussed relative to a refund of premium.

Employee Death Benefit

A benefit can be paid as the result of the death of an employee where the death benefit is in recognition of service in an office or employment. In such a situation, the first $10,000 of the benefit is exempt from income tax. The maximum cumulative exemption is $10,000, based on all sources related to a single taxpayer. In other words, if a death benefit is paid from two different sources, the $10,000 exemption is not available relative to each source that paid the death benefit, but is based on a cumulative exemption relative to each deceased taxpayer. The benefit amount can be paid out over more than one taxation year, even over a recipient's lifetime, but the $10,000 maximum exemption is cumulative and not applicable to each taxation year.

Qualifying Payments

Payments that qualify as a gross amount of a death benefit include:

- Payment in recognition of an employee's service, whether paid as a lump-sum or periodic amount, including a lifetime payment to a recipient, provided the payment does not fall within the list of non-qualified payments (outlined below).
- Payment in recognition of service for an employee who dies prior to retirement where the amount may represent a settlement of the deceased's accumulated sick-leave credits.

Non-Qualifying Payments

Payments that do not qualify as death benefits include:

- a payment from a retirement compensation arrangement;
- payments out of a salary deferral program or those out of a superannuation or pension fund;
- a Canada/Quebec Pension Plan death benefit; and
- payment in respect of accumulated vacation leave or representing overtime payable to the employee.

Application of Exemption

- When the surviving spouse is the sole beneficiary, the amount of the qualifying payment, up to a cumulative maximum of $10,000, is treated as exempt from taxation.

- When an individual other than a surviving spouse is the sole beneficiary, the amount of the qualifying payment, up to a cumulative maximum of $10,000, is treated as exempt from taxation.

- When the surviving spouse and a person other than the surviving spouse are beneficiaries, the surviving spouse's portion, up to $10,000, is exempt from taxation. If the surviving spouse's payment is less than $10,000, the non-spouse beneficiary's amount that exceeds the payment to the spouse up to the $10,000 maximum is exempt from taxation.

However, where payments cross into a subsequent taxation year, the surviving spouse retains the right to the $10,000 exemption. If, for example, a spouse received an amount equal to less than $10,000 in year one and a non-spouse beneficiary also claimed an exemption in year one, the non-spouse's exemption in year one will be affected by the surviving spouse's year-two claim. It is quite likely that the non-spouse beneficiary would need to file a revised tax return, reducing his exemption so not to infringe on an amount available to the surviving spouse.

CHERYL

Upon Cheryl's death, her employer paid a $10,000 benefit that qualified as a death benefit with up to $10,000 being exempt from taxation. The $10,000 payment was split as 60% to Cheryl's surviving spouse, Dan, and 40% to Cheryl's daughter, Heather, from a previous marriage. Both Dan and Heather's payments will be non-taxable because each is a qualifying payment and the combined maximum does not exceed $10,000.

DARLA

Upon Darla's death, her employer agreed to pay a $10,000 death benefit in each of Year 1 and Year 2. The payment amount was split equally between Darla's husband, Rod, and Darla's child from a previous marriage, Eddie.

In Year 1, both Rod and Eddie claimed their $5,000 payment as an exempt portion of the gross amount of the death benefit payable by Darla's employer.

In Year 2, Rod and Eddie each received a second payment of $5,000 from Darla's employer. When filing his income tax return, Rod will claim his second $5,000 payment as an exempt portion of the gross amount of the death benefit payable by Darla's employer. Rod does not have to claim any death benefit on his income tax return, because his total payments do not exceed the exempt portion.

Eddie's Year 1 income tax return will need to be revised to recognize Rod's claim for the exempt portion of the death benefit on his Year 2 income tax return.

Charitable Giving

Generally, charitable donations may be claimed up to a limit of 75% of the taxpayer's net income. Any charitable donation amount that a taxpayer cannot or does not claim in the taxation year, can be carried forward and used in any of the subsequent five years. In the year the taxpayer dies, charitable donations may be claimed up to a limit of 100% of the taxpayer's net income. Amounts that a deceased taxpayer cannot claim in the year of death, because of the net income maximum, can be carried back one year and claimed as a credit, up to 100% of net income.

Cultural and ecological gifts are an exception to these rules in that a charitable donation credit may be claimed for amounts up to 100% of the taxpayer's net income.

RUTHIE

Ruthie donated $200,000 to the local hospital, a registered charity. The same year, Ruthie earned net income of $63,000. How much of the $200,000 donation can her executor claim for charitable donations?

The executor can claim $63,000 (100% of her net income) on her terminal tax return and he can carryback $137,000 to claim on her prior year's tax return up to a maximum of her net income claim.

U.S. ESTATE TAXES

Unlike Canada, the United States imposes an estate tax, which should be carefully considered in any estate planning exercise when a Canadian owns U.S. property or when he is a regular visitor to the United States.

Residency Rules

For tax purposes, the United States utilizes the term *alien* in relationship to individuals who are not citizens of the United States. The residency of the alien plays a key role for income tax purposes with differing status for a *resident alien* and a *non-resident alien*. Aliens may be required to file a U.S. tax return. A resident alien is normally taxed on his worldwide income, similar to a U.S. citizen, and a non-resident alien is taxed only on his income from sources within the United States and on certain income connected with the conduct of a business in the United States.

From a U.S. estate tax perspective, a Canadian citizen would be considered a resident alien of the United States if he were resident in the United States either permanently or with the intention of making it permanent. Alternatively, a Canadian citizen who resides temporarily in the United States, and does not meet the definition of a resident alien, may fall in the status of a non-resident alien. Typically, Canadians who enjoy a break from Canada's cold winter months by taking up U.S. residence are treated as non-resident aliens.

U.S. Estate Tax

The United States employs an estate tax based on the gross estate value less allowable deductions. The gross estate value includes the fair market value of all property in which the deceased held an interest at the time of his death, including life insurance proceeds payable to the estate, or if the deceased owned the life insurance policy, the proceeds payable to his heirs.

A Canadian who is not a U.S. citizen and is a non-resident of the U.S. but who owns property that is referred to as a U.S. situs asset, is subject to U.S. estate tax. U.S. situs assets include real estate and tangible personal property, normally located in the United States. For example, a Florida vacation home, the personal furnishings in the vacation home, as well as a boat or other recreational vehicle that is normally located in the United States, are considered U.S. situs assets. Shares of a U.S. corporation, regardless of where they were purchased, and corporate debt obligations, such as bonds or promissory notes issued by U.S. corporations, are also considered U.S. situs assets.

Canadian mutual funds that hold U.S. investments are not considered U.S. situs assets because the investor holds an asset in a Canadian entity.

Funds on deposit with a U.S. bank are not considered a U.S. situs asset provided the funds are not connected with a business or trade, although currency held in a safety deposit box within a U.S. bank is a U.S. situs asset.

Given the relationship between U.S. situs assets and U.S. estate tax, the situs rules form a significant part of any strategy to avoid U.S. estate tax.

HARVEY

When Harvey died, his estate included: his home located in XYZ province; his condominium located in Arizona; a portfolio of Canadian mutual funds; shares of PQR Inc, a newly formed American corporation, which were purchased on the Toronto Stock Exchange; and the furnishings in his home as well as the furnishings in his Arizona condominium.

Harvey is a Canadian citizen who visits the United States each winter for four months.

Which of Harvey's assets are subject to U.S. estate tax?

Harvey's Arizona condominium, the furnishings in the condominium and the shares of PQR Inc. are all U.S. situs assets subject to U.S. estate tax.

For individuals who want to increase holdings in U.S. corporations while avoiding the U.S. estate tax implication, a common strategy is to purchase Canadian mutual funds that have a specific U.S. focus.

Canada-U.S. Tax Treaty

The Canada-U.S. tax treaty provides Canadians with the opportunity to claim an exemption, which provides some relief from the U.S. estate tax. The calculation of the exemption amount is based on a ratio of the deceased's U.S. property relative to his worldwide estate assets.

In 2010, a Canadian owning assets upon death is not subject to any U.S. estate tax. In 2011, the exemption is US$1 million and the top estate tax rate is 55%.

In 2011, Canadians with smaller worldwide estates valued at less than US$1 million will generally not be subject to estate tax. However, if a Canadian owns U.S. property and has a worldwide estate that exceeds US$1 million, even if the U.S. property is small in proportion to the total value of the estate, he may well be subject to U.S. estate tax.

Unit 7
Applications

HOLDING COMPANIES

A holding company can be a valuable place to accumulate and diversify investments so that when the shareholder/taxpayer dies, only the shares of the holding company are to be dealt with in his will. The assets within the holding company continue uninterrupted, reducing the need to liquidate or transfer many different investment holdings.

Upon the death of the taxpayer, the shares of the holding company can pass through the shareholder's estate in accordance with the provisions of the shareholder's will or can pass through the intestate succession laws if there is no will. Using a holding company makes the transfer simple and easily managed with minimal work for the estate executor or administrator.

LAURA

Laura has created a holding company in which she maintains a large array of investment assets. Included are shares of 50 different companies, 40 different bonds, a series of term deposits and a group of mutual funds.

In her will, Laura has bequeathed the shares of her holding company to her two sons and three nephews in equal amounts so that each of the five heirs will own 20% of the holding company. Using the holding company helps to balance the equitable distribution of assets, eliminates any liquidation issues and makes the transfer of ownership a simple transaction.

ESTATE FREEZE

An estate freeze is a planning technique that allows the owner of an operating company to freeze the growth of his interest in an operating company in order to avoid further capital gain on his shares that would be triggered at his death. Implementing an estate freeze is common when a shareholder has accumulated sufficient long-term wealth and would like future growth of the corporation to accumulate for the benefit of his intended heirs.

A holding company can be used to effect an estate freeze where the holding company becomes the owner of the common shares of an operating company. The shareholder of the operating company transfers his shares of the operating company to the holding company and takes back fixed value preferred shares of the holding company in exchange. The next generation of the family are allowed to subscribe to the common shares of the holding company, usually acquiring the stock at a nominal cost. The fixed value preferred shares taken back on the exchange are usually dividend bearing and carrying sufficient voting rights to control the holding company.

The payment of dividends on the preferred shares would provide continued income in an amount sufficient to meet the preferred shareholder's needs. Dividends paid on the common shares of the operating company to the holding company would be received tax-free provided the operating company had no investment income or portfolio dividends to cause a dividend refund while the two companies were connected.

The transfer of common shares into the holding company is permitted as a rollover without triggering a disposition or realization of capital gains to the original shareholder. This tax-free rollover is referred to as a *section 85 rollover.*

TOM

Tom owns Carpenters Inc., a successful operating company. Tom feels that he is ready to freeze the value of the business and allow the next generation to own some of the equity of the business.

Section 85 Rollover

Tom could accomplish an estate freeze by transferring his common shares of Carpenters Inc. into a holding company, taking back fixed value voting preferred shares of the holding company that bear dividends. The children involved in the business would be allowed to subscribe to common shares of the holding company. This is known as a Section 85 rollover.

Section 86 Reorganization

Alternatively, Tom could use a technique that does not involve a second company, but rather utilizes an exchange of shares within the operating company. Tom could transfer his common shares of Carpenters Inc. into Carpenters Inc. and take back fixed value voting preferred shares of Carpenters Inc. The children involved in the business would be allowed to subscribe to common shares of Carpenters. This is known as a Section 86 reorganization.

Both of these estate freezes can be accomplished on a tax-free rollover basis, such that the fixed value preferred shares that Tom takes back in exchange for his common shares have the same tax attributes (same fair market value, same adjusted cost base, and same paid-up capital).

INSURANCE

Estate Planning

Life insurance can be valuable when developing an estate plan. As discussed in Module 10, life insurance is a primary means by which to address any financial shortfall in an individual's estate that has the potential to threaten the deceased's family's standard of living. The proceeds of life insurance are payable immediately, which can assist with the issue of liquidity, so heirs are not forced to liquidate assets such as a family home or business in order to pay outstanding debts and expenses.

The use of life insurance is an excellent way to ensure outstanding expenses at death do not detract from inheritances established through an individual's estate. For example, the debts of the estate must be paid before a bequest can be fulfilled. Using life insurance, an individual can ensure that the taxes on capital gains resulting from the deemed disposition of capital property at death are covered, as well as any other taxes owing. Where there is no rollover opportunity, registered funds (i.e., RRSP, RRIF) are deemed to have been disposed of immediately upon death for proceeds equal to the fair market value. Insurance can be used to fund the tax liability that results with any registered funds or the capital gain on an asset that may be building during an individual's lifetime and is realized upon his death.

Life insurance is commonly used to fund bequests to family members or other beneficiaries. The proceeds of a life insurance benefit pass tax-free to the beneficiary, providing the insured with the opportunity to ensure beneficiaries are well cared for financially.

Using life insurance, individuals can ensure that equity prevails within their overall estate. For example, if an individual owns a family business that is intended to pass to the oldest son, who happens to be the only family member working in the business, the other siblings may feel the decision is inequitable. To ensure fairness across the family, insurance can be used to fund an equitable inheritance for all children within the family.

Students who have completed Course 3, Module 10, "Life Insurance and Living Benefits", of the CFP Education Program, will be familiar with the concept of Capital needs analysis relative to the use of life insurance in estate planning. Appendix Three, *Capital Needs Analysis*, has been incorporated into this module for those who did not complete Module 10, or for those who would like to refresh their knowledge in this area.

Buy-Sell Arrangements

A buy-sell arrangement is a subset of a shareholders' agreement and is a written document that outlines the terms relative to the succession of a business. A buy-sell arrangement is established during the business owners/partners' lifetimes and can address a variety of situations where the business transfers from an owner/partner to a successive owner/partner, based on specified triggering events. In Module 10, an extensive discussion of buy-sell arrangements looked at different buy-sell arrangements relative to the death of a corporate shareholder.

Insured Annuity/Back-to-Back

An *insured annuity*, also commonly referred to as a *back-to-back* strategy, is a unique financial plan that utilizes the purchase of an annuity and life insurance policy into an integrated plan. Through the use of these two products, an individual may be able to provide a higher guaranteed level of income throughout his retirement years relative to comparable interest-bearing investments, while ensuring the availability of assets to pass to the next generation.

In simple terms, the back-to-back strategy involves the purchase of a prescribed annuity. This generates a regular stream of income, a portion of which is used to purchase an insurance policy. The insurance policy provides a cash payment upon the insured's death to replace the capital that was originally invested in the annuity.

The products used to accomplish this strategy include a life annuity purchased with non-registered funds and a permanent life insurance product, typically a term-to-100 policy. The strategy can be implemented on a single or joint life basis.

Using prescribed taxation, the annuitant receives favourable tax treatment on the annuity income and the life insurance benefit passes tax-free to the beneficiary of the life insurance policy. Typically, this type of estate planning strategy is integrated into an individual's overall investment and estate plan. Annuities are a suitable investment product for individuals with low risk tolerance and who seek the highest possible income with the lowest amount of risk. The added layer of the insurance policy provides the individual with guaranteed preservation of the capital component.

RALPH

Seventy-one-year-old Ralph, a non-smoker, has approached his financial advisor to discuss alternatives for the investment of $1,000,000 of non-registered funds. A regular income flow is an essential investment objective for Ralph because he is highly dependent on the income in order to maintain his lifestyle. Safety of principal is a second primary objective, as Ralph intends to use the capital to support a bequest to his children, upon his death.

In order to address these two objectives, Ralph's financial planner presents two options:

- a GIC that provides a regular income flow from the interest earnings; and

- a back-to-back strategy.

The results of these two options are shown in Table 6.

continued . . .

---

continued . . .

Table 6
Investment Comparison

Total invested - $1,000,000

	GIC Option	Back-to-Back Strategy
Income	$40,000	$97,414
Taxable portion	$40,000	$19,913
Income taxes	$16,000	$7,965
Insurance premium	$0	$45,072
Net cash flow	$24,000	$44,377

Based on this analysis, the back-to-back strategy produces a higher annual cash flow than the GIC option, and preservation of principal is addressed through the use of insurance.

The primary shortcoming of a back-to-back strategy is the loss of liquidity; once committed, the strategy cannot be unwound and capital cannot be returned to the client.

Funding a Trust with Insurance

A testamentary trust is frequently used as a tool to control the assets after death in respect of the testator's beneficiaries. In certain circumstances an individual may want the proceeds of a life insurance policy to end up in a testamentary trust, as the proceeds are intended to fund the purpose of the trust, but may not want the insurance proceeds to pass through his estate. By passing through his estate the insurance proceeds become exposed to creditors of the estate, the probate process and public scrutiny.

One solution to the above dilemma is to have the insurance proceeds paid into a trust settled by the estate. In this fashion, the insurance proceeds do not pass through the estate, but go directly into the trust. To achieve this outcome, the individual would name the trustees of the testamentary trust as the beneficiaries of his life insurance policy.

ESTATE PLANNING REVIEW

Estate Planning Process

Similar to the broad concept of financial planning, the process of estate planning should utilize a clearly defined framework to ensure a thorough and comprehensive approach. The five-step process is generic and can be applied across the breadth of many different individuals, regardless of the complexity of the individual's estate.

Similar to financial planning, estate planning is concerned with: identifying or defining estate planning objectives; identifying and evaluating issues specific to the individual's situation; evaluating alternatives that lead to the selection of strategies that address the client's objectives; implementation of the selected strategies, which frequently involves other professionals; and monitoring the client's personal circumstances through periodic reviews to identify issues or changes that may impact the estate plan.

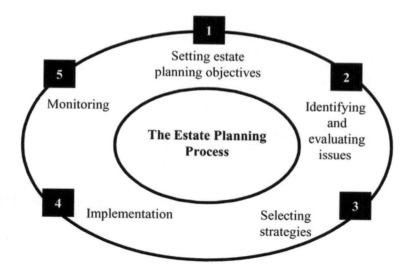

Estate Planning Checklist

Incapacity

Is there a power of attorney for property? Are there additional power of attorney documents to deal with property in other jurisdictions? Does the power of attorney for property have an enduring/continuing provision in the event of the individual's incapacity? Is there a power of attorney for health care?

Rollover Rules/Deferred Tax Liability

If assets are to pass to a successive generation, what rollover rules are permitted to defer the tax liability? What income tax implications does the rollover have for the recipient of the asset? What is the potential tax liability that arises upon the individual's death, including such items as a cottage, investment portfolio, deferred income plans, assets owned as joint tenants with the right of survivorship or as tenants in common, or shares of a business corporation? Does the individual own U.S. real property or investments that fall in the U.S. situs definition?

Beneficiary Designation

How up-to-date are the beneficiary designations on any product where a named beneficiary is permitted? Have beneficiary designations for life insurance, investment products (i.e., segregated funds) and registered investments been used effectively to meet the individual's testamentary objectives?

Will

Does the individual have a will? Has any event occurred that could cause the will to be invalid? Has any event occurred that could cause single issues or provisions to be invalid or that may affect the intended outcome? Are all assets accounted for in the will or through a will substitute arrangement? Does any bequest for minor children include provisions for a trustee to manage the assets? If a spousal trust is utilized in the will, does the structure meet the qualifying criteria from a tax perspective? Have testamentary trusts been explored and/or utilized in the will? Is there an opportunity to use multiple testamentary trusts for income splitting?

Inter Vivos Trusts

Do *inter vivos* trusts have any role or value in the individual's estate plan? Have appropriate provisions been incorporated for any testamentary trusts? If a spousal trust is utilized, are there any provisions that could taint it?

Liquidity

Does the estate provide for sufficient liquidity to meet the testator's testamentary intentions? Has there been a recent capital needs analysis completed? Are the assumptions used for assessing liquidity appropriate? Are there sufficient funds to meet the ongoing needs of the surviving family?

Ownership Structure

Does the individual understand the implications of any joint ownership structures currently in place, as it relates to distribution of the assets upon his death? Is there any opportunity to adjust the asset ownership structure to better meet the client's estate planning objectives? If so, have the implications including tax and softer issues been considered? Have successive-owner provisions been used, where possible and appropriate?

Probate

Does the individual understand the concept of probate? Does probate create issues or concerns (financial or softer issues) that need to be considered in any estate plan?

Unit 8
Self-Test Questions

QUESTIONS

The following background should be used with questions 1 through 6, inclusive.

JOHN

In the fall of 2010, just prior to his business trip to England, John completed an enduring general power of attorney for property in which he appointed his sister, Ashley, as his attorney. While in England, John became critically ill and was flown home in grave health. Upon returning home, John told his special friend, Adam, that in the event he succumbs to his current illness, Adam is to receive John's antique dining room suite.

Prior to his trip, John had initiated discussions about a will and his lawyer had prepared a draft will, but it had not yet been signed. John had no prior will.

John is an employee of an international firm of architects and is a single fellow who has never been married and has no children. Ashley is John's only sibling, and their parents are deceased. The siblings live in a province other than Quebec.

In 1998, a family cottage passed from John's parents to him and Ashley, which they now own as joint tenants with the right of survivorship. The adjusted cost base of the cottage is $200,000 while the current market value is $275,000. John has sole ownership of the townhouse condominium in which he lives.

Question 1

Given that John is gravely ill in the hospital, which of the following activities will Ashley typically have the automatic authority to undertake on John's behalf?

1. Pay John's bills during his sickness.

2. Re-negotiate John's car lease.

3. Make decisions regarding John's health care.

4. Sign John's will.

5. Re-invest John's maturing term deposit.

      a. 1 and 3 only

      b. 3 and 5 only

      c. 2 and 4 only

      d. 1, 2 and 5 only

Question 2

If John succumbs to his illness and dies, what role would Ashley automatically assume relative to John's estate?

      a. None

      b. Administrator of John's estate

      c. Executor of John's estate

      d. Trustee of John's estate

Question 3

If John succumbs to his illness, which of the following statements is true with regard to John's estate?

    a. If John lives in a province that incorporates a preferential share as part of the distribution of an intestate estate, Ashley will be entitled to a preferential share of John's estate.

    b. To avoid John dying intestate, Ashley, as John's power of attorney, could complete his will by signing it on his behalf.

    c. Because John had a partially completed will, he is considered to have an estate that is only partially intestate.

    d. Prior to the court appointment of an administrator for John's estate, no one, not even Ashley, has the power to transact on behalf of the estate.

Question 4

With regard to the cottage and John's home, which of the following statements is/are true, if John succumbs to his illness?

1. John's estate representative has the opportunity to decide whether it is more tax effective to apply the principal residence exemption to John's portion of the cottage or to his home.

2. The cottage will automatically pass to Ashley, outside of John's estate.

3. The ownership structure of the cottage makes it exempt from any capital gains tax at the time of John's death.

4. John's home will automatically pass to Ashley, outside of John's estate, because Ashley is John's nearest living relative.

    a. 2 only

    b. 1 and 2 only

    c. 1 and 3 only

    d. 3 and 4 only

Question 5

If John dies December 10, 2010, what are the due dates for John's final income tax return and for the balance of taxes owing on his final return?

    a. Both items are due on April 30, 2011.

    b. Both items are due on June 10, 2011.

    c. The balance of taxes owing is due on April 30, 2011, while the final income tax return is due June 10, 2011.

    d. The final income tax return is due on April 30, 2011, while the balance of taxes owing is due June 10, 2011.

Question 6

Assume that John survives his illness and fully recovers. However, on his way home from the hospital, a car strikes John and he dies instantly. How will the antique dining room suite be disbursed?

    a. Adam will automatically receive the dining room suite.

    b. Adam must apply to the courts to have his right to the dining room suite fulfilled because John made the gift as a condition of his death.

    c. The suite will be disbursed as an asset of John's estate under the provincial jurisdiction of an intestate estate.

    d. The dining room suite will automatically be placed under trusteeship and the courts will decide how it will be disbursed.

Question 7

Six years ago, Eleanor completely hand wrote what she viewed as her personal will. She signed and dated the document at that time, but did not review or discuss it with anyone else. Since that time, Eleanor has never updated the document or undertaken any additional steps in the completion of any other type of will. If Eleanor were to die today, it is likely that her handwritten will would be treated as:

    a. void because she did not have her signature witnessed by two people.

    b. a holograph will.

    c. a notarial will.

    d. void because it was completed more than five years prior to her death.

Question 8

Maxine inherited substantial assets from her wealthy parents when they died a few years ago. She and her husband, Tom, want to pass a significant portion of Maxine's inheritance on to their children, but Maxine wants Tom to be provided for fully before any assets pass on to the children. To address this issue, Maxine's will provides for the creation of a testamentary spousal trust that entitles Tom to all income from the trust assets throughout his lifetime. This trust also includes provisions that allow the children to access the capital of the trust prior to Tom's death, if he should become incapacitated. The family resides in Canada. With regard to this situation, which one of the following statements is true?

    a. Maxine's will establishes a qualified spousal trust.

    b. Maxine has set up an *alter ego* trust for Tom's benefit.

    c. There is no opportunity for a spousal rollover of assets into the trust.

    d. The trust that Maxine has established allows Tom to access any of the capital, as needed for his own benefit.

Question 9

Herb and Hannah, ages 30 and 28 respectively, are very private people who were quite unnerved to realize that they will lose their sense of privacy when their wills go through probate. To address this issue, Herb is investigating the possibility of establishing an *inter vivos* discretionary family trust where he is the settlor. Herb intends to make himself, Hannah and their three minor children discretionary beneficiaries of the trust. With regard to the establishment of such a strategy, which of the following statements are true?

1. Herb may lose some tax advantages that would be available if he were not both a settlor and beneficiary of the trust.

2. The strategy addresses the couple's concern regarding issues of privacy.

3. Income earned by the trust and distributed to the children will be taxed in the hands of the children, at their marginal tax rate.

4. The trust is exempt from the 21-year deemed disposition rule.

5. Capital gains realized by the trust and allocated to the children will be attributed back to Herb.

    a. 1 and 2 only

    b. 3 and 5 only

    c. 1, 2 and 5 only

    d. 2, 3 and 4 only

Question 10

Samantha has decided to file a rights or things return as part of the income tax filings on behalf of her deceased husband's estate. Samantha's husband died on July 1, 2010. Which of the following are considered rights or things income?

1. XYZ bonds that matured June 30, 2010, but which were only cashed on September 12, 2010.

2. Interest coupon on XYZ bonds payable June 30, 2010, that was received in mid-July but has not yet been included in the husband's income.

3. Payments received from her husband's RRIF for the period of January to June 2010.

4. Capital gains on her husband's investment portfolio as of his date of death.

5. Income her husband's employer paid to the estate as a salary continuance, for a three-month period following his death.

    a. 1 and 2 only

    b. 4 and 5 only

    c. 1, 2 and 3 only

    d. 3, 4 and 5 only

QUESTIONS & SOLUTIONS

The following background should be used with questions 1 through 6, inclusive.

JOHN

In the fall of 2010, just prior to his business trip to England, John completed an enduring general power of attorney for property in which he appointed his sister, Ashley, as his attorney. While in England, John became critically ill and was flown home in grave health. Upon returning home, John told his special friend, Adam, that in the event he succumbs to his current illness, Adam is to receive John's antique dining room suite.

Prior to his trip, John had initiated discussions about a will and his lawyer had prepared a draft will, but it had not yet been signed. John had no prior will.

John is an employee of an international firm of architects and is a single fellow who has never been married and has no children. Ashley is John's only sibling, and their parents are deceased. The siblings live in a province other than Quebec.

In 1998, a family cottage passed from John's parents to him and Ashley, which they now own as joint tenants with the right of survivorship. The adjusted cost base of the cottage is $200,000 while the current market value is $275,000. John has sole ownership of the townhouse condominium in which he lives.

Question 1

Given that John is gravely ill in the hospital, which of the following activities will Ashley typically have the automatically authority to undertake on John's behalf?

1. Pay John's bills during his sickness.

2. Re-negotiate John's car lease.

3. Make decisions regarding John's health care.

4. Sign John's will.

5. Re-invest John's maturing term deposit.

     a. 1 and 3 only

     b. 3 and 5 only

     c. 2 and 4 only

     d. 1, 2 and 5 only

Answer: d

     ⇨ 1. Pay John's bills during his sickness.

     ⇨ 2. Re-negotiate John's car lease.

     ⇨ 5. Re-invest John's maturing term deposit.

Reference: Pages 19-8 to 19-11

Question 2

If John succumbs to his illness and dies, what role would Ashley automatically assume relative to John's estate?

     a. None

     b. Administrator of John's estate

     c. Executor of John's estate

     d. Trustee of John's estate

Answer: a

     ⇨ None

Reference: Page 19-46

Question 3

If John succumbs to his illness, which of the following statements is true with regard to John's estate?

  a. If John lives in a province that incorporates a preferential share as part of the distribution of an intestate estate, Ashley will be entitled to a preferential share of John's estate.

  b. To avoid John dying intestate, Ashley, as John's power of attorney, could complete his will by signing it on his behalf.

  c. Because John had a partially completed will, he is considered to have an estate that is only partially intestate

  d. Prior to the court appointment of an administrator for John's estate, no one, not even Ashley, has the power to transact on behalf of the estate.

Answer: d

  ⇨   Prior to the court appointment of an administrator for John's estate, no one, not even Ashley, has the power to transact on behalf of the estate.

Reference: Pages 19-9 to 19-11 and 19-40 to 19-46

Question 4

With regard to the cottage and John's home, which of the following statements is/are true, if John succumbs to his illness?

1. John's estate representative has the opportunity to decide whether it is more tax effective to apply the principal residence exemption to John's portion of the cottage or to his home.

2. The cottage will automatically pass to Ashley, outside of John's estate.

3. The ownership structure of the cottage makes it exempt from any capital gains tax at the time of John's death.

4. John's home will automatically pass to Ashley, outside of John's estate, because Ashley is John's nearest living relative.

  a. 2 only

  b. 1 and 2 only

  c. 1 and 3 only

  d. 3 and 4 only

Answer: b

  ⇨   1. John's estate representative has the opportunity to decide whether it is more tax effective to apply the principal residence exemption to John's portion of the cottage or to his home.

  ⇨   2. The cottage will automatically pass to Ashley, outside of John's estate.

Reference: Integrated throughout the module

Question 5

If John dies December 10, 2010, what are the due dates for John's final income tax return and for the balance of taxes owing on his final return?

    a. Both items are due on April 30, 2011.

    b. Both items are due on June 10, 2011.

    c. The balance of taxes owing is due on April 30, 2011, while the final income tax return is due June 10, 2011.

    d. The final income tax return is due on April 30, 2011, while the balance of taxes owing is due June 10, 2011.

Answer: b

    ⇨   Both items are due on June 10, 2011.

Reference: Pages 19-64 to 19-66

Question 6

Assume that John survives his illness and fully recovers. However, on his way home from the hospital, a car strikes John and he dies instantly. How will the antique dining room suite be disbursed?

    a. Adam will automatically receive the dining room suite.

    b. Adam must apply to the courts to have his right to the dining room suite fulfilled because John made the gift as a condition of his death.

    c. The suite will be disbursed as an asset of John's estate under the provincial jurisdiction of an intestate estate.

    d. The dining room suite will automatically be placed under trusteeship and the courts will decide how it will be disbursed.

Answer: c

    ⇨   The suite will be disbursed as an asset of John's estate under the provincial jurisdiction of an intestate estate.

Reference: Page 19-41

Question 7

Six years ago, Eleanor completely hand wrote what she viewed as her personal will. She signed and dated the document at that time, but did not review or discuss it with anyone else. Since that time, Eleanor has never updated the document or undertaken any additional steps in the completion of any other type of will. If Eleanor were to die today, it is likely that her handwritten will would be treated as:

    a. void because she did not have her signature witnessed by two people.

    b. a holograph will.

    c. a notarial will.

    d. void because it was completed more than five years prior to her death.

Answer: b

    ⇨   a holograph will.

Reference: Page 19-13

Question 8

Maxine inherited substantial assets from her wealthy parents when they died a few years ago. She and her husband, Tom, want to pass a significant portion of Maxine's inheritance on to their children, but Maxine wants Tom to be provided for fully before any assets pass on to the children. To address this issue, Maxine's will provides for the creation of a testamentary spousal trust that entitles Tom to all income from the trust assets throughout his lifetime. This trust also includes provisions that allow the children to access the capital of the trust prior to Tom's death, if he should become incapacitated. The family resides in Canada. With regard to this situation, which one of the following statements is true?

    a. Maxine's will establishes a qualified spousal trust.

    b. Maxine has set up an *alter ego* trust for Tom's benefit.

    c. There is no opportunity for a spousal rollover of assets into the trust.

    d. The trust that Maxine has established allows Tom to access any of the capital, as needed for his own benefit.

Answer: c

    ⇨   There is no opportunity for a spousal rollover of assets into the trust.

Reference: Pages 19-31 to 19-33

Question 9

Herb and Hannah, ages 30 and 28 respectively, are very private people who were quite unnerved to realize that they will lose their sense of privacy when their wills go through probate. To address this issue, Herb is investigating the possibility of settling an *inter vivos* discretionary family trust. He intends to make himself, Hannah and their three minor children discretionary beneficiaries of the trust. With regard to the establishment of such a strategy, which of the following statements are true?

1. Herb may lose some tax advantages that would be available if he were not both a settlor and beneficiary of the trust.

2. The strategy addresses the couple's concern regarding issues of privacy.

3. Income earned by the trust and distributed to the children will be taxed in the hands of the children, at their marginal tax rate.

4. The trust is exempt from the 21-year deemed disposition rule.

5. Capital gains realized by the trust and allocated to the children will be attributed back to Herb.

    a. 1 and 2 only

    b. 3 and 5 only

    c. 1, 2 and 5 only

    d. 2, 3 and 4 only

Answer: c

    ⇨   1. Herb may loose some tax advantages that would be available if he were not both a settlor and beneficiary of the trust.

    ⇨   2. The strategy addresses the couple's concern regarding issues of privacy.

    ⇨   5. Capital gains realized by the trust and allocated to the children will be attributed back to Herb.

Reference: Pages 19-56 to 19-60

Question 10

Samantha has decided to file a rights or things return as part of the income tax filings on behalf of her deceased husband's estate. Samantha's husband died on July 1, 2010. Which of the following are considered rights or things income?

1. XYZ bonds that matured June 30, 2010, but which were only cashed on September 12, 2010.

2. Interest coupon on XYZ bonds payable June 30, 2010, that was received in mid-July but has not yet been included in the husband's income.

3. Payments received from her husband's RRIF for the period of January to June 2010.

4. Capital gains on her husband's investment portfolio as of his date of death.

5. Income her husband's employer paid to the estate as a salary continuance, for a three-month period following his death.

    a. 1 and 2 only

    b. 4 and 5 only

    c. 1, 2 and 3 only

    d. 3, 4 and 5 only

Answer: a

⇨ 1. XYZ bonds that matured June 30, 2010, but which were only cashed on September 12, 2010.

⇨ 2. Interest coupon on XYZ bonds payable June 30, 2010, that was received in mid-July but has not yet been included in the husband's income.

Reference: Pages 19-61 to 19-62

Unit 9
Module 19 Exercises and Case Study

MODULE 19 EXERCISES

1. Explain the two primary types of power of attorney. Why are both recommended?

2. What are the differences among limited, general and continuing, or enduring, power of attorney for property?

3. Explain the differences among the four basic types of wills.

4. Explain the differences among the four classifications of a legacy, or testamentary, disposition: general, specific, demonstrative, and residual bequests.

5. What is the difference between "ademption" and "abatement"?

6. Two important phases, *"per stirpes"* and *"per capita"*, are commonly used in a will to govern the distribution of assets. Explain the differences between the two terms.

7. Outline three activities that an executor may be responsible for performing.

8. What are the specific conditions that must apply for a testamentary trust to be a qualified spousal trust?

9. What are the two benefits of using a qualified spousal trust?

10. The role of trustee is a fiduciary relationship between the trust and beneficiaries. What is a trustee legally obligated to do in regard to the fiduciary relationship?

11. If an individual dies intestate, how is his estate distributed?

12. What steps are involved in probating a will?

13. Assets that do not form part of the deceased's estate are not subject to probate. List some common strategies for establishing assets that are not subject to probate.

14. In addition to the terminal income tax return, there is an opportunity to file three elective returns on behalf of the deceased. What are some reasons for filing the three elective returns? Briefly describe each of the three elective returns.

15. When is the final income tax return for a deceased taxpayer due?

16. When is the balance of taxes due for a deceased taxpayer?

17. What are the tax consequences on the death of a taxpayer under the following situations?

    a. Spousal rollover of assets

    b. Property owned as joint tenants

    c. Principle residence

    d. Alternative minimum tax

    e. Capital and terminal losses

18. The term "refund of premiums" is used to define assets from an unmatured RRSP that result from the death of the RRSP annuitant and are paid to qualified beneficiaries under specific conditions. Name the three categories of qualified beneficiaries.

19. What are the rules for charitable donations in the year of a taxpayer's death?

20. List some of the elements of a good estate planning framework or checklist.

CASE STUDY — TOTALLY CONFUSED ABOUT WILLS

As financial planner, you have developed a reputation as being quite knowledgeable about estate planning. One of your clients sent you the following letter. Prepare a response to the client.

Dear Financial Planner,

An article I read on estate planning stated that it is important for everyone to have a will and that one should talk to a financial planner prior to meeting with a lawyer. Why? What benefits can a financial planner offer regarding wills? The article mentioned that I need to appoint an executor as part of my will. What does an executor do, and what criteria should I use to appoint someone?

Yours truly,

Totally Confused

Appendix One
Sample Will

ITEM A   THIS IS THE LAST WILL AND TESTAMENT of me, ASHLEY CHRISTINE RACHEL THOMAS, of the City of ABC, in the Regional Municipality of DEF, and in the Province of XYZ.

ITEM B

1. I HEREBY REVOKE all former Wills, Codicils and other testamentary dispositions by me at any time heretofore made and declare this only to be and contain my last Will and Testament.

ITEM C

2. I NOMINATE, CONSTITUTE AND APPOINT my husband, DONALD WILSON THOMAS, to be the sole Executor of this my Will and Trustee of my estate, but if my husband should predecease me, or die within a period of thirty (30) days following my decease, or without having proved this my Will, then on the death of the survivor of me and my husband, I NOMINATE, CONSTITUTE AND APPOINT DARLENE WILEY to be the Executrix of this my Will and Trustee of my estate in the place and stead of my husband, and if the said DARLENE WILEY should then be deceased, or should die before having proved my Will, I NOMINATE, CONSTITUTE AND APPOINT JACK DARLING to be Executor of my Will and Trustee of my Estate in the place and stead of the said DARLENE WILEY, and I hereinafter refer to my Executor and Trustee or my Executrix and Trustee for the time being as my "Trustee".

ITEM D

3. I DIRECT AND DECLARE that any funds that are payable to my estate on my death as a refund of premiums from a Registered Retirement Savings Plan or Plans, or like approved Plans, with any insurance company, trust company or other corporation from whom such Plans may have been purchased by me shall be paid to my husband, DONALD THOMAS outright and absolutely. I recommend to him that he deposit the monies so received in a Registered Retirement Savings Plan or Plans of his own or applied by him in the purchase of a single premium Annuity on his life.

4. I GIVE, DEVISE AND BEQUEATH all of my property of every nature and kind and wheresoever situate, including any property over which I may have a general power to appoint, to my said Trustee upon the following trusts, namely:

ITEM E

(a) TO PAY OUT OF and charge to the capital of my general estate my just debts, funeral and testamentary expenses and all estate, inheritance and succession duties or taxes whether imposed by or pursuant to the law of this and any other jurisdiction in connection with any property passing (or deemed so to pass by any governing law) on my death or in connection with any insurance on my life or any gift or benefit given or conferred by me either during my lifetime or by survivorship or by this my Will or any Codicil thereto and whether such duties or taxes be payable in respect of estate or interest which fall into possession at my death or at any subsequent time; and I hereby authorize the commutation or prepayment of any such taxes or duties.

ITEM F

(b) TO PAY OR TRANSFER the residue of my estate to my husband, DONALD THOMAS, if he survives me for a period of thirty (30) days for his own use absolutely.

ITEM G

(c) IF MY SAID HUSBAND should predecease me, or should survive me but die within a period of thirty (30) days after my decease, I direct my Trustee to divide the residue of my estate equally amongst my children surviving and then alive, provided, however, that if any child of mine shall then be dead, but shall have left issue surviving and then alive, such child shall be considered alive for the purpose of this division and the issue of such child shall take, in equal shares *per stirpes*, the share to which their parent would have been entitled if living.

ITEM H

(d) IF MY SAID HUSBAND should predecease me, or should survive me but die within a period of thirty (30) days after my decease, and if there should be no children of mine or issue surviving and then alive, I direct my Trustee to pay or transfer the residue of my estate to CANDICE SHERMAN for her own use absolutely.

5. I HERBY GIVE the following authority and power to my Trustee:

ITEM I

With respect to the assets of my estate, except any assets hereinbefore specifically dealt with and to the extent so dealt with, I direct that any such asset or assets, even though not Trustee Investments, may be retained in my Estate for such unrestricted length of time as deemed advisable, with power and authority to sell any assets, privately or otherwise (including to any beneficiary hereunder without requiring the approval of others of them) at such time or times, at such price and upon such terms, conditions and arrangements as deemed to be in the best interest of my estate. In addition to the foregoing specific powers it is also my intention herein to give full power and authority to deal with and manage all real and personal property in my estate, or any trust thereof, to the full and same extent I could do as owner were I alive, including the power to execute all deeds, conveyances and other documents required from time to time in the administration of my estate.

ITEM J

6. IF ANY PERSON should become entitled to any share in my estate before attaining the age of majority, the share of such person shall be held and kept invested by my Trustee and the income and capital or so much thereof as my Trustee in her absolute sole discretion may consider to be necessary or advisable shall be used for the benefit of such person until he or she attains the age of majority.

ITEM K

7. I AUTHORIZE my Trustee to make any payments for any person under the age of majority to a parent or guardian of such person or to any other person they may consider to be a proper recipient therefore, whose receipt shall be sufficient discharge to my Trustee.

ITEM L

8. ANY REFERENCE in this Will or in any Codicil hereto to a person in terms of a relationship to another person determined by blood or marriage shall not include a person born outside of marriage nor a person who comes with the description traced through another person who was born outside marriage, provided that any person who has been legally adopted shall be regarded as having been born in lawful wedlock to his or her adopting parent.

ITEM M

9. ANY BENEFIT, whether as to income or capital or both, or income from capital to which any person shall become entitled in accordance with the provisions of this my Will and any Codicil thereto, shall not fall into any community property which may exist between any such person and his or her spouse and shall not form part of his or her net family property for any purpose or purposes of the FAMILY LAW ACT 1986, in the Province of XYZ and any amendments thereto, or any successor legislation thereto, but shall only be paid by my Trustee to such person on the condition that the same shall remain the separate property of such person, free from the control of his or her spouse. The separate receipt of such person shall be a discharge to my Trustee in respect of such payment.

ITEM N

10. IN THE CASE OF DEATH of my said husband, DONALD THOMAS, I HEREBY APPOINT DARLENE WILEY to be the guardian of the persons and estates of my children during their respective minorities, and in the event that DARLENE WILEY is unable or unwilling so to act for any reason, I THEN APPOINT CANDICE SHERMAN as such guardian.

ITEM O

IN TESTIMONY WHEREOF I have to this my last Will and Testament, written upon this and the two (2) preceding pages of paper, subscribe my name this <u>11</u> day of <u>Jan.</u> 1992.

SIGNED, PUBLISHED AND DECLARED by the above-named Testatrix ASHLEY CHRISTINE RACHEL THOMAS, as and for her last Will and Testament, in the presence of us, both present at the same time, who at her request, in her presence and in the presence of each other, have hereunto subscribed our names as witnesses.	))))))))))	Signed: *Ashley Christine* *Rachel Thomas*

Signed: *Darrin Rogers*   Jan. 11/92

Signed: *Emily Pythe*   Jan. 11/92

Appendix Two
Provincial Probate Fee Overview[1,2]

Province	Estate Size	Fee/Tax
British Columbia	First $25,000 $25,001–$50,000 Over $50,000	No fee 0.60 $150+ 1.40%
Alberta	First $10,000 $10,001–$250,000 Over $250,000	$25 Progressive to $300 $400 (maximum)
Saskatchewan	All estates	0.70%
Manitoba	First $10,000 Over $10,000	$70 $70 + 0.70%
Ontario	First $50,000 Over $50,000	0.50% $250+ 1.50%
Quebec	Notarial wills Holograph/witnessed	No fee $93
New Brunswick	First $5,000 $5,001–$20,000 Over $20,000	$25 Progressive to $100 0.50%
Nova Scotia	First $10,000 $10,001–$100,000 Over $100,000	$74.76 Progressive to $875.76 $875.76 + 1.479%
Prince Edward Island	First $10,000 $10,001–$100,000 Over $100,000	$50 Progressive to $400 $400 + 0.40%
Newfoundland	First $1,000 Over $1,000	$60 $60 + 0.50%
Yukon	First $25,000 Over $25,000	No fee $140
Northwest Territories	First $10,000 $10,001–$250,000 Over $250,000	$25 Progressive to $300 $400 (maximum)
Nunavut	First $10,000 $10,001–$250,000 Over $250,000	$25 Progressive to $300 $400 (maximum)

[1] As of December 31, 2009.

[2] These rates are quoted for use in estimating probate costs. Actual costs of probate may vary.

Appendix Three
Capital Needs Analysis

(*Note:* Students who have completed Course 3, Module 10, "Life Insurance and Living Benefits", of the CFP Education Program will be familiar with the concept of Capital Needs Analysis in relationship to the use of life insurance in estate planning and can use this information simply for review.)

How much is enough? This is a question often asked when considering the purchase of life insurance. To address this question, a process referred to as a *capital needs analysis* (CNA) should be undertaken. A capital needs analysis looks at the family's assets and liabilities along with the continuing income needs of the surviving family in the event that the individual (i.e., spouse) should die prematurely.

The possibility of premature death is a given fact for everyone, and few people have the current financial resources to ensure that their survivors can maintain a lifestyle to which they have become accustomed. A capital needs analysis, sometimes referred to as an *insurance needs analysis*, is a systematic approach to determine how much investment capital the survivors need to assist in the replacement of income that will support the survivors' lifestyle. To the extent that the family's investment capital is insufficient to address the financial gap identified in the capital needs analysis, life insurance is commonly used as a valued solution.

The typical need for income and assets can be divided into three areas:

- immediate cash needs upon death;
- debts and lump-sum needs/obligations; and
- the need for longer-term income.

The total amount of capital required to fulfill these three areas is compared to the total amount of capital currently held within the family unit. Where the current capital is less than the amount required, the difference is known as the "need for insurance".

Immediate Cash Needs

Immediate cash needs generally include funeral expenses, income taxes owing and administrative costs that the estate may incur.

Debts and Lump-Sum Needs/Obligations

A lump-sum amount is often targeted to pay off outstanding debts such as a mortgage, line of credit, credit card balances and any larger size debts that the deceased's family may owe. The lump sum amount is also helpful to establish provisions for an ongoing emergency cash reserve fund for the survivors and to establish provisions for known longer-term financial needs such as the children's education. This category would also include bequests, if any, set out in the deceased's will.

Long Term Income

Longer-term income considers the ongoing income needs that the surviving spouse and family will have, and should carefully incorporate assumptions as to how much the surviving spouse can contribute through work activities.

Income generated through government benefit programs may be considered, as it too can help to defray the ongoing income needs of the family. For example, survivor and children's benefits under the Canada Pension Plan may become payable under specific circumstances. Government benefits were examined extensively in Module 4 and discussions with the client should determine how much of these potential benefits, if any, the client wants included in the analysis.

It is important to ensure that any assumptions built into the income model are reasonable for the circumstances.

Estimating the amount of income needed by the surviving family can become quite complex because the model should address several periods:

- income needs while any children are young;
- income needs while any children are attaining an education;
- income needs for the surviving spouse during her working years (if there is an assumption that the spouse will earn an income); and
- income needs during retirement.

The income assumptions need to address a reasonable life expectancy for the surviving spouse. As well, the income need should consider some level of expectation relative to the anticipated annual inflation rate throughout the surviving spouse's lifetime.

The surviving family's income needs are compared to the known or expected sources of income. Expected sources of income will generally include the surviving spouse's annual earnings, government benefits, other income sources (i.e., pensions), and investment income from any assets remaining after immediate and lump-sum needs have been met. The difference between the income needs and expected income flow is identified as an income gap.

This exercise is intended to measure the amount of capital that is required by the surviving family to address the income gap. Assumptions are needed relative to the rate of investment return that the capital will produce in order to fulfill the income gap over the surviving spouse's lifetime. Life insurance can be used as the vehicle to create the capital that is necessary to address the family's income gap.

Monitoring

Completing a capital needs analysis is not a one-time activity because a family's situation is constantly evolving. Periodic reviews of the capital needs analysis are important to ensure that the family will not meet unexpected financial uncertainty.

FRED AND MARG BING

Fred and Marg Bing, both aged 36, have two small children, ages four and six. The Bings want to ensure that they have adequate resources in place to complete their estate plans should Fred pass away prematurely.

Considering the Bings' current resources and expressed needs as noted below, what is an appropriate amount of life insurance?

Needs

- fund a $25,000 bequest to their alumni association
- fund final expenses of $15,000
- repay credit cards and car loan of $30,000
- repay mortgage on home of $100,000
- fund an education fund of $50,000
- assume retirement at age 60

Current Resources/Assets

- $120,000 group life insurance coverage
- Marg, the surviving spouse earns $45,000 (and participates in a pension plan)

Objectives

Maintain the surviving family's income at $90,000 while the children are minors and then $60,000 thereafter. For planning purposes, the Bings have chosen to disregard any provisions for government-sponsored benefits arising from a premature death.

Note: For the sake of simplicity in explaining the capital needs analysis, inflation has not been incorporated into the calculations.

continued . . .

---

continued . . .

Analysis

A.   Immediate Cash Position

- current cash assets   0
- receipt of group insurance $120,000
- payment of last expenses $15,000
- cash available after immediate needs $105,000

B.   Debts and Lump-Sum Needs/Obligations

- cash available after immediate needs $105,000
- pay off short-term debts $30,000
- pay bequest $25,000
- set up education fund $50,000
- repay mortgage $100,000
- cash available after immediate and lump-
  sum needs/obligations   ($100,000)

Fred and Marg do not have sufficient financial resources to meet their immediate and short-term needs. They have a $100,000 shortfall relative to financing their immediate and short-term goals.

Long-Term Needs

The Bings' goal is to ensure that the surviving family has $90,000 of income during the children's minority years. It has been assumed that the surviving spouse can earn $45,000 annually, which leaves the family in need of another $45,000 of income for each of 14 years.

Once the youngest child reaches age 18, Marg begins the second income period, from age 49 to 60. This is the period after the children's minority and before Marg's retirement at age 60. The identified need is to provide $60,000 of annual income during this period, which is offset by the assumption of Marg's ability to earn $45,000. This leaves an annual shortfall of $15,000.

The last period is Marg's retirement. While the facts have not clearly set out the pension plan income, an assumption could be made in order to complete the analysis. Marg may have worked for 25 years earning $45,000, which could mean a pension of $22,500 ($45,000 × 25 years of service × 2%). This results in an annual shortfall of $37,500 ($60,000 - $22,500) from the annual goal of $60,000.

Income Shortfall

Years 1 to 14	$45,000	children's minority (up to age 50)
Years 15 to 25	$15,000	pre-retirement (up to age 60)
Years 26 to 56	$37,500	post-retirement (up to age 90)

The income shortfall can only be replaced with investment income. In order to determine the amount of investment capital required to replace the income shortfall, a rate of return assumption must be made. Because the capital being created is to protect an income shortfall and there is no room for mistakes, a conservative assumption should be made, say 4.5%.

The present value of the capital required to satisfy this income stream shortfall is $769,649 (using simple time value of money assumptions including P/YR = 1, I/YR = 4.5 and MODE = BEG).

To determine the required capital, calculate the present value of each period starting with the last period of up to age 90. The present value of the cash flows required during retirement is $638,320.

P/YR = 1

XP/YR = 30

I/YR = 4.5

PMT = 37,500

FV = 0

MODE = BEG

SOLVE FOR PV, which equals -638,320.82

The present value of the cash flows required at the start the pre-retirement phase, taking into account 30 years of retirement after age 60, is $535,064.

continued . . .

continued . . .

P/YR = 1

XP/YR = 10

I/YR = 4.5

PMT = 15,000

FV = 638,320.82

MODE = BEG

SOLVE FOR PV, which equals -535,064.31

Assuming Marg needs $535,064 at age 60 and $45,000 each year for 14 years until the youngest child reaches age 18, she will need $769,649 in insurance today.

P/YR = 1

XP/YR = 14

I/YR = 4.5

PMT = 45,000

FV = 535,064.31

MODE = BEG

SOLVE FOR PV, which equals -769,648.57

In summary, Fred and Marg need $100,000 of insurance to satisfy their short-term needs, and an additional $769,649 to fulfill their income replacement needs. In total, the insurance needed is $869,649.

Software is commonly used to perform this type of analysis and allows for incorporation of different variables and assumptions. In the Fred and Marg SNAP, the calculations have been kept as simple as possible to demonstrate the flow-through of the capital needs analysis.

The capital needs analysis is a logical process of determining a client's financial shortfall based on the facts, objectives and needs specific to their circumstances. Ongoing, regular review is important to ensure that all current and relevant circumstances are considered and appropriate solutions are put in place.

Topical Index

Topical Index — Course 4